Gnus 5.10 Reference Manual

A catalogue record for this book is available from the Hong Kong Public Libraries.

Published by Samurai Media Limited.

Email: info@@samuraimedia.org

ISBN 978-988-13277-7-2

Short Contents

Table of Contents

The Gnus Newsreader

Gnus is the advanced, self-documenting, customizable, extensible unreal-time newsreader for GNU Emacs.

Oops. That sounds oddly familiar, so let's start over again to avoid being accused of plagiarism:

Gnus is a message-reading laboratory. It will let you look at just about anything as if it were a newsgroup. You can read mail with it, you can browse directories with it, you can `ftp` with it—you can even read news with it!

Gnus tries to empower people who read news the same way Emacs empowers people who edit text. Gnus sets no limits to what the user should be allowed to do. Users are encouraged to extend Gnus to make it behave like they want it to behave. A program should not control people; people should be empowered to do what they want by using (or abusing) the program.

This manual corresponds to Ma Gnus v0.12

Other related manuals

- Message manual: Composing messages
- Emacs-MIME: Composing messages; MIME-specific parts.
- Sieve: Managing Sieve scripts in Emacs.
- EasyPG: PGP/MIME with Gnus.
- SASL: SASL authentication in Emacs.

1 Starting Gnus

If you haven't used Emacs much before using Gnus, read Section 11.9 [Emacs for Heathens], page 356 first.

If your system administrator has set things up properly, starting Gnus and reading news is extremely easy—you just type *M-x gnus* in your Emacs. If not, you should customize the variable `gnus-select-method` as described in Section 1.1 [Finding the News], page 2. For a minimal setup for posting should also customize the variables `user-full-name` and `user-mail-address`.

If you want to start Gnus in a different frame, you can use the command *M-x gnus-other-frame* instead.

If things do not go smoothly at startup, you have to twiddle some variables in your `~/.gnus.el` file. This file is similar to `~/.emacs`, but is read when Gnus starts.

If you puzzle at any terms used in this manual, please refer to the terminology section (see Section 11.5 [Terminology], page 329).

1.1 Finding the News

First of all, you should know that there is a special buffer called `*Server*` that lists all the servers Gnus knows about. You can press ^ from the Group buffer to see it. In the Server buffer, you can press *RET* on a defined server to see all the groups it serves (subscribed or not!). You can also add or delete servers, edit a foreign server's definition, agentize or de-agentize a server, and do many other neat things. See Section 6.1 [Server Buffer], page 136. See Section 2.9 [Foreign Groups], page 20. See Section 6.9.1 [Agent Basics], page 199.

The `gnus-select-method` variable says where Gnus should look for news. This variable should be a list where the first element says *how* and the second element says *where*. This method is your native method. All groups not fetched with this method are secondary or foreign groups.

For instance, if the 'news.somewhere.edu' NNTP server is where you want to get your daily dosage of news from, you'd say:

```
(setq gnus-select-method '(nntp "news.somewhere.edu"))
```

If you want to read directly from the local spool, say:

```
(setq gnus-select-method '(nnspool ""))
```

If you can use a local spool, you probably should, as it will almost certainly be much faster. But do not use the local spool if your server is running Leafnode (which is a simple, standalone private news server); in this case, use `(nntp "localhost")`.

If this variable is not set, Gnus will take a look at the `NNTPSERVER` environment variable. If that variable isn't set, Gnus will see whether `gnus-nntpserver-file` (`/etc/nntpserver` by default) has any opinions on the matter. If that fails as well, Gnus will try to use the machine running Emacs as an NNTP server. That's a long shot, though.

However, if you use one NNTP server regularly and are just interested in a couple of groups from a different server, you would be better served by using the *B* command in the group buffer. It will let you have a look at what groups are available, and you can subscribe to any of the groups you want to. This also makes `.newsrc` maintenance much tidier. See Section 2.9 [Foreign Groups], page 20.

A slightly different approach to foreign groups is to set the **gnus-secondary-select-methods** variable. The select methods listed in this variable are in many ways just as native as the **gnus-select-method** server. They will also be queried for active files during startup (if that's required), and new newsgroups that appear on these servers will be subscribed (or not) just as native groups are.

For instance, if you use the **nnmbox** back end to read your mail, you would typically set this variable to

```
(setq gnus-secondary-select-methods '((nnmbox "")))
```

1.2 The Server is Down

If the default server is down, Gnus will understandably have some problems starting. However, if you have some mail groups in addition to the news groups, you may want to start Gnus anyway.

Gnus, being the trusting sort of program, will ask whether to proceed without a native select method if that server can't be contacted. This will happen whether the server doesn't actually exist (i.e., you have given the wrong address) or the server has just momentarily taken ill for some reason or other. If you decide to continue and have no foreign groups, you'll find it difficult to actually do anything in the group buffer. But, hey, that's your problem. Blllrph!

If you know that the server is definitely down, or you just want to read your mail without bothering with the server at all, you can use the **gnus-no-server** command to start Gnus. That might come in handy if you're in a hurry as well. This command will not attempt to contact your primary server—instead, it will just activate all groups on level 1 and 2. (You should preferably keep no native groups on those two levels.) Also see Section 2.6 [Group Levels], page 17.

1.3 Slave Gnusae

You might want to run more than one Emacs with more than one Gnus at the same time. If you are using different `.newsrc` files (e.g., if you are using the two different Gnusae to read from two different servers), that is no problem whatsoever. You just do it.

The problem appears when you want to run two Gnusae that use the same `.newsrc` file.

To work around that problem some, we here at the Think-Tank at the Gnus Towers have come up with a new concept: *Masters* and *slaves*. (We have applied for a patent on this concept, and have taken out a copyright on those words. If you wish to use those words in conjunction with each other, you have to send $1 per usage instance to me. Usage of the patent (*Master/Slave Relationships In Computer Applications*) will be much more expensive, of course.)

Anyway, you start one Gnus up the normal way with *M-x gnus* (or however you do it). Each subsequent slave Gnusae should be started with *M-x gnus-slave*. These slaves won't save normal `.newsrc` files, but instead save *slave files* that contain information only on what groups have been read in the slave session. When a master Gnus starts, it will read (and delete) these slave files, incorporating all information from them. (The slave files will be read in the sequence they were created, so the latest changes will have precedence.)

Information from the slave files has, of course, precedence over the information in the normal (i.e., master) `.newsrc` file.

If the `.newsrc*` files have not been saved in the master when the slave starts, you may be prompted as to whether to read an auto-save file. If you answer "yes", the unsaved changes to the master will be incorporated into the slave. If you answer "no", the slave may see some messages as unread that have been read in the master.

1.4 New Groups

If you are satisfied that you really never want to see any new groups, you can set `gnus-check-new-newsgroups` to `nil`. This will also save you some time at startup. Even if this variable is `nil`, you can always subscribe to the new groups just by pressing *U* in the group buffer (see Section 2.13 [Group Maintenance], page 32). This variable is `ask-server` by default. If you set this variable to `always`, then Gnus will query the back ends for new groups even when you do the *g* command (see Section 2.18.1 [Scanning New Messages], page 41).

1.4.1 Checking New Groups

Gnus normally determines whether a group is new or not by comparing the list of groups from the active file(s) with the lists of subscribed and dead groups. This isn't a particularly fast method. If `gnus-check-new-newsgroups` is `ask-server`, Gnus will ask the server for new groups since the last time. This is both faster and cheaper. This also means that you can get rid of the list of killed groups (see Section 2.6 [Group Levels], page 17) altogether, so you may set `gnus-save-killed-list` to `nil`, which will save time both at startup, at exit, and all over. Saves disk space, too. Why isn't this the default, then? Unfortunately, not all servers support this command.

I bet I know what you're thinking now: How do I find out whether my server supports `ask-server`? No? Good, because I don't have a fail-safe answer. I would suggest just setting this variable to `ask-server` and see whether any new groups appear within the next few days. If any do, then it works. If none do, then it doesn't work. I could write a function to make Gnus guess whether the server supports `ask-server`, but it would just be a guess. So I won't. You could `telnet` to the server and say HELP and see whether it lists 'NEWGROUPS' among the commands it understands. If it does, then it might work. (But there are servers that lists 'NEWGROUPS' without supporting the function properly.)

This variable can also be a list of select methods. If so, Gnus will issue an `ask-server` command to each of the select methods, and subscribe them (or not) using the normal methods. This might be handy if you are monitoring a few servers for new groups. A side effect is that startup will take much longer, so you can meditate while waiting. Use the mantra "dingnusdingnusdingnus" to achieve permanent bliss.

1.4.2 Subscription Methods

What Gnus does when it encounters a new group is determined by the `gnus-subscribe-newsgroup-method` variable.

This variable should contain a function. This function will be called with the name of the new group as the only parameter.

Some handy pre-fab functions are:

`gnus-subscribe-zombies`

> Make all new groups zombies (see Section 2.6 [Group Levels], page 17). This is the default. You can browse the zombies later (with `A z`) and either kill them all off properly (with `S z`), or subscribe to them (with `u`).

`gnus-subscribe-randomly`

> Subscribe all new groups in arbitrary order. This really means that all new groups will be added at "the top" of the group buffer.

`gnus-subscribe-alphabetically`

> Subscribe all new groups in alphabetical order.

`gnus-subscribe-hierarchically`

> Subscribe all new groups hierarchically. The difference between this function and `gnus-subscribe-alphabetically` is slight. `gnus-subscribe-alphabetically` will subscribe new groups in a strictly alphabetical fashion, while this function will enter groups into its hierarchy. So if you want to have the 'rec' hierarchy before the 'comp' hierarchy, this function will not mess that configuration up. Or something like that.

`gnus-subscribe-interactively`

> Subscribe new groups interactively. This means that Gnus will ask you about **all** new groups. The groups you choose to subscribe to will be subscribed hierarchically.

`gnus-subscribe-killed`

> Kill all new groups.

`gnus-subscribe-topics`

> Put the groups into the topic that has a matching `subscribe` topic parameter (see Section 2.16.5 [Topic Parameters], page 37). For instance, a `subscribe` topic parameter that looks like
>
>   "nnml"
>
> will mean that all groups that match that regex will be subscribed under that topic.
>
> If no topics match the groups, the groups will be subscribed in the top-level topic.

A closely related variable is **gnus-subscribe-hierarchical-interactive**. (That's quite a mouthful.) If this variable is non-**nil**, Gnus will ask you in a hierarchical fashion whether to subscribe to new groups or not. Gnus will ask you for each sub-hierarchy whether you want to descend the hierarchy or not.

One common mistake is to set the variable a few paragraphs above (**gnus-subscribe-newsgroup-method**) to **gnus-subscribe-hierarchical-interactive**. This is an error. This will not work. This is ga-ga. So don't do it.

1.4.3 Filtering New Groups

A nice and portable way to control which new newsgroups should be subscribed (or ignored) is to put an *options* line at the start of the `.newsrc` file. Here's an example:

```
options -n !alt.all !rec.all sci.all
```

This line obviously belongs to a serious-minded intellectual scientific person (or she may just be plain old boring), because it says that all groups that have names beginning with 'alt' and 'rec' should be ignored, and all groups with names beginning with 'sci' should be subscribed. Gnus will not use the normal subscription method for subscribing these groups. `gnus-subscribe-options-newsgroup-method` is used instead. This variable defaults to `gnus-subscribe-alphabetically`.

The "options -n" format is very simplistic. The syntax above is all that is supports: you can force-subscribe hierarchies, or you can deny hierarchies, and that's it.

If you don't want to mess with your `.newsrc` file, you can just set the two variables `gnus-options-subscribe` and `gnus-options-not-subscribe`. These two variables do exactly the same as the `.newsrc` 'options -n' trick. Both are regexps, and if the new group matches the former, it will be unconditionally subscribed, and if it matches the latter, it will be ignored.

Yet another variable that meddles here is `gnus-auto-subscribed-groups`. It works exactly like `gnus-options-subscribe`, and is therefore really superfluous, but I thought it would be nice to have two of these. This variable is more meant for setting some ground rules, while the other variable is used more for user fiddling. By default this variable makes all new groups that come from mail back ends (`nnml`, `nnbabyl`, `nnfolder`, `nnmbox`, `nnmh`, `nnimap`, and `nnmaildir`) subscribed. If you don't like that, just set this variable to `nil`.

As if that wasn't enough, `gnus-auto-subscribed-categories` also allows you to specify that new groups should be subscribed based on the category their select methods belong to. The default is '(mail post-mail)', meaning that all new groups from mail-like backends should be subscribed automatically.

New groups that match these variables are subscribed using `gnus-subscribe-options-newsgroup-method`.

1.5 Changing Servers

Sometimes it is necessary to move from one NNTP server to another. This happens very rarely, but perhaps you change jobs, or one server is very flaky and you want to use another.

Changing the server is pretty easy, right? You just change `gnus-select-method` to point to the new server?

Wrong!

Article numbers are not (in any way) kept synchronized between different NNTP servers, and the only way Gnus keeps track of what articles you have read is by keeping track of article numbers. So when you change `gnus-select-method`, your `.newsrc` file becomes worthless.

You can use the *M-x gnus-group-clear-data-on-native-groups* command to clear out all data that you have on your native groups. Use with caution.

Clear the data from the current group only—nix out marks and the list of read articles (`gnus-group-clear-data`).

After changing servers, you **must** move the cache hierarchy away, since the cached articles will have wrong article numbers, which will affect which articles Gnus thinks are read.

`gnus-group-clear-data-on-native-groups` will ask you if you want to have it done automatically; for `gnus-group-clear-data`, you can use *M-x gnus-cache-move-cache* (but beware, it will move the cache for all groups).

1.6 Startup Files

Most common Unix news readers use a shared startup file called `.newsrc`. This file contains all the information about what groups are subscribed, and which articles in these groups have been read.

Things got a bit more complicated with GNUS. In addition to keeping the `.newsrc` file updated, it also used a file called `.newsrc.el` for storing all the information that didn't fit into the `.newsrc` file. (Actually, it also duplicated everything in the `.newsrc` file.) GNUS would read whichever one of these files was the most recently saved, which enabled people to swap between GNUS and other newsreaders.

That was kinda silly, so Gnus went one better: In addition to the `.newsrc` and `.newsrc.el` files, Gnus also has a file called `.newsrc.eld`. It will read whichever of these files that are most recent, but it will never write a `.newsrc.el` file. You should never delete the `.newsrc.eld` file—it contains much information not stored in the `.newsrc` file.

You can turn off writing the `.newsrc` file by setting **gnus-save-newsrc-file** to **nil**, which means you can delete the file and save some space, as well as exiting from Gnus faster. However, this will make it impossible to use other newsreaders than Gnus. But hey, who would want to, right? Similarly, setting **gnus-read-newsrc-file** to **nil** makes Gnus ignore the `.newsrc` file and any `.newsrc-SERVER` files, which can be convenient if you use a different news reader occasionally, and you want to read a different subset of the available groups with that news reader.

If **gnus-save-killed-list** (default t) is **nil**, Gnus will not save the list of killed groups to the startup file. This will save both time (when starting and quitting) and space (on disk). It will also mean that Gnus has no record of what groups are new or old, so the automatic new groups subscription methods become meaningless. You should always set **gnus-check-new-newsgroups** to **nil** or **ask-server** if you set this variable to **nil** (see Section 1.4 [New Groups], page 4). This variable can also be a regular expression. If that's the case, remove all groups that do not match this regexp before saving. This can be useful in certain obscure situations that involve several servers where not all servers support **ask-server**.

The **gnus-startup-file** variable says where the startup files are. The default value is `~/.newsrc`, with the Gnus (El Dingo) startup file being whatever that one is, with a '.eld' appended. If you want to keep multiple numbered backups of this file, set **gnus-backup-startup-file**. It respects the same values as the **version-control** variable.

gnus-save-newsrc-hook is called before saving any of the newsrc files, while **gnus-save-quick-newsrc-hook** is called just before saving the `.newsrc.eld` file, and **gnus-save-standard-newsrc-hook** is called just before saving the `.newsrc` file. The latter two are commonly used to turn version control on or off. Version control is on by default when saving the startup files. If you want to turn backup creation off, say something like:

```
(defun turn-off-backup ()
  (set (make-local-variable 'backup-inhibited) t))
```

```
(add-hook 'gnus-save-quick-newsrc-hook 'turn-off-backup)
(add-hook 'gnus-save-standard-newsrc-hook 'turn-off-backup)
```

When Gnus starts, it will read the **gnus-site-init-file** (.../site-lisp/gnus-init by default) and **gnus-init-file** (~/.gnus by default) files. These are normal Emacs Lisp files and can be used to avoid cluttering your ~/.emacs and site-init files with Gnus stuff. Gnus will also check for files with the same names as these, but with .elc and .el suffixes. In other words, if you have set **gnus-init-file** to ~/.gnus, it will look for ~/.gnus.elc, ~/.gnus.el, and finally ~/.gnus (in this order). If Emacs was invoked with the -q or --no-init-file options (see Section "Initial Options" in *The Emacs Manual*), Gnus doesn't read **gnus-init-file**.

1.7 Auto Save

Whenever you do something that changes the Gnus data (reading articles, catching up, killing/subscribing groups), the change is added to a special *dribble buffer*. This buffer is auto-saved the normal Emacs way. If your Emacs should crash before you have saved the .newsrc files, all changes you have made can be recovered from this file.

If Gnus detects this file at startup, it will ask the user whether to read it. The auto save file is deleted whenever the real startup file is saved.

If **gnus-use-dribble-file** is **nil**, Gnus won't create and maintain a dribble buffer. The default is **t**.

Gnus will put the dribble file(s) in **gnus-dribble-directory**. If this variable is **nil**, which it is by default, Gnus will dribble into the directory where the .newsrc file is located. (This is normally the user's home directory.) The dribble file will get the same file permissions as the .newsrc file.

If **gnus-always-read-dribble-file** is non-**nil**, Gnus will read the dribble file on startup without querying the user.

1.8 The Active File

When Gnus starts, or indeed whenever it tries to determine whether new articles have arrived, it reads the active file. This is a very large file that lists all the active groups and articles on the server.

Before examining the active file, Gnus deletes all lines that match the regexp **gnus-ignored-newsgroups**. This is done primarily to reject any groups with bogus names, but you can use this variable to make Gnus ignore hierarchies you aren't ever interested in. However, this is not recommended. In fact, it's highly discouraged. Instead, see Section 1.4 [New Groups], page 4 for an overview of other variables that can be used instead.

The active file can be rather Huge, so if you have a slow network, you can set **gnus-read-active-file** to **nil** to prevent Gnus from reading the active file. This variable is **some** by default.

Gnus will try to make do by getting information just on the groups that you actually subscribe to.

Note that if you subscribe to lots and lots of groups, setting this variable to `nil` will probably make Gnus slower, not faster. At present, having this variable `nil` will slow Gnus down considerably, unless you read news over a 2400 baud modem.

This variable can also have the value `some`. Gnus will then attempt to read active info only on the subscribed groups. On some servers this is quite fast (on sparkling, brand new INN servers that support the `LIST ACTIVE group` command), on others this isn't fast at all. In any case, `some` should be faster than `nil`, and is certainly faster than `t` over slow lines.

Some news servers (old versions of Leafnode and old versions of INN, for instance) do not support the `LIST ACTIVE group`. For these servers, `nil` is probably the most efficient value for this variable.

If this variable is `nil`, Gnus will ask for group info in total lock-step, which isn't very fast. If it is `some` and you use an NNTP server, Gnus will pump out commands as fast as it can, and read all the replies in one swoop. This will normally result in better performance, but if the server does not support the aforementioned `LIST ACTIVE group` command, this isn't very nice to the server.

If you think that starting up Gnus takes too long, try all the three different values for this variable and see what works best for you.

In any case, if you use `some` or `nil`, you should definitely kill all groups that you aren't interested in to speed things up.

Note that this variable also affects active file retrieval from secondary select methods.

1.9 Startup Variables

`gnus-load-hook`

> A hook run while Gnus is being loaded. Note that this hook will normally be run just once in each Emacs session, no matter how many times you start Gnus.

`gnus-before-startup-hook`

> A hook called as the first thing when Gnus is started.

`gnus-before-resume-hook`

> A hook called as the first thing when Gnus is resumed after a suspend.

`gnus-startup-hook`

> A hook run as the very last thing after starting up Gnus

`gnus-started-hook`

> A hook that is run as the very last thing after starting up Gnus successfully.

`gnus-setup-news-hook`

> A hook that is run after reading the `.newsrc` file(s), but before generating the group buffer.

`gnus-check-bogus-newsgroups`

> If non-`nil`, Gnus will check for and delete all bogus groups at startup. A *bogus group* is a group that you have in your `.newsrc` file, but doesn't exist on the news server. Checking for bogus groups can take quite a while, so to save time and resources it's best to leave this option off, and do the checking for bogus groups once in a while from the group buffer instead (see Section 2.13 [Group Maintenance], page 32).

`gnus-inhibit-startup-message`

> If non-`nil`, the startup message won't be displayed. That way, your boss might not notice as easily that you are reading news instead of doing your job. Note that this variable is used before `~/.gnus.el` is loaded, so it should be set in `.emacs` instead.

`gnus-no-groups-message`

> Message displayed by Gnus when no groups are available.

`gnus-use-backend-marks`

> If non-`nil`, Gnus will store article marks both in the `.newsrc.eld` file and in the backends. This will slow down group operation some.

2 Group Buffer

The *group buffer* lists all (or parts) of the available groups. It is the first buffer shown when Gnus starts, and will never be killed as long as Gnus is active.

2.1 Group Buffer Format

You can customize the Group Mode tool bar, see `M-x customize-apropos RET gnus-group-tool-bar`. This feature is only available in Emacs.

The tool bar icons are now (de)activated correctly depending on the cursor position. Therefore, moving around in the Group Buffer is slower. You can disable this via the variable `gnus-group-update-tool-bar`. Its default value depends on your Emacs version.

2.1.1 Group Line Specification

The default format of the group buffer is nice and dull, but you can make it as exciting and ugly as you feel like.

Here's a couple of example group lines:

```
      25: news.announce.newusers
 *     0: alt.fan.andrea-dworkin
```

Quite simple, huh?

You can see that there are 25 unread articles in 'news.announce.newusers'. There are no unread articles, but some ticked articles, in 'alt.fan.andrea-dworkin' (see that little asterisk at the beginning of the line?).

You can change that format to whatever you want by fiddling with the `gnus-group-line-format` variable. This variable works along the lines of a `format` specification, which is pretty much the same as a `printf` specifications, for those of you who use (feh!) C. See Section 9.4 [Formatting Variables], page 250.

'`%M%S%5y:%B%(%g%)\n`' is the value that produced those lines above.

There should always be a colon on the line; the cursor always moves to the colon after performing an operation. See Section 9.4.6 [Positioning Point], page 253. Nothing else is required—not even the group name. All displayed text is just window dressing, and is never examined by Gnus. Gnus stores all real information it needs using text properties.

(Note that if you make a really strange, wonderful, spreadsheet-like layout, everybody will believe you are hard at work with the accounting instead of wasting time reading news.)

Here's a list of all available format characters:

'M'   An asterisk if the group only has marked articles.

'S'   Whether the group is subscribed.

'L'   Level of subscribedness.

'N'   Number of unread articles.

'I'   Number of dormant articles.

'T'   Number of ticked articles.

'R'   Number of read articles.

'U'   Number of unseen articles.

't'   Estimated total number of articles. (This is really *max-number* minus *min-number* plus 1.)

               Gnus uses this estimation because the NNTP protocol provides efficient access to *max-number* and *min-number* but getting the true unread message count is not possible efficiently. For hysterical raisins, even the mail back ends, where the true number of unread messages might be available efficiently, use the same limited interface. To remove this restriction from Gnus means that the back end interface has to be changed, which is not an easy job.

               The nnml backend (see Section 6.4.13.3 [Mail Spool], page 174) has a feature called "group compaction" which circumvents this deficiency: the idea is to renumber all articles from 1, removing all gaps between numbers, hence getting a correct total count. Other backends may support this in the future. In order to keep your total article count relatively up to date, you might want to compact your groups (or even directly your server) from time to time. See Section 2.18 [Misc Group Stuff], page 40, See Section 6.1.2 [Server Commands], page 137.

'y'   Number of unread, unticked, non-dormant articles.

'i'   Number of ticked and dormant articles.

'g'   Full group name.

'G'   Group name.

'C'   Group comment (see Section 2.10 [Group Parameters], page 22) or group name if there is no comment element in the group parameters.

'D'   Newsgroup description. You need to read the group descriptions before these will appear, and to do that, you either have to set `gnus-read-active-file` or use the group buffer *M-d* command.

'o'   'm' if moderated.

'O'   '(m)' if moderated.

's'   Select method.

'B'   If the summary buffer for the group is open or not.

'n'   Select from where.

'z'   A string that looks like '<%s:%n>' if a foreign select method is used.

'P'   Indentation based on the level of the topic (see Section 2.16 [Group Topics], page 33).

'c'   Short (collapsed) group name. The `gnus-group-uncollapsed-levels` variable says how many levels to leave at the end of the group name. The default is 1—this will mean that group names like 'gnu.emacs.gnus' will be shortened to 'g.e.gnus'.

'm'   '%' (`gnus-new-mail-mark`) if there has arrived new mail to the group lately.

'p'   '#' (`gnus-process-mark`) if the group is process marked.

'd'   A string that says when you last read the group (see Section 2.18.3 [Group Timestamp], page 42).

'F'   The disk space used by the articles fetched by both the cache and agent. The value is automatically scaled to bytes(B), kilobytes(K), megabytes(M), or gigabytes(G) to minimize the column width. A format of %7F is sufficient for a fixed-width column.

'u'   User defined specifier. The next character in the format string should be a letter. Gnus will call the function `gnus-user-format-function-'X'`, where 'X' is the letter following '%u'. The function will be passed a single dummy parameter as argument. The function should return a string, which will be inserted into the buffer just like information from any other specifier.

All the "number-of" specs will be filled with an asterisk ('*') if no infc is available—for instance, if it is a non-activated foreign group, or a bogus native group.

2.1.2 Group Mode Line Specification

The mode line can be changed by setting `gnus-group-mode-line-format` (see Section 9.4.2 [Mode Line Formatting], page 251). It doesn't understand that many format specifiers:

'S'   The native news server.

'M'   The native select method.

2.1.3 Group Highlighting

Highlighting in the group buffer is controlled by the `gnus-group-highlight` variable. This is an alist with elements that look like (*form . face*). If *form* evaluates to something non-`nil`, the *face* will be used on the line.

Here's an example value for this variable that might look nice if the background is dark:

```
(cond (window-system
       (setq custom-background-mode 'light)
       (defface my-group-face-1
         '((t (:foreground "Red" :bold t))) "First group face")
       (defface my-group-face-2
         '((t (:foreground "DarkSeaGreen4" :bold t)))
         "Second group face")
       (defface my-group-face-3
         '((t (:foreground "Green4" :bold t))) "Third group face")
       (defface my-group-face-4
         '((t (:foreground "SteelBlue" :bold t))) "Fourth group face")
       (defface my-group-face-5
         '((t (:foreground "Blue" :bold t))) "Fifth group face")))

(setq gnus-group-highlight
      '(((> unread 200) . my-group-face-1)
        ((and (< level 3) (zerop unread)) . my-group-face-2)
        ((< level 3) . my-group-face-3)
        ((zerop unread) . my-group-face-4)
```

```
(t . my-group-face-5)))
```

Also see Section 9.6 [Faces and Fonts], page 258.

Variables that are dynamically bound when the forms are evaluated include:

group   The group name.

unread   The number of unread articles in the group.

method   The select method.

mailp   Whether the group is a mail group.

level   The level of the group.

score   The score of the group.

ticked   The number of ticked articles in the group.

total   The total number of articles in the group. Or rather, *max-number* minus *min-number* plus one.

topic   When using the topic minor mode, this variable is bound to the current topic being inserted.

When the forms are evaled, point is at the beginning of the line of the group in question, so you can use many of the normal Gnus functions for snarfing info on the group.

gnus-group-update-hook is called when a group line is changed. It will not be called when gnus-visual is nil.

2.2 Group Maneuvering

All movement commands understand the numeric prefix and will behave as expected, hopefully.

n   Go to the next group that has unread articles (**gnus-group-next-unread-group**).

p
DEL   Go to the previous group that has unread articles (**gnus-group-prev-unread-group**).

N   Go to the next group (**gnus-group-next-group**).

P   Go to the previous group (**gnus-group-prev-group**).

M-n   Go to the next unread group on the same (or lower) level (**gnus-group-next-unread-group-same-level**).

M-p   Go to the previous unread group on the same (or lower) level (**gnus-group-prev-unread-group-same-level**).

Three commands for jumping to groups:

j   Jump to a group (and make it visible if it isn't already) (**gnus-group-jump-to-group**). Killed groups can be jumped to, just like living groups.

,   Jump to the unread group with the lowest level (**gnus-group-best-unread-group**).

. Jump to the first group with unread articles (`gnus-group-first-unread-group`).

If `gnus-group-goto-unread` is `nil`, all the movement commands will move to the next group, not the next unread group. Even the commands that say they move to the next unread group. The default is `t`.

If `gnus-summary-next-group-on-exit` is `t`, when a summary is exited, the point in the group buffer is moved to the next unread group. Otherwise, the point is set to the group just exited. The default is `t`.

2.3 Selecting a Group

SPACE   Select the current group, switch to the summary buffer and display the first unread article (`gnus-group-read-group`). If there are no unread articles in the group, or if you give a non-numerical prefix to this command, Gnus will offer to fetch all the old articles in this group from the server. If you give a numerical prefix n, n determines the number of articles Gnus will fetch. If n is positive, Gnus fetches the n newest articles, if n is negative, Gnus fetches the `abs(n)` oldest articles.

Thus, *SPC* enters the group normally, *C-u SPC* offers old articles, *C-u 4 2 SPC* fetches the 42 newest articles, and *C-u - 4 2 SPC* fetches the 42 oldest ones.

When you are in the group (in the Summary buffer), you can type *M-g* to fetch new articles, or *C-u M-g* to also show the old ones.

RET   Select the current group and switch to the summary buffer (`gnus-group-select-group`). Takes the same arguments as `gnus-group-read-group`—the only difference is that this command does not display the first unread article automatically upon group entry.

M-RET   This does the same as the command above, but tries to do it with the minimum amount of fuzz (`gnus-group-quick-select-group`). No scoring/killing will be performed, there will be no highlights and no expunging. This might be useful if you're in a real hurry and have to enter some humongous group. If you give a 0 prefix to this command (i.e., *0 M-RET*), Gnus won't even generate the summary buffer, which is useful if you want to toggle threading before generating the summary buffer (see Section 3.27.3 [Summary Generation Commands], page 110).

M-SPACE This is yet one more command that does the same as the *RET* command, but this one does it without expunging and hiding dormants (`gnus-group-visible-select-group`).

C-M-RET Finally, this command selects the current group ephemerally without doing any processing of its contents (`gnus-group-select-group-ephemerally`). Even threading has been turned off. Everything you do in the group after selecting it in this manner will have no permanent effects.

The `gnus-large-newsgroup` variable says what Gnus should consider to be a big group. If it is `nil`, no groups are considered big. The default value is 200. If the group has more (unread and/or ticked) articles than this, Gnus will query the user before entering the group.

The user can then specify how many articles should be fetched from the server. If the user specifies a negative number (-n), the n oldest articles will be fetched. If it is positive, the n articles that have arrived most recently will be fetched.

`gnus-large-ephemeral-newsgroup` is the same as `gnus-large-newsgroup`, but is only used for ephemeral newsgroups.

In groups in some news servers, there might be a big gap between a few very old articles that will never be expired and the recent ones. In such a case, the server will return the data like (1 . 30000000) for the LIST ACTIVE group command, for example. Even if there are actually only the articles 1–10 and 29999900–30000000, Gnus doesn't know it at first and prepares for getting 30000000 articles. However, it will consume hundreds megabytes of memories and might make Emacs get stuck as the case may be. If you use such news servers, set the variable `gnus-newsgroup-maximum-articles` to a positive number. The value means that Gnus ignores articles other than this number of the latest ones in every group. For instance, the value 10000 makes Gnus get only the articles 29990001–30000000 (if the latest article number is 30000000 in a group). Note that setting this variable to a number might prevent you from reading very old articles. The default value of the variable `gnus-newsgroup-maximum-articles` is `nil`, which means Gnus never ignores old articles.

If `gnus-auto-select-first` is non-`nil`, select an article automatically when entering a group with the *SPACE* command. Which article this is controlled by the `gnus-auto-select-subject` variable. Valid values for this variable are:

unread   Place point on the subject line of the first unread article.

first   Place point on the subject line of the first article.

unseen   Place point on the subject line of the first unseen article.

unseen-or-unread
            Place point on the subject line of the first unseen article, and if there is no such article, place point on the subject line of the first unread article.

best   Place point on the subject line of the highest-scored unread article.

This variable can also be a function. In that case, that function will be called to place point on a subject line.

If you want to prevent automatic selection in some group (say, in a binary group with Huge articles) you can set the `gnus-auto-select-first` variable to `nil` in `gnus-select-group-hook`, which is called when a group is selected.

2.4 Subscription Commands

The following commands allow for managing your subscriptions in the Group buffer. If you want to subscribe to many groups, it's probably more convenient to go to the Section 6.1 [Server Buffer], page 136, and choose the server there using *RET* or *SPC*. Then you'll have the commands listed in Section 2.14 [Browse Foreign Server], page 32 at hand.

S t

u   Toggle subscription to the current group (`gnus-group-unsubscribe-current-group`).

S s	
U	Prompt for a group to subscribe, and then subscribe it. If it was subscribed already, unsubscribe it instead (**gnus-group-unsubscribe-group**).
S k	
C-k	Kill the current group (**gnus-group-kill-group**).
S y	
C-y	Yank the last killed group (**gnus-group-yank-group**).
C-x C-t	Transpose two groups (**gnus-group-transpose-groups**). This isn't really a subscription command, but you can use it instead of a kill-and-yank sequence sometimes.
S w	
C-w	Kill all groups in the region (**gnus-group-kill-region**).
S z	Kill all zombie groups (**gnus-group-kill-all-zombies**).
S C-k	Kill all groups on a certain level (**gnus-group-kill-level**). These groups can't be yanked back after killing, so this command should be used with some caution. The only time where this command comes in really handy is when you have a .newsrc with lots of unsubscribed groups that you want to get rid off. *S C-k* on level 7 will kill off all unsubscribed groups that do not have message numbers in the .newsrc file.

Also see Section 2.6 [Group Levels], page 17.

2.5 Group Data

c	Mark all unticked articles in this group as read (**gnus-group-catchup-current**). **gnus-group-catchup-group-hook** is called when catching up a group from the group buffer.
C	Mark all articles in this group, even the ticked ones, as read (**gnus-group-catchup-current-all**).
M-c	Clear the data from the current group—nix out marks and the list of read articles (**gnus-group-clear-data**).
M-x gnus-group-clear-data-on-native-groups	
	If you have switched from one NNTP server to another, all your marks and read ranges have become worthless. You can use this command to clear out all data that you have on your native groups. Use with caution.

2.6 Group Levels

All groups have a level of *subscribedness*. For instance, if a group is on level 2, it is more subscribed than a group on level 5. You can ask Gnus to just list groups on a given level or lower (see Section 2.11 [Listing Groups], page 29), or to just check for new articles in groups on a given level or lower (see Section 2.18.1 [Scanning New Messages], page 41).

Remember: The higher the level of the group, the less important it is.

S l   Set the level of the current group. If a numeric prefix is given, the next *n* groups
              will have their levels set. The user will be prompted for a level.

Gnus considers groups from levels 1 to **gnus-level-subscribed** (inclusive) (default
5) to be subscribed, **gnus-level-subscribed** (exclusive) and **gnus-level-unsubscribed**
(inclusive) (default 7) to be unsubscribed, **gnus-level-zombie** to be zombies (walking
dead) (default 8) and **gnus-level-killed** to be killed (completely dead) (default 9). Gnus
treats subscribed and unsubscribed groups exactly the same, but zombie and killed groups
store no information on what articles you have read, etc. This distinction between dead and
living groups isn't done because it is nice or clever, it is done purely for reasons of efficiency.

It is recommended that you keep all your mail groups (if any) on quite low levels (e.g.,
1 or 2).

Maybe the following description of the default behavior of Gnus helps to understand
what these levels are all about. By default, Gnus shows you subscribed nonempty groups,
but by hitting *L* you can have it show empty subscribed groups and unsubscribed groups,
too. Type *l* to go back to showing nonempty subscribed groups again. Thus, unsubscribed
groups are hidden, in a way.

Zombie and killed groups are similar to unsubscribed groups in that they are hidden
by default. But they are different from subscribed and unsubscribed groups in that Gnus
doesn't ask the news server for information (number of messages, number of unread messages) on zombie and killed groups. Normally, you use *C-k* to kill the groups you aren't
interested in. If most groups are killed, Gnus is faster.

Why does Gnus distinguish between zombie and killed groups? Well, when a new group
arrives on the server, Gnus by default makes it a zombie group. This means that you are
normally not bothered with new groups, but you can type *A z* to get a list of all new groups.
Subscribe the ones you like and kill the ones you don't want. (*A k* shows a list of killed
groups.)

If you want to play with the level variables, you should show some care. Set them once,
and don't touch them ever again. Better yet, don't touch them at all unless you know
exactly what you're doing.

Two closely related variables are **gnus-level-default-subscribed** (default 3) and
gnus-level-default-unsubscribed (default 6), which are the levels that new groups will
be put on if they are (un)subscribed. These two variables should, of course, be inside the
relevant valid ranges.

If **gnus-keep-same-level** is non-**nil**, some movement commands will only move to
groups of the same level (or lower). In particular, going from the last article in one group
to the next group will go to the next group of the same level (or lower). This might be
handy if you want to read the most important groups before you read the rest.

If this variable is **best**, Gnus will make the next newsgroup the one with the best level.

All groups with a level less than or equal to **gnus-group-default-list-level** will be
listed in the group buffer by default. This variable can also be a function. In that case,
that function will be called and the result will be used as value.

If **gnus-group-list-inactive-groups** is non-**nil**, non-active groups will be listed along
with the unread groups. This variable is **t** by default. If it is **nil**, inactive groups won't be
listed.

If `gnus-group-use-permanent-levels` is non-`nil`, once you give a level prefix to *g* or *l*, all subsequent commands will use this level as the "work" level.

Gnus will normally just activate (i.e., query the server about) groups on level `gnus-activate-level` or less. If you don't want to activate unsubscribed groups, for instance, you might set this variable to 5. The default is 6.

2.7 Group Score

You would normally keep important groups on high levels, but that scheme is somewhat restrictive. Don't you wish you could have Gnus sort the group buffer according to how often you read groups, perhaps? Within reason?

This is what *group score* is for. You can have Gnus assign a score to each group through the mechanism described below. You can then sort the group buffer based on this score. Alternatively, you can sort on score and then level. (Taken together, the level and the score is called the *rank* of the group. A group that is on level 4 and has a score of 1 has a higher rank than a group on level 5 that has a score of 300. (The level is the most significant part and the score is the least significant part.))

If you want groups you read often to get higher scores than groups you read seldom you can add the `gnus-summary-bubble-group` function to the `gnus-summary-exit-hook` hook. This will result (after sorting) in a bubbling sort of action. If you want to see that in action after each summary exit, you can add `gnus-group-sort-groups-by-rank` or `gnus-group-sort-groups-by-score` to the same hook, but that will slow things down somewhat.

2.8 Marking Groups

If you want to perform some command on several groups, and they appear subsequently in the group buffer, you would normally just give a numerical prefix to the command. Most group commands will then do your bidding on those groups.

However, if the groups are not in sequential order, you can still perform a command on several groups. You simply mark the groups first with the process mark and then execute the command.

#
M m   Set the mark on the current group (`gnus-group-mark-group`).

M-#
M u   Remove the mark from the current group (`gnus-group-unmark-group`).

M U   Remove the mark from all groups (`gnus-group-unmark-all-groups`).

M w   Mark all groups between point and mark (`gnus-group-mark-region`).

M b   Mark all groups in the buffer (`gnus-group-mark-buffer`).

M r   Mark all groups that match some regular expression (`gnus-group-mark-regexp`).

Also see Section 9.1 [Process/Prefix], page 249.

If you want to execute some command on all groups that have been marked with the process mark, you can use the *M-&* (`gnus-group-universal-argument`) command. It will prompt you for the command to be executed.

2.9 Foreign Groups

If you recall how to subscribe to servers (see Section 1.1 [Finding the News], page 2) you will remember that **gnus-secondary-select-methods** and **gnus-select-method** let you write a definition in Emacs Lisp of what servers you want to see when you start up. The alternate approach is to use foreign servers and groups. "Foreign" here means they are not coming from the select methods. All foreign server configuration and subscriptions are stored only in the `~/.newsrc.eld` file.

Below are some group mode commands for making and editing general foreign groups, as well as commands to ease the creation of a few special-purpose groups. All these commands insert the newly created groups under point—**gnus-subscribe-newsgroup-method** is not consulted.

Changes from the group editing commands are stored in `~/.newsrc.eld` (**gnus-startup-file**). An alternative is the variable **gnus-parameters**, See Section 2.10 [Group Parameters], page 22.

G m   Make a new group (**gnus-group-make-group**). Gnus will prompt you for a name, a method and possibly an *address*. For an easier way to subscribe to NNTP groups (see Section 2.14 [Browse Foreign Server], page 32).

G M   Make an ephemeral group (**gnus-group-read-ephemeral-group**). Gnus will prompt you for a name, a method and an *address*.

G r   Rename the current group to something else (**gnus-group-rename-group**). This is valid only on some groups—mail groups mostly. This command might very well be quite slow on some back ends.

G c   Customize the group parameters (**gnus-group-customize**).

G e   Enter a buffer where you can edit the select method of the current group (**gnus-group-edit-group-method**).

G p   Enter a buffer where you can edit the group parameters (**gnus-group-edit-group-parameters**).

G E   Enter a buffer where you can edit the group info (**gnus-group-edit-group**).

G d   Make a directory group (see Section 6.6.1 [Directory Groups], page 187). You will be prompted for a directory name (**gnus-group-make-directory-group**).

G h   Make the Gnus help group (**gnus-group-make-help-group**).

G D   Read an arbitrary directory as if it were a newsgroup with the **nneething** back end (**gnus-group-enter-directory**). See Section 6.6.2 [Anything Groups], page 187.

G f   Make a group based on some file or other (**gnus-group-make-doc-group**). If you give a prefix to this command, you will be prompted for a file name and a file type. Currently supported types are **mbox**, **babyl**, **digest**, **news**, **rnews**, **mmdf**, **forward**, **rfc934**, **rfc822-forward**, **mime-parts**, **standard-digest**, **slack-digest**, **clari-briefs**, **nsmail**, **outlook**, **oe-dbx**, and **mailman**. If you run this command without a prefix, Gnus will guess at the file type. See Section 6.6.3 [Document Groups], page 188.

G u   Create one of the groups mentioned in `gnus-useful-groups` (`gnus-group-make-useful-group`).

G w   Make an ephemeral group based on a web search (`gnus-group-make-web-group`). If you give a prefix to this command, make a solid group instead. You will be prompted for the search engine type and the search string. Valid search engine types include `google`, `dejanews`, and `gmane`. See Section 6.5.2 [Web Searches], page 184.

               If you use the `google` search engine, you can limit the search to a particular group by using a match string like 'shaving group:`alt.sysadmin.recovery`'.

G R   Make a group based on an RSS feed (`gnus-group-make-rss-group`). You will be prompted for an URL. See Section 6.5.3 [RSS], page 185.

G DEL   This function will delete the current group (`gnus-group-delete-group`). If given a prefix, this function will actually delete all the articles in the group, and forcibly remove the group itself from the face of the Earth. Use a prefix only if you are absolutely sure of what you are doing. This command can't be used on read-only groups (like `nntp` groups), though.

G V   Make a new, fresh, empty `nnvirtual` group (`gnus-group-make-empty-virtual`). See Section 6.7.1 [Virtual Groups], page 193.

G v   Add the current group to an `nnvirtual` group (`gnus-group-add-to-virtual`). Uses the process/prefix convention.

See Chapter 6 [Select Methods], page 136, for more information on the various select methods.

If `gnus-activate-foreign-newsgroups` is a positive number, Gnus will check all foreign groups with this level or lower at startup. This might take quite a while, especially if you subscribe to lots of groups from different NNTP servers. Also see Section 2.6 [Group Levels], page 17; `gnus-activate-level` also affects activation of foreign newsgroups.

The following commands create ephemeral groups. They can be called not only from the Group buffer, but in any Gnus buffer.

`gnus-read-ephemeral-gmane-group`
               Read an ephemeral group on Gmane.org. The articles are downloaded via HTTP using the URL specified by `gnus-gmane-group-download-format`. Gnus will prompt you for a group name, the start article number and an the article range.

`gnus-read-ephemeral-gmane-group-url`
               This command is similar to `gnus-read-ephemeral-gmane-group`, but the group name and the article number and range are constructed from a given URL. Supported URL formats include: '`http://thread.gmane.org/gmane.foo.bar/12300/focus=12399`', '`http://thread.gmane.org/gmane.foo.bar/12345/`', '`http://article.gmane.org/gmane.foo`' '`http://permalink.gmane.org/gmane.foo.bar/12345/`', and '`http://news.gmane.org/group/gmane.foo.bar/thread=12345`'.

gnus-read-ephemeral-emacs-bug-group
> Read an Emacs bug report in an ephemeral group. Gnus will prompt for a bug number. The default is the number at point. The URL is specified in gnus-bug-group-download-format-alist.

gnus-read-ephemeral-debian-bug-group
> Read a Debian bug report in an ephemeral group. Analog to gnus-read-ephemeral-emacs-bug-group.

Some of these command are also useful for article buttons, See Section 3.18.6 [Article Buttons], page 92.

Here is an example:

```
(require 'gnus-art)
(add-to-list
 'gnus-button-alist
 '("#\\([0-9]+\\)\\>" 1
   (string-match "\\<emacs\\>" (or gnus-newsgroup-name ""))
   gnus-read-ephemeral-emacs-bug-group 1))
```

2.10 Group Parameters

The group parameters store information local to a particular group.

Use the *G p* or the *G c* command to edit group parameters of a group. (*G p* presents you with a Lisp-based interface, *G c* presents you with a Customize-like interface. The latter helps avoid silly Lisp errors.) You might also be interested in reading about topic parameters (see Section 2.16.5 [Topic Parameters], page 37). Additionally, you can set group parameters via the gnus-parameters variable, see below.

Here's an example group parameter list:

```
((to-address . "ding@gnus.org")
 (auto-expire . t))
```

We see that each element consists of a "dotted pair"—the thing before the dot is the key, while the thing after the dot is the value. All the parameters have this form *except* local variable specs, which are not dotted pairs, but proper lists.

Some parameters have correspondent customizable variables, each of which is an alist of regexps and values.

The following group parameters can be used:

to-address
> Address used by when doing followups and new posts.
>
> ```
> (to-address . "some@where.com")
> ```
>
> This is primarily useful in mail groups that represent closed mailing lists— mailing lists where it's expected that everybody that writes to the mailing list is subscribed to it. Since using this parameter ensures that the mail only goes to the mailing list itself, it means that members won't receive two copies of your followups.
>
> Using to-address will actually work whether the group is foreign or not. Let's say there's a group on the server that is called 'fa.4ad-1'. This is a real

newsgroup, but the server has gotten the articles from a mail-to-news gateway. Posting directly to this group is therefore impossible—you have to send mail to the mailing list address instead.

See also `gnus-parameter-to-address-alist`.

to-list   Address used when doing `a` in that group.

> ```
> (to-list . "some@where.com")
> ```

It is totally ignored when doing a followup—except that if it is present in a news group, you'll get mail group semantics when doing `f`.

If you do an `a` command in a mail group and you have neither a `to-list` group parameter nor a `to-address` group parameter, then a `to-list` group parameter will be added automatically upon sending the message if `gnus-add-to-list` is set to `t`.

If this variable is set, `gnus-mailing-list-mode` is turned on when entering summary buffer.

See also `gnus-parameter-to-list-alist`.

subscribed

If this parameter is set to `t`, Gnus will consider the to-address and to-list parameters for this group as addresses of mailing lists you are subscribed to. Giving Gnus this information is (only) a first step in getting it to generate correct Mail-Followup-To headers for your posts to these lists. The second step is to put the following in your `.gnus.el`

> ```
> (setq message-subscribed-address-functions
>       '(gnus-find-subscribed-addresses))
> ```

See Section "Mailing Lists" in *The Message Manual*, for a complete treatment of available MFT support.

visible   If the group parameter list has the element `(visible . t)`, that group will always be visible in the Group buffer, regardless of whether it has any unread articles.

This parameter cannot be set via `gnus-parameters`. See `gnus-permanently-visible-groups` as an alternative.

broken-reply-to

Elements like `(broken-reply-to . t)` signals that `Reply-To` headers in this group are to be ignored, and for the header to be hidden if `reply-to` is part of `gnus-boring-article-headers`. This can be useful if you're reading a mailing list group where the listserv has inserted `Reply-To` headers that point back to the listserv itself. That is broken behavior. So there!

to-group   Elements like `(to-group . "some.group.name")` means that all posts in that group will be sent to `some.group.name`.

newsgroup

If you have `(newsgroup . t)` in the group parameter list, Gnus will treat all responses as if they were responses to news articles. This can be useful if you have a mail group that's really a mirror of a news group.

gcc-self   If (`gcc-self . t`) is present in the group parameter list, newly composed mes-
            sages will be `gcc`d to the current group. If (`gcc-self . none`) is present,
            no `Gcc:` header will be generated, if (`gcc-self . "group"`) is present, this
            string will be inserted literally as a `Gcc:` header. It should be a group name.
            The `gcc-self` value may also be a list of strings and `t`, e.g., (`gcc-self`
            `"group1" "group2" t`) means to `gcc` the newly composed message into the
            groups `"group1"` and `"group2"`, and into the current group. The `gcc-self`
            parameter takes precedence over any default `Gcc` rules as described later (see
            Section 5.5 [Archived Messages], page 128), with the exception for messages to
            resend.

            Caveat: Adding (`gcc-self . t`) to the parameter list of **nntp** groups (or the
            like) isn't valid. An **nntp** server doesn't accept articles.

auto-expire
            If the group parameter has an element that looks like (`auto-expire . t`), all
            articles read will be marked as expirable. For an alternative approach, see
            Section 6.4.9 [Expiring Mail], page 168.

            See also **gnus-auto-expirable-newsgroups**.

total-expire
            If the group parameter has an element that looks like (`total-expire . t`), all
            read articles will be put through the expiry process, even if they are not marked
            as expirable. Use with caution. Unread, ticked and dormant articles are not
            eligible for expiry.

            See also **gnus-total-expirable-newsgroups**.

expiry-wait
            If the group parameter has an element that looks like (`expiry-wait . 10`),
            this value will override any **nnmail-expiry-wait** and **nnmail-expiry-wait-**
            function (see Section 6.4.9 [Expiring Mail], page 168) when expiring expirable
            messages. The value can either be a number of days (not necessarily an integer)
            or the symbols **never** or **immediate**.

expiry-target
            Where expired messages end up. This parameter overrides **nnmail-expiry-**
            target.

score-file
            Elements that look like (`score-file . "file"`) will make `file` into the current
            score file for the group in question. All interactive score entries will be put into
            this file.

adapt-file
            Elements that look like (`adapt-file . "file"`) will make `file` into the current
            adaptive file for the group in question. All adaptive score entries will be put
            into this file.

admin-address
            When unsubscribing from a mailing list you should never send the unsubscrip-
            tion notice to the mailing list itself. Instead, you'd send messages to the ad-

ministrative address. This parameter allows you to put the admin address somewhere convenient.

display   Elements that look like (`display . MODE`) say which articles to display on entering the group. Valid values are:

all   Display all articles, both read and unread.

an integer

Display the last *integer* articles in the group. This is the same as entering the group with `C-u integer`.

default   Display the default visible articles, which normally includes unread and ticked articles.

an array Display articles that satisfy a predicate.

Here are some examples:

[unread]   Display only unread articles.

[not expire]

Display everything except expirable articles.

[and (not reply) (not expire)]

Display everything except expirable and articles you've already responded to.

The available operators are **not**, **and** and **or**. Predicates include **tick**, **unsend**, **undownload**, **unread**, **dormant**, **expire**, **reply**, **killed**, **bookmark**, **score**, **save**, **cache**, **forward**, and **unseen**.

The **display** parameter works by limiting the summary buffer to the subset specified. You can pop the limit by using the `/ w` command (see Section 3.8 [Limiting], page 63).

comment   Elements that look like (`comment . "This is a comment"`) are arbitrary comments on the group. You can display comments in the group line (see Section 2.1.1 [Group Line Specification], page 11).

charset   Elements that look like (`charset . iso-8859-1`) will make `iso-8859-1` the default charset; that is, the charset that will be used for all articles that do not specify a charset.

See also **gnus-group-charset-alist**.

ignored-charsets

Elements that look like (`ignored-charsets x-unknown iso-8859-1`) will make `iso-8859-1` and `x-unknown` ignored; that is, the default charset will be used for decoding articles.

See also **gnus-group-ignored-charsets-alist**.

posting-style

You can store additional posting style information for this group here (see Section 5.6 [Posting Styles], page 131). The format is that of an entry in the **gnus-posting-styles** alist, except that there's no regexp matching the group name (of course). Style elements in this group parameter will take precedence over the ones found in `gnus-posting-styles`.

For instance, if you want a funky name and signature in this group only, instead of hacking `gnus-posting-styles`, you could put something like this in the group parameters:

```
(posting-style
  (name "Funky Name")
  ("X-Message-SMTP-Method" "smtp smtp.example.org 587")
  ("X-My-Header" "Funky Value")
  (signature "Funky Signature"))
```

If you're using topics to organize your group buffer (see Section 2.16 [Group Topics], page 33), note that posting styles can also be set in the topics parameters. Posting styles in topic parameters apply to all groups in this topic. More precisely, the posting-style settings for a group result from the hierarchical merging of all posting-style entries in the parameters of this group and all the topics it belongs to.

`post-method`

If it is set, the value is used as the method for posting message instead of `gnus-post-method`.

`mail-source`

If it is set, and the setting of `mail-sources` includes a `group` mail source (see Section 6.4.4 [Mail Sources], page 154), the value is a mail source for this group.

`banner`   An item like (`banner . ` *regexp*) causes any part of an article that matches the regular expression *regexp* to be stripped. Instead of *regexp*, you can also use the symbol `signature` which strips the last signature or any of the elements of the alist `gnus-article-banner-alist`.

`sieve`   This parameter contains a Sieve test that should match incoming mail that should be placed in this group. From this group parameter, a Sieve 'IF' control structure is generated, having the test as the condition and 'fileinto "group.name";' as the body.

For example, if the 'INBOX.list.sieve' group has the (`sieve address "sender" "sieve-admin@extundo.com"`) group parameter, when translating the group parameter into a Sieve script (see Section 2.18.5 [Sieve Commands], page 43) the following Sieve code is generated:

```
if address "sender" "sieve-admin@extundo.com" {
        fileinto "INBOX.list.sieve";
}
```

To generate tests for multiple email-addresses use a group parameter like (`sieve address "sender" ("name@one.org" else@two.org")`). When generating a sieve script (see Section 2.18.5 [Sieve Commands], page 43) Sieve code like the following is generated:

```
if address "sender" ["name@one.org", "else@two.org"] {
        fileinto "INBOX.list.sieve";
}
```

You can also use regexp expansions in the rules:

```
(sieve header :regex "list-id" "<c++std-\\1.accu.org>")
```

See see Section 2.18.5 [Sieve Commands], page 43 for commands and variables that might be of interest in relation to the sieve parameter.

The Sieve language is described in RFC 3028. See *Emacs Sieve*.

`(agent parameters)`

If the agent has been enabled, you can set any of its parameters to control the behavior of the agent in individual groups. See Agent Parameters in Section 6.9.2.1 [Category Syntax], page 201. Most users will choose to set agent parameters in either an agent category or group topic to minimize the configuration effort.

`(variable form)`

You can use the group parameters to set variables local to the group you are entering. If you want to turn threading off in 'news.answers', you could put (gnus-show-threads nil) in the group parameters of that group. gnus-show-threads will be made into a local variable in the summary buffer you enter, and the form nil will be evaled there.

Note that this feature sets the variable locally to the summary buffer if and only if *variable* has been bound as a variable. Otherwise, only evaluating the form will take place. So, you may want to bind the variable in advance using defvar or other if the result of the form needs to be set to it.

But some variables are evaluated in the article buffer, or in the message buffer (of a reply or followup or otherwise newly created message). As a workaround, it might help to add the variable in question to gnus-newsgroup-variables. See Section 3.27 [Various Summary Stuff], page 108. So if you want to set message-from-style via the group parameters, then you may need the following statement elsewhere in your ~/.gnus.el file:

```
(add-to-list 'gnus-newsgroup-variables 'message-from-style)
```

A use for this feature is to remove a mailing list identifier tag in the subject fields of articles. E.g., if the news group

```
nntp+news.gnus.org:gmane.text.docbook.apps
```

has the tag 'DOC-BOOK-APPS:' in the subject of all articles, this tag can be removed from the article subjects in the summary buffer for the group by putting (gnus-list-identifiers "DOCBOOK-APPS:") into the group parameters for the group.

This can also be used as a group-specific hook function. If you want to hear a beep when you enter a group, you could put something like (dummy-variable (ding)) in the parameters of that group. If dummy-variable has been bound (see above), it will be set to the (meaningless) result of the (ding) form.

Alternatively, since the VARIABLE becomes local to the group, this pattern can be used to temporarily change a hook. For example, if the following is added to a group parameter

```
(gnus-summary-prepared-hook
```

```
          (lambda nil (local-set-key "d" (local-key-binding "n")))))
```
when the group is entered, the 'd' key will not mark the article as expired.

Group parameters can be set via the **gnus-parameters** variable too. But some variables, such as **visible**, have no effect (For this case see **gnus-permanently-visible-groups** as an alternative.). For example:

```
(setq gnus-parameters
      '(("mail\\..*"
         (gnus-show-threads nil)
         (gnus-use-scoring nil)
         (gnus-summary-line-format
          "%U%R%z%I%(%[%d:%ub%-23,23f%]%) %s\n")
         (gcc-self . t)
         (display . all))

        ("^nnimap:\\(foo.bar\\)$"
         (to-group . "\\1"))

        ("mail\\.me"
         (gnus-use-scoring t))

        ("list\\..*"
         (total-expire . t)
         (broken-reply-to . t))))
```

All clauses that matches the group name will be used, but the last setting "wins". So if you have two clauses that both match the group name, and both set, say **display**, the last setting will override the first.

Parameters that are strings will be subjected to regexp substitution, as the **to-group** example shows.

By default, whether comparing the group name and one of those regexps specified in **gnus-parameters** is done in a case-sensitive manner or a case-insensitive manner depends on the value of **case-fold-search** at the time when the comparison is done. The value of **case-fold-search** is typically **t**; it means, for example, the element (`"INBOX\\.FOO"` (total-expire . t)) might be applied to both the 'INBOX.FOO' group and the 'INBOX.foo' group. If you want to make those regexps always case-sensitive, set the value of the **gnus-parameters-case-fold-search** variable to **nil**. Otherwise, set it to **t** if you want to compare them always in a case-insensitive manner.

You can define different sorting to different groups via **gnus-parameters**. Here is an example to sort an NNTP group by reverse date to see the latest news at the top and an RSS group by subject. In this example, the first group is the Debian daily news group **gmane.linux.debian.user.news** from news.gmane.org. The RSS group corresponds to the Debian weekly news RSS feed http://packages.debian.org/unstable/newpkg_main.en.rdf, See Section 6.5.3 [RSS], page 185.

```
(setq
 gnus-parameters
 '(("nntp.*gmane\\.debian\\.user\\.news"
```

```
    (gnus-show-threads nil)
    (gnus-article-sort-functions '((not gnus-article-sort-by-date)))
    (gnus-use-adaptive-scoring nil)
    (gnus-use-scoring nil))
   ("nnrss.*debian"
    (gnus-show-threads nil)
    (gnus-article-sort-functions 'gnus-article-sort-by-subject)
    (gnus-use-adaptive-scoring nil)
    (gnus-use-scoring t)
    (gnus-score-find-score-files-function 'gnus-score-find-single)
    (gnus-summary-line-format "%U%R%z%d %I%(%[ %s %]%)\n"))))
```

2.11 Listing Groups

These commands all list various slices of the groups available.

l

A s   List all groups that have unread articles (**gnus-group-list-groups**). If the numeric prefix is used, this command will list only groups of level ARG and lower. By default, it only lists groups of level five (i.e., **gnus-group-default-list-level**) or lower (i.e., just subscribed groups).

L

A u   List all groups, whether they have unread articles or not (**gnus-group-list-all-groups**). If the numeric prefix is used, this command will list only groups of level ARG and lower. By default, it lists groups of level seven or lower (i.e., just subscribed and unsubscribed groups).

A l   List all unread groups on a specific level (**gnus-group-list-level**). If given a prefix, also list the groups with no unread articles.

A k   List all killed groups (**gnus-group-list-killed**). If given a prefix argument, really list all groups that are available, but aren't currently (un)subscribed. This could entail reading the active file from the server.

A z   List all zombie groups (**gnus-group-list-zombies**).

A m   List all unread, subscribed groups with names that match a regexp (**gnus-group-list-matching**).

A M   List groups that match a regexp (**gnus-group-list-all-matching**).

A A   List absolutely all groups in the active file(s) of the server(s) you are connected to (**gnus-group-list-active**). This might very well take quite a while. It might actually be a better idea to do a **A M** to list all matching, and just give '.' as the thing to match on. Also note that this command may list groups that don't exist (yet)—these will be listed as if they were killed groups. Take the output with some grains of salt.

A a   List all groups that have names that match a regexp (**gnus-group-apropos**).

A d   List all groups that have names or descriptions that match a regexp (**gnus-group-description-apropos**).

A c   List all groups with cached articles (**gnus-group-list-cached**).

A ?   List all groups with dormant articles (**gnus-group-list-dormant**).

A !   List all groups with ticked articles (**gnus-group-list-ticked**).

A /   Further limit groups within the current selection (**gnus-group-list-limit**).
            If you've first limited to groups with dormant articles with A ?, you can then
            further limit with A / c, which will then limit to groups with cached articles,
            giving you the groups that have both dormant articles and cached articles.

A f   Flush groups from the current selection (**gnus-group-list-flush**).

A p   List groups plus the current selection (**gnus-group-list-plus**).

Groups that match the **gnus-permanently-visible-groups** regexp will always be shown, whether they have unread articles or not. You can also add the **visible** element to the group parameters in question to get the same effect.

Groups that have just ticked articles in it are normally listed in the group buffer. If **gnus-list-groups-with-ticked-articles** is **nil**, these groups will be treated just like totally empty groups. It is **t** by default.

2.12 Sorting Groups

The *C-c C-s* (**gnus-group-sort-groups**) command sorts the group buffer according to the function(s) given by the **gnus-group-sort-function** variable. Available sorting functions include:

gnus-group-sort-by-alphabet
            Sort the group names alphabetically. This is the default.

gnus-group-sort-by-real-name
            Sort the group alphabetically on the real (unprefixed) group names.

gnus-group-sort-by-level
            Sort by group level.

gnus-group-sort-by-score
            Sort by group score. See Section 2.7 [Group Score], page 19.

gnus-group-sort-by-rank
            Sort by group score and then the group level. The level and the score are, when
            taken together, the group's *rank*. See Section 2.7 [Group Score], page 19.

gnus-group-sort-by-unread
            Sort by number of unread articles.

gnus-group-sort-by-method
            Sort alphabetically on the select method.

gnus-group-sort-by-server
            Sort alphabetically on the Gnus server name.

gnus-group-sort-function can also be a list of sorting functions. In that case, the most significant sort key function must be the last one.

There are also a number of commands for sorting directly according to some sorting criteria:

G S a   Sort the group buffer alphabetically by group name (`gnus-group-sort-groups-by-alphabet`).

G S u   Sort the group buffer by the number of unread articles (`gnus-group-sort-groups-by-unread`).

G S l   Sort the group buffer by group level (`gnus-group-sort-groups-by-level`).

G S v   Sort the group buffer by group score (`gnus-group-sort-groups-by-score`). See Section 2.7 [Group Score], page 19.

G S r   Sort the group buffer by group rank (`gnus-group-sort-groups-by-rank`). See Section 2.7 [Group Score], page 19.

G S m   Sort the group buffer alphabetically by back end name (`gnus-group-sort-groups-by-method`).

G S n   Sort the group buffer alphabetically by real (unprefixed) group name (`gnus-group-sort-groups-by-real-name`).

All the commands below obey the process/prefix convention (see Section 9.1 [Process/Prefix], page 249).

When given a symbolic prefix (see Section 9.3 [Symbolic Prefixes], page 250), all these commands will sort in reverse order.

You can also sort a subset of the groups:

G P a   Sort the groups alphabetically by group name (`gnus-group-sort-selected-groups-by-alphabet`).

G P u   Sort the groups by the number of unread articles (`gnus-group-sort-selected-groups-by-unread`).

G P l   Sort the groups by group level (`gnus-group-sort-selected-groups-by-level`).

G P v   Sort the groups by group score (`gnus-group-sort-selected-groups-by-score`). See Section 2.7 [Group Score], page 19.

G P r   Sort the groups by group rank (`gnus-group-sort-selected-groups-by-rank`). See Section 2.7 [Group Score], page 19.

G P m   Sort the groups alphabetically by back end name (`gnus-group-sort-selected-groups-by-method`).

G P n   Sort the groups alphabetically by real (unprefixed) group name (`gnus-group-sort-selected-groups-by-real-name`).

G P s   Sort the groups according to `gnus-group-sort-function`.

And finally, note that you can use *C-k* and *C-y* to manually move groups around.

2.13 Group Maintenance

b   Find bogus groups and delete them (**gnus-group-check-bogus-groups**).

F   Find new groups and process them (**gnus-group-find-new-groups**). With 1
                C-u, use the **ask-server** method to query the server for new groups. With 2
                C-u's, use most complete method possible to query the server for new groups,
                and subscribe the new groups as zombies.

C-c C-x   Run all expirable articles in the current group through the expiry process (if
                any) (**gnus-group-expire-articles**). That is, delete all expirable articles in
                the group that have been around for a while. (see Section 6.4.9 [Expiring Mail],
                page 168).

C-c C-M-x   Run all expirable articles in all groups through the expiry process (**gnus-group-
                expire-all-groups**).

2.14 Browse Foreign Server

B   You will be queried for a select method and a server name. Gnus will then at-
                tempt to contact this server and let you browse the groups there (**gnus-group-
                browse-foreign-server**).

A new buffer with a list of available groups will appear. This buffer will use the
gnus-browse-mode. This buffer looks a bit (well, a lot) like a normal group buffer.

Here's a list of keystrokes available in the browse mode:

n   Go to the next group (**gnus-group-next-group**).

p   Go to the previous group (**gnus-group-prev-group**).

SPACE   Enter the current group and display the first article (**gnus-browse-read-
                group**).

RET   Enter the current group (**gnus-browse-select-group**).

u   Unsubscribe to the current group, or, as will be the case here, subscribe to
                it (**gnus-browse-unsubscribe-current-group**). You can affect the way the
                new group is entered into the Group buffer using the variable **gnus-browse-
                subscribe-newsgroup-method**. See see Section 1.4.2 [Subscription Methods],
                page 4 for available options.

l
q   Exit browse mode (**gnus-browse-exit**).

d   Describe the current group (**gnus-browse-describe-group**).

?   Describe browse mode briefly (well, there's not much to describe, is there)
                (**gnus-browse-describe-briefly**).

DEL   This function will delete the current group (**gnus-browse-delete-group**). If
                given a prefix, this function will actually delete all the articles in the group,
                and forcibly remove the group itself from the face of the Earth. Use a prefix
                only if you are absolutely sure of what you are doing.

2.15 Exiting Gnus

Yes, Gnus is ex(c)iting.

z   Suspend Gnus (`gnus-group-suspend`). This doesn't really exit Gnus, but it
            kills all buffers except the Group buffer. I'm not sure why this is a gain, but
            then who am I to judge?

q   Quit Gnus (`gnus-group-exit`).

Q   Quit Gnus without saving the `.newsrc` files (`gnus-group-quit`). The dribble
            file will be saved, though (see Section 1.7 [Auto Save], page 8).

`gnus-suspend-gnus-hook` is called when you suspend Gnus and `gnus-exit-gnus-hook`
is called when you quit Gnus, while `gnus-after-exiting-gnus-hook` is called as the final
item when exiting Gnus.

Note:

> Miss Lisa Cannifax, while sitting in English class, felt her feet go numbly heavy
> and herself fall into a hazy trance as the boy sitting behind her drew repeated
> lines with his pencil across the back of her plastic chair.

2.16 Group Topics

If you read lots and lots of groups, it might be convenient to group them hierarchically
according to topics. You put your Emacs groups over here, your sex groups over there, and
the rest (what, two groups or so?) you put in some misc section that you never bother
with anyway. You can even group the Emacs sex groups as a sub-topic to either the Emacs
groups or the sex groups—or both! Go wild!

Here's an example:

```
Gnus
    Emacs -- I wuw it!
       3: comp.emacs
       2: alt.religion.emacs
    Naughty Emacs
     452: alt.sex.emacs
       0: comp.talk.emacs.recovery
  Misc
       8: comp.binaries.fractals
      13: comp.sources.unix
```

To get this *fab* functionality you simply turn on (ooh!) the **gnus-topic** minor mode—
type *t* in the group buffer. (This is a toggling command.)

Go ahead, just try it. I'll still be here when you get back. La de dum... Nice tune,
that... la la la... What, you're back? Yes, and now press *l*. There. All your groups are
now listed under 'misc'. Doesn't that make you feel all warm and fuzzy? Hot and bothered?

If you want this permanently enabled, you should add that minor mode to the hook for
the group mode. Put the following line in your `~/.gnus.el` file:

```
(add-hook 'gnus-group-mode-hook 'gnus-topic-mode)
```

2.16.1 Topic Commands

When the topic minor mode is turned on, a new *T* submap will be available. In addition, a few of the standard keys change their definitions slightly.

In general, the following kinds of operations are possible on topics. First of all, you want to create topics. Secondly, you want to put groups in topics and to move them around until you have an order you like. The third kind of operation is to show/hide parts of the whole shebang. You might want to hide a topic including its subtopics and groups, to get a better overview of the other groups.

Here is a list of the basic keys that you might need to set up topics the way you like.

T n   Prompt for a new topic name and create it (**gnus-topic-create-topic**).

T TAB
TAB   "Indent" the current topic so that it becomes a sub-topic of the previous topic (**gnus-topic-indent**). If given a prefix, "un-indent" the topic instead.

M-TAB   "Un-indent" the current topic so that it becomes a sub-topic of the parent of its current parent (**gnus-topic-unindent**).

The following two keys can be used to move groups and topics around. They work like the well-known cut and paste. *C-k* is like cut and *C-y* is like paste. Of course, this being Emacs, we use the terms kill and yank rather than cut and paste.

C-k   Kill a group or topic (**gnus-topic-kill-group**). All groups in the topic will be removed along with the topic.

C-y   Yank the previously killed group or topic (**gnus-topic-yank-group**). Note that all topics will be yanked before all groups.

So, to move a topic to the beginning of the list of topics, just hit *C-k* on it. This is like the "cut" part of cut and paste. Then, move the cursor to the beginning of the buffer (just below the "Gnus" topic) and hit *C-y*. This is like the "paste" part of cut and paste. Like I said—E-Z.

You can use *C-k* and *C-y* on groups as well as on topics. So you can move topics around as well as groups.

After setting up the topics the way you like them, you might wish to hide a topic, or to show it again. That's why we have the following key.

RET
SPACE   Either select a group or fold a topic (**gnus-topic-select-group**). When you perform this command on a group, you'll enter the group, as usual. When done on a topic line, the topic will be folded (if it was visible) or unfolded (if it was folded already). So it's basically a toggling command on topics. In addition, if you give a numerical prefix, group on that level (and lower) will be displayed.

Now for a list of other commands, in no particular order.

T m   Move the current group to some other topic (**gnus-topic-move-group**). This command uses the process/prefix convention (see Section 9.1 [Process/Prefix], page 249).

T j   Go to a topic (**gnus-topic-jump-to-topic**).

T c	Copy the current group to some other topic (**gnus-topic-copy-group**). This command uses the process/prefix convention (see Section 9.1 [Process/Prefix], page 249).
T h	Hide the current topic (**gnus-topic-hide-topic**). If given a prefix, hide the topic permanently.
T s	Show the current topic (**gnus-topic-show-topic**). If given a prefix, show the topic permanently.
T D	Remove a group from the current topic (**gnus-topic-remove-group**). This command is mainly useful if you have the same group in several topics and wish to remove it from one of the topics. You may also remove a group from all topics, but in that case, Gnus will add it to the root topic the next time you start Gnus. In fact, all new groups (which, naturally, don't belong to any topic) will show up in the root topic.
	This command uses the process/prefix convention (see Section 9.1 [Process/Prefix], page 249).
T M	Move all groups that match some regular expression to a topic (**gnus-topic-move-matching**).
T C	Copy all groups that match some regular expression to a topic (**gnus-topic-copy-matching**).
T H	Toggle hiding empty topics (**gnus-topic-toggle-display-empty-topics**).
T #	Mark all groups in the current topic with the process mark (**gnus-topic-mark-topic**). This command works recursively on sub-topics unless given a prefix.
T M-#	Remove the process mark from all groups in the current topic (**gnus-topic-unmark-topic**). This command works recursively on sub-topics unless given a prefix.
C-c C-x	Run all expirable articles in the current group or topic through the expiry process (if any) (**gnus-topic-expire-articles**). (see Section 6.4.9 [Expiring Mail], page 168).
T r	Rename a topic (**gnus-topic-rename**).
T DEL	Delete an empty topic (**gnus-topic-delete**).
A T	List all groups that Gnus knows about in a topics-ified way (**gnus-topic-list-active**).
T M-n	Go to the next topic (**gnus-topic-goto-next-topic**).
T M-p	Go to the previous topic (**gnus-topic-goto-previous-topic**).
G p	Edit the topic parameters (**gnus-topic-edit-parameters**). See Section 2.16.5 [Topic Parameters], page 37.

2.16.2 Topic Variables

The previous section told you how to tell Gnus which topics to display. This section explains how to tell Gnus what to display about each topic.

The topic lines themselves are created according to the **gnus-topic-line-format** variable (see Section 9.4 [Formatting Variables], page 250). Valid elements are:

'i'   Indentation.

'n'   Topic name.

'v'   Visibility.

'l'   Level.

'g'   Number of groups in the topic.

'a'   Number of unread articles in the topic.

'A'   Number of unread articles in the topic and all its subtopics.

Each sub-topic (and the groups in the sub-topics) will be indented with **gnus-topic-indent-level** times the topic level number of spaces. The default is 2.

gnus-topic-mode-hook is called in topic minor mode buffers.

The **gnus-topic-display-empty-topics** says whether to display even topics that have no unread articles in them. The default is **t**.

2.16.3 Topic Sorting

You can sort the groups in each topic individually with the following commands:

T S a   Sort the current topic alphabetically by group name (**gnus-topic-sort-groups-by-alphabet**).

T S u   Sort the current topic by the number of unread articles (**gnus-topic-sort-groups-by-unread**).

T S l   Sort the current topic by group level (**gnus-topic-sort-groups-by-level**).

T S v   Sort the current topic by group score (**gnus-topic-sort-groups-by-score**). See Section 2.7 [Group Score], page 19.

T S r   Sort the current topic by group rank (**gnus-topic-sort-groups-by-rank**). See Section 2.7 [Group Score], page 19.

T S m   Sort the current topic alphabetically by back end name (**gnus-topic-sort-groups-by-method**).

T S e   Sort the current topic alphabetically by server name (**gnus-topic-sort-groups-by-server**).

T S s   Sort the current topic according to the function(s) given by the **gnus-group-sort-function** variable (**gnus-topic-sort-groups**).

When given a prefix argument, all these commands will sort in reverse order. See Section 2.12 [Sorting Groups], page 30, for more information about group sorting.

2.16.4 Topic Topology

So, let's have a look at an example group buffer:

```
Gnus
   Emacs -- I wuw it!
      3: comp.emacs
      2: alt.religion.emacs
    Naughty Emacs
    452: alt.sex.emacs
      0: comp.talk.emacs.recovery
  Misc
      8: comp.binaries.fractals
     13: comp.sources.unix
```

So, here we have one top-level topic ('Gnus'), two topics under that, and one sub-topic under one of the sub-topics. (There is always just one (1) top-level topic). This topology can be expressed as follows:

```
(("Gnus" visible)
 (("Emacs -- I wuw it!" visible)
  (("Naughty Emacs" visible)))
 (("Misc" visible)))
```

This is in fact how the variable `gnus-topic-topology` would look for the display above. That variable is saved in the `.newsrc.eld` file, and shouldn't be messed with manually—unless you really want to. Since this variable is read from the `.newsrc.eld` file, setting it in any other startup files will have no effect.

This topology shows what topics are sub-topics of what topics (right), and which topics are visible. Two settings are currently allowed—`visible` and `invisible`.

2.16.5 Topic Parameters

All groups in a topic will inherit group parameters from the parent (and ancestor) topic parameters. All valid group parameters are valid topic parameters (see Section 2.10 [Group Parameters], page 22). When the agent is enabled, all agent parameters (See Agent Parameters in Section 6.9.2.1 [Category Syntax], page 201) are also valid topic parameters.

In addition, the following parameters are only valid as topic parameters:

subscribe

> When subscribing new groups by topic (see Section 1.4.2 [Subscription Methods], page 4), the `subscribe` topic parameter says what groups go in what topic. Its value should be a regexp to match the groups that should go in that topic.

subscribe-level

> When subscribing new groups by topic (see the `subscribe` parameter), the group will be subscribed with the level specified in the `subscribe-level` instead of `gnus-level-default-subscribed`.

Group parameters (of course) override topic parameters, and topic parameters in sub-topics override topic parameters in super-topics. You know. Normal inheritance rules. (*Rules* is here a noun, not a verb, although you may feel free to disagree with me here.)

```
Gnus
  Emacs
       3: comp.emacs
       2: alt.religion.emacs
     452: alt.sex.emacs
     Relief
       452: alt.sex.emacs
         0: comp.talk.emacs.recovery
  Misc
       8: comp.binaries.fractals
      13: comp.sources.unix
     452: alt.sex.emacs
```

The 'Emacs' topic has the topic parameter (score-file . "emacs.SCORE"); the 'Relief' topic has the topic parameter (score-file . "relief.SCORE"); and the 'Misc' topic has the topic parameter (score-file . "emacs.SCORE"). In addition, 'alt.religion.emacs' has the group parameter (score-file . "religion.SCORE").

Now, when you enter 'alt.sex.emacs' in the 'Relief' topic, you will get the relief.SCORE home score file. If you enter the same group in the 'Emacs' topic, you'll get the emacs.SCORE home score file. If you enter the group 'alt.religion.emacs', you'll get the religion.SCORE home score file.

This seems rather simple and self-evident, doesn't it? Well, yes. But there are some problems, especially with the total-expiry parameter. Say you have a mail group in two topics; one with total-expiry and one without. What happens when you do *M-x gnus-expire-all-expirable-groups*? Gnus has no way of telling which one of these topics you mean to expire articles from, so anything may happen. In fact, I hereby declare that it is *undefined* what happens. You just have to be careful if you do stuff like that.

2.17 Accessing groups of non-English names

There are some news servers that provide groups of which the names are expressed with their native languages in the world. For instance, in a certain news server there are some newsgroups of which the names are spelled in Chinese, where people are talking in Chinese. You can, of course, subscribe to such news groups using Gnus. Currently Gnus supports non-ASCII group names not only with the **nntp** back end but also with the **nnml** back end and the **nnrss** back end.

Every such group name is encoded by a certain charset in the server side (in an NNTP server its administrator determines the charset, but for groups in the other back ends it is determined by you). Gnus has to display the decoded ones for you in the group buffer and the article buffer, and needs to use the encoded ones when communicating with servers. However, Gnus doesn't know what charset is used for each non-ASCII group name. The following two variables are just the ones for telling Gnus what charset should be used for each group:

gnus-group-name-charset-method-alist

> An alist of select methods and charsets. The default value is **nil**. The names of groups in the server specified by that select method are all supposed to use the corresponding charset. For example:

```
(setq gnus-group-name-charset-method-alist
      '(((nntp "news.com.cn") . cn-gb-2312)))
```

Charsets specified for groups with this variable are preferred to the ones specified for the same groups with the `gnus-group-name-charset-group-alist` variable (see below).

A select method can be very long, like:

```
(nntp "gmane"
      (nntp-address "news.gmane.org")
      (nntp-end-of-line "\n")
      (nntp-open-connection-function
       nntp-open-via-rlogin-and-telnet)
      (nntp-via-rlogin-command "ssh")
      (nntp-via-rlogin-command-switches
       ("-C" "-t" "-e" "none"))
      (nntp-via-address ...))
```

In that case, you can truncate it into `(nntp "gmane")` in this variable. That is, it is enough to contain only the back end name and the server name.

gnus-group-name-charset-group-alist

> An alist of regexp of group name and the charset for group names. `((".*" . utf-8))` is the default value if UTF-8 is supported, otherwise the default is `nil`. For example:
>
> ```
> (setq gnus-group-name-charset-group-alist
>       '(("\\.com\\.cn:" . cn-gb-2312)
>         (".*" . utf-8)))
> ```
>
> Note that this variable is ignored if the match is made with `gnus-group-name-charset-method-alist`.

Those two variables are used also to determine the charset for encoding and decoding non-ASCII group names that are in the back ends other than `nntp`. It means that it is you who determine it. If you do nothing, the charset used for group names in those back ends will all be `utf-8` because of the last element of `gnus-group-name-charset-group-alist`.

There is one more important variable for non-ASCII group names:

nnmail-pathname-coding-system

> The value of this variable should be a coding system or `nil`. The default is `nil` in Emacs, or is the aliasee of the coding system named `file-name` (a certain coding system of which an alias is `file-name`) in XEmacs.
>
> The `nnml` back end, the `nnrss` back end, the agent, and the cache use non-ASCII group names in those files and directories. This variable overrides the value of `file-name-coding-system` which specifies the coding system used when encoding and decoding those file names and directory names.
>
> In XEmacs (with the `mule` feature), `file-name-coding-system` is the only means to specify the coding system used to encode and decode file names. On the other hand, Emacs uses the value of `default-file-name-coding-system` if `file-name-coding-system` is `nil` or it is bound to the value of `nnmail-pathname-coding-system` which is `nil`.

Normally the value of `default-file-name-coding-system` in Emacs or `nnmail-pathname-coding-system` in XEmacs is initialized according to the locale, so you will need to do nothing if the value is suitable to encode and decode non-ASCII group names.

The value of this variable (or `default-file-name-coding-system`) does not necessarily need to be the same value that is determined by `gnus-group-name-charset-method-alist` and `gnus-group-name-charset-group-alist`.

If `default-file-name-coding-system` or this variable is initialized by default to `iso-latin-1` for example, although you want to subscribe to the groups spelled in Chinese, that is the most typical case where you have to customize `nnmail-pathname-coding-system`. The `utf-8` coding system is a good candidate for it. Otherwise, you may change the locale in your system so that `default-file-name-coding-system` or this variable may be initialized to an appropriate value.

Note that when you copy or move articles from a non-ASCII group to another group, the charset used to encode and decode group names should be the same in both groups. Otherwise the Newsgroups header will be displayed incorrectly in the article buffer.

2.18 Misc Group Stuff

v   The key v is reserved for users. You can bind it to some command or better use it as a prefix key. For example:

```
(define-key gnus-group-mode-map (kbd "v j d")
  (lambda ()
    (interactive)
    (gnus-group-jump-to-group "nndraft:drafts")))
```

On keys reserved for users in Emacs and on keybindings in general See Section "Keymaps" in *The Emacs Editor*.

^   Enter the server buffer (**gnus-group-enter-server-mode**). See Section 6.1 [Server Buffer], page 136.

a   Start composing a message (a news by default) (**gnus-group-post-news**). If given a prefix, post to the group under the point. If the prefix is 1, prompt for a group to post to. Contrary to what the name of this function suggests, the prepared article might be a mail instead of a news, if a mail group is specified with the prefix argument. See Chapter 5 [Composing Messages], page 126.

m   Mail a message somewhere (**gnus-group-mail**). If given a prefix, use the posting style of the group under the point. If the prefix is 1, prompt for a group name to find the posting style. See Chapter 5 [Composing Messages], page 126.

i   Start composing a news (**gnus-group-news**). If given a prefix, post to the group under the point. If the prefix is 1, prompt for group to post to. See Chapter 5 [Composing Messages], page 126.

This function actually prepares a news even when using mail groups. This is useful for "posting" messages to mail groups without actually sending them over the network: they're just saved directly to the group in question. The corresponding back end must have a request-post method for this to work though.

G z

Compact the group under point (**gnus-group-compact-group**). Currently implemented only in nnml (see Section 6.4.13.3 [Mail Spool], page 174). This removes gaps between article numbers, hence getting a correct total article count.

Variables for the group buffer:

gnus-group-mode-hook
is called after the group buffer has been created.

gnus-group-prepare-hook
is called after the group buffer is generated. It may be used to modify the buffer in some strange, unnatural way.

gnus-group-prepared-hook
is called as the very last thing after the group buffer has been generated. It may be used to move point around, for instance.

gnus-permanently-visible-groups
Groups matching this regexp will always be listed in the group buffer, whether they are empty or not.

2.18.1 Scanning New Messages

g

Check the server(s) for new articles. If the numerical prefix is used, this command will check only groups of level *arg* and lower (**gnus-group-get-new-news**). If given a non-numerical prefix, this command will force a total re-reading of the active file(s) from the back end(s).

M-g

Check whether new articles have arrived in the current group (**gnus-group-get-new-news-this-group**). **gnus-goto-next-group-when-activating** says whether this command is to move point to the next group or not. It is **t** by default.

C-c M-g   Activate absolutely all groups (**gnus-activate-all-groups**).

R

Restart Gnus (**gnus-group-restart**). This saves the .newsrc file(s), closes the connection to all servers, clears up all run-time Gnus variables, and then starts Gnus all over again.

gnus-get-new-news-hook is run just before checking for new news.

gnus-after-getting-new-news-hook is run after checking for new news.

2.18.2 Group Information

H d
C-c C-d   Describe the current group (**gnus-group-describe-group**). If given a prefix, force Gnus to re-read the description from the server.

| M-d | Describe all groups (`gnus-group-describe-all-groups`). If given a prefix, force Gnus to re-read the description file from the server. |

| H v | |
| V | Display current Gnus version numbers (`gnus-version`). |

| ? | Give a very short help message (`gnus-group-describe-briefly`). |

| C-c C-i | Go to the Gnus info node (`gnus-info-find-node`). |

2.18.3 Group Timestamp

It can be convenient to let Gnus keep track of when you last read a group. To set the ball rolling, you should add `gnus-group-set-timestamp` to `gnus-select-group-hook`:

```
(add-hook 'gnus-select-group-hook 'gnus-group-set-timestamp)
```

After doing this, each time you enter a group, it'll be recorded.

This information can be displayed in various ways—the easiest is to use the '%d' spec in the group line format:

```
(setq gnus-group-line-format
      "%M\%S\%p\%P\%5y: %(%-40,40g%) %d\n")
```

This will result in lines looking like:

```
*       0: mail.ding                              19961002T012943
        0: custom                                19961002T012713
```

As you can see, the date is displayed in compact ISO 8601 format. This may be a bit too much, so to just display the date, you could say something like:

```
(setq gnus-group-line-format
      "%M\%S\%p\%P\%5y: %(%-40,40g%) %6,6~(cut 2)d\n")
```

If you would like greater control of the time format, you can use a user-defined format spec. Something like the following should do the trick:

```
(setq gnus-group-line-format
      "%M\%S\%p\%P\%5y: %(%-40,40g%) %ud\n")
(defun gnus-user-format-function-d (headers)
  (let ((time (gnus-group-timestamp gnus-tmp-group)))
    (if time
        (format-time-string "%b %d  %H:%M" time)
      "")))
```

To see what variables are dynamically bound (like `gnus-tmp-group`), you have to look at the source code. The variable names aren't guaranteed to be stable over Gnus versions, either.

2.18.4 File Commands

| r | Re-read the init file (`gnus-init-file`, which defaults to `~/.gnus.el`) (`gnus-group-read-init-file`). |

| s | Save the `.newsrc.eld` file (and `.newsrc` if wanted) (`gnus-group-save-newsrc`). If given a prefix, force saving the file(s) whether Gnus thinks it is necessary or not. |

2.18.5 Sieve Commands

Sieve is a server-side mail filtering language. In Gnus you can use the `sieve` group parameter (see Section 2.10 [Group Parameters], page 22) to specify sieve rules that should apply to each group. Gnus provides two commands to translate all these group parameters into a proper Sieve script that can be transferred to the server somehow.

The generated Sieve script is placed in `gnus-sieve-file` (by default `~/.sieve`). The Sieve code that Gnus generate is placed between two delimiters, `gnus-sieve-region-start` and `gnus-sieve-region-end`, so you may write additional Sieve code outside these delimiters that will not be removed the next time you regenerate the Sieve script.

The variable `gnus-sieve-crosspost` controls how the Sieve script is generated. If it is non-`nil` (the default) articles is placed in all groups that have matching rules, otherwise the article is only placed in the group with the first matching rule. For example, the group parameter '`(sieve address "sender" "owner-ding@hpc.uh.edu")`' will generate the following piece of Sieve code if `gnus-sieve-crosspost` is `nil`. (When `gnus-sieve-crosspost` is non-`nil`, it looks the same except that the line containing the call to `stop` is removed.)

```
if address "sender" "owner-ding@hpc.uh.edu" {
        fileinto "INBOX.ding";
        stop;
}
```

See *Emacs Sieve*.

D g   Regenerate a Sieve script from the `sieve` group parameters and put you into the `gnus-sieve-file` without saving it.

D u   Regenerates the Gnus managed part of `gnus-sieve-file` using the `sieve` group parameters, save the file and upload it to the server using the `sieveshell` program.

3 Summary Buffer

A line for each article is displayed in the summary buffer. You can move around, read articles, post articles and reply to articles.

The most common way to a summary buffer is to select a group from the group buffer (see Section 2.3 [Selecting a Group], page 15).

You can have as many summary buffers open as you wish.

You can customize the Summary Mode tool bar, see *M-x customize-apropos RET gnus-summary-tool-bar*. This feature is only available in Emacs.

The key *v* is reserved for users. You can bind it to some command or better use it as a prefix key. For example:

```
(define-key gnus-summary-mode-map (kbd "v -") "LrS") ;; lower subthread
```

3.1 Summary Buffer Format

Gnus will use the value of the `gnus-extract-address-components` variable as a function for getting the name and address parts of a `From` header. Two pre-defined functions exist: `gnus-extract-address-components`, which is the default, quite fast, and too simplistic solution; and `mail-extract-address-components`, which works very nicely, but is slower. The default function will return the wrong answer in 5% of the cases. If this is unacceptable to you, use the other function instead:

```
(setq gnus-extract-address-components
      'mail-extract-address-components)
```

`gnus-summary-same-subject` is a string indicating that the current article has the same subject as the previous. This string will be used with those specs that require it. The default is `""`.

3.1.1 Summary Buffer Lines

You can change the format of the lines in the summary buffer by changing the `gnus-summary-line-format` variable. It works along the same lines as a normal `format` string, with some extensions (see Section 9.4 [Formatting Variables], page 250).

There should always be a colon or a point position marker on the line; the cursor always moves to the point position marker or the colon after performing an operation. (Of course, Gnus wouldn't be Gnus if it wasn't possible to change this. Just write a new function `gnus-goto-colon` which does whatever you like with the cursor.) See Section 9.4.6 [Positioning Point], page 253.

The default string is '%U%R%z%I%(%[%4L: %-23,23f%]%) %s\n'.

The following format specification characters and extended format specification(s) are understood:

'N'   Article number.

'S'   Subject string. List identifiers stripped, `gnus-list-identifiers`. See Section 3.18.3 [Article Hiding], page 86.

'S'   Subject if the article is the root of the thread or the previous article had a differ-
            ent subject, **gnus-summary-same-subject** otherwise. (**gnus-summary-same-
            subject** defaults to **""**.)

'F'   Full **From** header.

'n'   The name (from the **From** header).

'f'   The name, **To** header or the **Newsgroups** header (see Section 3.1.2 [To From
            Newsgroups], page 47).

'a'   The name (from the **From** header). This differs from the **n** spec in that it uses
            the function designated by the **gnus-extract-address-components** variable,
            which is slower, but may be more thorough.

'A'   The address (from the **From** header). This works the same way as the **a** spec.

'L'   Number of lines in the article.

'c'   Number of characters in the article. This specifier is not supported in some
            methods (like nnfolder).

'k'   Pretty-printed version of the number of characters in the article; for example,
            '**1.2k**' or '**0.4M**'.

'I'   Indentation based on thread level (see Section 3.9.1 [Customizing Threading],
            page 65).

'B'   A complex trn-style thread tree, showing response-connecting trace lines. A
            thread could be drawn like this:

```
>
+->
| +->
| | \->
| |   \->
| \->
+->
\->
```

            You can customize the appearance with the following options. Note that it is
            possible to make the thread display look really neat by replacing the default
            ASCII characters with graphic line-drawing glyphs.

            gnus-sum-thread-tree-root
                    Used for the root of a thread. If **nil**, use subject instead. The
                    default is '**> **'.

            gnus-sum-thread-tree-false-root
                    Used for the false root of a thread (see Section 3.9.1.1 [Loose
                    Threads], page 65). If **nil**, use subject instead. The default is '**> **'.

            gnus-sum-thread-tree-single-indent
                    Used for a thread with just one message. If **nil**, use subject instead.
                    The default is '**'.

       `gnus-sum-thread-tree-vertical`
           Used for drawing a vertical line. The default is '| '.

       `gnus-sum-thread-tree-indent`
           Used for indenting. The default is ' '.

       `gnus-sum-thread-tree-leaf-with-other`
           Used for a leaf with brothers. The default is '+-> '.

       `gnus-sum-thread-tree-single-leaf`
           Used for a leaf without brothers. The default is '\-> '

'T'   Nothing if the article is a root and lots of spaces if it isn't (it pushes everything after it off the screen).

'['   Opening bracket, which is normally '[', but can also be '<' for adopted articles (see Section 3.9.1 [Customizing Threading], page 65).

']'   Closing bracket, which is normally ']', but can also be '>' for adopted articles.

'>'   One space for each thread level.

'<'   Twenty minus thread level spaces.

'U'   Unread. See Section 3.7.2 [Read Articles], page 58.

'R'   This misleadingly named specifier is the *secondary mark*. This mark will say whether the article has been replied to, has been cached, or has been saved. See Section 3.7.3 [Other Marks], page 59.

'i'   Score as a number (see Chapter 7 [Scoring], page 214).

'z'   Zcore, '+' if above the default level and '-' if below the default level. If the difference between `gnus-summary-default-score` and the score is less than `gnus-summary-zcore-fuzz`, this spec will not be used.

'V'   Total thread score.

'x'   `Xref`.

'D'   `Date`.

'd'   The `Date` in DD-MMM format.

'o'   The `Date` in *YYYYMMDDTHHMMSS* format.

'M'   `Message-ID`.

'r'   `References`.

't'   Number of articles in the current sub-thread. Using this spec will slow down summary buffer generation somewhat.

'e'   An '=' (`gnus-not-empty-thread-mark`) will be displayed if the article has any children.

'P'   The line number.

'O'   Download mark.

'*'   Desired cursor position (instead of after first colon).

'&user-date;'
                Age sensitive date format. Various date format is defined in **gnus-user-date-format-alist**.

'u'   User defined specifier. The next character in the format string should be a letter. Gnus will call the function **gnus-user-format-function-x**, where x is the letter following '%u'. The function will be passed the current header as argument. The function should return a string, which will be inserted into the summary just like information from any other summary specifier.

Text between '%(' and '%)' will be highlighted with **gnus-mouse-face** when the mouse point is placed inside the area. There can only be one such area.

The '%U' (status), '%R' (replied) and '%z' (zcore) specs have to be handled with care. For reasons of efficiency, Gnus will compute what column these characters will end up in, and "hard-code" that. This means that it is invalid to have these specs after a variable-length spec. Well, you might not be arrested, but your summary buffer will look strange, which is bad enough.

The smart choice is to have these specs as far to the left as possible. (Isn't that the case with everything, though? But I digress.)

This restriction may disappear in later versions of Gnus.

3.1.2 To From Newsgroups

In some groups (particularly in archive groups), the **From** header isn't very interesting, since all the articles there are written by you. To display the information in the **To** or **Newsgroups** headers instead, you need to decide three things: What information to gather; where to display it; and when to display it.

1. The reading of extra header information is controlled by the **gnus-extra-headers**. This is a list of header symbols. For instance:

   ```
   (setq gnus-extra-headers
         '(To Newsgroups X-Newsreader))
   ```

   This will result in Gnus trying to obtain these three headers, and storing it in header structures for later easy retrieval.

2. The value of these extra headers can be accessed via the **gnus-extra-header** function. Here's a format line spec that will access the **X-Newsreader** header:

   ```
   "%~(form (gnus-extra-header 'X-Newsreader))@"
   ```

3. The **gnus-ignored-from-addresses** variable says when the '%f' summary line spec returns the **To**, **Newsreader** or **From** header. If this regexp matches the contents of the **From** header, the value of the **To** or **Newsreader** headers are used instead.

   To distinguish regular articles from those where the **From** field has been swapped, a string is prefixed to the **To** or **Newsgroups** header in the summary line. By default the string is '-> ' for **To** and '=> ' for **Newsgroups**, you can customize these strings with **gnus-summary-to-prefix** and **gnus-summary-newsgroup-prefix**.

A related variable is **nnmail-extra-headers**, which controls when to include extra headers when generating overview (NOV) files. If you have old overview files, you should regenerate them after changing this variable, by entering the server buffer using `, and then **g** on the appropriate mail server (e.g., nnml) to cause regeneration.

You also have to instruct Gnus to display the data by changing the `%n` spec to the `%f` spec in the `gnus-summary-line-format` variable.

In summary, you'd typically put something like the following in `~/.gnus.el`:

```
(setq gnus-extra-headers
      '(To Newsgroups))
(setq nnmail-extra-headers gnus-extra-headers)
(setq gnus-summary-line-format
      "%U%R%z%I%(%[%4L: %-23,23f%]%) %s\n")
(setq gnus-ignored-from-addresses
      "Your Name Here")
```

(The values listed above are the default values in Gnus. Alter them to fit your needs.)

A note for news server administrators, or for users who wish to try to convince their news server administrator to provide some additional support:

The above is mostly useful for mail groups, where you have control over the NOV files that are created. However, if you can persuade your nntp admin to add (in the usual implementation, notably INN):

```
Newsgroups:full
```

to the end of her `overview.fmt` file, then you can use that just as you would the extra headers from the mail groups.

3.1.3 Summary Buffer Mode Line

You can also change the format of the summary mode bar (see Section 9.4.2 [Mode Line Formatting], page 251). Set `gnus-summary-mode-line-format` to whatever you like. The default is 'Gnus: %%b [%A] %Z'.

Here are the elements you can play with:

'G'   Group name.

'p'   Unprefixed group name.

'A'   Current article number.

'z'   Current article score.

'V'   Gnus version.

'U'   Number of unread articles in this group.

'e'   Number of unread articles in this group that aren't displayed in the summary buffer.

'Z'   A string with the number of unread and unselected articles represented either as '<%U(+%e) more>' if there are both unread and unselected articles, and just as '<%U more>' if there are just unread articles and no unselected ones.

'g'   Shortish group name. For instance, 'rec.arts.anime' will be shortened to 'r.a.anime'.

'S'   Subject of the current article.

'u'   User-defined spec (see Section 9.4.4 [User-Defined Specs], page 252).

's'   Name of the current score file (see Chapter 7 [Scoring], page 214).

'd'   Number of dormant articles (see Section 3.7.1 [Unread Articles], page 58).

't'   Number of ticked articles (see Section 3.7.1 [Unread Articles], page 58).

'r'   Number of articles that have been marked as read in this session.

'E'   Number of articles expunged by the score files.

3.1.4 Summary Highlighting

gnus-visual-mark-article-hook
                This hook is run after selecting an article. It is meant to be used for highlighting
                the article in some way. It is not run if **gnus-visual** is **nil**.

gnus-summary-update-hook
                This hook is called when a summary line is changed. It is not run if
                gnus-visual is **nil**.

gnus-summary-selected-face
                This is the face (or *font* as some people call it) used to highlight the current
                article in the summary buffer.

gnus-summary-highlight
                Summary lines are highlighted according to this variable, which is a list where
                the elements are of the format (*form . face*). If you would, for instance, like
                ticked articles to be italic and high-scored articles to be bold, you could set this
                variable to something like

                      (((eq mark gnus-ticked-mark) . italic)
                       ((> score default) . bold))

                As you may have guessed, if *form* returns a non-**nil** value, *face* will be applied
                to the line.

3.2 Summary Maneuvering

All the straight movement commands understand the numeric prefix and behave pretty
much as you'd expect.

    None of these commands select articles.

G M-n
M-n   Go to the next summary line of an unread article (**gnus-summary-next-unread-subject**).

G M-p
M-p   Go to the previous summary line of an unread article (**gnus-summary-prev-unread-subject**).

G g   Ask for an article number and then go to the summary line of that article
                without displaying the article (**gnus-summary-goto-subject**).

If Gnus asks you to press a key to confirm going to the next group, you can use the `C-n` and `C-p` keys to move around the group buffer, searching for the next group to read without actually returning to the group buffer.

Variables related to summary movement:

`gnus-auto-select-next`

> If you issue one of the movement commands (like `n`) and there are no more unread articles after the current one, Gnus will offer to go to the next group. If this variable is `t` and the next group is empty, Gnus will exit summary mode and return to the group buffer. If this variable is neither `t` nor `nil`, Gnus will select the next group with unread articles. As a special case, if this variable is `quietly`, Gnus will select the next group without asking for confirmation. If this variable is `almost-quietly`, the same will happen only if you are located on the last article in the group. Finally, if this variable is `slightly-quietly`, the `Z n` command will go to the next group without confirmation. Also see Section 2.6 [Group Levels], page 17.

`gnus-auto-select-same`

> If non-`nil`, all the movement commands will try to go to the next article with the same subject as the current. (*Same* here might mean *roughly equal*. See `gnus-summary-gather-subject-limit` for details (see Section 3.9.1 [Customizing Threading], page 65).) If there are no more articles with the same subject, go to the first unread article.
>
> This variable is not particularly useful if you use a threaded display.

`gnus-summary-check-current`

> If non-`nil`, all the "unread" movement commands will not proceed to the next (or previous) article if the current article is unread. Instead, they will choose the current article.

`gnus-auto-center-summary`

> If non-`nil`, Gnus will keep the point in the summary buffer centered at all times. This makes things quite tidy, but if you have a slow network connection, or simply do not like this un-Emacsism, you can set this variable to `nil` to get the normal Emacs scrolling action. This will also inhibit horizontal re-centering of the summary buffer, which might make it more inconvenient to read extremely long threads.
>
> This variable can also be a number. In that case, center the window at the given number of lines from the top.

`gnus-summary-stop-at-end-of-message`

> If non-`nil`, don't go to the next article when hitting `SPC`, and you're at the end of the article.

3.3 Choosing Articles

3.3.1 Choosing Commands

None of the following movement commands understand the numeric prefix, and they all select and display an article.

If you want to fetch new articles or redisplay the group, see Section 3.28 [Exiting the Summary Buffer], page 111.

SPACE   Select the current article, or, if that one's read already, the next unread article (**gnus-summary-next-page**).

                   If you have an article window open already and you press *SPACE* again. the article will be scrolled. This lets you conveniently *SPACE* through an entire newsgroup. See Section 3.4 [Paging the Article], page 52.

G n
n   Go to next unread article (**gnus-summary-next-unread-article**).

G p
p   Go to previous unread article (**gnus-summary-prev-unread-article**).

G N
N   Go to the next article (**gnus-summary-next-article**).

G P
P   Go to the previous article (**gnus-summary-prev-article**).

G C-n   Go to the next article with the same subject (**gnus-summary-next-subject**).

G C-p   Go to the previous article with the same subject (**gnus-summary-prev-subject**).

G f
.   Go to the first unread article (**gnus-summary-first-unread-article**).

G b
,   Go to the unread article with the highest score (**gnus-summary-best-unread-article**). If given a prefix argument, go to the first unread article that has a score over the default score.

G l
l   Go to the previous article read (**gnus-summary-goto-last-article**).

G o   Pop an article off the summary history and go to this article (**gnus-summary-pop-article**). This command differs from the command above in that you can pop as many previous articles off the history as you like, while *l* toggles the two last read articles. For a somewhat related issue (if you use these commands a lot), see Section 3.15 [Article Backlog], page 76.

G j
j   Ask for an article number or **Message-ID**, and then go to that article (**gnus-summary-goto-article**).

3.3.2 Choosing Variables

Some variables relevant for moving and selecting articles:

gnus-auto-extend-newsgroup

                   All the movement commands will try to go to the previous (or next) article, even if that article isn't displayed in the Summary buffer if this variable is non-nil. Gnus will then fetch the article from the server and display it in the article buffer.

`gnus-select-article-hook`

> This hook is called whenever an article is selected. The default is `nil`. If you would like each article to be saved in the Agent as you read it, putting `gnus-agent-fetch-selected-article` on this hook will do so.

`gnus-mark-article-hook`

> This hook is called whenever an article is selected. It is intended to be used for marking articles as read. The default value is `gnus-summary-mark-read-and-unread-as-read`, and will change the mark of almost any article you read to `gnus-read-mark`. The only articles not affected by this function are ticked, dormant, and expirable articles. If you'd instead like to just have unread articles marked as read, you can use `gnus-summary-mark-unread-as-read` instead. It will leave marks like `gnus-low-score-mark`, `gnus-del-mark` (and so on) alone.

3.4 Scrolling the Article

SPACE

> Pressing *SPACE* will scroll the current article forward one page, or, if you have come to the end of the current article, will choose the next article (`gnus-summary-next-page`).
>
> If `gnus-article-skip-boring` is non-`nil` and the rest of the article consists only of citations and signature, then it will be skipped; the next article will be shown instead. You can customize what is considered uninteresting with `gnus-article-boring-faces`. You can manually view the article's pages, no matter how boring, using *C-M-v*.

DEL

> Scroll the current article back one page (`gnus-summary-prev-page`).

RET

> Scroll the current article one line forward (`gnus-summary-scroll-up`).

M-RET

> Scroll the current article one line backward (`gnus-summary-scroll-down`).

A g
g

> (Re)fetch the current article (`gnus-summary-show-article`). If given a prefix, show a completely "raw" article, just the way it came from the server. If given a prefix twice (i.e., *C-u C-u g'*), fetch the current article, but don't run any of the article treatment functions.
>
> If given a numerical prefix, you can do semi-manual charset stuff. *C-u 0 g cn-gb-2312 RET* will decode the message as if it were encoded in the `cn-gb-2312` charset. If you have
>
> ```
> (setq gnus-summary-show-article-charset-alist
>       '((1 . cn-gb-2312)
>         (2 . big5)))
> ```
>
> then you can say *C-u 1 g* to get the same effect.

A <
<

> Scroll to the beginning of the article (`gnus-summary-beginning-of-article`).

A >

>   Scroll to the end of the article (`gnus-summary-end-of-article`).

A s

s   Perform an isearch in the article buffer (`gnus-summary-isearch-article`).

h   Select the article buffer (`gnus-summary-select-article-buffer`).

3.5 Reply, Followup and Post

3.5.1 Summary Mail Commands

Commands for composing a mail message:

S r

r   Mail a reply to the author of the current article (`gnus-summary-reply`).

S R

R   Mail a reply to the author of the current article and include the original message (`gnus-summary-reply-with-original`). This command uses the process/prefix convention.

S w   Mail a wide reply to the author of the current article (`gnus-summary-wide-reply`). A *wide reply* is a reply that goes out to all people listed in the `To`, `From` (or `Reply-to`) and `Cc` headers. If `Mail-Followup-To` is present, that's used instead.

S W   Mail a wide reply to the current article and include the original message (`gnus-summary-wide-reply-with-original`). This command uses the process/prefix convention, but only uses the headers from the first article to determine the recipients.

S L   When replying to a message from a mailing list, send a reply to that message to the mailing list, and include the original message (`gnus-summary-reply-to-list-with-original`).

S v   Mail a very wide reply to the author of the current article (`gnus-summary-wide-reply`). A *very wide reply* is a reply that goes out to all people listed in the `To`, `From` (or `Reply-to`) and `Cc` headers in all the process/prefixed articles. This command uses the process/prefix convention.

S V   Mail a very wide reply to the author of the current article and include the original message (`gnus-summary-very-wide-reply-with-original`). This command uses the process/prefix convention.

S B r   Mail a reply to the author of the current article but ignore the `Reply-To` field (`gnus-summary-reply-broken-reply-to`). If you need this because a mailing list incorrectly sets a `Reply-To` header pointing to the list, you probably want to set the `broken-reply-to` group parameter instead, so things will work correctly. See Section 2.10 [Group Parameters], page 22.

S B R   Mail a reply to the author of the current article and include the original message but ignore the `Reply-To` field (`gnus-summary-reply-broken-reply-to-with-original`).

S o m

C-c C-f   Forward the current article to some other person (`gnus-summary-mail-forward`). If no prefix is given, the message is forwarded according to the value of (`message-forward-as-mime`) and (`message-forward-show-mml`); if the prefix is 1, decode the message and forward directly inline; if the prefix is 2, forward message as an rfc822 MIME section; if the prefix is 3, decode message and forward as an rfc822 MIME section; if the prefix is 4, forward message directly inline; otherwise, the message is forwarded as no prefix given but use the flipped value of (`message-forward-as-mime`). By default, the message is decoded and forwarded as an rfc822 MIME section.

S m

m   Prepare a mail (`gnus-summary-mail-other-window`). By default, use the posting style of the current group. If given a prefix, disable that. If the prefix is 1, prompt for a group name to find the posting style.

S i   Prepare a news (`gnus-summary-news-other-window`). By default, post to the current group. If given a prefix, disable that. If the prefix is 1, prompt for a group to post to.

            This function actually prepares a news even when using mail groups. This is useful for "posting" messages to mail groups without actually sending them over the network: they're just saved directly to the group in question. The corresponding back end must have a request-post method for this to work though.

S D b   If you have sent a mail, but the mail was bounced back to you for some reason (wrong address, transient failure), you can use this command to resend that bounced mail (`gnus-summary-resend-bounced-mail`). You will be popped into a mail buffer where you can edit the headers before sending the mail off again. If you give a prefix to this command, and the bounced mail is a reply to some other mail, Gnus will try to fetch that mail and display it for easy perusal of its headers. This might very well fail, though.

S D r   Not to be confused with the previous command, `gnus-summary-resend-message` will prompt you for an address to send the current message off to, and then send it to that place. The headers of the message won't be altered—but lots of headers that say `Resent-To`, `Resent-From` and so on will be added. This means that you actually send a mail to someone that has a `To` header that (probably) points to yourself. This will confuse people. So, natcherly you'll only do that if you're really eVIl.

            This command is mainly used if you have several accounts and want to ship a mail to a different account of yours. (If you're both `root` and `postmaster` and get a mail for `postmaster` to the `root` account, you may want to resend it to `postmaster`. Ordnung muss sein!

            This command understands the process/prefix convention (see Section 9.1 [Process/Prefix], page 249).

S D e

            Like the previous command, but will allow you to edit the message as if it were a new message before resending.

S O m   Digest the current series (see Section 3.17 [Decoding Articles], page 80) and for-
                 ward the result using mail (`gnus-uu-digest-mail-forward`). This command
                 uses the process/prefix convention (see Section 9.1 [Process/Prefix], page 249).

S M-c   Send a complaint about excessive crossposting to the author of the current
                 article (`gnus-summary-mail-crosspost-complaint`).

                 This command is provided as a way to fight back against the current cross-
                 posting pandemic that's sweeping Usenet. It will compose a reply using the
                 `gnus-crosspost-complaint` variable as a preamble. This command under-
                 stands the process/prefix convention (see Section 9.1 [Process/Prefix], page 249)
                 and will prompt you before sending each mail.

Also See Section "Header Commands" in *The Message Manual*, for more information.

3.5.2 Summary Post Commands

Commands for posting a news article:

S p
a   Prepare for posting an article (`gnus-summary-post-news`). By default, post to
                 the current group. If given a prefix, disable that. If the prefix is 1, prompt for
                 another group instead.

S f
f   Post a followup to the current article (`gnus-summary-followup`).

S F
F   Post a followup to the current article and include the original message
                 (`gnus-summary-followup-with-original`).   This   command   uses   the
                 process/prefix convention.

S n   Post a followup to the current article via news, even if you got the message
                 through mail (`gnus-summary-followup-to-mail`).

S N   Post a followup to the current article via news, even if you got the message
                 through mail and include the original message (`gnus-summary-followup-to-`
                 `mail-with-original`). This command uses the process/prefix convention.

S o p   Forward the current article to a newsgroup (`gnus-summary-post-forward`).
                 If no prefix is given, the message is forwarded according to the value of
                 (`message-forward-as-mime`) and (`message-forward-show-mml`); if the prefix
                 is 1, decode the message and forward directly inline; if the prefix is 2, forward
                 message as an rfc822 MIME section; if the prefix is 3, decode message and
                 forward as an rfc822 MIME section; if the prefix is 4, forward message directly
                 inline; otherwise, the message is forwarded as no prefix given but use the
                 flipped value of (`message-forward-as-mime`). By default, the message is
                 decoded and forwarded as an rfc822 MIME section.

S O p   Digest the current series and forward the result to a newsgroup (`gnus-uu-`
                 `digest-post-forward`). This command uses the process/prefix convention.

S u   Uuencode a file, split it into parts, and post it as a series (`gnus-uu-post-news`).
                 (see Section 3.17.5.3 [Uuencoding and Posting], page 83).

Also See Section "Header Commands" in *The Message Manual*, for more information.

3.5.3 Summary Message Commands

S y   Yank the current article into an already existing Message composition buffer
               (`gnus-summary-yank-message`). This command prompts for what message
               buffer you want to yank into, and understands the process/prefix convention
               (see Section 9.1 [Process/Prefix], page 249).

3.5.4 Canceling Articles

Have you ever written something, and then decided that you really, really, really wish you
hadn't posted that?

Well, you can't cancel mail, but you can cancel posts.

Find the article you wish to cancel (you can only cancel your own articles, so don't try
any funny stuff). Then press *C* or *S c* (`gnus-summary-cancel-article`). Your article will
be canceled—machines all over the world will be deleting your article. This command uses
the process/prefix convention (see Section 9.1 [Process/Prefix], page 249).

Be aware, however, that not all sites honor cancels, so your article may live on here and
there, while most sites will delete the article in question.

Gnus will use the "current" select method when canceling. If you want to use the
standard posting method, use the 'a' symbolic prefix (see Section 9.3 [Symbolic Prefixes],
page 250).

Gnus ensures that only you can cancel your own messages using a `Cancel-Lock` header
(see Section "Canceling News" in *Message Manual*).

If you discover that you have made some mistakes and want to do some corrections, you
can post a *superseding* article that will replace your original article.

Go to the original article and press *S s* (`gnus-summary-supersede-article`). You will
be put in a buffer where you can edit the article all you want before sending it off the usual
way.

The same goes for superseding as for canceling, only more so: Some sites do not honor
superseding. On those sites, it will appear that you have posted almost the same article
twice.

If you have just posted the article, and change your mind right away, there is a trick you
can use to cancel/supersede the article without waiting for the article to appear on your
site first. You simply return to the post buffer (which is called `*sent ...*`). There you
will find the article you just posted, with all the headers intact. Change the `Message-ID`
header to a `Cancel` or `Supersedes` header by substituting one of those words for the word
`Message-ID`. Then just press *C-c C-c* to send the article as you would do normally. The
previous article will be canceled/superseded.

Just remember, kids: There is no 'c' in 'supersede'.

3.6 Delayed Articles

Sometimes, you might wish to delay the sending of a message. For example, you might wish
to arrange for a message to turn up just in time to remind your about the birthday of your
Significant Other. For this, there is the `gnus-delay` package. Setup is simple:

`(gnus-delay-initialize)`

Normally, to send a message you use the *C-c C-c* command from Message mode. To delay a message, use *C-c C-j* (`gnus-delay-article`) instead. This will ask you for how long the message should be delayed. Possible answers are:

- A time span. Consists of an integer and a letter. For example, `42d` means to delay for 42 days. Available letters are `m` (minutes), `h` (hours), `d` (days), `w` (weeks), `M` (months) and `Y` (years).

- A specific date. Looks like `YYYY-MM-DD`. The message will be delayed until that day, at a specific time (eight o'clock by default). See also `gnus-delay-default-hour`.

- A specific time of day. Given in `hh:mm` format, 24h, no am/pm stuff. The deadline will be at that time today, except if that time has already passed, then it's at the given time tomorrow. So if it's ten o'clock in the morning and you specify `11:15`, then the deadline is one hour and fifteen minutes hence. But if you specify `9:20`, that means a time tomorrow.

The action of the **gnus-delay-article** command is influenced by a couple of variables:

gnus-delay-default-hour

When you specify a specific date, the message will be due on that hour on the given date. Possible values are integers 0 through 23.

gnus-delay-default-delay

This is a string and gives the default delay. It can be of any of the formats described above.

gnus-delay-group

Delayed articles will be kept in this group on the drafts server until they are due. You probably don't need to change this. The default value is `"delayed"`.

gnus-delay-header

The deadline for each article will be stored in a header. This variable is a string and gives the header name. You probably don't need to change this. The default value is `"X-Gnus-Delayed"`.

The way delaying works is like this: when you use the **gnus-delay-article** command, you give a certain delay. Gnus calculates the deadline of the message and stores it in the `X-Gnus-Delayed` header and puts the message in the `nndraft:delayed` group.

And whenever you get new news, Gnus looks through the group for articles which are due and sends them. It uses the **gnus-delay-send-queue** function for this. By default, this function is added to the hook `gnus-get-new-news-hook`. But of course, you can change this. Maybe you want to use the demon to send drafts? Just tell the demon to execute the **gnus-delay-send-queue** function.

gnus-delay-initialize

By default, this function installs **gnus-delay-send-queue** in `gnus-get-new-news-hook`. But it accepts the optional second argument `nc-check`. If it is non-nil, `gnus-get-new-news-hook` is not changed. The optional first argument is ignored.

For example, (gnus-delay-initialize nil t) means to do nothing. Presumably, you want to use the demon for sending due delayed articles. Just don't forget to set that up :-)

When delaying an article with C-c C-j, Message mode will automatically add a "Date" header with the current time. In many cases you probably want the "Date" header to reflect the time the message is sent instead. To do this, you have to delete Date from message-draft-headers.

3.7 Marking Articles

There are several marks you can set on an article.

You have marks that decide the *readedness* (whoo, neato-keano neologism ohoy!) of the article. Alphabetic marks generally mean *read*, while non-alphabetic characters generally mean *unread*.

In addition, you also have marks that do not affect readedness.

3.7.1 Unread Articles

The following marks mark articles as (kinda) unread, in one form or other.

'!'   Marked as ticked (gnus-ticked-mark).

           Ticked articles are articles that will remain visible always. If you see an article that you find interesting, or you want to put off reading it, or replying to it, until sometime later, you'd typically tick it. However, articles can be expired (from news servers by the news server software, Gnus itself never expires ticked messages), so if you want to keep an article forever, you'll have to make it persistent (see Section 3.13 [Persistent Articles], page 75).

'?'   Marked as dormant (gnus-dormant-mark).

           Dormant articles will only appear in the summary buffer if there are followups to it. If you want to see them even if they don't have followups, you can use the / D command (see Section 3.8 [Limiting], page 63). Otherwise (except for the visibility issue), they are just like ticked messages.

'SPACE'   Marked as unread (gnus-unread-mark).

           Unread articles are articles that haven't been read at all yet.

3.7.2 Read Articles

All the following marks mark articles as read.

'r'   These are articles that the user has marked as read with the d command manually, more or less (gnus-del-mark).

'R'   Articles that have actually been read (gnus-read-mark).

'O'   Articles that were marked as read in previous sessions and are now *old* (gnus-ancient-mark).

'K'   Marked as killed (gnus-killed-mark).

'X'   Marked as killed by kill files (gnus-kill-file-mark).

'Y'   Marked as read by having too low a score (`gnus-low-score-mark`).

'C'   Marked as read by a catchup (`gnus-catchup-mark`).

'G'   Canceled article (`gnus-canceled-mark`)

'Q'   Sparsely reffed article (`gnus-sparse-mark`). See Section 3.9.1 [Customizing Threading], page 65.

'M'   Article marked as read by duplicate suppression (`gnus-duplicate-mark`). See Section 3.30 [Duplicate Suppression], page 113.

All these marks just mean that the article is marked as read, really. They are interpreted differently when doing adaptive scoring, though.

One more special mark, though:

'E'   Marked as expirable (`gnus-expirable-mark`).

            Marking articles as *expirable* (or have them marked as such automatically) doesn't make much sense in normal groups—a user doesn't control expiring of news articles, but in mail groups, for instance, articles marked as *expirable* can be deleted by Gnus at any time.

3.7.3 Other Marks

There are some marks that have nothing to do with whether the article is read or not.

*   You can set a bookmark in the current article. Say you are reading a long thesis on cats' urinary tracts, and have to go home for dinner before you've finished reading the thesis. You can then set a bookmark in the article, and Gnus will jump to this bookmark the next time it encounters the article. See Section 3.7.4 [Setting Marks], page 60.

*   All articles that you have replied to or made a followup to (i.e., have answered) will be marked with an 'A' in the second column (`gnus-replied-mark`).

*   All articles that you have forwarded will be marked with an 'F' in the second column (`gnus-forwarded-mark`).

*   Articles stored in the article cache will be marked with an '*' in the second column (`gnus-cached-mark`). See Section 3.12 [Article Caching], page 74.

*   Articles "saved" (in some manner or other; not necessarily religiously) are marked with an 'S' in the second column (`gnus-saved-mark`).

*   Articles that haven't been seen before in Gnus by the user are marked with a '.' in the second column (`gnus-unseen-mark`).

*   When using the Gnus agent (see Section 6.9.1 [Agent Basics], page 199), articles may be downloaded for unplugged (offline) viewing. If you are using the '%O' spec, these articles get the '+' mark in that spec. (The variable `gnus-downloaded-mark` controls which character to use.)

*   When using the Gnus agent (see Section 6.9.1 [Agent Basics], page 199), some articles might not have been downloaded. Such articles cannot be viewed while you are unplugged (offline). If you are using the '%O' spec, these articles get the '-' mark in that spec. (The variable `gnus-undownloaded-mark` controls which character to use.)

- The Gnus agent (see Section 6.9.1 [Agent Basics], page 199) downloads some articles automatically, but it is also possible to explicitly mark articles for download, even if they would not be downloaded automatically. Such explicitly-marked articles get the '%' mark in the first column. (The variable `gnus-downloadable-mark` controls which character to use.)

- If the '%e' spec is used, the presence of threads or not will be marked with `gnus-not-empty-thread-mark` and `gnus-empty-thread-mark` in the third column, respectively.

- Finally we have the *process mark* (`gnus-process-mark`). A variety of commands react to the presence of the process mark. For instance, *X u* (`gnus-uu-decode-uu`) will uudecode and view all articles that have been marked with the process mark. Articles marked with the process mark have a '#' in the second column.

You might have noticed that most of these "non-readedness" marks appear in the second column by default. So if you have a cached, saved, replied article that you have process-marked, what will that look like?

Nothing much. The precedence rules go as follows: process -> cache -> replied -> saved. So if the article is in the cache and is replied, you'll only see the cache mark and not the replied mark.

3.7.4 Setting Marks

All the marking commands understand the numeric prefix.

M c
M-u   Clear all readedness-marks from the current article (`gnus-summary-clear-mark-forward`). In other words, mark the article as unread.

M t
!   Tick the current article (`gnus-summary-tick-article-forward`). See Section 3.12 [Article Caching], page 74.

M ?
?   Mark the current article as dormant (`gnus-summary-mark-as-dormant`). See Section 3.12 [Article Caching], page 74.

M d
d   Mark the current article as read (`gnus-summary-mark-as-read-forward`).

D   Mark the current article as read and move point to the previous line (`gnus-summary-mark-as-read-backward`).

M k
k   Mark all articles that have the same subject as the current one as read, and then select the next unread article (`gnus-summary-kill-same-subject-and-select`).

M K
C-k   Mark all articles that have the same subject as the current one as read (`gnus-summary-kill-same-subject`).

M C   Mark all unread articles as read (`gnus-summary-catchup`).

M C-c	Mark all articles in the group as read—even the ticked and dormant articles (`gnus-summary-catchup-all`).
M H	Catchup the current group to point (before the point) (`gnus-summary-catchup-to-here`).
M h	Catchup the current group from point (after the point) (`gnus-summary-catchup-from-here`).
C-w	Mark all articles between point and mark as read (`gnus-summary-mark-region-as-read`).
M V k	Kill all articles with scores below the default score (or below the numeric prefix) (`gnus-summary-kill-below`).
M e *E*	Mark the current article as expirable (`gnus-summary-mark-as-expirable`).
M b	Set a bookmark in the current article (`gnus-summary-set-bookmark`).
M B	Remove the bookmark from the current article (`gnus-summary-remove-bookmark`).
M V c	Clear all marks from articles with scores over the default score (or over the numeric prefix) (`gnus-summary-clear-above`).
M V u	Tick all articles with scores over the default score (or over the numeric prefix) (`gnus-summary-tick-above`).
M V m	Prompt for a mark, and mark all articles with scores over the default score (or over the numeric prefix) with this mark (`gnus-summary-clear-above`).

The `gnus-summary-goto-unread` variable controls what action should be taken after setting a mark. If non-`nil`, point will move to the next/previous unread article. If `nil`, point will just move one line up or down. As a special case, if this variable is `never`, all the marking commands as well as other commands (like *SPACE*) will move to the next article, whether it is unread or not. The default is `t`.

3.7.5 Generic Marking Commands

Some people would like the command that ticks an article (*!*) to go to the next article. Others would like it to go to the next unread article. Yet others would like it to stay on the current article. And even though I haven't heard of anybody wanting it to go to the previous (unread) article, I'm sure there are people that want that as well.

Multiply these five behaviors with five different marking commands, and you get a potentially complex set of variable to control what each command should do.

To sidestep that mess, Gnus provides commands that do all these different things. They can be found on the *M M* map in the summary buffer. Type *M M C-h* to see them all—there are too many of them to list in this manual.

While you can use these commands directly, most users would prefer altering the summary mode keymap. For instance, if you would like the *!* command to go to the next article instead of the next unread article, you could say something like:

```
(add-hook 'gnus-summary-mode-hook 'my-alter-summary-map)
(defun my-alter-summary-map ()
  (local-set-key "!" 'gnus-summary-put-mark-as-ticked-next))
```

or

```
(defun my-alter-summary-map ()
  (local-set-key "!" "MM!n"))
```

3.7.6 Setting Process Marks

Process marks are displayed as # in the summary buffer, and are used for marking articles in such a way that other commands will process these articles. For instance, if you process mark four articles and then use the * command, Gnus will enter these four articles into the cache. For more information, see Section 9.1 [Process/Prefix], page 249.

M P p

\#   Mark the current article with the process mark (**gnus-summary-mark-as-processable**).

M P u

M-\#   Remove the process mark, if any, from the current article (**gnus-summary-unmark-as-processable**).

M P U   Remove the process mark from all articles (**gnus-summary-unmark-all-processable**).

M P i   Invert the list of process marked articles (**gnus-uu-invert-processable**).

M P R   Mark articles that have a **Subject** header that matches a regular expression (**gnus-uu-mark-by-regexp**).

M P G   Unmark articles that have a **Subject** header that matches a regular expression (**gnus-uu-unmark-by-regexp**).

M P r   Mark articles in region (**gnus-uu-mark-region**).

M P g   Unmark articles in region (**gnus-uu-unmark-region**).

M P t   Mark all articles in the current (sub)thread (**gnus-uu-mark-thread**).

M P T   Unmark all articles in the current (sub)thread (**gnus-uu-unmark-thread**).

M P v   Mark all articles that have a score above the prefix argument (**gnus-uu-mark-over**).

M P s   Mark all articles in the current series (**gnus-uu-mark-series**).

M P S   Mark all series that have already had some articles marked (**gnus-uu-mark-sparse**).

M P a   Mark all articles in series order (**gnus-uu-mark-all**).

M P b   Mark all articles in the buffer in the order they appear (**gnus-uu-mark-buffer**).

M P k   Push the current process mark set onto the stack and unmark all articles (**gnus-summary-kill-process-mark**).

M P y   Pop the previous process mark set from the stack and restore it (**gnus-summary-yank-process-mark**).

M P w   Push the current process mark set onto the stack (**gnus-summary-save-process-mark**).

Also see the *&* command in Section 3.27.2 [Searching for Articles], page 110, for how to set process marks based on article body contents.

3.8 Limiting

It can be convenient to limit the summary buffer to just show some subset of the articles currently in the group. The effect most limit commands have is to remove a few (or many) articles from the summary buffer.

Limiting commands work on subsets of the articles already fetched from the servers. These commands don't query the server for additional articles.

/ /

/ s   Limit the summary buffer to articles that match some subject (**gnus-summary-limit-to-subject**). If given a prefix, exclude matching articles.

/ a   Limit the summary buffer to articles that match some author (**gnus-summary-limit-to-author**). If given a prefix, exclude matching articles.

/ R   Limit the summary buffer to articles that match some recipient (**gnus-summary-limit-to-recipient**). If given a prefix, exclude matching articles.

/ A   Limit the summary buffer to articles in which contents of From, To or Cc header match a given address (**gnus-summary-limit-to-address**). If given a prefix, exclude matching articles.

/ S   Limit the summary buffer to articles that aren't part of any displayed threads (**gnus-summary-limit-to-singletons**). If given a prefix, limit to articles that are part of displayed threads.

/ x   Limit the summary buffer to articles that match one of the "extra" headers (see Section 3.1.2 [To From Newsgroups], page 47) (**gnus-summary-limit-to-extra**). If given a prefix, exclude matching articles.

/ u

x   Limit the summary buffer to articles not marked as read (**gnus-summary-limit-to-unread**). If given a prefix, limit the buffer to articles strictly unread. This means that ticked and dormant articles will also be excluded.

/ m   Ask for a mark and then limit to all articles that have been marked with that mark (**gnus-summary-limit-to-marks**).

/ t   Ask for a number and then limit the summary buffer to articles older than (or equal to) that number of days (**gnus-summary-limit-to-age**). If given a prefix, limit to articles younger than that number of days.

/ n   With prefix 'n', limit the summary buffer to the next 'n' articles. If not given a prefix, use the process marked articles instead. (**gnus-summary-limit-to-articles**).

/ w   Pop the previous limit off the stack and restore it (`gnus-summary-pop-limit`).
             If given a prefix, pop all limits off the stack.

/ .   Limit the summary buffer to the unseen articles (`gnus-summary-limit-to-unseen`).

/ v   Limit the summary buffer to articles that have a score at or above some score
             (`gnus-summary-limit-to-score`).

/ p   Limit the summary buffer to articles that satisfy the `display` group parameter
             predicate (`gnus-summary-limit-to-display-predicate`). See Section 2.10
             [Group Parameters], page 22, for more on this predicate.

/ r   Limit the summary buffer to replied articles (`gnus-summary-limit-to-replied`). If given a prefix, exclude replied articles.

/ E
M S   Include all expunged articles in the limit (`gnus-summary-limit-include-expunged`).

/ D   Include all dormant articles in the limit (`gnus-summary-limit-include-dormant`).

/ *   Include all cached articles in the limit (`gnus-summary-limit-include-cached`).

/ d   Exclude all dormant articles from the limit (`gnus-summary-limit-exclude-dormant`).

/ M   Exclude all marked articles (`gnus-summary-limit-exclude-marks`).

/ T   Include all the articles in the current thread in the limit.

/ c   Exclude all dormant articles that have no children from the limit
             (`gnus-summary-limit-exclude-childless-dormant`).

/ C   Mark all excluded unread articles as read (`gnus-summary-limit-mark-excluded-as-read`). If given a prefix, also mark excluded ticked and dormant
             articles as read.

/ b   Limit the summary buffer to articles that have bodies that match a certain
             regexp (`gnus-summary-limit-to-bodies`). If given a prefix, reverse the limit.
             This command is quite slow since it requires selecting each article to find the
             matches.

/ h   Like the previous command, only limit to headers instead (`gnus-summary-limit-to-headers`).

The following commands aren't limiting commands, but use the / prefix as well.

/ N   Insert all new articles in the summary buffer. It scans for new emails if *back-end*-`get-new-mail` is non-`nil`.

/ o   Insert all old articles in the summary buffer. If given a numbered prefix, fetch
             this number of articles.

3.9 Threading

Gnus threads articles by default. *To thread* is to put responses to articles directly after the articles they respond to—in a hierarchical fashion.

Threading is done by looking at the `References` headers of the articles. In a perfect world, this would be enough to build pretty trees, but unfortunately, the `References` header is often broken or simply missing. Weird news propagation exacerbates the problem, so one has to employ other heuristics to get pleasing results. A plethora of approaches exists, as detailed in horrible detail in Section 3.9.1 [Customizing Threading], page 65.

First, a quick overview of the concepts:

root   The top-most article in a thread; the first article in the thread.

thread   A tree-like article structure.

sub-thread

        A small(er) section of this tree-like structure.

loose threads

        Threads often lose their roots due to article expiry, or due to the root already having been read in a previous session, and not displayed in the summary buffer. We then typically have many sub-threads that really belong to one thread, but are without connecting roots. These are called loose threads.

thread gathering

        An attempt to gather loose threads into bigger threads.

sparse threads

        A thread where the missing articles have been "guessed" at, and are displayed as empty lines in the summary buffer.

3.9.1 Customizing Threading

3.9.1.1 Loose Threads

`gnus-summary-make-false-root`

        If non-`nil`, Gnus will gather all loose subtrees into one big tree and create a dummy root at the top. (Wait a minute. Root at the top? Yup.) Loose subtrees occur when the real root has expired, or you've read or killed the root in a previous session.

        When there is no real root of a thread, Gnus will have to fudge something. This variable says what fudging method Gnus should use. There are four possible values:

        `adopt`   Gnus will make the first of the orphaned articles the parent. This parent will adopt all the other articles. The adopted articles will be marked as such by pointy brackets ('`<>`') instead of the standard square brackets ('`[]`'). This is the default method.

        `dummy`   Gnus will create a dummy summary line that will pretend to be the parent. This dummy line does not correspond to any real article, so selecting it will just select the first real article after the dummy article. `gnus-summary-dummy-line-format` is used to specify the format of the dummy roots. It accepts only one format spec: 'S', which is the subject of the article. See Section 9.4 [Formatting Variables], page 250. If you want all threads to have a dummy root, even the non-gathered ones, set `gnus-summary-make-false-root-always` to t.

empty   Gnus won't actually make any article the parent, but simply leave the subject field of all orphans except the first empty. (Actually, it will use `gnus-summary-same-subject` as the subject (see Section 3.1 [Summary Buffer Format], page 44).)

none   Don't make any article parent at all. Just gather the threads and display them after one another.

nil   Don't gather loose threads.

`gnus-summary-gather-subject-limit`

Loose threads are gathered by comparing subjects of articles. If this variable is `nil`, Gnus requires an exact match between the subjects of the loose threads before gathering them into one big super-thread. This might be too strict a requirement, what with the presence of stupid newsreaders that chop off long subject lines. If you think so, set this variable to, say, 20 to require that only the first 20 characters of the subjects have to match. If you set this variable to a really low number, you'll find that Gnus will gather everything in sight into one thread, which isn't very helpful.

If you set this variable to the special value `fuzzy`, Gnus will use a fuzzy string comparison algorithm on the subjects (see Section 9.15 [Fuzzy Matching], page 267).

`gnus-simplify-subject-fuzzy-regexp`

This can either be a regular expression or list of regular expressions that match strings that will be removed from subjects if fuzzy subject simplification is used.

`gnus-simplify-ignored-prefixes`

If you set `gnus-summary-gather-subject-limit` to something as low as 10, you might consider setting this variable to something sensible:

```
(setq gnus-simplify-ignored-prefixes
  (concat
   "\\`\\[?\\("
   (mapconcat
    'identity
    '("looking"
      "wanted" "followup" "summary\\( of\\)?"
      "help" "query" "problem" "question"
      "answer" "reference" "announce"
      "How can I" "How to" "Comparison of"
      ;; ...
      )
    "\\|")
```

```
"\\)\\s *\\("
(mapconcat 'identity
              '("for" "for reference" "with" "about")
              "\\|")
"\\)?\\]?:?[ \t]*"))
```

All words that match this regexp will be removed before comparing two subjects.

`gnus-simplify-subject-functions`

If non-nil, this variable overrides `gnus-summary-gather-subject-limit`. This variable should be a list of functions to apply to the `Subject` string iteratively to arrive at the simplified version of the string.

Useful functions to put in this list include:

`gnus-simplify-subject-re`
> Strip the leading 'Re:'.

`gnus-simplify-subject-fuzzy`
> Simplify fuzzily.

`gnus-simplify-whitespace`
> Remove excessive whitespace.

`gnus-simplify-all-whitespace`
> Remove all whitespace.

You may also write your own functions, of course.

`gnus-summary-gather-exclude-subject`

Since loose thread gathering is done on subjects only, that might lead to many false hits, especially with certain common subjects like '' and '(none)'. To make the situation slightly better, you can use the regexp `gnus-summary-gather-exclude-subject` to say what subjects should be excluded from the gathering process.

The default is '^ *$\\|^(none)$'.

`gnus-summary-thread-gathering-function`

Gnus gathers threads by looking at `Subject` headers. This means that totally unrelated articles may end up in the same "thread", which is confusing. An alternate approach is to look at all the `Message-IDs` in all the `References` headers to find matches. This will ensure that no gathered threads ever include unrelated articles, but it also means that people who have posted with broken newsreaders won't be gathered properly. The choice is yours—plague or cholera:

`gnus-gather-threads-by-subject`
> This function is the default gathering function and looks at `Subjects` exclusively.

`gnus-gather-threads-by-references`
> This function looks at `References` headers exclusively.

If you want to test gathering by `References`, you could say something like:

```
(setq gnus-summary-thread-gathering-function
      'gnus-gather-threads-by-references)
```

3.9.1.2 Filling In Threads

`gnus-fetch-old-headers`

> If non-`nil`, Gnus will attempt to build old threads by fetching more old headers—headers to articles marked as read. If you would like to display as few summary lines as possible, but still connect as many loose threads as possible, you should set this variable to `some` or a number. If you set it to a number, no more than that number of extra old headers will be fetched. In either case, fetching old headers only works if the back end you are using carries overview files—this would normally be `nntp`, `nnspool`, `nnml`, and `nnmaildir`. Also remember that if the root of the thread has been expired by the server, there's not much Gnus can do about that.
>
> This variable can also be set to `invisible`. This won't have any visible effects, but is useful if you use the *A T* command a lot (see Section 3.23 [Finding the Parent], page 102).
>
> The server has to support NOV for any of this to work.
>
> This feature can seriously impact performance it ignores all locally cached header entries. Setting it to `t` for groups for a server that doesn't expire articles (such as news.gmane.org), leads to very slow summary generation.

`gnus-fetch-old-ephemeral-headers`

> Same as `gnus-fetch-old-headers`, but only used for ephemeral newsgroups.

`gnus-build-sparse-threads`

> Fetching old headers can be slow. A low-rent similar effect can be gotten by setting this variable to `some`. Gnus will then look at the complete `References` headers of all articles and try to string together articles that belong in the same thread. This will leave *gaps* in the threading display where Gnus guesses that an article is missing from the thread. (These gaps appear like normal summary lines. If you select a gap, Gnus will try to fetch the article in question.) If this variable is `t`, Gnus will display all these "gaps" without regard for whether they are useful for completing the thread or not. Finally, if this variable is `more`, Gnus won't cut off sparse leaf nodes that don't lead anywhere. This variable is `nil` by default.

`gnus-read-all-available-headers`

> This is a rather obscure variable that few will find useful. It's intended for those non-news newsgroups where the back end has to fetch quite a lot to present the summary buffer, and where it's impossible to go back to parents of articles. This is mostly the case in the web-based groups.
>
> If you don't use those, then it's safe to leave this as the default `nil`. If you want to use this variable, it should be a regexp that matches the group name, or `t` for all groups.

3.9.1.3 More Threading

`gnus-show-threads`

> If this variable is `nil`, no threading will be done, and all of the rest of the variables here will have no effect. Turning threading off will speed group selection up a bit, but it is sure to make reading slower and more awkward.

`gnus-thread-hide-subtree`

> If non-`nil`, all threads will be hidden when the summary buffer is generated.
>
> This can also be a predicate specifier (see Section 9.11 [Predicate Specifiers], page 262). Available predicates are `gnus-article-unread-p` and `gnus-article-unseen-p`.
>
> Here's an example:
>
> ```
> (setq gnus-thread-hide-subtree
>       '(or gnus-article-unread-p
>            gnus-article-unseen-p))
> ```
>
> (It's a pretty nonsensical example, since all unseen articles are also unread, but you get my drift.)

`gnus-thread-expunge-below`

> All threads that have a total score (as defined by `gnus-thread-score-function`) less than this number will be expunged. This variable is `nil` by default, which means that no threads are expunged.

`gnus-thread-hide-killed`

> if you kill a thread and this variable is non-`nil`, the subtree will be hidden.

`gnus-thread-ignore-subject`

> Sometimes somebody changes the subject in the middle of a thread. If this variable is non-`nil`, which is the default, the subject change is ignored. If it is `nil`, a change in the subject will result in a new thread.

`gnus-thread-indent-level`

> This is a number that says how much each sub-thread should be indented. The default is 4.

`gnus-sort-gathered-threads-function`

> Sometimes, particularly with mailing lists, the order in which mails arrive locally is not necessarily the same as the order in which they arrived on the mailing list. Consequently, when sorting sub-threads using the default `gnus-thread-sort-by-number`, responses can end up appearing before the article to which they are responding to. Setting this variable to an alternate value (e.g., `gnus-thread-sort-by-date`), in a group's parameters or in an appropriate hook (e.g., `gnus-summary-generate-hook`) can produce a more logical sub-thread ordering in such instances.

3.9.1.4 Low-Level Threading

`gnus-parse-headers-hook`

> Hook run before parsing any headers.

`gnus-alter-header-function`

> If non-`nil`, this function will be called to allow alteration of article header structures. The function is called with one parameter, the article header vector, which it may alter in any way. For instance, if you have a mail-to-news gateway which alters the `Message-IDs` in systematic ways (by adding prefixes and such), you can use this variable to un-scramble the `Message-IDs` so that they are more meaningful. Here's one example:

```
(setq gnus-alter-header-function 'my-alter-message-id)

(defun my-alter-message-id (header)
  (let ((id (mail-header-id header)))
    (when (string-match
           "\\(<[^<>@]*\\)\\.?cygnus\\..*@\\([^<>@]*>\\)" id)
      (mail-header-set-id
       (concat (match-string 1 id) "@" (match-string 2 id))
       header))))
```

3.9.2 Thread Commands

T k

C-M-k   Mark all articles in the current (sub-)thread as read (`gnus-summary-kill-thread`). If the prefix argument is positive, remove all marks instead. If the prefix argument is negative, tick articles instead.

T l

C-M-l   Lower the score of the current (sub-)thread (`gnus-summary-lower-thread`).

T i   Increase the score of the current (sub-)thread (`gnus-summary-raise-thread`).

T #   Set the process mark on the current (sub-)thread (`gnus-uu-mark-thread`).

T M-#   Remove the process mark from the current (sub-)thread (`gnus-uu-unmark-thread`).

T T   Toggle threading (`gnus-summary-toggle-threads`).

T s   Expose the (sub-)thread hidden under the current article, if any (`gnus-summary-show-thread`).

T h   Hide the current (sub-)thread (`gnus-summary-hide-thread`).

T S   Expose all hidden threads (`gnus-summary-show-all-threads`).

T H   Hide all threads (`gnus-summary-hide-all-threads`).

T t   Re-thread the current article's thread (`gnus-summary-rethread-current`). This works even when the summary buffer is otherwise unthreaded.

T ^   Make the current article the child of the marked (or previous) article (`gnus-summary-reparent-thread`).

*T M-^*   Make the current article the parent of the marked articles (`gnus-summary-reparent-children`).

The following commands are thread movement commands. They all understand the numeric prefix.

T n
C-M-f
M-down   Go to the next thread (`gnus-summary-next-thread`).

T p
C-M-b
M-up   Go to the previous thread (`gnus-summary-prev-thread`).

T d   Descend the thread (`gnus-summary-down-thread`).

T u   Ascend the thread (`gnus-summary-up-thread`).

T o   Go to the top of the thread (`gnus-summary-top-thread`).

If you ignore subject while threading, you'll naturally end up with threads that have several different subjects in them. If you then issue a command like *T k* (`gnus-summary-kill-thread`) you might not wish to kill the entire thread, but just those parts of the thread that have the same subject as the current article. If you like this idea, you can fiddle with `gnus-thread-operation-ignore-subject`. If it is non-`nil` (which it is by default), subjects will be ignored when doing thread commands. If this variable is `nil`, articles in the same thread with different subjects will not be included in the operation in question. If this variable is `fuzzy`, only articles that have subjects fuzzily equal will be included (see Section 9.15 [Fuzzy Matching], page 267).

3.10 Sorting the Summary Buffer

If you are using a threaded summary display, you can sort the threads by setting `gnus-thread-sort-functions`, which can be either a single function, a list of functions, or a list containing functions and (`not some-function`) elements.

By default, sorting is done on article numbers. Ready-made sorting predicate functions include `gnus-thread-sort-by-number`, `gnus-thread-sort-by-author`, `gnus-thread-sort-by-recipient`, `gnus-thread-sort-by-subject`, `gnus-thread-sort-by-date`, `gnus-thread-sort-by-score`, `gnus-thread-sort-by-most-recent-number`, `gnus-thread-sort-by-most-recent-date`, `gnus-thread-sort-by-random` and `gnus-thread-sort-by-total-score`.

Each function takes two threads and returns non-`nil` if the first thread should be sorted before the other. Note that sorting really is normally done by looking only at the roots of each thread. Exceptions to this rule are `gnus-thread-sort-by-most-recent-number` and `gnus-thread-sort-by-most-recent-date`.

If you use more than one function, the primary sort key should be the last function in the list. You should probably always include `gnus-thread-sort-by-number` in the list of sorting functions—preferably first. This will ensure that threads that are equal with respect to the other sort criteria will be displayed in ascending article order.

If you would like to sort by reverse score, then by subject, and finally by number, you could do something like:

```
(setq gnus-thread-sort-functions
```

```
'(gnus-thread-sort-by-number
  gnus-thread-sort-by-subject
  (not gnus-thread-sort-by-total-score)))
```

The threads that have highest score will be displayed first in the summary buffer. When threads have the same score, they will be sorted alphabetically. The threads that have the same score and the same subject will be sorted by number, which is (normally) the sequence in which the articles arrived.

If you want to sort by score and then reverse arrival order, you could say something like:

```
(setq gnus-thread-sort-functions
      '((not gnus-thread-sort-by-number)
        gnus-thread-sort-by-score))
```

By default, threads including their subthreads are sorted according to the value of `gnus-thread-sort-functions`. By customizing `gnus-subthread-sort-functions` you can define a custom sorting order for subthreads. This allows for example to sort threads from high score to low score in the summary buffer, but to have subthreads still sorted chronologically from old to new without taking their score into account.

The function in the `gnus-thread-score-function` variable (default +) is used for calculating the total score of a thread. Useful functions might be `max`, `min`, or squared means, or whatever tickles your fancy.

If you are using an unthreaded display for some strange reason or other, you have to fiddle with the `gnus-article-sort-functions` variable. It is very similar to the `gnus-thread-sort-functions`, except that it uses slightly different functions for article comparison. Available sorting predicate functions are `gnus-article-sort-by-number`, `gnus-article-sort-by-author`, `gnus-article-sort-by-subject`, `gnus-article-sort-by-date`, `gnus-article-sort-by-random`, and `gnus-article-sort-by-score`.

If you want to sort an unthreaded summary display by subject, you could say something like:

```
(setq gnus-article-sort-functions
      '(gnus-article-sort-by-number
        gnus-article-sort-by-subject))
```

You can define group specific sorting via `gnus-parameters`, See Section 2.10 [Group Parameters], page 22.

3.11 Asynchronous Article Fetching

If you read your news from an NNTP server that's far away, the network latencies may make reading articles a chore. You have to wait for a while after pressing **n** to go to the next article before the article appears. Why can't Gnus just go ahead and fetch the article while you are reading the previous one? Why not, indeed.

First, some caveats. There are some pitfalls to using asynchronous article fetching, especially the way Gnus does it.

Let's say you are reading article 1, which is short, and article 2 is quite long, and you are not interested in reading that. Gnus does not know this, so it goes ahead and fetches article 2. You decide to read article 3, but since Gnus is in the process of fetching article 2, the connection is blocked.

To avoid these situations, Gnus will open two (count 'em two) connections to the server. Some people may think this isn't a very nice thing to do, but I don't see any real alternatives. Setting up that extra connection takes some time, so Gnus startup will be slower.

Gnus will fetch more articles than you will read. This will mean that the link between your machine and the NNTP server will become more loaded than if you didn't use article pre-fetch. The server itself will also become more loaded—both with the extra article requests, and the extra connection.

Ok, so now you know that you shouldn't really use this thing... unless you really want to.

Here's how: Set `gnus-asynchronous` to `t`. The rest should happen automatically.

You can control how many articles are to be pre-fetched by setting `gnus-use-article-prefetch`. This is 30 by default, which means that when you read an article in the group, the back end will pre-fetch the next 30 articles. If this variable is `t`, the back end will pre-fetch all the articles it can without bound. If it is `nil`, no pre-fetching will be done.

There are probably some articles that you don't want to pre-fetch—read articles, for instance. The `gnus-async-prefetch-article-p` variable controls whether an article is to be pre-fetched. This function should return non-`nil` when the article in question is to be pre-fetched. The default is `gnus-async-unread-p`, which returns `nil` on read articles. The function is called with an article data structure as the only parameter.

If, for instance, you wish to pre-fetch only unread articles shorter than 100 lines, you could say something like:

```
(defun my-async-short-unread-p (data)
  "Return non-nil for short, unread articles."
  (and (gnus-data-unread-p data)
       (< (mail-header-lines (gnus-data-header data))
          100)))


(setq gnus-async-prefetch-article-p 'my-async-short-unread-p)
```

These functions will be called many, many times, so they should preferably be short and sweet to avoid slowing down Gnus too much. It's probably a good idea to byte-compile things like this.

After an article has been prefetched, this `gnus-async-post-fetch-function` will be called. The buffer will be narrowed to the region of the article that was fetched. A useful value would be `gnus-html-prefetch-images`, which will prefetch and store images referenced in the article, so that you don't have to wait for them to be fetched when you read the article. This is useful for HTML messages that have external images.

Articles have to be removed from the asynch buffer sooner or later. The `gnus-prefetched-article-deletion-strategy` says when to remove articles. This is a list that may contain the following elements:

read   Remove articles when they are read.

exit   Remove articles when exiting the group.

The default value is (`read exit`).

3.12 Article Caching

If you have an *extremely* slow NNTP connection, you may consider turning article caching on. Each article will then be stored locally under your home directory. As you may surmise, this could potentially use *huge* amounts of disk space, as well as eat up all your inodes so fast it will make your head swim. In vodka.

Used carefully, though, it could be just an easier way to save articles.

To turn caching on, set `gnus-use-cache` to `t`. By default, all articles ticked or marked as dormant will then be copied over to your local cache (`gnus-cache-directory`). Whether this cache is flat or hierarchical is controlled by the `gnus-use-long-file-name` variable, as usual.

When re-selecting a ticked or dormant article, it will be fetched from the cache instead of from the server. As articles in your cache will never expire, this might serve as a method of saving articles while still keeping them where they belong. Just mark all articles you want to save as dormant, and don't worry.

When an article is marked as read, is it removed from the cache.

The entering/removal of articles from the cache is controlled by the `gnus-cache-enter-articles` and `gnus-cache-remove-articles` variables. Both are lists of symbols. The first is (`ticked dormant`) by default, meaning that ticked and dormant articles will be put in the cache. The latter is (`read`) by default, meaning that articles marked as read are removed from the cache. Possibly symbols in these two lists are `ticked`, `dormant`, `unread` and `read`.

So where does the massive article-fetching and storing come into the picture? The `gnus-jog-cache` command will go through all subscribed newsgroups, request all unread articles, score them, and store them in the cache. You should only ever, ever ever ever, use this command if 1) your connection to the NNTP server is really, really, really slow and 2) you have a really, really, really huge disk. Seriously. One way to cut down on the number of articles downloaded is to score unwanted articles down and have them marked as read. They will not then be downloaded by this command.

It is likely that you do not want caching on all groups. For instance, if your `nnml` mail is located under your home directory, it makes no sense to cache it somewhere else under your home directory. Unless you feel that it's neat to use twice as much space.

To limit the caching, you could set `gnus-cacheable-groups` to a regexp of groups to cache, '`^nntp`' for instance, or set the `gnus-uncacheable-groups` regexp to '`^nnml`', for instance. Both variables are `nil` by default. If a group matches both variables, the group is not cached.

The cache stores information on what articles it contains in its active file (`gnus-cache-active-file`). If this file (or any other parts of the cache) becomes all messed up for some reason or other, Gnus offers two functions that will try to set things right. *M-x gnus-cache-generate-nov-databases* will (re)build all the NOV files, and *gnus-cache-generate-active* will (re)generate the active file.

`gnus-cache-move-cache` will move your whole `gnus-cache-directory` to some other location. You get asked to where, isn't that cool?

3.13 Persistent Articles

Closely related to article caching, we have *persistent articles*. In fact, it's just a different way of looking at caching, and much more useful in my opinion.

Say you're reading a newsgroup, and you happen on to some valuable gem that you want to keep and treasure forever. You'd normally just save it (using one of the many saving commands) in some file. The problem with that is that it's just, well, yucky. Ideally you'd prefer just having the article remain in the group where you found it forever; untouched by the expiry going on at the news server.

This is what a *persistent article* is—an article that just won't be deleted. It's implemented using the normal cache functions, but you use two explicit commands for managing persistent articles:

`*`   Make the current article persistent (**gnus-cache-enter-article**).

`M-*`   Remove the current article from the persistent articles (**gnus-cache-remove-article**). This will normally delete the article.

Both these commands understand the process/prefix convention.

To avoid having all ticked articles (and stuff) entered into the cache, you should set **gnus-use-cache** to `passive` if you're just interested in persistent articles:

```
(setq gnus-use-cache 'passive)
```

3.14 Sticky Articles

When you select an article the current article buffer will be reused according to the value of the variable **gnus-single-article-buffer**. If its value is non-`nil` (the default) all articles reuse the same article buffer. Else each group has its own article buffer.

This implies that it's not possible to have more than one article buffer in a group at a time. But sometimes you might want to display all the latest emails from your mother, your father, your aunt, your uncle and your 17 cousins to coordinate the next Christmas party.

That's where sticky articles come in handy. A sticky article buffer basically is a normal article buffer, but it won't be reused when you select another article. You can make an article sticky with:

`A S`   Make the current article sticky. If a prefix arg is given, ask for a name for this sticky article buffer.

To close a sticky article buffer you can use these commands:

`q`   Puts this sticky article buffer at the end of the list of all buffers.

`k`   Kills this sticky article buffer.

To kill all sticky article buffers you can use:

gnus-kill-sticky-article-buffers *ARG*   [Function]
    Kill all sticky article buffers. If a prefix ARG is given, ask for confirmation.

3.15 Article Backlog

If you have a slow connection, but the idea of using caching seems unappealing to you (and it is, really), you can help the situation some by switching on the *backlog*. This is where Gnus will buffer already read articles so that it doesn't have to re-fetch articles you've already read. This only helps if you are in the habit of re-selecting articles you've recently read, of course. If you never do that, turning the backlog on will slow Gnus down a little bit, and increase memory usage some.

If you set **gnus-keep-backlog** to a number *n*, Gnus will store at most *n* old articles in a buffer for later re-fetching. If this variable is non-**nil** and is not a number, Gnus will store *all* read articles, which means that your Emacs will grow without bound before exploding and taking your machine down with you. I put that in there just to keep y'all on your toes.

The default value is 20.

3.16 Saving Articles

Gnus can save articles in a number of ways. Below is the documentation for saving articles in a fairly straight-forward fashion (i.e., little processing of the article is done before it is saved). For a different approach (uudecoding, unsharing) you should use **gnus-uu** (see Section 3.17 [Decoding Articles], page 80).

For the commands listed here, the target is a file. If you want to save to a group, see the *B c* (**gnus-summary-copy-article**) command (see Section 3.26 [Mail Group Commands], page 107).

If **gnus-save-all-headers** is non-**nil**, Gnus will not delete unwanted headers before saving the article.

If the preceding variable is **nil**, all headers that match the **gnus-saved-headers** regexp will be kept, while the rest will be deleted before saving.

O o

o   Save the current article using the default article saver (**gnus-summary-save-article**).

O m   Save the current article in a Unix mail box (mbox) file (**gnus-summary-save-article-mail**).

O r   Save the current article in Rmail format (**gnus-summary-save-article-rmail**). This is mbox since Emacs 23, Babyl in older versions.

O f   Save the current article in plain file format (**gnus-summary-save-article-file**).

O F   Write the current article in plain file format, overwriting any previous file contents (**gnus-summary-write-article-file**).

O b   Save the current article body in plain file format (**gnus-summary-save-article-body-file**).

O h   Save the current article in mh folder format (**gnus-summary-save-article-folder**).

O v   Save the current article in a VM folder (**gnus-summary-save-article-vm**).

O p
|
Save the current article in a pipe. Uhm, like, what I mean is—Pipe the current article to a process (`gnus-summary-pipe-output`). If given a symbolic prefix (see Section 9.3 [Symbolic Prefixes], page 250), include the complete headers in the piped output. The symbolic prefix **r** is special; it lets this command pipe a raw article including all headers. The `gnus-summary-pipe-output-default-command` variable can be set to a string containing the default command and options (default `nil`).

O P
Save the current article into muttprint. That is, print it using the external program Muttprint. The program name and options to use is controlled by the variable `gnus-summary-muttprint-program`. (`gnus-summary-muttprint`).

All these commands use the process/prefix convention (see Section 9.1 [Process/Prefix], page 249). If you save bunches of articles using these functions, you might get tired of being prompted for files to save each and every article in. The prompting action is controlled by the `gnus-prompt-before-saving` variable, which is **always** by default, giving you that excessive prompting action you know and loathe. If you set this variable to **t** instead, you'll be prompted just once for each series of articles you save. If you like to really have Gnus do all your thinking for you, you can even set this variable to `nil`, which means that you will never be prompted for files to save articles in. Gnus will simply save all the articles in the default files.

You can customize the `gnus-default-article-saver` variable to make Gnus do what you want it to. You can use any of the eight ready-made functions below, or you can create your own.

`gnus-summary-save-in-rmail`
This is the default format, that used by the Rmail package. Since Emacs 23, Rmail uses standard mbox format. Before this, it used the *Babyl* format. Accordingly, this command writes mbox format since Emacs 23, unless appending to an existing Babyl file. In older versions of Emacs, it always uses Babyl format. Uses the function in the `gnus-rmail-save-name` variable to get a file name to save the article in. The default is **gnus-plain-save-name**.

`gnus-summary-save-in-mail`
Save in a Unix mail (mbox) file. Uses the function in the **gnus-mail-save-name** variable to get a file name to save the article in. The default is **gnus-plain-save-name**.

`gnus-summary-save-in-file`
Append the article straight to an ordinary file. Uses the function in the **gnus-file-save-name** variable to get a file name to save the article in. The default is **gnus-numeric-save-name**.

`gnus-summary-write-to-file`
Write the article straight to an ordinary file. The file is overwritten if it exists. Uses the function in the **gnus-file-save-name** variable to get a file name to save the article in. The default is **gnus-numeric-save-name**.

`gnus-summary-save-body-in-file`
> Append the article body to an ordinary file. Uses the function in the `gnus-file-save-name` variable to get a file name to save the article in. The default is **gnus-numeric-save-name**.

`gnus-summary-write-body-to-file`
> Write the article body straight to an ordinary file. The file is overwritten if it exists. Uses the function in the `gnus-file-save-name` variable to get a file name to save the article in. The default is **gnus-numeric-save-name**.

`gnus-summary-save-in-folder`
> Save the article to an MH folder using `rcvstore` from the MH library. Uses the function in the `gnus-folder-save-name` variable to get a file name to save the article in. The default is **gnus-folder-save-name**, but you can also use **gnus-Folder-save-name**, which creates capitalized names.

`gnus-summary-save-in-vm`
> Save the article in a VM folder. You have to have the VM mail reader to use this setting.

`gnus-summary-save-in-pipe`
> Pipe the article to a shell command. This function takes optional two arguments COMMAND and RAW. Valid values for COMMAND include:
>
> - a string
>   The executable command name and possibly arguments.
> - `nil`
>   You will be prompted for the command in the minibuffer.
> - the symbol `default`
>   It will be replaced with the command which the variable **gnus-summary-pipe-output-default-command** holds or the command last used for saving.
>
> Non-`nil` value for RAW overrides `:decode` and `:headers` properties (see below) and the raw article including all headers will be piped.

The symbol of each function may have the following properties:

`:decode`   The value non-`nil` means save decoded articles. This is meaningful only with `gnus-summary-save-in-file`, `gnus-summary-save-body-in-file`, `gnus-summary-write-to-file`, `gnus-summary-write-body-to-file`, and `gnus-summary-save-in-pipe`.

`:function`
> The value specifies an alternative function which appends, not overwrites, articles to a file. This implies that when saving many articles at a time, `gnus-prompt-before-saving` is bound to `t` and all articles are saved in a single file. This is meaningful only with `gnus-summary-write-to-file` and `gnus-summary-write-body-to-file`.

`:headers`   The value specifies the symbol of a variable of which the value specifies headers to be saved. If it is omitted, **gnus-save-all-headers** and **gnus-saved-headers** control what headers should be saved.

All of these functions, except for the last one, will save the article in the `gnus-article-save-directory`, which is initialized from the `SAVEDIR` environment variable. This is ~/News/ by default.

As you can see above, the functions use different functions to find a suitable name of a file to save the article in. Below is a list of available functions that generate names:

`gnus-Numeric-save-name`
>   File names like ~/News/Alt.andrea-dworkin/45.

`gnus-numeric-save-name`
>   File names like ~/News/alt.andrea-dworkin/45.

`gnus-Plain-save-name`
>   File names like ~/News/Alt.andrea-dworkin.

`gnus-plain-save-name`
>   File names like ~/News/alt.andrea-dworkin.

`gnus-sender-save-name`
>   File names like ~/News/larsi.

You can have Gnus suggest where to save articles by plonking a regexp into the `gnus-split-methods` alist. For instance, if you would like to save articles related to Gnus in the file `gnus-stuff`, and articles related to VM in `vm-stuff`, you could set this variable to something like:

```
(("^Subject:.*gnus\\|^Newsgroups:.*gnus" "gnus-stuff")
 ("^Subject:.*vm\\|^Xref:.*vm" "vm-stuff")
 (my-choosing-function "../other-dir/my-stuff")
 ((equal gnus-newsgroup-name "mail.misc") "mail-stuff"))
```

We see that this is a list where each element is a list that has two elements—the *match* and the *file*. The match can either be a string (in which case it is used as a regexp to match on the article head); it can be a symbol (which will be called as a function with the group name as a parameter); or it can be a list (which will be `eval`ed). If any of these actions have a non-`nil` result, the *file* will be used as a default prompt. In addition, the result of the operation itself will be used if the function or form called returns a string or a list of strings.

You basically end up with a list of file names that might be used when saving the current article. (All "matches" will be used.) You will then be prompted for what you really want to use as a name, with file name completion over the results from applying this variable.

This variable is `((gnus-article-archive-name))` by default, which means that Gnus will look at the articles it saves for an `Archive-name` line and use that as a suggestion for the file name.

Here's an example function to clean up file names somewhat. If you have lots of mail groups called things like 'nnml:mail.whatever', you may want to chop off the beginning of these group names before creating the file name to save to. The following will do just that:

```
(defun my-save-name (group)
  (when (string-match "^nnml:mail." group)
    (substring group (match-end 0))))
```

```
(setq gnus-split-methods
      '((gnus-article-archive-name)
        (my-save-name)))
```

Finally, you have the **gnus-use-long-file-name** variable. If it is **nil**, all the preceding functions will replace all periods ('.') in the group names with slashes ('/')—which means that the functions will generate hierarchies of directories instead of having all the files in the top level directory (**~/News/alt/andrea-dworkin** instead of **~/News/alt.andrea-dworkin**.) This variable is **t** by default on most systems. However, for historical reasons, this is **nil** on Xenix and usg-unix-v machines by default.

This function also affects kill and score file names. If this variable is a list, and the list contains the element **not-score**, long file names will not be used for score files, if it contains the element **not-save**, long file names will not be used for saving, and if it contains the element **not-kill**, long file names will not be used for kill files.

If you'd like to save articles in a hierarchy that looks something like a spool, you could

```
(setq gnus-use-long-file-name '(not-save)) ; to get a hierarchy
(setq gnus-default-article-saver
      'gnus-summary-save-in-file)              ; no encoding
```

Then just save with *o*. You'd then read this hierarchy with ephemeral **nneething** groups—*G D* in the group buffer, and the top level directory as the argument (**~/News/**). Then just walk around to the groups/directories with **nneething**.

3.17 Decoding Articles

Sometime users post articles (or series of articles) that have been encoded in some way or other. Gnus can decode them for you.

All these functions use the process/prefix convention (see Section 9.1 [Process/Prefix], page 249) for finding out what articles to work on, with the extension that a "single article" means "a single series". Gnus can find out by itself what articles belong to a series, decode all the articles and unpack/view/save the resulting file(s).

Gnus guesses what articles are in the series according to the following simplish rule: The subjects must be (nearly) identical, except for the last two numbers of the line. (Spaces are largely ignored, however.)

For example: If you choose a subject called 'cat.gif (2/3)', Gnus will find all the articles that match the regexp '^cat.gif ([0-9]+/[0-9]+).*$'.

Subjects that are non-standard, like 'cat.gif (2/3) Part 6 of a series', will not be properly recognized by any of the automatic viewing commands, and you have to mark the articles manually with **#**.

3.17.1 Uuencoded Articles

X u   Uudecodes the current series (**gnus-uu-decode-uu**).

X U   Uudecodes and saves the current series (**gnus-uu-decode-uu-and-save**).

X v u   Uudecodes and views the current series (**gnus-uu-decode-uu-view**).

X v U   Uudecodes, views and saves the current series (**gnus-uu-decode-uu-and-save-view**).

Remember that these all react to the presence of articles marked with the process mark. If, for instance, you'd like to decode and save an entire newsgroup, you'd typically do *M P a* (`gnus-uu-mark-all`) and then *X U* (`gnus-uu-decode-uu-and-save`).

All this is very much different from how **gnus-uu** worked with GNUS 4.1, where you had explicit keystrokes for everything under the sun. This version of **gnus-uu** generally assumes that you mark articles in some way (see Section 3.7.6 [Setting Process Marks], page 62) and then press *X u*.

Note: When trying to decode articles that have names matching `gnus-uu-notify-files`, which is hard-coded to '`[Cc][Ii][Nn][Dd][Yy][0-9]+.\\(gif\\|jpg\\)`', **gnus-uu** will automatically post an article on '`comp.unix.wizards`' saying that you have just viewed the file in question. This feature can't be turned off.

3.17.2 Shell Archives

Shell archives ("shar files") used to be a popular way to distribute sources, but it isn't used all that much today. In any case, we have some commands to deal with these:

X s	Unshars the current series (`gnus-uu-decode-unshar`).
X S	Unshars and saves the current series (`gnus-uu-decode-unshar-and-save`).
X v s	Unshars and views the current series (`gnus-uu-decode-unshar-view`).
X v S	Unshars, views and saves the current series (`gnus-uu-decode-unshar-and-save-view`).

3.17.3 PostScript Files

X p	Unpack the current PostScript series (`gnus-uu-decode-postscript`).
X P	Unpack and save the current PostScript series (`gnus-uu-decode-postscript-and-save`).
X v p	View the current PostScript series (`gnus-uu-decode-postscript-view`).
X v P	View and save the current PostScript series (`gnus-uu-decode-postscript-and-save-view`).

3.17.4 Other Files

X o	Save the current series (`gnus-uu-decode-save`).
X b	Unbinhex the current series (`gnus-uu-decode-binhex`). This doesn't really work yet.
X Y	yEnc-decode the current series and save it (`gnus-uu-decode-yenc`).

3.17.5 Decoding Variables

Adjective, not verb.

3.17.5.1 Rule Variables

Gnus uses *rule variables* to decide how to view a file. All these variables are of the form

```
(list '(regexp1 command2)
      '(regexp2 command2)
      ...)
```

`gnus-uu-user-view-rules`

> This variable is consulted first when viewing files. If you wish to use, for instance, `sox` to convert an `.au` sound file, you could say something like:

```
(setq gnus-uu-user-view-rules
      (list '("\\\\.au$" "sox %s -t .aiff > /dev/audio")))
```

`gnus-uu-user-view-rules-end`

> This variable is consulted if Gnus couldn't make any matches from the user and default view rules.

`gnus-uu-user-archive-rules`

> This variable can be used to say what commands should be used to unpack archives.

3.17.5.2 Other Decode Variables

`gnus-uu-grabbed-file-functions`

> All functions in this list will be called right after each file has been successfully decoded—so that you can move or view files right away, and don't have to wait for all files to be decoded before you can do anything. Ready-made functions you can put in this list are:
>
> `gnus-uu-grab-view`
>> View the file.
>
> `gnus-uu-grab-move`
>> Move the file (if you're using a saving function.)

`gnus-uu-be-dangerous`

> Specifies what to do if unusual situations arise during decoding. If `nil`, be as conservative as possible. If `t`, ignore things that didn't work, and overwrite existing files. Otherwise, ask each time.

`gnus-uu-ignore-files-by-name`

> Files with name matching this regular expression won't be viewed.

`gnus-uu-ignore-files-by-type`

> Files with a MIME type matching this variable won't be viewed. Note that Gnus tries to guess what type the file is based on the name. **gnus-uu** is not a MIME package (yet), so this is slightly kludgy.

`gnus-uu-tmp-dir`

> Where **gnus-uu** does its work.

`gnus-uu-do-not-unpack-archives`

> Non-`nil` means that **gnus-uu** won't peek inside archives looking for files to display.

`gnus-uu-view-and-save`

> Non-`nil` means that the user will always be asked to save a file after viewing it.

`gnus-uu-ignore-default-view-rules`

> Non-`nil` means that `gnus-uu` will ignore the default viewing rules.

`gnus-uu-ignore-default-archive-rules`

> Non-`nil` means that `gnus-uu` will ignore the default archive unpacking commands.

`gnus-uu-kill-carriage-return`

> Non-`nil` means that `gnus-uu` will strip all carriage returns from articles.

`gnus-uu-unmark-articles-not-decoded`

> Non-`nil` means that `gnus-uu` will mark unsuccessfully decoded articles as unread.

`gnus-uu-correct-stripped-uucode`

> Non-`nil` means that `gnus-uu` will *try* to fix uuencoded files that have had trailing spaces deleted.

`gnus-uu-pre-uudecode-hook`

> Hook run before sending a message to `uudecode`.

`gnus-uu-view-with-metamail`

> Non-`nil` means that `gnus-uu` will ignore the viewing commands defined by the rule variables and just fudge a MIME content type based on the file name. The result will be fed to `metamail` for viewing.

`gnus-uu-save-in-digest`

> Non-`nil` means that `gnus-uu`, when asked to save without decoding, will save in digests. If this variable is `nil`, `gnus-uu` will just save everything in a file without any embellishments. The digesting almost conforms to RFC 1153—no easy way to specify any meaningful volume and issue numbers were found, so I simply dropped them.

3.17.5.3 Uuencoding and Posting

`gnus-uu-post-include-before-composing`

> Non-`nil` means that `gnus-uu` will ask for a file to encode before you compose the article. If this variable is `t`, you can either include an encoded file with `C-c C-i` or have one included for you when you post the article.

`gnus-uu-post-length`

> Maximum length of an article. The encoded file will be split into how many articles it takes to post the entire file.

`gnus-uu-post-threaded`

> Non-`nil` means that `gnus-uu` will post the encoded file in a thread. This may not be smart, as no other decoder I have seen is able to follow threads when collecting uuencoded articles. (Well, I have seen one package that does that—`gnus-uu`, but somehow, I don't think that counts...) Default is `nil`.

`gnus-uu-post-separate-description`

> Non-`nil` means that the description will be posted in a separate article. The first article will typically be numbered (0/x). If this variable is `nil`, the de-

scription the user enters will be included at the beginning of the first article, which will be numbered (1/x). Default is `t`.

3.17.6 Viewing Files

After decoding, if the file is some sort of archive, Gnus will attempt to unpack the archive and see if any of the files in the archive can be viewed. For instance, if you have a gzipped tar file `pics.tar.gz` containing the files `pic1.jpg` and `pic2.gif`, Gnus will uncompress and de-tar the main file, and then view the two pictures. This unpacking process is recursive, so if the archive contains archives of archives, it'll all be unpacked.

Finally, Gnus will normally insert a *pseudo-article* for each extracted file into the summary buffer. If you go to these "articles", you will be prompted for a command to run (usually Gnus will make a suggestion), and then the command will be run.

If `gnus-view-pseudo-asynchronously` is `nil`, Emacs will wait until the viewing is done before proceeding.

If `gnus-view-pseudos` is `automatic`, Gnus will not insert the pseudo-articles into the summary buffer, but view them immediately. If this variable is `not-confirm`, the user won't even be asked for a confirmation before viewing is done.

If `gnus-view-pseudos-separately` is non-`nil`, one pseudo-article will be created for each file to be viewed. If `nil`, all files that use the same viewing command will be given as a list of parameters to that command.

If `gnus-insert-pseudo-articles` is non-`nil`, insert pseudo-articles when decoding. It is `t` by default.

So; there you are, reading your *pseudo-articles* in your *virtual newsgroup* from the *virtual server*; and you think: Why isn't anything real anymore? How did we get here?

3.18 Article Treatment

Reading through this huge manual, you may have quite forgotten that the object of news-readers is to actually, like, read what people have written. Reading articles. Unfortunately, people are quite bad at writing, so there are tons of functions and variables to make reading these articles easier.

3.18.1 Article Highlighting

Not only do you want your article buffer to look like fruit salad, but you want it to look like technicolor fruit salad.

W H a   Do much highlighting of the current article (`gnus-article-highlight`). This function highlights header, cited text, the signature, and adds buttons to the body and the head.

W H h   Highlight the headers (`gnus-article-highlight-headers`). The highlighting will be done according to the `gnus-header-face-alist` variable, which is a list where each element has the form (*regexp name content*). *regexp* is a regular expression for matching the header, *name* is the face used for highlighting the header name (see Section 9.6 [Faces and Fonts], page 258) and *content* is the face for highlighting the header value. The first match made will be used. Note that *regexp* shouldn't have '`^`' prepended—Gnus will add one.

W H c   Highlight cited text (`gnus-article-highlight-citation`).

Some variables to customize the citation highlights:

`gnus-cite-parse-max-size`
> If the article size in bytes is bigger than this variable (which is 25000 by default), no citation highlighting will be performed.

`gnus-cite-max-prefix`
> Maximum possible length for a citation prefix (default 20).

`gnus-cite-face-list`
> List of faces used for highlighting citations (see Section 9.6 [Faces and Fonts], page 258). When there are citations from multiple articles in the same message, Gnus will try to give each citation from each article its own face. This should make it easier to see who wrote what.

`gnus-supercite-regexp`
> Regexp matching normal Supercite attribution lines.

`gnus-supercite-secondary-regexp`
> Regexp matching mangled Supercite attribution lines.

`gnus-cite-minimum-match-count`
> Minimum number of identical prefixes we have to see before we believe that it's a citation.

`gnus-cite-attribution-prefix`
> Regexp matching the beginning of an attribution line.

`gnus-cite-attribution-suffix`
> Regexp matching the end of an attribution line.

`gnus-cite-attribution-face`
> Face used for attribution lines. It is merged with the face for the cited text belonging to the attribution.

`gnus-cite-ignore-quoted-from`
> If non-`nil`, no citation highlighting will be performed on lines beginning with '`>From `'. Those lines may have been quoted by MTAs in order not to mix up with the envelope From line. The default value is `t`.

W H s   Highlight the signature (`gnus-article-highlight-signature`). Everything after `gnus-signature-separator` (see Section 3.18.10 [Article Signature], page 96) in an article will be considered a signature and will be highlighted with `gnus-signature-face`, which is *italic* by default.

See Section 4.4 [Customizing Articles], page 120, for how to highlight articles automatically.

3.18.2 Article Fontisizing

People commonly add emphasis to words in news articles by writing things like '_this_' or '*this*' or '/this/'. Gnus can make this look nicer by running the article through the `W e` (`gnus-article-emphasize`) command.

How the emphasis is computed is controlled by the `gnus-emphasis-alist` variable. This is an alist where the first element is a regular expression to be matched. The second is a number that says what regular expression grouping is used to find the entire emphasized word. The third is a number that says what regexp grouping should be displayed and highlighted. (The text between these two groupings will be hidden.) The fourth is the face used for highlighting.

```
(setq gnus-emphasis-alist
      '(("_\\(\\w+\\)_" 0 1 gnus-emphasis-underline)
        ("\\*\\(\\w+\\)\\*" 0 1 gnus-emphasis-bold)))
```

By default, there are seven rules, and they use the following faces: `gnus-emphasis-bold`, `gnus-emphasis-italic`, `gnus-emphasis-underline`, `gnus-emphasis-bold-italic`, `gnus-emphasis-underline-italic`, `gnus-emphasis-underline-bold`, and `gnus-emphasis-underline-bold-italic`.

If you want to change these faces, you can either use *M-x customize*, or you can use `copy-face`. For instance, if you want to make `gnus-emphasis-italic` use a red face instead, you could say something like:

```
(copy-face 'red 'gnus-emphasis-italic)
```

If you want to highlight arbitrary words, you can use the `gnus-group-highlight-words-alist` variable, which uses the same syntax as `gnus-emphasis-alist`. The `highlight-words` group parameter (see Section 2.10 [Group Parameters], page 22) can also be used.

See Section 4.4 [Customizing Articles], page 120, for how to fontize articles automatically.

3.18.3 Article Hiding

Or rather, hiding certain things in each article. There usually is much too much cruft in most articles.

W W a   Do quite a lot of hiding on the article buffer (*gnus-article-hide*). In particular, this function will hide headers, PGP, cited text and the signature.

W W h   Hide headers (`gnus-article-hide-headers`). See Section 4.1 [Hiding Headers], page 116.

W W b   Hide headers that aren't particularly interesting (`gnus-article-hide-boring-headers`). See Section 4.1 [Hiding Headers], page 116.

W W s   Hide signature (`gnus-article-hide-signature`). See Section 3.18.10 [Article Signature], page 96.

W W l   Strip list identifiers specified in `gnus-list-identifiers`. These are strings some mailing list servers add to the beginning of all `Subject` headers—for example, '`[zebra 4711]`'. Any leading '`Re: `' is skipped before stripping. `gnus-list-identifiers` may not contain `\\(..\\)`.

`gnus-list-identifiers`

> A regular expression that matches list identifiers to be removed from subject. This can also be a list of regular expressions.

W W P   Hide PEM (privacy enhanced messages) cruft (`gnus-article-hide-pem`).

W W B   Strip the banner specified by the `banner` group parameter (`gnus-article-strip-banner`). This is mainly used to hide those annoying banners and/or signatures that some mailing lists and moderated groups adds to all the messages. The way to use this function is to add the `banner` group parameter (see Section 2.10 [Group Parameters], page 22) to the group you want banners stripped from. The parameter either be a string, which will be interpreted as a regular expression matching text to be removed, or the symbol `signature`, meaning that the (last) signature should be removed, or other symbol, meaning that the corresponding regular expression in `gnus-article-banner-alist` is used.

For instance:

```
(setq gnus-article-banner-alist
      ((googleGroups .
        "^\n*--~--~---------\\(.+\n\\)+")))
```

Regardless of a group, you can hide things like advertisements only when the sender of an article has a certain mail address specified in `gnus-article-address-banner-alist`.

`gnus-article-address-banner-alist`

> Alist of mail addresses and banners. Each element has the form (*address . banner*), where *address* is a regexp matching a mail address in the From header, *banner* is one of a symbol `signature`, an item in `gnus-article-banner-alist`, a regexp and `nil`. If *address* matches author's mail address, it will remove things like advertisements. For example, if a sender has the mail address 'hail@yoo-hoo.co.jp' and there is a banner something like 'Do You Yoo-hoo!?' in all articles he sends, you can use the following element to remove them:
>
> ```
> ("@yoo-hoo\\.co\\.jp\\'" .
>  "\n_+\nDo You Yoo-hoo!\\?\n.*\n.*\n")
> ```

W W c   Hide citation (`gnus-article-hide-citation`). Some variables for customizing the hiding:

`gnus-cited-opened-text-button-line-format`
`gnus-cited-closed-text-button-line-format`

> Gnus adds buttons to show where the cited text has been hidden, and to allow toggle hiding the text. The format of the variable is specified by these format-like variable (see Section 9.4 [Formatting Variables], page 250). These specs are valid:
>
> 'b'   Starting point of the hidden text.
>
> 'e'   Ending point of the hidden text.

'l'   Number of characters in the hidden region.

'n'   Number of lines of hidden text.

`gnus-cited-lines-visible`

The number of lines at the beginning of the cited text to leave shown. This can also be a cons cell with the number of lines at the top and bottom of the text, respectively, to remain visible.

W W C-c

Hide citation (`gnus-article-hide-citation-maybe`) depending on the following two variables:

`gnus-cite-hide-percentage`

If the cited text is of a bigger percentage than this variable (default 50), hide the cited text.

`gnus-cite-hide-absolute`

The cited text must have at least this length (default 10) before it is hidden.

W W C   Hide cited text in articles that aren't roots (`gnus-article-hide-citation-in-followups`). This isn't very useful as an interactive command, but might be a handy function to stick have happen automatically (see Section 4.4 [Customizing Articles], page 120).

All these "hiding" commands are toggles, but if you give a negative prefix to these commands, they will show what they have previously hidden. If you give a positive prefix, they will always hide.

Also see Section 3.18.1 [Article Highlighting], page 84 for further variables for citation customization.

See Section 4.4 [Customizing Articles], page 120, for how to hide article elements automatically.

3.18.4 Article Washing

We call this "article washing" for a really good reason. Namely, the A key was taken, so we had to use the W key instead.

Washing is defined by us as "changing something from something to something else", but normally results in something looking better. Cleaner, perhaps.

See Section 4.4 [Customizing Articles], page 120, if you want to change how Gnus displays articles by default.

C-u g   This is not really washing, it's sort of the opposite of washing. If you type this, you see the article exactly as it exists on disk or on the server.

g   Force redisplaying of the current article (`gnus-summary-show-article`). This is also not really washing. If you type this, you see the article without any previously applied interactive Washing functions but with all default treatments (see Section 4.4 [Customizing Articles], page 120).

W l
Remove page breaks from the current article (gnus-summary-stop-page-breaking). See Section 4.6 [Misc Article], page 124, for page delimiters.

W r
Do a Caesar rotate (rot13) on the article buffer (gnus-summary-caesar-message). Unreadable articles that tell you to read them with Caesar rotate or rot13. (Typically offensive jokes and such.)

It's commonly called "rot13" because each letter is rotated 13 positions in the alphabet, e.g., 'B' (letter #2) -> 'O' (letter #15). It is sometimes referred to as "Caesar rotate" because Caesar is rumored to have employed this form of, uh, somewhat weak encryption.

W m
Morse decode the article buffer (gnus-summary-morse-message).

W i
Decode IDNA encoded domain names in the current articles. IDNA encoded domain names looks like 'xn--bar'. If a string remain unencoded after running invoking this, it is likely an invalid IDNA string ('xn--bar' is invalid). You must have GNU Libidn (http://www.gnu.org/software/libidn/) installed for this command to work.

W t

t
Toggle whether to display all headers in the article buffer (gnus-summary-toggle-header).

W v
Toggle whether to display all headers in the article buffer permanently (gnus-summary-verbose-headers).

W o
Treat overstrike (gnus-article-treat-overstrike).

W d
Treat M****s*** sm*rtq**t*s according to gnus-article-dumbquotes-map (gnus-article-treat-dumbquotes). Note that this function guesses whether a character is a sm*rtq**t* or not, so it should only be used interactively.

Sm*rtq**t*s are M****s***'s unilateral extension to the character map in an attempt to provide more quoting characters. If you see something like \222 or \264 where you're expecting some kind of apostrophe or quotation mark, then try this wash.

W U
Translate many non-ASCII characters into their ASCII equivalents (gnus-article-treat-non-ascii). This is mostly useful if you're on a terminal that has a limited font and doesn't show accented characters, "advanced" punctuation, and the like. For instance, '»' is translated into '>>', and so on.

W Y f
Full deuglify of broken Outlook (Express) articles: Treat dumbquotes, unwrap lines, repair attribution and rearrange citation. (gnus-article-outlook-deuglify-article).

W Y u
Unwrap lines that appear to be wrapped citation lines. You can control what lines will be unwrapped by frobbing gnus-outlook-deuglify-unwrap-min and gnus-outlook-deuglify-unwrap-max, indicating the minimum and maximum length of an unwrapped citation line. (gnus-article-outlook-unwrap-lines).

W Y a   Repair a broken attribution line.
               (gnus-article-outlook-repair-attribution).

W Y c   Repair broken citations by rearranging the text. (gnus-article-outlook-
               rearrange-citation).

W w   Do word wrap (gnus-article-fill-cited-article).

               You can give the command a numerical prefix to specify the width to use when
               filling.

W Q   Fill long lines (gnus-article-fill-long-lines).

W C   Capitalize the first word in each sentence (gnus-article-capitalize-
               sentences).

W c   Translate CRLF pairs (i.e., '^M's on the end of the lines) into LF (this takes
               care of DOS line endings), and then translate any remaining CRs into LF (this
               takes care of Mac line endings) (gnus-article-remove-cr).

W q   Treat quoted-printable (gnus-article-de-quoted-unreadable).   Quoted-
               Printable is one common MIME encoding employed when sending non-ASCII
               (i.e., 8-bit) articles.   It typically makes strings like 'déjà vu' look like
               'd=E9j=E0 vu', which doesn't look very readable to me.   Note that this
               is usually done automatically by Gnus if the message in question has a
               Content-Transfer-Encoding header that says that this encoding has been
               done. If a prefix is given, a charset will be asked for.

W 6   Treat base64 (gnus-article-de-base64-unreadable). Base64 is one common
               MIME encoding employed when sending non-ASCII (i.e., 8-bit) articles. Note
               that this is usually done automatically by Gnus if the message in question has
               a Content-Transfer-Encoding header that says that this encoding has been
               done. If a prefix is given, a charset will be asked for.

W Z   Treat HZ or HZP (gnus-article-decode-HZ). HZ (or HZP) is one common
               encoding employed when sending Chinese articles. It typically makes strings
               look like '~{<:Ky2;S{#,NpJ)16HK!#~}'.

W A   Translate ANSI SGR control sequences into overlays or extents (gnus-article-
               treat-ansi-sequences). ANSI sequences are used in some Chinese hierarchies
               for highlighting.

W u   Remove newlines from within URLs. Some mailers insert newlines into outgoing
               email messages to keep lines short. This reformatting can split long URLs onto
               multiple lines. Repair those URLs by removing the newlines (gnus-article-
               unsplit-urls).

W h   Treat HTML (gnus-article-wash-html). Note that this is usually done auto-
               matically by Gnus if the message in question has a Content-Type header that
               says that the message is HTML.

               If a prefix is given, a charset will be asked for. If it is a number, the charset de-
               fined in gnus-summary-show-article-charset-alist (see Section 3.4 [Paging
               the Article], page 52) will be used.

The default is to use the function specified by `mm-text-html-renderer` (see Section "Display Customization" in *The Emacs MIME Manual*) to convert the HTML. Pre-defined functions you can use include:

`shr`   Use Gnus simple html renderer.

`gnus-w3m`   Use Gnus rendered based on w3m.

`w3m`   Use emacs-w3m.

`w3m-standalone`
        Use w3m.

`links`   Use Links.

`lynx`   Use Lynx.

`html2text`
        Use html2text—a simple HTML converter included with Gnus.

W b   Add clickable buttons to the article (`gnus-article-add-buttons`). See Section 3.18.6 [Article Buttons], page 92.

W B   Add clickable buttons to the article headers (`gnus-article-add-buttons-to-head`).

W p   Verify a signed control message (`gnus-article-verify-x-pgp-sig`). Control messages such as `newgroup` and `checkgroups` are usually signed by the hierarchy maintainer. You need to add the PGP public key of the maintainer to your keyring to verify the message.[1]

W s   Verify a signed (PGP, PGP/MIME or S/MIME) message (`gnus-summary-force-verify-and-decrypt`). See Section 3.31 [Security], page 114.

W a   Strip headers like the `X-No-Archive` header from the beginning of article bodies (`gnus-article-strip-headers-in-body`).

W E l   Remove all blank lines from the beginning of the article (`gnus-article-strip-leading-blank-lines`).

W E m   Replace all blank lines with empty lines and then all multiple empty lines with a single empty line. (`gnus-article-strip-multiple-blank-lines`).

W E t   Remove all blank lines at the end of the article (`gnus-article-remove-trailing-blank-lines`).

W E a   Do all the three commands above (`gnus-article-strip-blank-lines`).

W E A   Remove all blank lines (`gnus-article-strip-all-blank-lines`).

W E s   Remove all white space from the beginning of all lines of the article body (`gnus-article-strip-leading-space`).

W E e   Remove all white space from the end of all lines of the article body (`gnus-article-strip-trailing-space`).

See Section 4.4 [Customizing Articles], page 120, for how to wash articles automatically.

---

[1] PGP keys for many hierarchies are available at `ftp://ftp.isc.org/pub/pgpcontrol/README.html`

3.18.5 Article Header

These commands perform various transformations of article header.

W G u   Unfold folded header lines (gnus-article-treat-unfold-headers).

W G n   Fold the Newsgroups and Followup-To headers (gnus-article-treat-fold-newsgroups).

W G f   Fold all the message headers (gnus-article-treat-fold-headers).

W E w   Remove excessive whitespace from all headers (gnus-article-remove-leading-whitespace).

3.18.6 Article Buttons

People often include references to other stuff in articles, and it would be nice if Gnus could just fetch whatever it is that people talk about with the minimum of fuzz when you hit RET or use the middle mouse button on these references.

Gnus adds *buttons* to certain standard references by default: Well-formed URLs, mail addresses, Message-IDs, Info links, man pages and Emacs or Gnus related references. This is controlled by two variables, one that handles article bodies and one that handles article heads:

gnus-button-alist

This is an alist where each entry has this form:

(*regexp button-par use-p function data-par*)

regexp   All text that match this regular expression (case insensitive) will be considered an external reference. Here's a typical regexp that matches embedded URLs: '<URL:\\([^\n\r>]*\\)>'. This can also be a variable containing a regexp, useful variables to use include gnus-button-url-regexp and gnus-button-mid-or-mail-regexp.

button-par

Gnus has to know which parts of the matches is to be highlighted. This is a number that says what sub-expression of the regexp is to be highlighted. If you want it all highlighted, you use 0 here.

use-p   This form will be evaled, and if the result is non-nil, this is considered a match. This is useful if you want extra sifting to avoid false matches. Often variables named gnus-button-*-level are used here, See Section 3.18.7 [Article Button Levels], page 94, but any other form may be used too.

function   This function will be called when you click on this button.

data-par   As with *button-par*, this is a sub-expression number, but this one says which part of the match is to be sent as data to *function*.

So the full entry for buttonizing URLs is then

("<URL:\\([^\n\r>]*\\)>" 0 t gnus-button-url 1)

`gnus-header-button-alist`

> This is just like the other alist, except that it is applied to the article head only, and that each entry has an additional element that is used to say what headers to apply the buttonize coding to:
>
> (*header regexp button-par use-p function data-par*)
>
> *header* is a regular expression.

3.18.6.1 Related variables and functions

`gnus-button-*-level`

> See Section 3.18.7 [Article Button Levels], page 94.

`gnus-button-url-regexp`

> A regular expression that matches embedded URLs. It is used in the default values of the variables above.

`gnus-button-man-handler`

> The function to use for displaying man pages. It must take at least one argument with a string naming the man page.

`gnus-button-mid-or-mail-regexp`

> Regular expression that matches a message ID or a mail address.

`gnus-button-prefer-mid-or-mail`

> This variable determines what to do when the button on a string as 'foo123@bar.invalid' is pushed. Strings like this can be either a message ID or a mail address. If it is one of the symbols **mid** or **mail**, Gnus will always assume that the string is a message ID or a mail address, respectively. If this variable is set to the symbol **ask**, always query the user what to do. If it is a function, this function will be called with the string as its only argument. The function must return **mid**, **mail**, **invalid** or **ask**. The default value is the function `gnus-button-mid-or-mail-heuristic`.

`gnus-button-mid-or-mail-heuristic`

> Function that guesses whether its argument is a message ID or a mail address. Returns **mid** if it's a message IDs, **mail** if it's a mail address, **ask** if unsure and **invalid** if the string is invalid.

`gnus-button-mid-or-mail-heuristic-alist`

> An alist of (RATE . REGEXP) pairs used by the function `gnus-button-mid-or-mail-heuristic`.

`gnus-article-button-face`

> Face used on buttons.

`gnus-article-mouse-face`

> Face used when the mouse cursor is over a button.

See Section 4.4 [Customizing Articles], page 120, for how to buttonize articles automatically.

3.18.7 Article button levels

The higher the value of the variables `gnus-button-*-level`, the more buttons will appear.
If the level is zero, no corresponding buttons are displayed. With the default value (which
is 5) you should already see quite a lot of buttons. With higher levels, you will see more
buttons, but you may also get more false positives. To avoid them, you can set the variables `gnus-button-*-level` local to specific groups (see Section 2.10 [Group Parameters],
page 22). Here's an example for the variable `gnus-parameters`:

```
;; increase gnus-button-*-level in some groups:
(setq gnus-parameters
        '(("\\<\\(emacs\\|gnus\\)\\>" (gnus-button-emacs-level 10))
          ("\\<unix\\>"                (gnus-button-man-level 10))
          ("\\<tex\\>"                 (gnus-button-tex-level 10))))
```

`gnus-button-browse-level`

> Controls the display of references to message IDs, mail addresses and news
> URLs. Related variables and functions include `gnus-button-url-regexp`,
> `browse-url`, and `browse-url-browser-function`.

`gnus-button-emacs-level`

> Controls the display of Emacs or Gnus references. Related functions are
> `gnus-button-handle-custom`, `gnus-button-handle-describe-function`,
> `gnus-button-handle-describe-variable`, `gnus-button-handle-symbol`,
> `gnus-button-handle-describe-key`, `gnus-button-handle-apropos`,
> `gnus-button-handle-apropos-command`, `gnus-button-handle-apropos-variable`, `gnus-button-handle-apropos-documentation`, and
> `gnus-button-handle-library`.

`gnus-button-man-level`

> Controls the display of references to (Unix) man pages. See `gnus-button-man-handler`.

`gnus-button-message-level`

> Controls the display of message IDs, mail addresses and news URLs.
> Related variables and functions include `gnus-button-mid-or-mail-regexp`,
> `gnus-button-prefer-mid-or-mail`, `gnus-button-mid-or-mail-heuristic`,
> and `gnus-button-mid-or-mail-heuristic-alist`.

3.18.8 Article Date

The date is most likely generated in some obscure timezone you've never heard of, so it's
quite nice to be able to find out what the time was when the article was sent.

W T u   Display the date in UT (aka. GMT, aka ZULU) (`gnus-article-date-ut`).

W T i   Display the date in international format, aka. ISO 8601 (`gnus-article-date-iso8601`).

W T l   Display the date in the local timezone (`gnus-article-date-local`).

W T p   Display the date in a format that's easily pronounceable in English
               (`gnus-article-date-english`).

W T s	Display the date using a user-defined format (`gnus-article-date-user`). The format is specified by the `gnus-article-time-format` variable, and is a string that's passed to `format-time-string`. See the documentation of that variable for a list of possible format specs.
W T e	Say how much time has elapsed between the article was posted and now (`gnus-article-date-lapsed`). It looks something like:

> Date: 6 weeks, 4 days, 1 hour, 3 minutes, 8 seconds ago

To make this line updated continually, set the `gnus-article-update-date-headers` variable to the frequency in seconds (the default is `nil`).

W T o	Display the original date (`gnus-article-date-original`). This can be useful if you normally use some other conversion function and are worried that it might be doing something totally wrong. Say, claiming that the article was posted in 1854. Although something like that is *totally* impossible. Don't you trust me? *titter*

See Section 4.4 [Customizing Articles], page 120, for how to display the date in your preferred format automatically.

3.18.9 Article Display

These commands add various frivolous display gimmicks to the article buffer in Emacs versions that support them.

`X-Face` headers are small black-and-white images supplied by the message headers (see Section 9.14.1 [X-Face], page 263).

`Face` headers are small colored images supplied by the message headers (see Section 9.14.2 [Face], page 264).

Smileys are those little ':-)' symbols that people like to litter their messages with (see Section 9.14.3 [Smileys], page 265).

Picons, on the other hand, reside on your own system, and Gnus will try to match the headers to what you have (see Section 9.14.4 [Picons], page 265).

Gravatars reside on-line and are fetched from `http://www.gravatar.com/` (see Section 9.14.5 [Gravatars], page 266).

All these functions are toggles—if the elements already exist, they'll be removed.

W D x	Display an X-Face in the `From` header. (`gnus-article-display-x-face`).
W D d	Display a Face in the `From` header. (`gnus-article-display-face`).
W D s	Display smileys (`gnus-treat-smiley`).
W D f	Piconify the `From` header (`gnus-treat-from-picon`).
W D m	Piconify all mail headers (i.e., Cc, To) (`gnus-treat-mail-picon`).
W D n	Piconify all news headers (i.e., `Newsgroups` and `Followup-To`) (`gnus-treat-newsgroups-picon`).
W D g	Gravatarify the `From` header (`gnus-treat-from-gravatar`).
W D h	Gravatarify all mail headers (i.e., Cc, To) (`gnus-treat-from-gravatar`).

W D D   Remove all images from the article buffer (`gnus-article-remove-images`).

W D W   If you're reading an HTML article rendered with `gnus-article-html`, then you can insert any blocked images in the buffer with this command. (`gnus-html-show-images`).

3.18.10 Article Signature

Each article is divided into two parts—the head and the body. The body can be divided into a signature part and a text part. The variable that says what is to be considered a signature is `gnus-signature-separator`. This is normally the standard '`^-- $`' as mandated by son-of-RFC 1036. However, many people use non-standard signature separators, so this variable can also be a list of regular expressions to be tested, one by one. (Searches are done from the end of the body towards the beginning.) One likely value is:

```
(setq gnus-signature-separator
      '("^-- $"           ; The standard
        "^-- *$"          ; A common mangling
        "^-------*S"      ; Many people just use a looong
                          ; line of dashes.  Shame!
        "^ *--------*$"   ; Double-shame!
        "^_____*$"     ; Underscores are also popular
        "^========*$"))   ; Pervert!
```

The more permissive you are, the more likely it is that you'll get false positives.

`gnus-signature-limit` provides a limit to what is considered a signature when displaying articles.

1. If it is an integer, no signature may be longer (in characters) than that integer.

2. If it is a floating point number, no signature may be longer (in lines) than that number.

3. If it is a function, the function will be called without any parameters, and if it returns nil, there is no signature in the buffer.

4. If it is a string, it will be used as a regexp. If it matches, the text in question is not a signature.

This variable can also be a list where the elements may be of the types listed above. Here's an example:

```
(setq gnus-signature-limit
      '(200.0 "^---*Forwarded article"))
```

This means that if there are more than 200 lines after the signature separator, or the text after the signature separator is matched by the regular expression '`^---*Forwarded article`', then it isn't a signature after all.

3.18.11 Article Miscellanea

A t   Translate the article from one language to another (`gnus-article-babel`).

3.19 MIME Commands

The following commands all understand the numerical prefix. For instance, *3 K v* means "view the third MIME part".

b

K v   View the MIME part.

K o   Save the MIME part.

K O   Prompt for a file name, then save the MIME part and strip it from the article. The stripped MIME object will be referred via the message/external-body MIME type.

K r   Replace the MIME part with an external body.

K d   Delete the MIME part and add some information about the removed part.

K c   Copy the MIME part.

K e   View the MIME part externally.

K i   View the MIME part internally.

K | Pipe the MIME part to an external command.

The rest of these MIME commands do not use the numerical prefix in the same manner:

K H   View 'text/html' parts of the current article with a WWW browser. Inline images embedded in a message using the cid scheme, as they are generally considered to be safe, will be processed properly. The message header is added to the beginning of every HTML part unless the prefix argument is given.

               Warning: Spammers use links to images (using the http scheme) in HTML articles to verify whether you have read the message. As this command passes the HTML content to the browser without eliminating these "web bugs" you should only use it for mails from trusted senders.

               If you always want to display HTML parts in the browser, set mm-text-html-renderer to nil.

               This command creates temporary files to pass HTML contents including images if any to the browser, and deletes them when exiting the group (if you want).

K b   Make all the MIME parts have buttons in front of them. This is mostly useful if you wish to save (or perform other actions) on inlined parts.

W M h   Display MIME part buttons in the end of the header of an article (gnus-mime-buttonize-attachments-in-header). This command toggles the display. Note that buttons to be added to the header are only the ones that aren't inlined in the body. If you want those buttons always to be displayed, set gnus-mime-display-attachment-buttons-in-header to non-nil. The default is t. To change the appearance of buttons, customize gnus-header-face-alist.

K m   Some multipart messages are transmitted with missing or faulty headers. This command will attempt to "repair" these messages so that they can be viewed in a more pleasant manner (gnus-summary-repair-multipart).

X m   Save all parts matching a MIME type to a directory (gnus-summary-save-parts). Understands the process/prefix convention (see Section 9.1 [Process/Prefix], page 249).

M-t   Toggle the buttonized display of the article buffer (gnus-summary-toggle-
                display-buttonized).

W M w   Decode RFC 2047-encoded words in the article headers (gnus-article-
                decode-mime-words).

W M c   Decode encoded article bodies as well as charsets (gnus-article-decode-
                charset).

                This command looks in the Content-Type header to determine the charset.
                If there is no such header in the article, you can give it a prefix, which will
                prompt for the charset to decode as. In regional groups where people post
                using some common encoding (but do not include MIME headers), you can set
                the charset group/topic parameter to the required charset (see Section 2.10
                [Group Parameters], page 22).

W M v   View all the MIME parts in the current article (gnus-mime-view-all-parts).

        Relevant variables:

gnus-ignored-mime-types
                This is a list of regexps. MIME types that match a regexp from this list will be
                completely ignored by Gnus. The default value is nil.

                To have all Vcards be ignored, you'd say something like this:

                        (setq gnus-ignored-mime-types
                              '("text/x-vcard"))

gnus-article-loose-mime
                If non-nil, Gnus won't require the 'MIME-Version' header before interpreting
                the message as a MIME message. This helps when reading messages from certain
                broken mail user agents. The default is t.

gnus-article-emulate-mime
                There are other non-MIME encoding methods used. The most common is
                'uuencode', but yEncode is also getting to be popular. If this variable is non-
                nil, Gnus will look in message bodies to see if it finds these encodings, and if
                so, it'll run them through the Gnus MIME machinery. The default is t. Only
                single-part yEnc encoded attachments can be decoded. There's no support for
                encoding in Gnus.

gnus-unbuttonized-mime-types
                This is a list of regexps. MIME types that match a regexp from this list won't
                have MIME buttons inserted unless they aren't displayed or this variable is
                overridden by gnus-buttonized-mime-types. The default value is (".*/.*").
                This variable is only used when gnus-inhibit-mime-unbuttonizing is nil.

gnus-buttonized-mime-types
                This is a list of regexps. MIME types that match a regexp from this list will have
                MIME buttons inserted unless they aren't displayed. This variable overrides
                gnus-unbuttonized-mime-types. The default value is nil. This variable is
                only used when gnus-inhibit-mime-unbuttonizing is nil.

E.g., to see security buttons but no other buttons, you could set this variable to ("multipart/signed") and leave `gnus-unbuttonized-mime-types` at the default value.

You could also add "multipart/alternative" to this list to display radio buttons that allow you to choose one of two media types those mails include. See also `mm-discouraged-alternatives` (see Section "Display Customization" in *The Emacs MIME Manual*).

`gnus-inhibit-mime-unbuttonizing`
> If this is non-`nil`, then all MIME parts get buttons. The default value is `nil`.

`gnus-article-mime-part-function`
> For each MIME part, this function will be called with the MIME handle as the parameter. The function is meant to be used to allow users to gather information from the article (e.g., add Vcard info to the bbdb database) or to do actions based on parts (e.g., automatically save all jpegs into some directory).
>
> Here's an example function the does the latter:
> ```
> (defun my-save-all-jpeg-parts (handle)
>   (when (equal (car (mm-handle-type handle)) "image/jpeg")
>     (with-temp-buffer
>       (insert (mm-get-part handle))
>       (write-region (point-min) (point-max)
>                     (read-file-name "Save jpeg to: ")))))
> (setq gnus-article-mime-part-function
>       'my-save-all-jpeg-parts)
> ```

`gnus-mime-multipart-functions`
> Alist of MIME multipart types and functions to handle them.

`gnus-mime-display-multipart-alternative-as-mixed`
> Display "multipart/alternative" parts as "multipart/mixed".

`gnus-mime-display-multipart-related-as-mixed`
> Display "multipart/related" parts as "multipart/mixed".
>
> If displaying 'text/html' is discouraged, see `mm-discouraged-alternatives`, images or other material inside a "multipart/related" part might be overlooked when this variable is `nil`. Section "Display Customization" in *Emacs-Mime Manual*.

`gnus-mime-display-multipart-as-mixed`
> Display "multipart" parts as "multipart/mixed". If `t`, it overrides `nil` values of `gnus-mime-display-multipart-alternative-as-mixed` and `gnus-mime-display-multipart-related-as-mixed`.

`mm-file-name-rewrite-functions`
> List of functions used for rewriting file names of MIME parts. Each function takes a file name as input and returns a file name.
>
> Ready-made functions include
> `mm-file-name-delete-whitespace`, `mm-file-name-trim-whitespace`,

`mm-file-name-collapse-whitespace`, and `mm-file-name-replace-whitespace`. The later uses the value of the variable `mm-file-name-replace-whitespace` to replace each whitespace character in a file name with that string; default value is `"_"` (a single underscore).

The standard functions `capitalize`, `downcase`, `upcase`, and `upcase-initials` may be useful, too.

Everybody knows that whitespace characters in file names are evil, except those who don't know. If you receive lots of attachments from such unenlightened users, you can make live easier by adding

```
(setq mm-file-name-rewrite-functions
      '(mm-file-name-trim-whitespace
        mm-file-name-collapse-whitespace
        mm-file-name-replace-whitespace))
```

to your `~/.gnus.el` file.

3.20 Charsets

People use different charsets, and we have MIME to let us know what charsets they use. Or rather, we wish we had. Many people use newsreaders and mailers that do not understand or use MIME, and just send out messages without saying what character sets they use. To help a bit with this, some local news hierarchies have policies that say what character set is the default. For instance, the 'fj' hierarchy uses `iso-2022-jp`.

This knowledge is encoded in the `gnus-group-charset-alist` variable, which is an alist of regexps (use the first item to match full group names) and default charsets to be used when reading these groups.

In addition, some people do use soi-disant MIME-aware agents that aren't. These blithely mark messages as being in `iso-8859-1` even if they really are in `koi-8`. To help here, the `gnus-newsgroup-ignored-charsets` variable can be used. The charsets that are listed here will be ignored. The variable can be set on a group-by-group basis using the group parameters (see Section 2.10 [Group Parameters], page 22). The default value is (`unknown-8bit x-unknown`), which includes values some agents insist on having in there.

When posting, `gnus-group-posting-charset-alist` is used to determine which charsets should not be encoded using the MIME encodings. For instance, some hierarchies discourage using quoted-printable header encoding.

This variable is an alist of regexps and permitted unencoded charsets for posting. Each element of the alist has the form (*test header body-list*), where:

test   is either a regular expression matching the newsgroup header or a variable to query,

header   is the charset which may be left unencoded in the header (`nil` means encode all charsets),

body-list   is a list of charsets which may be encoded using 8bit content-transfer encoding in the body, or one of the special values `nil` (always encode using quoted-printable) or `t` (always use 8bit).

See Section "Encoding Customization" in *The Emacs MIME Manual*, for additional variables that control which MIME charsets are used when sending messages.

Other charset tricks that may be useful, although not Gnus-specific:

If there are several MIME charsets that encode the same Emacs charset, you can choose what charset to use by saying the following:

```
(put-charset-property 'cyrillic-iso8859-5
                      'preferred-coding-system 'koi8-r)
```

This means that Russian will be encoded using `koi8-r` instead of the default `iso-8859-5` MIME charset.

If you want to read messages in `koi8-u`, you can cheat and say

```
(define-coding-system-alias 'koi8-u 'koi8-r)
```

This will almost do the right thing.

And finally, to read charsets like `windows-1251`, you can say something like

```
(codepage-setup 1251)
(define-coding-system-alias 'windows-1251 'cp1251)
```

3.21 Article Commands

A P   Generate and print a PostScript image of the article buffer (`gnus-summary-print-article`). `gnus-ps-print-hook` will be run just before printing the buffer. An alternative way to print article is to use Muttprint (see Section 3.16 [Saving Articles], page 76).

A C   If `<backend>-fetch-partial-articles` is non-`nil`, Gnus will fetch partial articles, if the backend it fetches them from supports it. Currently only `nnimap` does. If you're looking at a partial article, and want to see the complete article instead, then the *A C* command (`gnus-summary-show-complete-article`) will do so.

3.22 Summary Sorting

You can have the summary buffer sorted in various ways, even though I can't really see why you'd want that.

C-c C-s C-n

Sort by article number (`gnus-summary-sort-by-number`).

C-c C-s C-m C-n

Sort by most recent article number (`gnus-summary-sort-by-most-recent-number`).

C-c C-s C-a

Sort by author (`gnus-summary-sort-by-author`).

C-c C-s C-t

Sort by recipient (`gnus-summary-sort-by-recipient`).

C-c C-s C-s

Sort by subject (`gnus-summary-sort-by-subject`).

`C-c C-s C-d`
> Sort by date (`gnus-summary-sort-by-date`).

`C-c C-s C-m C-d`
> Sort by most recent date (`gnus-summary-sort-by-most-recent-date`).

`C-c C-s C-l`
> Sort by lines (`gnus-summary-sort-by-lines`).

`C-c C-s C-c`
> Sort by article length (`gnus-summary-sort-by-chars`).

`C-c C-s C-i`
> Sort by score (`gnus-summary-sort-by-score`).

`C-c C-s C-r`
> Randomize (`gnus-summary-sort-by-random`).

`C-c C-s C-o`
> Sort using the default sorting method (`gnus-summary-sort-by-original`).

These functions will work both when you use threading and when you don't use threading. In the latter case, all summary lines will be sorted, line by line. In the former case, sorting will be done on a root-by-root basis, which might not be what you were looking for. To toggle whether to use threading, type *T T* (see Section 3.9.2 [Thread Commands], page 70).

If a prefix argument if given, the sort order is reversed.

3.23 Finding the Parent

`^`
> If you'd like to read the parent of the current article, and it is not displayed in the summary buffer, you might still be able to. That is, if the current group is fetched by NNTP, the parent hasn't expired and the **References** in the current article are not mangled, you can just press `^` or *A r* (`gnus-summary-refer-parent-article`). If everything goes well, you'll get the parent. If the parent is already displayed in the summary buffer, point will just move to this article.
>
> If given a positive numerical prefix, fetch that many articles back into the ancestry. If given a negative numerical prefix, fetch just that ancestor. So if you say *3 ^*, Gnus will fetch the parent, the grandparent and the great-grandparent of the current article. If you say *-3 ^*, Gnus will only fetch the great-grandparent of the current article.

`A R (Summary)`
> Fetch all articles mentioned in the **References** header of the article (`gnus-summary-refer-references`).

`A T (Summary)`
> Display the full thread where the current article appears (`gnus-summary-refer-thread`). This command has to fetch all the headers in the current group to work, so it usually takes a while. If you do it often, you may consider setting **gnus-fetch-old-headers** to **invisible** (see Section 3.9.1.2 [Filling In Threads], page 68). This won't have any visible effects normally, but it'll

make this command work a whole lot faster. Of course, it'll make group entry somewhat slow.

The `gnus-refer-thread-limit` variable says how many old (i.e., articles before the first displayed in the current group) headers to fetch when doing this command. The default is 200. If `t`, all the available headers will be fetched. This variable can be overridden by giving the *A T* command a numerical prefix.

M-^ (Summary)

You can also ask Gnus for an arbitrary article, no matter what group it belongs to. *M-^* (`gnus-summary-refer-article`) will ask you for a `Message-ID`, which is one of those long, hard-to-read thingies that look something like '`<38o6up$6f2@hymir.ifi.uio.no>`'. You have to get it all exactly right. No fuzzy searches, I'm afraid.

Gnus looks for the `Message-ID` in the headers that have already been fetched, but also tries all the select methods specified by `gnus-refer-article-method` if it is not found.

If the group you are reading is located on a back end that does not support fetching by `Message-ID` very well (like **nnspool**), you can set `gnus-refer-article-method` to an NNTP method. It would, perhaps, be best if the NNTP server you consult is the one updating the spool you are reading from, but that's not really necessary.

It can also be a list of select methods, as well as the special symbol `current`, which means to use the current select method. If it is a list, Gnus will try all the methods in the list until it finds a match.

Here's an example setting that will first try the current method, and then ask Google if that fails:

```
(setq gnus-refer-article-method
      '(current
        (nnweb "google" (nnweb-type google))))
```

Most of the mail back ends support fetching by `Message-ID`, but do not do a particularly excellent job at it. That is, **nnmbox**, **nnbabyl**, **nnmaildir**, **nnml**, are able to locate articles from any groups, while **nnfolder**, and **nnimap** are only able to locate articles that have been posted to the current group. **nnmh** does not support this at all.

Fortunately, the special **nnregistry** back end is able to locate articles in any groups, regardless of their back end (see Section 9.18.2 [Registry Article Refer Method], page 296).

3.24 Alternative Approaches

Different people like to read news using different methods. This being Gnus, we offer a small selection of minor modes for the summary buffers.

3.24.1 Pick and Read

Some newsreaders (like **nn** and, uhm, `Netnews` on VM/CMS) use a two-phased reading interface. The user first marks in a summary buffer the articles she wants to read. Then she starts reading the articles with just an article buffer displayed.

Gnus provides a summary buffer minor mode that allows this—**gnus-pick-mode**. This basically means that a few process mark commands become one-keystroke commands to allow easy marking, and it provides one additional command for switching to the summary buffer.

Here are the available keystrokes when using pick mode:

.   Pick the article or thread on the current line (**gnus-pick-article-or-thread**). If the variable **gnus-thread-hide-subtree** is true, then this key selects the entire thread when used at the first article of the thread. Otherwise, it selects just the article. If given a numerical prefix, go to that thread or article and pick it. (The line number is normally displayed at the beginning of the summary pick lines.)

SPACE   Scroll the summary buffer up one page (**gnus-pick-next-page**). If at the end of the buffer, start reading the picked articles.

u   Unpick the thread or article (**gnus-pick-unmark-article-or-thread**). If the variable **gnus-thread-hide-subtree** is true, then this key unpicks the thread if used at the first article of the thread. Otherwise it unpicks just the article. You can give this key a numerical prefix to unpick the thread or article at that line.

RET   Start reading the picked articles (**gnus-pick-start-reading**). If given a prefix, mark all unpicked articles as read first. If **gnus-pick-display-summary** is non-**nil**, the summary buffer will still be visible when you are reading.

All the normal summary mode commands are still available in the pick-mode, with the exception of *u*. However *!* is available which is mapped to the same function **gnus-summary-tick-article-forward**.

If this sounds like a good idea to you, you could say:

    (add-hook 'gnus-summary-mode-hook 'gnus-pick-mode)

gnus-pick-mode-hook is run in pick minor mode buffers.

If **gnus-mark-unpicked-articles-as-read** is non-**nil**, mark all unpicked articles as read. The default is **nil**.

The summary line format in pick mode is slightly different from the standard format. At the beginning of each line the line number is displayed. The pick mode line format is controlled by the **gnus-summary-pick-line-format** variable (see Section 9.4 [Formatting Variables], page 250). It accepts the same format specs that **gnus-summary-line-format** does (see Section 3.1.1 [Summary Buffer Lines], page 44).

3.24.2 Binary Groups

If you spend much time in binary groups, you may grow tired of hitting *X u*, *n*, *RET* all the time. *M-x gnus-binary-mode* is a minor mode for summary buffers that makes all ordinary Gnus article selection functions uudecode series of articles and display the result instead of just displaying the articles the normal way.

The only way, in fact, to see the actual articles is the *g* command, when you have turned on this mode (**gnus-binary-show-article**).

gnus-binary-mode-hook is called in binary minor mode buffers.

3.25 Tree Display

If you don't like the normal Gnus summary display, you might try setting `gnus-use-trees` to `t`. This will create (by default) an additional *tree buffer*. You can execute all summary mode commands in the tree buffer.

There are a few variables to customize the tree display, of course:

`gnus-tree-mode-hook`

        A hook called in all tree mode buffers.

`gnus-tree-mode-line-format`

        A format string for the mode bar in the tree mode buffers (see Section 9.4.2 [Mode Line Formatting], page 251). The default is 'Gnus: %%b %S %Z'. For a list of valid specs, see Section 3.1.3 [Summary Buffer Mode Line], page 48.

`gnus-selected-tree-face`

        Face used for highlighting the selected article in the tree buffer. The default is `modeline`.

`gnus-tree-line-format`

        A format string for the tree nodes. The name is a bit of a misnomer, though—it doesn't define a line, but just the node. The default value is '%(%[%3,3n%]%)', which displays the first three characters of the name of the poster. It is vital that all nodes are of the same length, so you *must* use '%4,4n'-like specifiers.

        Valid specs are:

        'n'   The name of the poster.

        'f'   The `From` header.

        'N'   The number of the article.

        '['   The opening bracket.

        ']'   The closing bracket.

        's'   The subject.

        See Section 9.4 [Formatting Variables], page 250.

        Variables related to the display are:

`gnus-tree-brackets`

        This is used for differentiating between "real" articles and "sparse" articles. The format is

```
((real-open . real-close)
 (sparse-open . sparse-close)
 (dummy-open . dummy-close))
```

        and the default is ((?[. ?]) (?(. ?)) (?{ . ?}) (?< . ?>)).

`gnus-tree-parent-child-edges`

        This is a list that contains the characters used for connecting parent nodes to their children. The default is (?- ?\\ ?|).

gnus-tree-minimize-windcw

>If this variable is non-nil, Gnus will try to keep the tree buffer as small as possible to allow more room for the other Gnus windows. If this variable is a number, the tree buffer will never be higher than that number. The default is t. Note that if you have several windows displayed side-by-side in a frame and the tree buffer is one of these, minimizing the tree window will also resize all other windows displayed next to it.

>You may also wish to add the following hook to keep the window minimized at all times:

```
(add-hook 'gnus-configure-windows-hook
          'gnus-tree-perhaps-minimize)
```

gnus-generate-tree-function

>The function that actually generates the thread tree. Two predefined functions are available: **gnus-generate-horizontal-tree** and **gnus-generate-vertical-tree** (which is the default).

Here's an example from a horizontal tree buffer:

```
{***}-(***)-[odd]-[Gun]
  |        \[Jan]
  |        \[odd]-[Eri]
  |        \(***)-[Eri]
  |              \[odd]-[Paa]
  \[Bjo]
  \[Gun]
  \[Gun]-[Jor]
```

Here's the same thread displayed in a vertical tree buffer:

```
{***}
  |------------------------\-----\-----\
(***)                    [Bjo] [Gun] [Gun]
  |--\-----\-----\                     |
[odd] [Jan] [odd] (***)              [Jor]
  |          |     |--\
[Gun]      [Eri] [Eri] [odd]
                         |
                       [Paa]
```

If you're using horizontal trees, it might be nice to display the trees side-by-side with the summary buffer. You could add something like the following to your ~/.gnus.el file:

```
(setq gnus-use-trees t
      gnus-generate-tree-function 'gnus-generate-horizontal-tree
      gnus-tree-minimize-window nil)
(gnus-add-configuration
 '(article
   (vertical 1.0
             (horizontal 0.25
                         (summary 0.75 point)
```

```
                      (tree 1.0))
            (article 1.0))))
```
See Section 9.5 [Window Layout], page 254.

3.26 Mail Group Commands

Some commands only make sense in mail groups. If these commands are invalid in the current group, they will raise a hell and let you know.

All these commands (except the expiry and edit commands) use the process/prefix convention (see Section 9.1 [Process/Prefix], page 249).

B e   Run all expirable articles in the current group through the expiry process (**gnus-summary-expire-articles**). That is, delete all expirable articles in the group that have been around for a while. (see Section 6.4.9 [Expiring Mail], page 168).

B C-M-e   Delete all the expirable articles in the group (**gnus-summary-expire-articles-now**). This means that **all** articles eligible for expiry in the current group will disappear forever into that big **/dev/null** in the sky.

B DEL   Delete the mail article. This is "delete" as in "delete it from your disk forever and ever, never to return again." Use with caution. (**gnus-summary-delete-article**).

B m   Move the article from one mail group to another (**gnus-summary-move-article**). Marks will be preserved if **gnus-preserve-marks** is non-**nil** (which is the default).

B c   Copy the article from one group (mail group or not) to a mail group (**gnus-summary-copy-article**). Marks will be preserved if **gnus-preserve-marks** is non-**nil** (which is the default).

B B   Crosspost the current article to some other group (**gnus-summary-crosspost-article**). This will create a new copy of the article in the other group, and the Xref headers of the article will be properly updated.

B i   Import an arbitrary file into the current mail newsgroup (**gnus-summary-import-article**). You will be prompted for a file name, a **From** header and a **Subject** header.

B I   Create an empty article in the current mail newsgroups (**gnus-summary-create-article**). You will be prompted for a **From** header and a **Subject** header.

B r   Respool the mail article (**gnus-summary-respool-article**). **gnus-summary-respool-default-method** will be used as the default select method when respooling. This variable is **nil** by default, which means that the current group select method will be used instead. Marks will be preserved if **gnus-preserve-marks** is non-**nil** (which is the default).

B w
e   Edit the current article (**gnus-summary-edit-article**). To finish editing and make the changes permanent, type *C-c C-c* (**gnus-summary-edit-article-**

done). If you give a prefix to the *C-c C-c* command, Gnus won't re-highlight the article.

B q   If you want to re-spool an article, you might be curious as to what group the article will end up in before you do the re-spooling. This command will tell you (**gnus-summary-respool-query**).

B t   Similarly, this command will display all fancy splitting patterns used when respooling, if any (**gnus-summary-respool-trace**).

B p   Some people have a tendency to send you "courtesy" copies when they follow up to articles you have posted. These usually have a **Newsgroups** header in them, but not always. This command (**gnus-summary-article-posted-p**) will try to fetch the current article from your news server (or rather, from **gnus-refer-article-method** or **gnus-select-method**) and will report back whether it found the article or not. Even if it says that it didn't find the article, it may have been posted anyway—mail propagation is much faster than news propagation, and the news copy may just not have arrived yet.

K E   Encrypt the body of an article (**gnus-article-encrypt-body**). The body is encrypted with the encryption protocol specified by the variable **gnus-article-encrypt-protocol**.

If you move (or copy) articles regularly, you might wish to have Gnus suggest where to put the articles. **gnus-move-split-methods** is a variable that uses the same syntax as **gnus-split-methods** (see Section 3.16 [Saving Articles], page 76). You may customize that variable to create suggestions you find reasonable. (Note that **gnus-move-split-methods** uses group names where **gnus-split-methods** uses file names.)

```
(setq gnus-move-split-methods
      '(("^From:.*Lars Magne" "nnml:junk")
        ("^Subject:.*gnus" "nnfolder:important")
        (".*" "nnml:misc")))
```

3.27 Various Summary Stuff

gnus-summary-display-while-building
>If non-**nil**, show and update the summary buffer as it's being built. If **t**, update the buffer after every line is inserted. If the value is an integer, *n*, update the display every *n* lines. The default is **nil**.

gnus-summary-display-arrow
>If non-**nil**, display an arrow in the fringe to indicate the current article.

gnus-summary-mode-hook
>This hook is called when creating a summary mode buffer.

gnus-summary-generate-hook
>This is called as the last thing before doing the threading and the generation of the summary buffer. It's quite convenient for customizing the threading variables based on what data the newsgroup has. This hook is called from the summary buffer after most summary buffer variables have been set.

gnus-summary-prepare-hook

> It is called after the summary buffer has been generated. You might use it to, for instance, highlight lines or modify the look of the buffer in some other ungodly manner. I don't care.

gnus-summary-prepared-hook

> A hook called as the very last thing after the summary buffer has been generated.

gnus-summary-ignore-duplicates

> When Gnus discovers two articles that have the same Message-ID, it has to do something drastic. No articles are allowed to have the same Message-ID, but this may happen when reading mail from some sources. Gnus allows you to customize what happens with this variable. If it is nil (which is the default), Gnus will rename the Message-ID (for display purposes only) and display the article as any other article. If this variable is t, it won't display the article—it'll be as if it never existed.

gnus-alter-articles-to-read-function

> This function, which takes two parameters (the group name and the list of articles to be selected), is called to allow the user to alter the list of articles to be selected.
>
> For instance, the following function adds the list of cached articles to the list in one particular group:

```
(defun my-add-cached-articles (group articles)
  (if (string= group "some.group")
      (append gnus-newsgroup-cached articles)
    articles))
```

gnus-newsgroup-variables

> A list of newsgroup (summary buffer) local variables, or cons of variables and their default expressions to be evalled (when the default values are not nil), that should be made global while the summary buffer is active.
>
> Note: The default expressions will be evaluated (using function eval) before assignment to the local variable rather than just assigned to it. If the default expression is the symbol global, that symbol will not be evaluated but the global value of the local variable will be used instead.
>
> These variables can be used to set variables in the group parameters while still allowing them to affect operations done in other buffers. For example:

```
(setq gnus-newsgroup-variables
      '(message-use-followup-to
        (gnus-visible-headers .
 "^From:\\|^Newsgroups:\\|^Subject:\\|^Date:\\|^To:")))
```

> Also see Section 2.10 [Group Parameters], page 22.

3.27.1 Summary Group Information

H d   Give a brief description of the current group (gnus-summary-describe-group). If given a prefix, force rereading the description from the server.

H h   Give an extremely brief description of the most important summary keystrokes (gnus-summary-describe-briefly).

H i   Go to the Gnus info node (gnus-info-find-node).

3.27.2 Searching for Articles

M-s   Search through all subsequent (raw) articles for a regexp (gnus-summary-search-article-forward).

M-r   Search through all previous (raw) articles for a regexp (gnus-summary-search-article-backward).

M-S   Repeat the previous search forwards (gnus-summary-repeat-search-article-forward).

M-R   Repeat the previous search backwards (gnus-summary-repeat-search-article-backward).

&   This command will prompt you for a header, a regular expression to match on this field, and a command to be executed if the match is made (gnus-summary-execute-command). If the header is an empty string, the match is done on the entire article. If given a prefix, search backward instead.

             For instance, *& RET some.*string RET #* will put the process mark on all articles that have heads or bodies that match 'some.*string'.

M-&   Perform any operation on all articles that have been marked with the process mark (gnus-summary-universal-argument).

3.27.3 Summary Generation Commands

Y g   Regenerate the current summary buffer (gnus-summary-prepare).

Y c   Pull all cached articles (for the current group) into the summary buffer (gnus-summary-insert-cached-articles).

Y d   Pull all dormant articles (for the current group) into the summary buffer (gnus-summary-insert-dormant-articles).

Y t   Pull all ticked articles (for the current group) into the summary buffer (gnus-summary-insert-ticked-articles).

3.27.4 Really Various Summary Commands

A D
C-d   If the current article is a collection of other articles (for instance, a digest), you might use this command to enter a group based on the that article (gnus-summary-enter-digest-group). Gnus will try to guess what article type is currently displayed unless you give a prefix to this command, which forces a "digest" interpretation. Basically, whenever you see a message that is a collection of other messages of some format, you *C-d* and read these messages in a more convenient fashion.

             The variable gnus-auto-select-on-ephemeral-exit controls what article should be selected after exiting a digest group. Valid values include:

next   Select the next article.

next-unread
        Select the next unread article.

next-noselect
        Move the cursor to the next article. This is the default.

next-unread-noselect
        Move the cursor to the next unread article.

If it has any other value or there is no next (unread) article, the article selected before entering to the digest group will appear.

C-M-d   This command is very similar to the one above, but lets you gather several documents into one biiig group (**gnus-summary-read-document**). It does this by opening several **nndoc** groups for each document, and then opening an **nnvirtual** group on top of these **nndoc** groups. This command understands the process/prefix convention (see Section 9.1 [Process/Prefix], page 249).

C-t   Toggle truncation of summary lines (**gnus-summary-toggle-truncation**). This will probably confuse the line centering function in the summary buffer, so it's not a good idea to have truncation switched off while reading articles.

=   Expand the summary buffer window (**gnus-summary-expand-window**). If given a prefix, force an **article** window configuration.

C-M-e   Edit the group parameters (see Section 2.10 [Group Parameters], page 22) of the current group (**gnus-summary-edit-parameters**).

C-M-a   Customize the group parameters (see Section 2.10 [Group Parameters], page 22) of the current group (**gnus-summary-customize-parameters**).

3.28 Exiting the Summary Buffer

Exiting from the summary buffer will normally update all info on the group and return you to the group buffer.

Z Z
Z Q
q   Exit the current group and update all information on the group (**gnus-summary-exit**). **gnus-summary-prepare-exit-hook** is called before doing much of the exiting, which calls **gnus-summary-expire-articles** by default. **gnus-summary-exit-hook** is called after finishing the exit process. **gnus-group-no-more-groups-hook** is run when returning to group mode having no more (unread) groups.

Z E
Q   Exit the current group without updating any information on the group (**gnus-summary-exit-no-update**).

Z c
c   Mark all unticked articles in the group as read and then exit (**gnus-summary-catchup-and-exit**).

Z C   Mark all articles, even the ticked ones, as read and then exit (**gnus-summary-catchup-all-and-exit**).

Z n   Mark all articles as read and go to the next group (**gnus-summary-catchup-and-goto-next-group**).

Z p   Mark all articles as read and go to the previous group (**gnus-summary-catchup-and-goto-prev-group**).

Z R
C-x C-s   Exit this group. and then enter it again (**gnus-summary-reselect-current-group**). If given a prefix, select all articles, both read and unread.

Z G
M-g   Exit the group, check for new articles in the group, and select the group (**gnus-summary-rescan-group**). If given a prefix, select all articles, both read and unread.

Z N   Exit the group and go to the next group (**gnus-summary-next-group**).

Z P   Exit the group and go to the previous group (**gnus-summary-prev-group**).

Z s   Save the current number of read/marked articles in the dribble buffer and then save the dribble buffer (**gnus-summary-save-newsrc**). If given a prefix, also save the .**newsrc** file(s). Using this command will make exit without updating (the *Q* command) worthless.

gnus-exit-group-hook is called when you exit the current group with an "updating" exit. For instance *Q* (**gnus-summary-exit-no-update**) does not call this hook.

If you're in the habit of exiting groups, and then changing your mind about it, you might set **gnus-kill-summary-on-exit** to **nil**. If you do that, Gnus won't kill the summary buffer when you exit it. (Quelle surprise!) Instead it will change the name of the buffer to something like *Dead Summary ... * and install a minor mode called **gnus-dead-summary-mode**. Now, if you switch back to this buffer, you'll find that all keys are mapped to a function called **gnus-summary-wake-up-the-dead**. So tapping any keys in a dead summary buffer will result in a live, normal summary buffer.

There will never be more than one dead summary buffer at any one time.

The data on the current group will be updated (which articles you have read, which articles you have replied to, etc.) when you exit the summary buffer. If the **gnus-use-cross-reference** variable is **t** (which is the default), articles that are cross-referenced to this group and are marked as read, will also be marked as read in the other subscribed groups they were cross-posted to. If this variable is neither **nil** nor **t**, the article will be marked as read in both subscribed and unsubscribed groups (see Section 3.29 [Crosspost Handling], page 112).

3.29 Crosspost Handling

Marking cross-posted articles as read ensures that you'll never have to read the same article more than once. Unless, of course, somebody has posted it to several groups separately. Posting the same article to several groups (not cross-posting) is called *spamming*, and you are by law required to send nasty-grams to anyone who perpetrates such a heinous crime.

Remember: Cross-posting is kinda ok, but posting the same article separately to several groups is not. Massive cross-posting (aka. *velveeta*) is to be avoided at all costs, and you can even use the `gnus-summary-mail-crosspost-complaint` command to complain about excessive crossposting (see Section 3.5.1 [Summary Mail Commands], page 53).

One thing that may cause Gnus to not do the cross-posting thing correctly is if you use an NNTP server that supports XOVER (which is very nice, because it speeds things up considerably) which does not include the `Xref` header in its NOV lines. This is Evil, but all too common, alas, alack. Gnus tries to Do The Right Thing even with XOVER by registering the `Xref` lines of all articles you actually read, but if you kill the articles, or just mark them as read without reading them, Gnus will not get a chance to snoop the `Xref` lines out of these articles, and will be unable to use the cross reference mechanism.

To check whether your NNTP server includes the `Xref` header in its overview files, try '`telnet your.nntp.server nntp`', '`MODE READER`' on `inn` servers, and then say '`LIST overview.fmt`'. This may not work, but if it does, and the last line you get does not read '`Xref:full`', then you should shout and whine at your news admin until she includes the `Xref` header in the overview files.

If you want Gnus to get the `Xref`s right all the time, you have to set `nntp-nov-is-evil` to `t`, which slows things down considerably. Also see Section 11.6.1 [Slow/Expensive Connection], page 332.

C'est la vie.

For an alternative approach, see Section 3.30 [Duplicate Suppression], page 113.

3.30 Duplicate Suppression

By default, Gnus tries to make sure that you don't have to read the same article more than once by utilizing the crossposting mechanism (see Section 3.29 [Crosspost Handling], page 112). However, that simple and efficient approach may not work satisfactory for some users for various reasons.

1. The NNTP server may fail to generate the `Xref` header. This is evil and not very common.

2. The NNTP server may fail to include the `Xref` header in the `.overview` data bases. This is evil and all too common, alas.

3. You may be reading the same group (or several related groups) from different NNTP servers.

4. You may be getting mail that duplicates articles posted to groups.

I'm sure there are other situations where `Xref` handling fails as well, but these four are the most common situations.

If, and only if, `Xref` handling fails for you, then you may consider switching on *duplicate suppression*. If you do so, Gnus will remember the `Message-ID`s of all articles you have read or otherwise marked as read, and then, as if by magic, mark them as read all subsequent times you see them—in *all* groups. Using this mechanism is quite likely to be somewhat inefficient, but not overly so. It's certainly preferable to reading the same articles more than once.

Duplicate suppression is not a very subtle instrument. It's more like a sledge hammer than anything else. It works in a very simple fashion—if you have marked an article as read, it adds this Message-ID to a cache. The next time it sees this Message-ID, it will mark the article as read with the 'M' mark. It doesn't care what group it saw the article in.

`gnus-suppress-duplicates`

>   If non-`nil`, suppress duplicates.

`gnus-save-duplicate-list`

>   If non-`nil`, save the list of duplicates to a file. This will make startup and shutdown take longer, so the default is `nil`. However, this means that only duplicate articles read in a single Gnus session are suppressed.

`gnus-duplicate-list-length`

>   This variable says how many `Message-IDs` to keep in the duplicate suppression list. The default is 10000.

`gnus-duplicate-file`

>   The name of the file to store the duplicate suppression list in. The default is `~/News/suppression`.

If you have a tendency to stop and start Gnus often, setting `gnus-save-duplicate-list` to `t` is probably a good idea. If you leave Gnus running for weeks on end, you may have it `nil`. On the other hand, saving the list makes startup and shutdown much slower, so that means that if you stop and start Gnus often, you should set `gnus-save-duplicate-list` to `nil`. Uhm. I'll leave this up to you to figure out, I think.

3.31 Security

Gnus is able to verify signed messages or decrypt encrypted messages. The formats that are supported are PGP, PGP/MIME and S/MIME, however you need some external programs to get things to work:

1. To handle PGP and PGP/MIME messages, you have to install an OpenPGP implementation such as GnuPG. The Lisp interface to GnuPG included with Emacs is called EasyPG (see Section 'EasyPG' in *EasyPG Assistant user's manual*), but PGG (see Section "PGG" in *PGG Manual*), and Mailcrypt are also supported.

2. To handle S/MIME message, you need to install OpenSSL. OpenSSL 0.9.6 or newer is recommended.

The variables that control security functionality on reading/composing messages include:

`mm-verify-option`

>   Option of verifying signed parts. **never**, not verify; **always**, always verify; **known**, only verify known protocols. Otherwise, ask user.

`mm-decrypt-option`

>   Option of decrypting encrypted parts. **never**, no decryption; **always**, always decrypt; **known**, only decrypt known protocols. Otherwise, ask user.

`mm-sign-option`

>   Option of creating signed parts. **nil**, use default signing keys; **guided**, ask user to select signing keys from the menu.

`mm-encrypt-option`

> Option of creating encrypted parts. `nil`, use the first public-key matching the 'From:' header as the recipient; `guided`, ask user to select recipient keys from the menu.

`mml1991-use`

> Symbol indicating elisp interface to OpenPGP implementation for PGP messages. The default is `epg`, but `pgg`, and `mailcrypt` are also supported although deprecated. By default, Gnus uses the first available interface in this order.

`mml2015-use`

> Symbol indicating elisp interface to OpenPGP implementation for PGP/MIME messages. The default is `epg`, but `pgg`, and `mailcrypt` are also supported although deprecated. By default, Gnus uses the first available interface in this order.

By default the buttons that display security information are not shown, because they clutter reading the actual e-mail. You can type *K b* manually to display the information. Use the `gnus-buttonized-mime-types` and `gnus-unbuttonized-mime-types` variables to control this permanently. Section 3.19 [MIME Commands], page 96 for further details, and hints on how to customize these variables to always display security information.

Snarfing OpenPGP keys (i.e., importing keys from articles into your key ring) is not supported explicitly through a menu item or command, rather Gnus do detect and label keys as 'application/pgp-keys', allowing you to specify whatever action you think is appropriate through the usual MIME infrastructure. You can use a `~/.mailcap` entry (see Section "mailcap" in *The Emacs MIME Manual*) such as the following to import keys using GNU Privacy Guard when you click on the MIME button (see Section 4.2 [Using MIME], page 117).

        application/pgp-keys; gpg --import --interactive --verbose; needsterminal

This happens to also be the default action defined in `mailcap-mime-data`.

More information on how to set things for sending outgoing signed and encrypted messages up can be found in the message manual (see Section "Security" in *Message Manual*).

3.32 Mailing List

Gnus understands some mailing list fields of RFC 2369. To enable it, add a `to-list` group parameter (see Section 2.10 [Group Parameters], page 22), possibly using *A M* (`gnus-mailing-list-insinuate`) in the summary buffer.

That enables the following commands to the summary buffer:

C-c C-n h Send a message to fetch mailing list help, if List-Help field exists.

C-c C-n s Send a message to subscribe the mailing list, if List-Subscribe field exists.

C-c C-n u Send a message to unsubscribe the mailing list, if List-Unsubscribe field exists.

C-c C-n p Post to the mailing list, if List-Post field exists.

C-c C-n o Send a message to the mailing list owner, if List-Owner field exists.

C-c C-n a Browse the mailing list archive, if List-Archive field exists.

4 Article Buffer

The articles are displayed in the article buffer, of which there is only one. All the summary buffers share the same article buffer unless you tell Gnus otherwise.

4.1 Hiding Headers

The top section of each article is the *head*. (The rest is the *body*, but you may have guessed that already.)

There is a lot of useful information in the head: the name of the person who wrote the article, the date it was written and the subject of the article. That's well and nice, but there's also lots of information most people do not want to see—what systems the article has passed through before reaching you, the `Message-ID`, the `References`, etc. ad nauseam—and you'll probably want to get rid of some of those lines. If you want to keep all those lines in the article buffer, you can set `gnus-show-all-headers` to `t`.

Gnus provides you with two variables for sifting headers:

`gnus-visible-headers`

>   If this variable is non-`nil`, it should be a regular expression that says what headers you wish to keep in the article buffer. All headers that do not match this variable will be hidden.
>
>   For instance, if you only want to see the name of the person who wrote the article and the subject, you'd say:
>
>   `(setq gnus-visible-headers "^From:\\|^Subject:")`
>
>   This variable can also be a list of regexps to match headers to remain visible.

`gnus-ignored-headers`

>   This variable is the reverse of `gnus-visible-headers`. If this variable is set (and `gnus-visible-headers` is `nil`), it should be a regular expression that matches all lines that you want to hide. All lines that do not match this variable will remain visible.
>
>   For instance, if you just want to get rid of the `References` line and the `Xref` line, you might say:
>
>   `(setq gnus-ignored-headers "^References:\\|^Xref:")`
>
>   This variable can also be a list of regexps to match headers to be removed.
>
>   Note that if `gnus-visible-headers` is non-`nil`, this variable will have no effect.

Gnus can also sort the headers for you. (It does this by default.) You can control the sorting by setting the `gnus-sorted-header-list` variable. It is a list of regular expressions that says in what order the headers are to be displayed.

For instance, if you want the name of the author of the article first, and then the subject, you might say something like:

`(setq gnus-sorted-header-list '("^From:" "^Subject:"))`

Any headers that are to remain visible, but are not listed in this variable, will be displayed in random order after all the headers listed in this variable.

You can hide further boring headers by setting `gnus-treat-hide-boring-headers` to `head`. What this function does depends on the `gnus-boring-article-headers` variable. It's a list, but this list doesn't actually contain header names. Instead it lists various *boring conditions* that Gnus can check and remove from sight.

These conditions are:

`empty`   Remove all empty headers.

`followup-to`
        Remove the `Followup-To` header if it is identical to the `Newsgroups` header.

`reply-to`   Remove the `Reply-To` header if it lists the same addresses as the `From` header, or if the `broken-reply-to` group parameter is set.

`newsgroups`
        Remove the `Newsgroups` header if it only contains the current group name.

`to-address`
        Remove the `To` header if it only contains the address identical to the current group's `to-address` parameter.

`to-list`   Remove the `To` header if it only contains the address identical to the current group's `to-list` parameter.

`cc-list`   Remove the `Cc` header if it only contains the address identical to the current group's `to-list` parameter.

`date`   Remove the `Date` header if the article is less than three days old.

`long-to`   Remove the `To` and/or `Cc` header if it is very long.

`many-to`   Remove all `To` and/or `Cc` headers if there are more than one.

To include these three elements, you could say something like:

```
(setq gnus-boring-article-headers
      '(empty followup-to reply-to))
```

This is also the default value for this variable.

4.2 Using MIME

Mime is a standard for waving your hands through the air, aimlessly, while people stand around yawning.

MIME, however, is a standard for encoding your articles, aimlessly, while all newsreaders die of fear.

MIME may specify what character set the article uses, the encoding of the characters, and it also makes it possible to embed pictures and other naughty stuff in innocent-looking articles.

Gnus pushes MIME articles through `gnus-display-mime-function` to display the MIME parts. This is `gnus-display-mime` by default, which creates a bundle of clickable buttons that can be used to display, save and manipulate the MIME objects.

The following commands are available when you have placed point over a MIME button:

RET (Article)
BUTTON-2 (Article)

> Toggle displaying of the MIME object (**gnus-article-press-button**). If built-in viewers can not display the object, Gnus resorts to external viewers in the **mailcap** files. If a viewer has the 'copiousoutput' specification, the object is displayed inline.

M-RET (Article)
v (Article)

> Prompt for a method, and then view the MIME object using this method (**gnus-mime-view-part**).

t (Article)

> View the MIME object as if it were a different MIME media type (**gnus-mime-view-part-as-type**).

C (Article)

> Prompt for a charset, and then view the MIME object using this charset (**gnus-mime-view-part-as-charset**).

o (Article)

> Prompt for a file name, and then save the MIME object (**gnus-mime-save-part**).

C-o (Article)

> Prompt for a file name, then save the MIME object and strip it from the article. Then proceed to article editing, where a reasonable suggestion is being made on how the altered article should look like. The stripped MIME object will be referred via the message/external-body MIME type. (**gnus-mime-save-part-and-strip**).

r (Article)

> Prompt for a file name, replace the MIME object with an external body referring to the file via the message/external-body MIME type. (**gnus-mime-replace-part**).

d (Article)

> Delete the MIME object from the article and replace it with some information about the removed MIME object (**gnus-mime-delete-part**).

c (Article)

> Copy the MIME object to a fresh buffer and display this buffer (**gnus-mime-copy-part**). If given a prefix, copy the raw contents without decoding. If given a numerical prefix, you can do semi-manual charset stuff (see **gnus-summary-show-article-charset-alist** in Section 3.4 [Paging the Article], page 52). Compressed files like .gz and .bz2 are automatically decompressed if **auto-compression-mode** is enabled (see Section "Accessing Compressed Files" in *The Emacs Editor*).

p (Article)

> Print the MIME object (**gnus-mime-print-part**). This command respects the 'print=' specifications in the .mailcap file.

i (Article)

> Insert the contents of the MIME object into the buffer (**gnus-mime-inline-part**) as 'text/plain'. If given a prefix, insert the raw contents without decoding. If given a numerical prefix, you can do semi-manual charset stuff (see **gnus-summary-show-article-charset-alist** in Section 3.4 [Paging the Article], page 52). Compressed files like .gz and .bz2 are automatically decompressed depending on **jka-compr** regardless of **auto-compression-mode** (see Section "Accessing Compressed Files" in *The Emacs Editor*).

E (Article)

> View the MIME object with an internal viewer. If no internal viewer is available, use an external viewer (**gnus-mime-view-part-internally**).

e (Article)

> View the MIME object with an external viewer. (**gnus-mime-view-part-externally**).

| (Article)

> Output the MIME object to a process (**gnus-mime-pipe-part**).

. (Article)

> Interactively run an action on the MIME object (**gnus-mime-action-on-part**).

Gnus will display some MIME objects automatically. The way Gnus determines which parts to do this with is described in the Emacs MIME manual.

It might be best to just use the toggling functions from the article buffer to avoid getting nasty surprises. (For instance, you enter the group 'alt.sing-a-long' and, before you know it, MIME has decoded the sound file in the article and some horrible sing-a-long song comes screaming out your speakers, and you can't find the volume button, because there isn't one, and people are starting to look at you, and you try to stop the program, but you can't, and you can't find the program to control the volume, and everybody else in the room suddenly decides to look at you disdainfully, and you'll feel rather stupid.)

Any similarity to real events and people is purely coincidental. Ahem.

Also see Section 3.19 [MIME Commands], page 96.

4.3 HTML

Gnus can display HTML articles nicely formatted in the article buffer. There are many methods for doing that, but two of them are kind of default methods.

If your Emacs copy has been built with libxml2 support, then Gnus uses Emacs' built-in, plain elisp Simple HTML Renderer **shr**[1] which is also used by Emacs' browser EWW (see Section "EWW" in *The Emacs Manual*).

If your Emacs copy lacks libxml2 support but you have **w3m** installed on your system, Gnus uses that to render HTML mail and display the results in the article buffer (**gnus-w3m**).

For a complete overview, consult See Section "Display Customization" in *The Emacs MIME Manual*. This section only describes the default method.

---

[1] **shr** displays colors as declared in the HTML article but tries to adjust them in order to be readable. If you prefer more contrast, See [FAQ 4-16], page 371.

`mm-text-html-renderer`

> If set to `shr`, Gnus uses its own simple HTML renderer. If set to `gnus-w3m`, it uses `w3m`.

`gnus-blocked-images`

> External images that have URLs that match this regexp won't be fetched and displayed. For instance, do block all URLs that have the string "ads" in them, do the following:
>
> > `(setq gnus-blocked-images "ads")`
>
> This can also be a function to be evaluated. If so, it will be called with the group name as the parameter. The default value is `gnus-block-private-groups`, which will return '"."' for anything that isn't a newsgroup. This means that no external images will be fetched as a result of reading mail, so that nobody can use web bugs (and the like) to track whether you've read email.
>
> Also see Section 4.6 [Misc Article], page 124 for `gnus-inhibit-images`.

`gnus-html-cache-directory`

> Gnus will download and cache images according to how `gnus-blocked-images` is set. These images will be stored in this directory.

`gnus-html-cache-size`

> When `gnus-html-cache-size` bytes have been used in that directory, the oldest files will be deleted. The default is 500MB.

`gnus-html-frame-width`

> The width to use when rendering HTML. The default is 70.

`gnus-max-image-proportion`

> How big pictures displayed are in relation to the window they're in. A value of 0.7 (the default) means that they are allowed to take up 70% of the width and height of the window. If they are larger than this, and Emacs supports it, then the images will be rescaled down to fit these criteria.

To use this, make sure that you have `w3m` and `curl` installed. If you have, then Gnus should display HTML automatically.

4.4 Customizing Articles

A slew of functions for customizing how the articles are to look like exist. You can call these functions interactively (see Section 3.18.4 [Article Washing], page 88), or you can have them called automatically when you select the articles.

To have them called automatically, you should set the corresponding "treatment" variable. For instance, to have headers hidden, you'd set `gnus-treat-hide-headers`. Below is a list of variables that can be set, but first we discuss the values these variables can have.

Note: Some values, while valid, make little sense. Check the list below for sensible values.

1. `nil`: Don't do this treatment.

2. `t`: Do this treatment on all body parts.

3. `head`: Do the treatment on the headers.

4. `first`: Do this treatment on the first body part.

5. `last`: Do this treatment on the last body part.

6. An integer: Do this treatment on all body parts that have a length less than this number.

7. A list of strings: Do this treatment on all body parts that are in articles that are read in groups that have names that match one of the regexps in the list.

8. A list where the first element is not a string:

   The list is evaluated recursively. The first element of the list is a predicate. The following predicates are recognized: `or`, `and`, `not` and `typep`. Here's an example:

   ```
   (or last
       (typep "text/x-vcard"))
   ```

9. A function: the function is called with no arguments and should return `nil` or non-`nil`. The current article is available in the buffer named by `gnus-article-buffer`.

You may have noticed that the word *part* is used here. This refers to the fact that some messages are MIME multipart articles that may be divided into several parts. Articles that are not multiparts are considered to contain just a single part.

Are the treatments applied to all sorts of multipart parts? Yes, if you want to, but by default, only 'text/plain' parts are given the treatment. This is controlled by the `gnus-article-treat-types` variable, which is a list of regular expressions that are matched to the type of the part. This variable is ignored if the value of the controlling variable is a predicate list, as described above.

The following treatment options are available. The easiest way to customize this is to examine the `gnus-article-treat` customization group. Values in parenthesis are suggested sensible values. Others are possible but those listed are probably sufficient for most people.

`gnus-treat-buttonize (t, integer)`
`gnus-treat-buttonize-head (head)`
>   See Section 3.18.6 [Article Buttons], page 92.

`gnus-treat-capitalize-sentences (t, integer)`
`gnus-treat-overstrike (t, integer)`
`gnus-treat-strip-cr (t, integer)`
`gnus-treat-strip-headers-in-body (t, integer)`
`gnus-treat-strip-leading-blank-lines (t, first, integer)`
`gnus-treat-strip-multiple-blank-lines (t, integer)`
`gnus-treat-strip-pem (t, last, integer)`
`gnus-treat-strip-trailing-blank-lines (t, last, integer)`
`gnus-treat-unsplit-urls (t, integer)`
`gnus-treat-wash-html (t, integer)`
>   See Section 3.18.4 [Article Washing], page 88.

`gnus-treat-date (head)`
>   This will transform/add date headers according to the `gnus-article-date-headers` variable. This is a list of Date headers to display. The formats available are:
>
>   ut   Universal time, aka GMT, aka ZULU.

local   The user's local time zone.

english   A semi-readable English sentence.

lapsed   The time elapsed since the message was posted.

combined-lapsed
             Both the original date header and a (shortened) elapsed time.

original   The original date header.

iso8601   ISO8601 format, i.e., "2010-11-23T22:05:21".

user-defined
             A format done according to the `gnus-article-time-format` variable.

See Section 3.18.8 [Article Date], page 94.

`gnus-treat-from-picon (head)`
`gnus-treat-mail-picon (head)`
`gnus-treat-newsgroups-picon (head)`
        See Section 9.14.4 [Picons], page 265.

`gnus-treat-from-gravatar (head)`
`gnus-treat-mail-gravatar (head)`
        See Section 9.14.5 [Gravatars], page 266.

`gnus-treat-display-smileys (t, integer)`
`gnus-treat-body-boundary (head)`
        Adds a delimiter between header and body, the string used as delimiter is
        controlled by `gnus-body-boundary-delimiter`.
        See Section 9.14.3 [Smileys], page 265.

`gnus-treat-display-x-face (head)`
        See Section 9.14.1 [X-Face], page 263.

`gnus-treat-display-face (head)`
        See Section 9.14.2 [Face], page 264.

`gnus-treat-emphasize (t, head, integer)`
`gnus-treat-fill-article (t, integer)`
`gnus-treat-fill-long-lines (t, integer)`
`gnus-treat-hide-boring-headers (head)`
`gnus-treat-hide-citation (t, integer)`
`gnus-treat-hide-citation-maybe (t, integer)`
`gnus-treat-hide-headers (head)`
`gnus-treat-hide-signature (t, last)`
`gnus-treat-strip-banner (t, last)`
`gnus-treat-strip-list-identifiers (head)`
        See Section 3.18.3 [Article Hiding], page 86.

`gnus-treat-highlight-citation (t, integer)`
`gnus-treat-highlight-headers (head)`
`gnus-treat-highlight-signature (t, last, integer)`
        See Section 3.18.1 [Article Highlighting], page 84.

```
gnus-treat-play-sounds
gnus-treat-ansi-sequences (t)
gnus-treat-x-pgp-sig (head)
gnus-treat-unfold-headers (head)
gnus-treat-fold-headers (head)
gnus-treat-fold-newsgroups (head)
gnus-treat-leading-whitespace (head)
```
See Section 3.18.5 [Article Header], page 92.

You can, of course, write your own functions to be called from **gnus-part-display-hook**. The functions are called narrowed to the part, and you can do anything you like, pretty much. There is no information that you have to keep in the buffer—you can change everything.

4.5 Article Keymap

Most of the keystrokes in the summary buffer can also be used in the article buffer. They should behave as if you typed them in the summary buffer, which means that you don't actually have to have a summary buffer displayed while reading. You can do it all from the article buffer.

The key *v* is reserved for users. You can bind it to some command or better use it as a prefix key.

A few additional keystrokes are available:

SPACE	Scroll forwards one page (**gnus-article-next-page**). This is exactly the same as *h SPACE h*.
DEL	Scroll backwards one page (**gnus-article-prev-page**). This is exactly the same as *h DEL h*.
C-c ^	If point is in the neighborhood of a **Message-ID** and you press *C-c ^*, Gnus will try to get that article from the server (**gnus-article-refer-article**).
C-c C-m	Send a reply to the address near point (**gnus-article-mail**). If given a prefix, include the mail.
s	Reconfigure the buffers so that the summary buffer becomes visible (**gnus-article-show-summary**).
?	Give a very brief description of the available keystrokes (**gnus-article-describe-briefly**).
TAB	Go to the next button, if any (**gnus-article-next-button**). This only makes sense if you have buttonizing turned on.
M-TAB	Go to the previous button, if any (**gnus-article-prev-button**).
R	Send a reply to the current article and yank the current article (**gnus-article-reply-with-original**). If the region is active, only yank the text in the region.
S W	Send a wide reply to the current article and yank the current article (**gnus-article-wide-reply-with-original**). If the region is active, only yank the text in the region.

F   Send a followup to the current article and yank the current article
           (`gnus-article-followup-with-original`). If the region is active, only yank
           the text in the region.

4.6 Misc Article

`gnus-single-article-buffer`
           If non-`nil`, use the same article buffer for all the groups. (This is the default.)
           If `nil`, each group will have its own article buffer.

`gnus-widen-article-window`
           If non-`nil`, selecting the article buffer with the *h* command will "widen" the
           article window to take the entire frame.

`gnus-article-decode-hook`
           Hook used to decode MIME articles. The default value is (`article-decode-`
           `charset article-decode-encoded-words`)

`gnus-article-prepare-hook`
           This hook is called right after the article has been inserted into the article
           buffer. It is mainly intended for functions that do something depending on the
           contents; it should probably not be used for changing the contents of the article
           buffer.

`gnus-article-mode-hook`
           Hook called in article mode buffers.

`gnus-article-mode-syntax-table`
           Syntax table used in article buffers. It is initialized from `text-mode-syntax-`
           `table`.

`gnus-article-over-scroll`
           If non-`nil`, allow scrolling the article buffer even when there no more new text
           to scroll in. The default is `nil`.

`gnus-article-mode-line-format`
           This variable is a format string along the same lines as `gnus-summary-mode-`
           `line-format` (see Section 3.1.3 [Summary Buffer Mode Line], page 48). It
           accepts the same format specifications as that variable, with two extensions:

           'w'   The *wash status* of the article. This is a short string with one
                        character for each possible article wash operation that may have
                        been performed. The characters and their meaning:

                        'c'   Displayed when cited text may be hidden in the article
                                     buffer.

                        'h'   Displayed when headers are hidden in the article buffer.

                        'p'   Displayed when article is digitally signed or encrypted,
                                     and Gnus has hidden the security headers. (N.B. does
                                     not tell anything about security status, i.e., good or
                                     bad signature.)

    's'   Displayed when the signature has been hidden in the Article buffer.

    'o'   Displayed when Gnus has treated overstrike characters in the article buffer.

    'e'   Displayed when Gnus has treated emphasized strings in the article buffer.

'm'   The number of MIME parts in the article.

`gnus-break-pages`

Controls whether *page breaking* is to take place. If this variable is non-`nil`, the articles will be divided into pages whenever a page delimiter appears in the article. If this variable is `nil`, paging will not be done.

`gnus-page-delimiter`

This is the delimiter mentioned above. By default, it is '`^L`' (formfeed).

`gnus-use-idna`

This variable controls whether Gnus performs IDNA decoding of internationalized domain names inside '`From`', '`To`' and '`Cc`' headers. See Section "IDNA" in *The Message Manual*, for how to compose such messages. This requires GNU Libidn, and this variable is only enabled if you have installed it.

`gnus-inhibit-images`

If this is non-`nil`, inhibit displaying of images inline in the article body. It is effective to images that are in articles as MIME parts, and images in HTML articles rendered when `mm-text-html-renderer` (see Section "Display Customization" in *The Emacs MIME Manual*) is `shr` or `gnus-w3m`.

5 Composing Messages

All commands for posting and mailing will put you in a message buffer where you can edit the article all you like, before you send the article by pressing *C-c C-c*. See Section "Overview" in *Message Manual*. Where the message will be posted/mailed to depends on your setup (see Section 5.2 [Posting Server], page 126).

Also see Section 3.5.4 [Canceling and Superseding], page 56 for information on how to remove articles you shouldn't have posted.

5.1 Mail

Variables for customizing outgoing mail:

`gnus-uu-digest-headers`

> List of regexps to match headers included in digested messages. The headers will be included in the sequence they are matched. If `nil` include all headers.

`gnus-add-to-list`

> If non-`nil`, add a `to-list` group parameter to mail groups that have none when you do a **a**.

`gnus-confirm-mail-reply-to-news`

> If non-`nil`, Gnus will ask you for a confirmation when you are about to reply to news articles by mail. If it is `nil`, nothing interferes in what you want to do. This can also be a function receiving the group name as the only parameter which should return non-`nil` if a confirmation is needed, or a regular expression matching group names, where confirmation should be asked for.

> If you find yourself never wanting to reply to mail, but occasionally press *R* anyway, this variable might be for you.

`gnus-confirm-treat-mail-like-news`

> If non-`nil`, Gnus also requests confirmation according to **gnus-confirm-mail-reply-to-news** when replying to mail. This is useful for treating mailing lists like newsgroups.

5.2 Posting Server

When you press those magical *C-c C-c* keys to ship off your latest (extremely intelligent, of course) article, where does it go?

Thank you for asking. I hate you.

It can be quite complicated.

When posting news, Message usually invokes **message-send-news** (see Section "News Variables" in *Message Manual*). Normally, Gnus will post using the same select method as you're reading from (which might be convenient if you're reading lots of groups from different private servers). However. If the server you're reading from doesn't allow posting, just reading, you probably want to use some other server to post your (extremely intelligent and fabulously interesting) articles. You can then set the **gnus-post-method** to some other method:

```
(setq gnus-post-method '(nnspool ""))
```

Now, if you've done this, and then this server rejects your article, or this server is down, what do you do then? To override this variable you can use a non-zero prefix to the *C-c C-c* command to force using the "current" server, to get back the default behavior, for posting.

If you give a zero prefix (i.e., *C-u 0 C-c C-c*) to that command, Gnus will prompt you for what method to use for posting.

You can also set `gnus-post-method` to a list of select methods. If that's the case, Gnus will always prompt you for what method to use for posting.

Finally, if you want to always post using the native select method, you can set this variable to `native`.

When sending mail, Message invokes the function specified by the variable `message-send-mail-function`. Gnus tries to set it to a value suitable for your system. See Section "Mail Variables" in *Message manual*, for more information.

5.3 POP before SMTP

Does your ISP use POP-before-SMTP authentication? This authentication method simply requires you to contact the POP server before sending email. To do that, put the following lines in your `~/.gnus.el` file:

```
(add-hook 'message-send-mail-hook 'mail-source-touch-pop)
```

The `mail-source-touch-pop` function does POP authentication according to the value of `mail-sources` without fetching mails, just before sending a mail. See Section 6.4.4 [Mail Sources], page 154.

If you have two or more POP mail servers set in `mail-sources`, you may want to specify one of them to `mail-source-primary-source` as the POP mail server to be used for the POP-before-SMTP authentication. If it is your primary POP mail server (i.e., you are fetching mails mainly from that server), you can set it permanently as follows:

```
(setq mail-source-primary-source
      '(pop :server "pop3.mail.server"
            :password "secret"))
```

Otherwise, bind it dynamically only when performing the POP-before-SMTP authentication as follows:

```
(add-hook 'message-send-mail-hook
          (lambda ()
            (let ((mail-source-primary-source
                   '(pop :server "pop3.mail.server"
                         :password "secret")))
              (mail-source-touch-pop))))
```

5.4 Mail and Post

Here's a list of variables relevant to both mailing and posting:

`gnus-mailing-list-groups`

> If your news server offers groups that are really mailing lists gatewayed to the NNTP server, you can read those groups without problems, but you can't

post/followup to them without some difficulty. One solution is to add a `to-address` to the group parameters (see Section 2.10 [Group Parameters], page 22). An easier thing to do is set the `gnus-mailing-list-groups` to a regexp that matches the groups that really are mailing lists. Then, at least, followups to the mailing lists will work most of the time. Posting to these groups (`a`) is still a pain, though.

`gnus-user-agent`

        This variable controls which information should be exposed in the User-Agent header. It can be a list of symbols or a string. Valid symbols are `gnus` (show Gnus version) and `emacs` (show Emacs version). In addition to the Emacs version, you can add `codename` (show (S)XEmacs codename) or either `config` (show system configuration) or `type` (show system type). If you set it to a string, be sure to use a valid format, see RFC 2616.

You may want to do spell-checking on messages that you send out. Or, if you don't want to spell-check by hand, you could add automatic spell-checking via the `ispell` package:

```
(add-hook 'message-send-hook 'ispell-message)
```

If you want to change the `ispell` dictionary based on what group you're in, you could say something like the following:

```
(add-hook 'gnus-select-group-hook
          (lambda ()
            (cond
             ((string-match
               "^de\\." (gnus-group-real-name gnus-newsgroup-name))
              (ispell-change-dictionary "deutsch"))
             (t
              (ispell-change-dictionary "english")))))
```

Modify to suit your needs.

If `gnus-message-highlight-citation` is `t`, different levels of citations are highlighted like in Gnus article buffers also in message mode buffers.

5.5 Archived Messages

Gnus provides a few different methods for storing the mail and news you send. The default method is to use the *archive virtual server* to store the messages. If you want to disable this completely, the `gnus-message-archive-group` variable should be `nil`. The default is `"sent.%Y-%m"`, which gives you one archive group per month.

For archiving interesting messages in a group you read, see the *B c* (`gnus-summary-copy-article`) command (see Section 3.26 [Mail Group Commands], page 107).

`gnus-message-archive-method` says what virtual server Gnus is to use to store sent messages. The default is `"archive"`, and when actually being used it is expanded into:

```
(nnfolder "archive"
          (nnfolder-directory   "~/Mail/archive")
          (nnfolder-active-file "~/Mail/archive/active")
          (nnfolder-get-new-mail nil)
          (nnfolder-inhibit-expiry t))
```

Note: a server like this is saved in the `~/.newsrc.eld` file first so that it may be used as a real method of the server which is named `"archive"` (that is, for the case where `gnus-message-archive-method` is set to `"archive"`) ever since. If it once has been saved, it will never be updated by default even if you change the value of `gnus-message-archive-method` afterward. Therefore, the server `"archive"` doesn't necessarily mean the `nnfolder` server like this at all times. If you want the saved method to reflect always the value of `gnus-message-archive-method`, set the `gnus-update-message-archive-method` variable to a non-`nil` value. The default value of this variable is `nil`.

You can, however, use any mail select method (`nnml`, `nnmbox`, etc.). `nnfolder` is a quite likable select method for doing this sort of thing, though. If you don't like the default directory chosen, you could say something like:

```
(setq gnus-message-archive-method
      '(nnfolder "archive"
                 (nnfolder-inhibit-expiry t)
                 (nnfolder-active-file "~/News/sent-mail/active")
                 (nnfolder-directory "~/News/sent-mail/")))
```

Gnus will insert `Gcc` headers in all outgoing messages that point to one or more group(s) on that server. Which group to use is determined by the `gnus-message-archive-group` variable.

This variable can be used to do the following:

a string   Messages will be saved in that group.

Note that you can include a select method in the group name, then the message will not be stored in the select method given by `gnus-message-archive-method`, but in the select method specified by the group name, instead. Suppose `gnus-message-archive-method` has the default value shown above. Then setting `gnus-message-archive-group` to `"foo"` means that outgoing messages are stored in 'nnfolder+archive:foo', but if you use the value `"nnml:foo"`, then outgoing messages will be stored in 'nnml:foo'.

a list of strings
Messages will be saved in all those groups.

an alist of regexps, functions and forms
When a key "matches", the result is used.

nil   No message archiving will take place.

Let's illustrate:

Just saving to a single group called 'MisK':

```
(setq gnus-message-archive-group "MisK")
```

Saving to two groups, 'MisK' and 'safe':

```
(setq gnus-message-archive-group '("MisK" "safe"))
```

Save to different groups based on what group you are in:

```
(setq gnus-message-archive-group
      '(("^alt" "sent-to-alt")
```

```
                    ("mail" "sent-to-mail")
                    (".*" "sent-to-misc")))
```

More complex stuff:

```
(setq gnus-message-archive-group
        '((if (message-news-p)
            "misc-news"
           "misc-mail")))
```

How about storing all news messages in one file, but storing all mail messages in one file per month:

```
(setq gnus-message-archive-group
        '((if (message-news-p)
            "misc-news"
          (concat "mail." (format-time-string "%Y-%m")))))
```

Now, when you send a message off, it will be stored in the appropriate group. (If you want to disable storing for just one particular message, you can just remove the Gcc header that has been inserted.) The archive group will appear in the group buffer the next time you start Gnus, or the next time you press F in the group buffer. You can enter it and read the articles in it just like you'd read any other group. If the group gets really big and annoying, you can simply rename if (using G r in the group buffer) to something nice—'misc-mail-september-1995', or whatever. New messages will continue to be stored in the old (now empty) group.

gnus-gcc-mark-as-read

> If non-nil, automatically mark Gcc articles as read.

gnus-gcc-externalize-attachments

> If nil, attach files as normal parts in Gcc copies; if a regexp and matches the Gcc group name, attach files as external parts; if it is all, attach local files as external parts; if it is other non-nil, the behavior is the same as all, but it may be changed in the future.

gnus-gcc-self-resent-messages

> Like the gcc-self group parameter, applied only for unmodified messages that gnus-summary-resend-message (see Section 3.5.1 [Summary Mail Commands], page 53) resends. Non-nil value of this variable takes precedence over any existing Gcc header.

> If this is none, no Gcc copy will be made. If this is t, messages resent will be Gcc copied to the current group. If this is a string, it specifies a group to which resent messages will be Gcc copied. If this is nil, Gcc will be done according to existing Gcc header(s), if any. If this is no-gcc-self, that is the default, resent messages will be Gcc copied to groups that existing Gcc header specifies, except for the current group.

gnus-gcc-pre-body-encode-hook
gnus-gcc-post-body-encode-hook

> These hooks are run before/after encoding the message body of the Gcc copy of a sent message. The current buffer (when the hook is run) contains the message including the message header. Changes made to the message will only affect

the Gcc copy, but not the original message. You can use these hooks to edit
the copy (and influence subsequent transformations), e.g., remove MML secure
tags (see Section 5.9 [Signing and encrypting], page 134).

5.6 Posting Styles

All them variables, they make my head swim.

So what if you want a different **Organization** and signature based on what groups you
post to? And you post both from your home machine and your work machine, and you
want different **From** lines, and so on?

One way to do stuff like that is to write clever hooks that change the variables you need
to have changed. That's a bit boring, so somebody came up with the bright idea of letting
the user specify these things in a handy alist. Here's an example of a **gnus-posting-styles**
variable:

```
((".*"
  (signature "Peace and happiness")
  (organization "What me?"))
 ("^comp"
  (signature "Death to everybody"))
 ("comp.emacs.i-love-it"
  (organization "Emacs is it")))
```

As you might surmise from this example, this alist consists of several *styles*. Each style
will be applicable if the first element "matches", in some form or other. The entire alist
will be iterated over, from the beginning towards the end, and each match will be applied,
which means that attributes in later styles that match override the same attributes in earlier
matching styles. So 'comp.programming.literate' will have the 'Death to everybody'
signature and the 'What me?' Organization header.

The first element in each style is called the **match**. If it's a string, then Gnus will try
to regexp match it against the group name. If it is the form (header *match regexp*), then
Gnus will look in the original article for a header whose name is *match* and compare that
regexp. *match* and *regexp* are strings. (The original article is the one you are replying
or following up to. If you are not composing a reply or a followup, then there is nothing
to match against.) If the **match** is a function symbol, that function will be called with no
arguments. If it's a variable symbol, then the variable will be referenced. If it's a list, then
that list will be **evaled**. In any case, if this returns a non-**nil** value, then the style is said
to *match*.

Each style may contain an arbitrary amount of *attributes*. Each attribute consists of
a (*name value*) pair. In addition, you can also use the (*name* :file *value*) form or the
(*name* :value *value*) form. Where :file signifies *value* represents a file name and its
contents should be used as the attribute value, :value signifies *value* does not represent a
file name explicitly. The attribute name can be one of:

- signature
- signature-file
- x-face-file
- address, overriding user-mail-address

- `name`, overriding (`user-full-name`)
- `body`

Note that the `signature-file` attribute honors the variable `message-signature-directory`.

The attribute name can also be a string or a symbol. In that case, this will be used as a header name, and the value will be inserted in the headers of the article; if the value is `nil`, the header name will be removed. If the attribute name is `eval`, the form is evaluated, and the result is thrown away.

The attribute value can be a string, a function with zero arguments (the return value will be used), a variable (its value will be used) or a list (it will be `evaled` and the return value will be used). The functions and sexps are called/`evaled` in the message buffer that is being set up. The headers of the current article are available through the `message-reply-headers` variable, which is a vector of the following headers: number subject from date id references chars lines xref extra.

In the case of a string value, if the `match` is a regular expression, or if it takes the form (`header match regexp`), a 'gnus-match-substitute-replacement' is proceed on the value to replace the positional parameters '\n' by the corresponding parenthetical matches (see See Section "Replacing the Text that Matched" in *The Emacs Lisp Reference Manual*.)

If you wish to check whether the message you are about to compose is meant to be a news article or a mail message, you can check the values of the `message-news-p` and `message-mail-p` functions.

So here's a new example:

```
(setq gnus-posting-styles
      '((".*"
         (signature-file "~/.signature")
         (name "User Name")
         (x-face-file "~/.xface")
         (x-url (getenv "WWW_HOME"))
         (organization "People's Front Against MWM"))
        ("^rec.humor"
         (signature my-funny-signature-randomizer))
        ((equal (system-name) "gnarly")  ;; A form
         (signature my-quote-randomizer))
        (message-news-p        ;; A function symbol
         (signature my-news-signature))
        (window-system         ;; A value symbol
         ("X-Window-System" (format "%s" window-system)))
        ;; If I'm replying to Larsi, set the Organization header.
        ((header "from" "larsi.*org")
         (Organization "Somewhere, Inc."))
        ;; Reply to a message from the same subaddress the message
        ;; was sent to.
        ((header "x-original-to" "me\\(\\+.+\\)@example.org")
         (address "me\\1@example.org"))
        ((posting-from-work-p) ;; A user defined function
```

```
        (signature-file "~/.work-signature")
        (address "user@bar.foo")
        (body "You are fired.\n\nSincerely, your boss.")
        ("X-Message-SMTP-Method" "smtp smtp.example.org 587")
        (organization "Important Work, Inc"))
       ("nnml:.*"
        (From (with-current-buffer gnus-article-buffer
                  (message-fetch-field "to"))))
       ("^nn.+:"
        (signature-file "~/.mail-signature"))))
```

The 'nnml:.*' rule means that you use the To address as the From address in all your outgoing replies, which might be handy if you fill many roles. You may also use **message-alternative-emails** instead. See Section "Message Headers" in *Message Manual*.

Of particular interest in the "work-mail" style is the 'X-Message-SMTP-Method' header. It specifies how to send the outgoing email. You may want to sent certain emails through certain SMTP servers due to company policies, for instance. See Section "Message Variables" in *Message Manual*.

5.7 Drafts

If you are writing a message (mail or news) and suddenly remember that you have a steak in the oven (or some pesto in the food processor, you craaazy vegetarians), you'll probably wish there was a method to save the message you are writing so that you can continue editing it some other day, and send it when you feel its finished.

Well, don't worry about it. Whenever you start composing a message of some sort using the Gnus mail and post commands, the buffer you get will automatically associate to an article in a special *draft* group. If you save the buffer the normal way (*C-x C-s*, for instance), the article will be saved there. (Auto-save files also go to the draft group.)

The draft group is a special group (which is implemented as an **nndraft** group, if you absolutely have to know) called 'nndraft:drafts'. The variable **nndraft-directory** says where **nndraft** is to store its files. What makes this group special is that you can't tick any articles in it or mark any articles as read—all articles in the group are permanently unread.

If the group doesn't exist, it will be created and you'll be subscribed to it. The only way to make it disappear from the Group buffer is to unsubscribe it. The special properties of the draft group comes from a group property (see Section 2.10 [Group Parameters], page 22), and if lost the group behaves like any other group. This means the commands below will not be available. To restore the special properties of the group, the simplest way is to kill the group, using *C-k*, and restart Gnus. The group is automatically created again with the correct parameters. The content of the group is not lost.

When you want to continue editing the article, you simply enter the draft group and push *D e* (**gnus-draft-edit-message**) to do that. You will be placed in a buffer where you left off.

Rejected articles will also be put in this draft group (see Section 5.8 [Rejected Articles], page 134).

If you have lots of rejected messages you want to post (or mail) without doing further editing, you can use the *D s* command (**gnus-draft-send-message**). This command understands the process/prefix convention (see Section 9.1 [Process/Prefix], page 249). The *D S* command (**gnus-draft-send-all-messages**) will ship off all messages in the buffer.

If you have some messages that you wish not to send, you can use the *D t* (**gnus-draft-toggle-sending**) command to mark the message as unsendable. This is a toggling command.

Finally, if you want to delete a draft, use the normal *B DEL* command (see Section 3.26 [Mail Group Commands], page 107).

5.8 Rejected Articles

Sometimes a news server will reject an article. Perhaps the server doesn't like your face. Perhaps it just feels miserable. Perhaps *there be demons*. Perhaps you have included too much cited text. Perhaps the disk is full. Perhaps the server is down.

These situations are, of course, totally beyond the control of Gnus. (Gnus, of course, loves the way you look, always feels great, has angels fluttering around inside of it, doesn't care about how much cited text you include, never runs full and never goes down.) So Gnus saves these articles until some later time when the server feels better.

The rejected articles will automatically be put in a special draft group (see Section 5.7 [Drafts], page 133). When the server comes back up again, you'd then typically enter that group and send all the articles off.

5.9 Signing and encrypting

Gnus can digitally sign and encrypt your messages, using vanilla PGP format or PGP/MIME or S/MIME. For decoding such messages, see the **mm-verify-option** and **mm-decrypt-option** options (see Section 3.31 [Security], page 114).

Often, you would like to sign replies to people who send you signed messages. Even more often, you might want to encrypt messages which are in reply to encrypted messages. Gnus offers **gnus-message-replysign** to enable the former, and **gnus-message-replyencrypt** for the latter. In addition, setting **gnus-message-replysignencrypted** (on by default) will sign automatically encrypted messages.

Instructing MML to perform security operations on a MIME part is done using the *C-c C-m s* key map for signing and the *C-c C-m c* key map for encryption, as follows.

C-c C-m s s

> Digitally sign current message using S/MIME.

C-c C-m s o

> Digitally sign current message using PGP.

C-c C-m s p

> Digitally sign current message using PGP/MIME.

C-c C-m c s

> Digitally encrypt current message using S/MIME.

C-c C-m c o

> Digitally encrypt current message using PGP.

`C-c C-m c p`
> Digitally encrypt current message using PGP/MIME.

`C-c C-m C-n`
> Remove security related MML tags from message.

See Section "Security" in *Message Manual*, for more information.

6 Select Methods

A *foreign group* is a group not read by the usual (or default) means. It could be, for instance, a group from a different NNTP server, it could be a virtual group, or it could be your own personal mail group.

A foreign group (or any group, really) is specified by a *name* and a *select method*. To take the latter first, a select method is a list where the first element says what back end to use (e.g., `nntp`, `nnspool`, `nnml`) and the second element is the *server name*. There may be additional elements in the select method, where the value may have special meaning for the back end in question.

One could say that a select method defines a *virtual server*—so we do just that (see Section 6.1 [Server Buffer], page 136).

The *name* of the group is the name the back end will recognize the group as.

For instance, the group 'soc.motss' on the NNTP server 'some.where.edu' will have the name 'soc.motss' and select method (`nntp "some.where.edu"`). Gnus will call this group 'nntp+some.where.edu:soc.motss', even though the `nntp` back end just knows this group as 'soc.motss'.

The different methods all have their peculiarities, of course.

6.1 Server Buffer

Traditionally, a *server* is a machine or a piece of software that one connects to, and then requests information from. Gnus does not connect directly to any real servers, but does all transactions through one back end or other. But that's just putting one layer more between the actual media and Gnus, so we might just as well say that each back end represents a virtual server.

For instance, the `nntp` back end may be used to connect to several different actual NNTP servers, or, perhaps, to many different ports on the same actual NNTP server. You tell Gnus which back end to use, and what parameters to set by specifying a *select method*.

These select method specifications can sometimes become quite complicated—say, for instance, that you want to read from the NNTP server 'news.funet.fi' on port number 13, which hangs if queried for NOV headers and has a buggy select. Ahem. Anyway, if you had to specify that for each group that used this server, that would be too much work, so Gnus offers a way of naming select methods, which is what you do in the server buffer.

To enter the server buffer, use the `^` (`gnus-group-enter-server-mode`) command in the group buffer.

`gnus-server-mode-hook` is run when creating the server buffer.

6.1.1 Server Buffer Format

You can change the look of the server buffer lines by changing the `gnus-server-line-format` variable. This is a `format`-like variable, with some simple extensions:

'h'   How the news is fetched—the back end name.

'n'   The name of this server.

'w'   Where the news is to be fetched from—the address.

‘s’   The opened/closed/denied status of the server.

‘a’   Whether this server is agentized.

The mode line can also be customized by using the **gnus-server-mode-line-format** variable (see Section 9.4.2 [Mode Line Formatting], page 251). The following specs are understood:

‘S’   Server name.

‘M’   Server method.

Also see Section 9.4 [Formatting Variables], page 250.

6.1.2 Server Commands

v   The key *v* is reserved for users. You can bind it to some command or better use it as a prefix key.

a   Add a new server (**gnus-server-add-server**).

e   Edit a server (**gnus-server-edit-server**).

S   Show the definition of a server (**gnus-server-show-server**).

SPACE   Browse the current server (**gnus-server-read-server**).

q   Return to the group buffer (**gnus-server-exit**).

k   Kill the current server (**gnus-server-kill-server**).

y   Yank the previously killed server (**gnus-server-yank-server**).

c   Copy the current server (**gnus-server-copy-server**).

l   List all servers (**gnus-server-list-servers**).

s   Request that the server scan its sources for new articles (**gnus-server-scan-server**). This is mainly sensible with mail servers.

g   Request that the server regenerate all its data structures (**gnus-server-regenerate-server**). This can be useful if you have a mail back end that has gotten out of sync.

z

             Compact all groups in the server under point (**gnus-server-compact-server**). Currently implemented only in nnml (see Section 6.4.13.3 [Mail Spool], page 174). This removes gaps between article numbers, hence getting a correct total article count.

Some more commands for closing, disabling, and re-opening servers are listed in Section 6.1.7 [Unavailable Servers], page 140.

6.1.3 Example Methods

Most select methods are pretty simple and self-explanatory:

```
(nntp "news.funet.fi")
```

Reading directly from the spool is even simpler:

```
(nnspool "")
```

As you can see, the first element in a select method is the name of the back end, and the second is the *address*, or *name*, if you will.

After these two elements, there may be an arbitrary number of (`variable form`) pairs.

To go back to the first example—imagine that you want to read from port 15 on that machine. This is what the select method should look like then:

```
(nntp "news.funet.fi" (nntp-port-number 15))
```

You should read the documentation to each back end to find out what variables are relevant, but here's an **nnmh** example:

nnmh is a mail back end that reads a spool-like structure. Say you have two structures that you wish to access: One is your private mail spool, and the other is a public one. Here's the possible spec for your private mail:

```
(nnmh "private" (nnmh-directory "~/private/mail/"))
```

(This server is then called 'private', but you may have guessed that.)

Here's the method for a public spool:

```
(nnmh "public"
      (nnmh-directory "/usr/information/spool/")
      (nnmh-get-new-mail nil))
```

If you are behind a firewall and only have access to the NNTP server from the firewall machine, you can instruct Gnus to **rlogin** on the firewall machine and connect with netcat from there to the NNTP server. Doing this can be rather fiddly, but your virtual server definition should probably look something like this:

```
(nntp "firewall"
      (nntp-open-connection-function nntp-open-via-rlogin-and-netcat)
      (nntp-via-address "the.firewall.machine")
      (nntp-address "the.real.nntp.host"))
```

If you want to use the wonderful **ssh** program to provide a compressed connection over the modem line, you could add the following configuration to the example above:

```
(nntp-via-rlogin-command "ssh")
```

See also **nntp-via-rlogin-command-switches**. Here's an example for an indirect connection:

```
(setq gnus-select-method
      '(nntp "indirect"
             (nntp-address "news.server.example")
             (nntp-via-user-name "intermediate_user_name")
             (nntp-via-address "intermediate.host.example")
             (nntp-via-rlogin-command "ssh")
             (nntp-via-rlogin-command-switches ("-C"))
```

```
(nntp-open-connection-function nntp-open-via-rlogin-and-netcat)))
```

This means that you have to have set up **ssh-agent** correctly to provide automatic authorization, of course.

If you're behind a firewall, but have direct access to the outside world through a wrapper command like "runsocks", you could open a socksified netcat connection to the news server as follows:

```
(nntp "outside"
      (nntp-pre-command "runsocks")
      (nntp-open-connection-function nntp-open-netcat-stream)
      (nntp-address "the.news.server"))
```

6.1.4 Creating a Virtual Server

If you're saving lots of articles in the cache by using persistent articles, you may want to create a virtual server to read the cache.

First you need to add a new server. The **a** command does that. It would probably be best to use **nnml** to read the cache. You could also use **nnspool** or **nnmh**, though.

Type **a** *nnml RET cache RET*.

You should now have a brand new **nnml** virtual server called 'cache'. You now need to edit it to have the right definitions. Type **e** to edit the server. You'll be entered into a buffer that will contain the following:

```
(nnml "cache")
```

Change that to:

```
(nnml "cache"
      (nnml-directory "~/News/cache/")
      (nnml-active-file "~/News/cache/active"))
```

Type *C-c C-c* to return to the server buffer. If you now press *RET* over this virtual server, you should be entered into a browse buffer, and you should be able to enter any of the groups displayed.

6.1.5 Server Variables

One sticky point when defining variables (both on back ends and in Emacs in general) is that some variables are typically initialized from other variables when the definition of the variables is being loaded. If you change the "base" variable after the variables have been loaded, you won't change the "derived" variables.

This typically affects directory and file variables. For instance, **nnml-directory** is `~/Mail/` by default, and all **nnml** directory variables are initialized from that variable, so **nnml-active-file** will be `~/Mail/active`. If you define a new virtual **nnml** server, it will *not* suffice to set just **nnml-directory**—you have to explicitly set all the file variables to be what you want them to be. For a complete list of variables for each back end, see each back end's section later in this manual, but here's an example **nnml** definition:

```
(nnml "public"
      (nnml-directory "~/my-mail/")
      (nnml-active-file "~/my-mail/active")
      (nnml-newsgroups-file "~/my-mail/newsgroups"))
```

Server variables are often called *server parameters*.

6.1.6 Servers and Methods

Wherever you would normally use a select method (e.g., **gnus-secondary-select-method**, in the group select method, when browsing a foreign server) you can use a virtual server name instead. This could potentially save lots of typing. And it's nice all over.

6.1.7 Unavailable Servers

If a server seems to be unreachable, Gnus will mark that server as **denied**. That means that any subsequent attempt to make contact with that server will just be ignored. "It can't be opened," Gnus will tell you, without making the least effort to see whether that is actually the case or not.

That might seem quite naughty, but it does make sense most of the time. Let's say you have 10 groups subscribed to on server 'nephelococcygia.com'. This server is located somewhere quite far away from you and the machine is quite slow, so it takes 1 minute just to find out that it refuses connection to you today. If Gnus were to attempt to do that 10 times, you'd be quite annoyed, so Gnus won't attempt to do that. Once it has gotten a single "connection refused", it will regard that server as "down".

So, what happens if the machine was only feeling unwell temporarily? How do you test to see whether the machine has come up again?

You jump to the server buffer (see Section 6.1 [Server Buffer], page 136) and poke it with the following commands:

O   Try to establish connection to the server on the current line (**gnus-server-open-server**).

C   Close the connection (if any) to the server (**gnus-server-close-server**).

D   Mark the current server as unreachable (**gnus-server-deny-server**).

M-o   Open the connections to all servers in the buffer (**gnus-server-open-all-servers**).

M-c   Close the connections to all servers in the buffer (**gnus-server-close-all-servers**).

R   Remove all marks to whether Gnus was denied connection from any servers (**gnus-server-remove-denials**).

c   Copy a server and give it a new name (**gnus-server-copy-server**). This can be useful if you have a complex method definition, and want to use the same definition towards a different (physical) server.

L   Set server status to offline (**gnus-server-offline-server**).

6.2 Getting News

A newsreader is normally used for reading news. Gnus currently provides only two methods of getting news—it can read from an NNTP server, or it can read from a local spool.

6.2.1 NNTP

Subscribing to a foreign group from an NNTP server is rather easy. You just specify `nntp` as method and the address of the NNTP server as the, uhm, address.

If the NNTP server is located at a non-standard port, setting the third element of the select method to this port number should allow you to connect to the right port. You'll have to edit the group info for that (see Section 2.9 [Foreign Groups], page 20).

The name of the foreign group can be the same as a native group. In fact, you can subscribe to the same group from as many different servers you feel like. There will be no name collisions.

The following variables can be used to create a virtual `nntp` server:

`nntp-server-opened-hook`

> is run after a connection has been made. It can be used to send commands to the NNTP server after it has been contacted. By default it sends the command **MODE READER** to the server with the `nntp-send-mode-reader` function. This function should always be present in this hook.

`nntp-authinfo-function`

> This function will be used to send 'AUTHINFO' to the NNTP server. The default function is `nntp-send-authinfo`, which looks through your `~/.authinfo` (or whatever you've set the `nntp-authinfo-file` variable to) for applicable entries. If none are found, it will prompt you for a login name and a password. The format of the `~/.authinfo` file is (almost) the same as the `ftp` `~/.netrc` file, which is defined in the `ftp` manual page, but here are the salient facts:
>
> 1. The file contains one or more line, each of which define one server.
> 2. Each line may contain an arbitrary number of token/value pairs.
>
>   The valid tokens include '`machine`', '`login`', '`password`', '`default`'. In addition Gnus introduces two new tokens, not present in the original `.netrc/ftp` syntax, namely '`port`' and '`force`'. (This is the only way the `.authinfo` file format deviates from the `.netrc` file format.) '`port`' is used to indicate what port on the server the credentials apply to and '`force`' is explained below.
>
> Here's an example file:
>
> ```
> machine news.uio.no login larsi password geheimnis
> machine nntp.ifi.uio.no login larsi force yes
> ```
>
> The token/value pairs may appear in any order; '`machine`' doesn't have to be first, for instance.
>
> In this example, both login name and password have been supplied for the former server, while the latter has only the login name listed, and the user will be prompted for the password. The latter also has the '`force`' tag, which means that the authinfo will be sent to the *nntp* server upon connection; the default (i.e., when there is not '`force`' tag) is to not send authinfo to the *nntp* server until the *nntp* server asks for it.
>
> You can also add '`default`' lines that will apply to all servers that don't have matching '`machine`' lines.

```
                    default force yes
```
This will force sending 'AUTHINFO' commands to all servers not previously mentioned.

Remember to not leave the `~/.authinfo` file world-readable.

nntp-server-action-alist

This is a list of regexps to match on server types and actions to be taken when matches are made. For instance, if you want Gnus to beep every time you connect to innd, you could say something like:

```
        (setq nntp-server-action-alist
              '(("innd" (ding))))
```
You probably don't want to do that, though.

The default value is

```
        '(("nntpd 1\\.5\\.11t"
           (remove-hook 'nntp-server-opened-hook
                        'nntp-send-mode-reader)))
```
This ensures that Gnus doesn't send the MODE READER command to nntpd 1.5.11t, since that command chokes that server, I've been told.

nntp-maximum-request

If the NNTP server doesn't support NOV headers, this back end will collect headers by sending a series of **head** commands. To speed things up, the back end sends lots of these commands without waiting for reply, and then reads all the replies. This is controlled by the **nntp-maximum-request** variable, and is 400 by default. If your network is buggy, you should set this to 1.

nntp-connection-timeout

If you have lots of foreign **nntp** groups that you connect to regularly, you're sure to have problems with NNTP servers not responding properly, or being too loaded to reply within reasonable time. This is can lead to awkward problems, which can be helped somewhat by setting **nntp-connection-timeout**. This is an integer that says how many seconds the **nntp** back end should wait for a connection before giving up. If it is **nil**, which is the default, no timeouts are done.

nntp-nov-is-evil

If the NNTP server does not support NOV, you could set this variable to **t**, but **nntp** usually checks automatically whether NOV can be used.

nntp-xover-commands

List of strings used as commands to fetch NOV lines from a server. The default value of this variable is ("XOVER" "XOVERVIEW").

nntp-nov-gap

nntp normally sends just one big request for NOV lines to the server. The server responds with one huge list of lines. However, if you have read articles 2–5000 in the group, and only want to read article 1 and 5001, that means that **nntp** will fetch 4999 NOV lines that you will not need. This variable says how big a gap between two consecutive articles is allowed to be before the XOVER request is split into several request. Note that if your network is fast, setting this variable to a really small number means that fetching will probably be slower. If this variable is `nil`, `nntp` will never split requests. The default is 5.

`nntp-xref-number-is-evil`

When Gnus refers to an article having the `Message-ID` that a user specifies or having the `Message-ID` of the parent article of the current one (see Section 3.23 [Finding the Parent], page 102), Gnus sends a `HEAD` command to the NNTP server to know where it is, and the server returns the data containing the pairs of a group and an article number in the `Xref` header. Gnus normally uses the article number to refer to the article if the data shows that that article is in the current group, while it uses the `Message-ID` otherwise. However, some news servers, e.g., ones running Diablo, run multiple engines having the same articles but article numbers are not kept synchronized between them. In that case, the article number that appears in the `Xref` header varies by which engine is chosen, so you cannot refer to the parent article that is in the current group, for instance. If you connect to such a server, set this variable to a non-`nil` value, and Gnus never uses article numbers. For example:

```
(setq gnus-select-method
      '(nntp "newszilla"
             (nntp-address "newszilla.example.com")
             (nntp-xref-number-is-evil t)
             ...))
```

The default value of this server variable is `nil`.

`nntp-prepare-server-hook`

A hook run before attempting to connect to an NNTP server.

`nntp-record-commands`

If non-`nil`, `nntp` will log all commands it sends to the NNTP server (along with a timestamp) in the `*nntp-log*` buffer. This is useful if you are debugging a Gnus/NNTP connection that doesn't seem to work.

`nntp-open-connection-function`

It is possible to customize how the connection to the nntp server will be opened. If you specify an `nntp-open-connection-function` parameter, Gnus will use that function to establish the connection. Seven pre-made functions are supplied. These functions can be grouped in two categories: direct connection functions (four pre-made), and indirect ones (three pre-made).

`nntp-never-echoes-commands`

Non-`nil` means the nntp server never echoes commands. It is reported that some nntps server doesn't echo commands. So, you may want to set this to non-`nil` in the method for such a server setting `nntp-open-connection-function` to `nntp-open-ssl-stream` for example. The default value is `nil`. Note that the `nntp-open-connection-functions-never-echo-commands` variable overrides the `nil` value of this variable.

`nntp-open-connection-functions-never-echo-commands`

> List of functions that never echo commands. Add or set a function which you set to `nntp-open-connection-function` to this list if it does not echo commands. Note that a non-`nil` value of the `nntp-never-echoes-commands` variable overrides this variable. The default value is (`nntp-open-network-stream`).

`nntp-prepare-post-hook`

> A hook run just before posting an article. If there is no `Message-ID` header in the article and the news server provides the recommended ID, it will be added to the article before running this hook. It is useful to make `Cancel-Lock` headers even if you inhibit Gnus to add a `Message-ID` header, you could say:

> ```
> (add-hook 'nntp-prepare-post-hook 'canlock-insert-header)
> ```

> Note that not all servers support the recommended ID. This works for INN versions 2.3.0 and later, for instance.

`nntp-server-list-active-group`

> If `nil`, then always use 'GROUP' instead of 'LIST ACTIVE'. This is usually slower, but on misconfigured servers that don't update their active files often, this can help.

6.2.1.1 Direct Functions

These functions are called direct because they open a direct connection between your machine and the NNTP server. The behavior of these functions is also affected by commonly understood variables (see Section 6.2.1.3 [Common Variables], page 147).

`nntp-open-network-stream`

> This is the default, and simply connects to some port or other on the remote system. If both Emacs and the server supports it, the connection will be upgraded to an encrypted STARTTLS connection automatically.

`network-only`

> The same as the above, but don't do automatic STARTTLS upgrades.

`nntp-open-tls-stream`

> Opens a connection to a server over a *secure* channel. To use this you must have GnuTLS installed. You then define a server as follows:

> ```
> ;; "nntps" is port 563 and is predefined in our /etc/services
> ;; however, 'gnutls-cli -p' doesn't like named ports.
> ;;
> (nntp "snews.bar.com"
>       (nntp-open-connection-function nntp-open-tls-stream)
>       (nntp-port-number 563)
>       (nntp-address "snews.bar.com"))
> ```

`nntp-open-ssl-stream`

> Opens a connection to a server over a *secure* channel. To use this you must have OpenSSL installed. You then define a server as follows:

> ```
> ;; "snews" is port 563 and is predefined in our /etc/services
> ```

```
;; however, 'openssl s_client -port' doesn't like named ports.
;;
(nntp "snews.bar.com"
      (nntp-open-connection-function nntp-open-ssl-stream)
      (nntp-port-number 563)
      (nntp-address "snews.bar.com"))
```

nntp-open-netcat-stream

Opens a connection to an NNTP server using the `netcat` program. You might wonder why this function exists, since we have the default `nntp-open-network-stream` which would do the job. (One of) the reason(s) is that if you are behind a firewall but have direct connections to the outside world thanks to a command wrapper like `runsocks`, you can use it like this:

```
(nntp "socksified"
      (nntp-pre-command "runsocks")
      (nntp-open-connection-function nntp-open-netcat-stream)
      (nntp-address "the.news.server"))
```

With the default method, you would need to wrap your whole Emacs session, which is not a good idea.

nntp-open-telnet-stream

Like `nntp-open-netcat-stream`, but uses `telnet` rather than `netcat`. `telnet` is a bit less robust because of things like line-end-conversion, but sometimes netcat is simply not available. The previous example would turn into:

```
(nntp "socksified"
      (nntp-pre-command "runsocks")
      (nntp-open-connection-function nntp-open-telnet-stream)
      (nntp-address "the.news.server")
      (nntp-end-of-line "\n"))
```

6.2.1.2 Indirect Functions

These functions are called indirect because they connect to an intermediate host before actually connecting to the NNTP server. All of these functions and related variables are also said to belong to the "via" family of connection: they're all prefixed with "via" to make things cleaner. The behavior of these functions is also affected by commonly understood variables (see Section 6.2.1.3 [Common Variables], page 147).

nntp-open-via-rlogin-and-netcat

Does an 'rlogin' on a remote system, and then uses `netcat` to connect to the real NNTP server from there. This is useful for instance if you need to connect to a firewall machine first.

nntp-open-via-rlogin-and-netcat-specific variables:

nntp-via-rlogin-command

Command used to log in on the intermediate host. The default is 'rsh', but 'ssh' is a popular alternative.

nntp-via-rlogin-command-switches

> List of strings to be used as the switches to `nntp-via-rlogin-command`. The default is `nil`. If you use 'ssh' for `nntp-via-rlogin-command`, you may set this to '`("-C")`' in order to compress all data connections.

nntp-open-via-rlogin-and-telnet

> Does essentially the same, but uses `telnet` instead of 'netcat' to connect to the real NNTP server from the intermediate host. `telnet` is a bit less robust because of things like line-end-conversion, but sometimes `netcat` is simply not available.

> `nntp-open-via-rlogin-and-telnet`-specific variables:

nntp-telnet-command

> Command used to connect to the real NNTP server from the intermediate host. The default is 'telnet'.

nntp-telnet-switches

> List of strings to be used as the switches to the `nntp-telnet-command` command. The default is `("-8")`.

nntp-via-rlogin-command

> Command used to log in on the intermediate host. The default is 'rsh', but 'ssh' is a popular alternative.

nntp-via-rlogin-command-switches

> List of strings to be used as the switches to `nntp-via-rlogin-command`. If you use 'ssh', you may need to set this to '`("-t" "-e" "none")`' or '`("-C" "-t" "-e" "none")`' if the telnet command requires a pseudo-tty allocation on an intermediate host. The default is `nil`.

> Note that you may want to change the value for `nntp-end-of-line` to '\n' (see Section 6.2.1.3 [Common Variables], page 147).

nntp-open-via-telnet-and-telnet

> Does essentially the same, but uses 'telnet' instead of 'rlogin' to connect to the intermediate host.

> `nntp-open-via-telnet-and-telnet`-specific variables:

nntp-via-telnet-command

> Command used to `telnet` the intermediate host. The default is 'telnet'.

nntp-via-telnet-switches

> List of strings to be used as the switches to the `nntp-via-telnet-command` command. The default is '`("-8")`'.

nntp-via-user-password

> Password to use when logging in on the intermediate host.

nntp-via-envuser
> If non-nil, the intermediate telnet session (client and server both) will support the ENVIRON option and not prompt for login name. This works for Solaris telnet, for instance.

nntp-via-shell-prompt
> Regexp matching the shell prompt on the intermediate host. The default is 'bash\\|\$ *\r?$\\|> *\r?'.

Note that you may want to change the value for nntp-end-of-line to '\n' (see Section 6.2.1.3 [Common Variables], page 147).

Here are some additional variables that are understood by all the above functions:

nntp-via-user-name
> User name to use when connecting to the intermediate host.

nntp-via-address
> Address of the intermediate host to connect to.

6.2.1.3 Common Variables

The following variables affect the behavior of all, or several of the pre-made connection functions. When not specified, all functions are affected (the values of the following variables will be used as the default if each virtual nntp server doesn't specify those server variables individually).

nntp-pre-command
> A command wrapper to use when connecting through a non native connection function (all except nntp-open-network-stream, nntp-open-tls-stream, and nntp-open-ssl-stream). This is where you would put a 'SOCKS' wrapper for instance.

nntp-address
> The address of the NNTP server.

nntp-port-number
> Port number to connect to the NNTP server. The default is 'nntp'. If you use NNTP over TLS/SSL, you may want to use integer ports rather than named ports (i.e., use '563' instead of 'snews' or 'nntps'), because external TLS/SSL tools may not work with named ports.

nntp-end-of-line
> String to use as end-of-line marker when talking to the NNTP server. This is '\r\n' by default, but should be '\n' when using a non native telnet connection function.

nntp-netcat-command
> Command to use when connecting to the NNTP server through 'netcat'. This is *not* for an intermediate host. This is just for the real NNTP server. The default is 'nc'.

nntp-netcat-switches
> A list of switches to pass to nntp-netcat-command. The default is '()'.

6.2.2 News Spool

Subscribing to a foreign group from the local spool is extremely easy, and might be useful, for instance, to speed up reading groups that contain very big articles—'alt.binaries.pictures.furniture', for instance.

Anyway, you just specify nnspool as the method and "" (or anything else) as the address.

If you have access to a local spool, you should probably use that as the native select method (see Section 1.1 [Finding the News], page 2). It is normally faster than using an nntp select method, but might not be. It depends. You just have to try to find out what's best at your site.

nnspool-inews-program
> Program used to post an article.

nnspool-inews-switches
> Parameters given to the inews program when posting an article.

nnspool-spool-directory
> Where nnspool looks for the articles. This is normally /usr/spool/news/.

nnspool-nov-directory
> Where nnspool will look for NOV files. This is normally
> /usr/spool/news/over.view/.

nnspool-lib-dir
> Where the news lib dir is (/usr/lib/news/ by default).

nnspool-active-file
> The name of the active file.

nnspool-newsgroups-file
> The name of the group descriptions file.

nnspool-history-file
> The name of the news history file.

nnspool-active-times-file
> The name of the active date file.

nnspool-nov-is-evil
> If non-nil, nnspool won't try to use any NOV files that it finds.

nnspool-sift-nov-with-sed
> If non-nil, which is the default, use sed to get the relevant portion from the overview file. If nil, nnspool will load the entire file into a buffer and process it there.

6.3 Using IMAP

The most popular mail backend is probably nnimap, which provides access to IMAP servers. IMAP servers store mail remotely, so the client doesn't store anything locally. This means that it's a convenient choice when you're reading your mail from different locations, or with different user agents.

6.3.1 Connecting to an IMAP Server

Connecting to an IMAP can be very easy. Type *B* in the group buffer, or (if your primary interest is reading email), say something like:

```
(setq gnus-select-method
      '(nnimap "imap.gmail.com"))
```

You'll be prompted for a user name and password. If you grow tired of that, then add the following to your ~/.authinfo file:

```
machine imap.gmail.com login <username> password <password> port imap
```

That should basically be it for most users.

6.3.2 Customizing the IMAP Connection

Here's an example method that's more complex:

```
(nnimap "imap.gmail.com"
        (nnimap-inbox "INBOX")
        (nnimap-split-methods default)
        (nnimap-expunge t)
        (nnimap-stream ssl))
```

nnimap-address

> The address of the server, like 'imap.gmail.com'.

nnimap-server-port

> If the server uses a non-standard port, that can be specified here. A typical port would be "imap" or "imaps".

nnimap-stream

> How nnimap should connect to the server. Possible values are:

> undecided
>> This is the default, and this first tries the ssl setting, and then tries the network setting.

> ssl   This uses standard TLS/SSL connections.

> network   Non-encrypted and unsafe straight socket connection, but will upgrade to encrypted STARTTLS if both Emacs and the server supports it.

> starttls Encrypted STARTTLS over the normal IMAP port.

> shell   If you need to tunnel via other systems to connect to the server, you can use this option, and customize nnimap-shell-program to be what you need.

nnimap-authenticator

> Some IMAP servers allow anonymous logins. In that case, this should be set to anonymous. If this variable isn't set, the normal login methods will be used. If you wish to specify a specific login method to be used, you can set this variable to either login (the traditional IMAP login method), plain or cram-md5.

`nnimap-expunge`

If non-`nil`, expunge articles after deleting them. This is always done if the server supports UID EXPUNGE, but it's not done by default on servers that doesn't support that command.

`nnimap-streaming`

Virtually all IMAP server support fast streaming of data. If you have problems connecting to the server, try setting this to `nil`.

`nnimap-fetch-partial-articles`

If non-`nil`, fetch partial articles from the server. If set to a string, then it's interpreted as a regexp, and parts that have matching types will be fetched. For instance, '`"text/"`' will fetch all textual parts, while leaving the rest on the server.

`nnimap-record-commands`

If non-`nil`, record all IMAP commands in the '`"*imap log*"`' buffer.

6.3.3 Client-Side IMAP Splitting

Many people prefer to do the sorting/splitting of mail into their mail boxes on the IMAP server. That way they don't have to download the mail they're not all that interested in.

If you do want to do client-side mail splitting, then the following variables are relevant:

`nnimap-inbox`

This is the IMAP mail box that will be scanned for new mail. This can also be a list of mail box names.

`nnimap-split-methods`

Uses the same syntax as `nnmail-split-methods` (see Section 6.4.3 [Splitting Mail], page 152), except the symbol `default`, which means that it should use the value of the `nnmail-split-methods` variable.

`nnimap-split-fancy`

Uses the same syntax as `nnmail-split-fancy`.

`nnimap-unsplittable-articles`

List of flag symbols to ignore when doing splitting. That is, articles that have these flags won't be considered when splitting. The default is '`(%Deleted %Seen)`'.

Here's a complete example `nnimap` backend with a client-side "fancy" splitting method:

```
(nnimap "imap.example.com"
        (nnimap-inbox "INBOX")
        (nnimap-split-methods
         (| ("MailScanner-SpamCheck" "spam" "spam.detected")
            (to "foo@bar.com" "foo")
            "undecided")))
```

6.4 Getting Mail

Reading mail with a newsreader—isn't that just plain WeIrD? But of course.

6.4.1 Mail in a Newsreader

If you are used to traditional mail readers, but have decided to switch to reading mail with Gnus, you may find yourself experiencing something of a culture shock.

Gnus does not behave like traditional mail readers. If you want to make it behave that way, you can, but it's an uphill battle.

Gnus, by default, handles all its groups using the same approach. This approach is very newsreaderly—you enter a group, see the new/unread messages, and when you read the messages, they get marked as read, and you don't see them any more. (Unless you explicitly ask for them.)

In particular, you do not do anything explicitly to delete messages.

Does this mean that all the messages that have been marked as read are deleted? How awful!

But, no, it means that old messages are *expired* according to some scheme or other. For news messages, the expire process is controlled by the news administrator; for mail, the expire process is controlled by you. The expire process for mail is covered in depth in Section 6.4.9 [Expiring Mail], page 168.

What many Gnus users find, after using it a while for both news and mail, is that the transport mechanism has very little to do with how they want to treat a message.

Many people subscribe to several mailing lists. These are transported via SMTP, and are therefore mail. But we might go for weeks without answering, or even reading these messages very carefully. We may not need to save them because if we should need to read one again, they are archived somewhere else.

Some people have local news groups which have only a handful of readers. These are transported via NNTP, and are therefore news. But we may need to read and answer a large fraction of the messages very carefully in order to do our work. And there may not be an archive, so we may need to save the interesting messages the same way we would personal mail.

The important distinction turns out to be not the transport mechanism, but other factors such as how interested we are in the subject matter, or how easy it is to retrieve the message if we need to read it again.

Gnus provides many options for sorting mail into "groups" which behave like newsgroups, and for treating each group (whether mail or news) differently.

Some users never get comfortable using the Gnus (ahem) paradigm and wish that Gnus should grow up and be a male, er, mail reader. It is possible to whip Gnus into a more mailreaderly being, but, as said before, it's not easy. People who prefer proper mail readers should try VM instead, which is an excellent, and proper, mail reader.

I don't mean to scare anybody off, but I want to make it clear that you may be required to learn a new way of thinking about messages. After you've been subjected to The Gnus Way, you will come to love it. I can guarantee it. (At least the guy who sold me the Emacs Subliminal Brain-Washing Functions that I've put into Gnus did guarantee it. You Will Be Assimilated. You Love Gnus. You Love The Gnus Mail Way. You Do.)

6.4.2 Getting Started Reading Mail

It's quite easy to use Gnus to read your new mail. You just plonk the mail back end of your choice into `gnus-secondary-select-methods`, and things will happen automatically.

For instance, if you want to use `nnml` (which is a "one file per mail" back end), you could put the following in your `~/.gnus.el` file:

```
(setq gnus-secondary-select-methods '((nnml "")))
```

Now, the next time you start Gnus, this back end will be queried for new articles, and it will move all the messages in your spool file to its directory, which is `~/Mail/` by default. The new group that will be created ('`mail.misc`') will be subscribed, and you can read it like any other group.

You will probably want to split the mail into several groups, though:

```
(setq nnmail-split-methods
      '(("junk" "^From:.*Lars Ingebrigtsen")
        ("crazy" "^Subject:.*die\\|^Organization:.*flabby")
        ("other" "")))
```

This will result in three new `nnml` mail groups being created: '`nnml:junk`', '`nnml:crazy`', and '`nnml:other`'. All the mail that doesn't fit into the first two groups will be placed in the last group.

This should be sufficient for reading mail with Gnus. You might want to give the other sections in this part of the manual a perusal, though. Especially see Section 6.4.13 [Choosing a Mail Back End], page 173 and see Section 6.4.9 [Expiring Mail], page 168.

6.4.3 Splitting Mail

The `nnmail-split-methods` variable says how the incoming mail is to be split into groups.

```
(setq nnmail-split-methods
      '(("mail.junk" "^From:.*Lars Ingebrigtsen")
        ("mail.crazy" "^Subject:.*die\\|^Organization:.*flabby")
        ("mail.other" "")))
```

This variable is a list of lists, where the first element of each of these lists is the name of the mail group (they do not have to be called something beginning with '`mail`', by the way), and the second element is a regular expression used on the header of each mail to determine if it belongs in this mail group. The first string may contain '`\\1`' forms, like the ones used by `replace-match` to insert sub-expressions from the matched text. For instance:

```
("list.\\1" "From:.* \\(.*\\)-list@majordomo.com")
```

In that case, `nnmail-split-lowercase-expanded` controls whether the inserted text should be made lowercase. See Section 6.4.6 [Fancy Mail Splitting], page 162.

The second element can also be a function. In that case, it will be called narrowed to the headers with the first element of the rule as the argument. It should return a non-`nil` value if it thinks that the mail belongs in that group.

The last of these groups should always be a general one, and the regular expression should *always* be '`""`' so that it matches any mails that haven't been matched by any of the other regexps. (These rules are processed from the beginning of the alist toward the end. The first rule to make a match will "win", unless you have crossposting enabled.

In that case, all matching rules will "win".) If no rule matched, the mail will end up in the 'bogus' group. When new groups are created by splitting mail, you may want to run gnus-group-find-new-groups to see the new groups. This also applies to the 'bogus' group.

If you like to tinker with this yourself, you can set this variable to a function of your choice. This function will be called without any arguments in a buffer narrowed to the headers of an incoming mail message. The function should return a list of group names that it thinks should carry this mail message.

This variable can also be a fancy split method. For the syntax, see Section 6.4.6 [Fancy Mail Splitting], page 162.

Note that the mail back ends are free to maul the poor, innocent, incoming headers all they want to. They all add Lines headers; some add X-Gnus-Group headers; most rename the Unix mbox From<SPACE> line to something else.

The mail back ends all support cross-posting. If several regexps match, the mail will be "cross-posted" to all those groups. nnmail-crosspost says whether to use this mechanism or not. Note that no articles are crossposted to the general ('""') group.

nnmh and nnml makes crossposts by creating hard links to the crossposted articles. However, not all file systems support hard links. If that's the case for you, set nnmail-crosspost-link-function to copy-file. (This variable is add-name-to-file by default.)

If you wish to see where the previous mail split put the messages, you can use the *M-x nnmail-split-history* command. If you wish to see where re-spooling messages would put the messages, you can use gnus-summary-respool-trace and related commands (see Section 3.26 [Mail Group Commands], page 107).

Header lines longer than the value of nnmail-split-header-length-limit are excluded from the split function.

By default, splitting does not decode headers, so you can not match on non-ASCII strings. But it is useful if you want to match articles based on the raw header data. To enable it, set the nnmail-mail-splitting-decodes variable to a non-nil value. In addition, the value of the nnmail-mail-splitting-charset variable is used for decoding non-MIME encoded string when nnmail-mail-splitting-decodes is non-nil. The default value is nil which means not to decode non-MIME encoded string. A suitable value for you will be undecided or be the charset used normally in mails you are interested in.

By default, splitting is performed on all incoming messages. If you specify a directory entry for the variable mail-sources (see Section 6.4.4.1 [Mail Source Specifiers], page 154), however, then splitting does *not* happen by default. You can set the variable nnmail-resplit-incoming to a non-nil value to make splitting happen even in this case. (This variable has no effect on other kinds of entries.)

Gnus gives you all the opportunity you could possibly want for shooting yourself in the foot. Let's say you create a group that will contain all the mail you get from your boss. And then you accidentally unsubscribe from the group. Gnus will still put all the mail from your boss in the unsubscribed group, and so, when your boss mails you "Have that report ready by Monday or you're fired!", you'll never see it and, come Tuesday. you'll still believe that you're gainfully employed while you really should be out collecting empty bottles to save up for next month's rent money.

6.4.4 Mail Sources

Mail can be gotten from many different sources—the mail spool, from a POP mail server, from a procmail directory, or from a maildir, for instance.

6.4.4.1 Mail Source Specifiers

You tell Gnus how to fetch mail by setting `mail-sources` (see Section 6.4.4.4 [Fetching Mail], page 160) to a *mail source specifier*.

Here's an example:

```
(pop :server "pop3.mailserver.com" :user "myname")
```

As can be observed, a mail source specifier is a list where the first element is a *mail source type*, followed by an arbitrary number of *keywords*. Keywords that are not explicitly specified are given default values.

The `mail-sources` is global for all mail groups. You can specify an additional mail source for a particular group by including the `group` mail specifier in `mail-sources`, and setting a `mail-source` group parameter (see Section 2.10 [Group Parameters], page 22) specifying a single mail source. When this is used, `mail-sources` is typically just `(group)`; the `mail-source` parameter for a group might look like this:

```
(mail-source . (file :path "home/user/spools/foo.spool"))
```

This means that the group's (and only this group's) messages will be fetched from the spool file '/user/spools/foo.spool'.

The following mail source types are available:

file   Get mail from a single file; typically from the mail spool.

            Keywords:

            :path   The file name. Defaults to the value of the MAIL environment vari-
                        able or the value of `rmail-spool-directory` (usually something
                        like /usr/mail/spool/user-name).

            :prescript
            :postscript
                        Script run before/after fetching mail.

            An example file mail source:

```
(file :path "/usr/spool/mail/user-name")
```

            Or using the default file name:

```
(file)
```

            If the mail spool file is not located on the local machine, it's best to use POP or
            IMAP or the like to fetch the mail. You can not use ange-ftp file names here—it
            has no way to lock the mail spool while moving the mail.

            If it's impossible to set up a proper server, you can use ssh instead.

```
(setq mail-sources
      '((file :prescript "ssh host bin/getmail >%t")))
```

            The 'getmail' script would look something like the following:

```
#!/bin/sh
#  getmail - move mail from spool to stdout
#  flu@iki.fi

MOVEMAIL=/usr/lib/emacs/20.3/i386-redhat-linux/movemail
TMP=$HOME/Mail/tmp
rm -f $TMP; $MOVEMAIL $MAIL $TMP >/dev/null && cat $TMP
```

Alter this script to fit the 'movemail' and temporary file you want to use.

directory

Get mail from several files in a directory. This is typically used when you have procmail split the incoming mail into several files. That is, there is a one-to-one correspondence between files in that directory and groups, so that mail from the file `foo.bar.spool` will be put in the group `foo.bar`. (You can change the suffix to be used instead of `.spool`.) Setting `nnmail-scan-directory-mail-source-once` to non-nil forces Gnus to scan the mail source only once. This is particularly useful if you want to scan mail groups at a specified level.

There is also the variable `nnmail-resplit-incoming`, if you set that to a non-nil value, then the normal splitting process is applied to all the files from the directory, Section 6.4.3 [Splitting Mail], page 152.

Keywords:

:path   The name of the directory where the files are. There is no default value.

:suffix   Only files ending with this suffix are used. The default is '`.spool`'.

:predicate
           Only files that have this predicate return non-`nil` are returned. The default is `identity`. This is used as an additional filter—only files that have the right suffix *and* satisfy this predicate are considered.

:prescript
:postscript
           Script run before/after fetching mail.

An example directory mail source:

```
(directory :path "/home/user-name/procmail-dir/"
           :suffix ".prcml")
```

pop   Get mail from a POP server.

Keywords:

:server   The name of the POP server. The default is taken from the `MAILHOST` environment variable.

:port   The port number of the POP server. This can be a number (e.g., ':port 1234') or a string (e.g., ':port "pop3"'). If it is a string, it should be a service name as listed in `/etc/services` on Unix systems. The default is '`"pop3"`'. On some systems you might need to specify it as '`"pop-3"`' instead.

:user   The user name to give to the POP server. The default is the login
               name.

:password
               The password to give to the POP server. If not specified, the user
               is prompted.

:program   The program to use to fetch mail from the POP server. This should
               be a `format`-like string. Here's an example:

                   `fetchmail %u@%s -P %p %t`

               The valid format specifier characters are:

               't'   The name of the file the mail is to be moved to. This
                                must always be included in this string.

               's'   The name of the server.

               'P'   The port number of the server.

               'u'   The user name to use.

               'p'   The password to use.

               The values used for these specs are taken from the values you give
               the corresponding keywords.

:prescript
               A script to be run before fetching the mail. The syntax is the same
               as the :program keyword. This can also be a function to be run.

               One popular way to use this is to set up an SSH tunnel to access
               the POP server. Here's an example:

```
(pop :server "127.0.0.1"
     :port 1234
     :user "foo"
     :password "secret"
     :prescript
     "nohup ssh -f -L 1234:pop.server:110
     remote.host sleep 3600 &")
```

:postscript
               A script to be run after fetching the mail. The syntax is the same
               as the :program keyword. This can also be a function to be run.

:function
               The function to use to fetch mail from the POP server. The function
               is called with one parameter—the name of the file where the mail
               should be moved to.

:authentication
               This can be either the symbol **password** or the symbol **apop** and
               says what authentication scheme to use. The default is **password**.

:leave   Non-nil if the mail is to be left on the POP server after fetching. Only the built-in pop3-movemail program (the default) supports this keyword.

If this is a number, leave mails on the server for this many days since you first checked new mails. In that case, mails once fetched will never be fetched again by the UIDL control. If this is nil (the default), mails will be deleted on the server right after fetching. If this is neither nil nor a number, all mails will be left on the server, and you will end up getting the same mails again and again.

The pop3-uidl-file variable specifies the file to which the UIDL data are locally stored. The default value is ~/.pop3-uidl.

Note that POP servers maintain no state information between sessions, so what the client believes is there and what is actually there may not match up. If they do not, then you may get duplicate mails or the whole thing can fall apart and leave you with a corrupt mailbox.

If the :program and :function keywords aren't specified, pop3-movemail will be used.

Here are some examples for getting mail from a POP server.

Fetch from the default POP server, using the default user name, and default fetcher:

```
(pop)
```

Fetch from a named server with a named user and password:

```
(pop :server "my.pop.server"
     :user "user-name" :password "secret")
```

Leave mails on the server for 14 days:

```
(pop :server "my.pop.server"
     :user "user-name" :password "secret"
     :leave 14)
```

Use 'movemail' to move the mail:

```
(pop :program "movemail po:%u %t %p")
```

maildir   Get mail from a maildir. This is a type of mailbox that is supported by at least qmail and postfix, where each file in a special directory contains exactly one mail.

Keywords:

:path   The name of the directory where the mails are stored. The default is taken from the MAILDIR environment variable or ~/Maildir/.

:subdirs   The subdirectories of the Maildir. The default is '("new" "cur")'.

You can also get mails from remote hosts (because maildirs don't suffer from locking problems).

Two example maildir mail sources:

```
(maildir :path "/home/user-name/Maildir/"
         :subdirs ("cur" "new"))
(maildir :path "/user@remotehost.org:~/Maildir/"
         :subdirs ("new"))
```

imap   Get mail from a IMAP server. If you don't want to use IMAP as intended, as a network mail reading protocol (i.e., with nnimap), for some reason or other, Gnus let you treat it similar to a POP server and fetches articles from a given IMAP mailbox. See Section 6.3 [Using IMAP], page 148, for more information.

Keywords:

:server   The name of the IMAP server. The default is taken from the MAILHOST environment variable.

:port   The port number of the IMAP server. The default is '143', or '993' for TLS/SSL connections.

:user   The user name to give to the IMAP server. The default is the login name.

:password

            The password to give to the IMAP server. If not specified, the user is prompted.

:stream   What stream to use for connecting to the server, this is one of the symbols in imap-stream-alist. Right now, this means 'gssapi', 'kerberos4', 'starttls', 'tls', 'ssl', 'shell' or the default 'network'.

:authentication

            Which authenticator to use for authenticating to the server, this is one of the symbols in imap-authenticator-alist. Right now, this means 'gssapi', 'kerberos4', 'digest-md5', 'cram-md5', 'anonymous' or the default 'login'.

:program   When using the 'shell' :stream, the contents of this variable is mapped into the imap-shell-program variable. This should be a format-like string (or list of strings). Here's an example:

                ssh %s imapd

            Make sure nothing is interfering with the output of the program, e.g., don't forget to redirect the error output to the void. The valid format specifier characters are:

            's'   The name of the server.

            'l'   User name from imap-default-user.

            'p'   The port number of the server.

            The values used for these specs are taken from the values you give the corresponding keywords.

:mailbox   The name of the mailbox to get mail from. The default is 'INBOX' which normally is the mailbox which receives incoming mail.

`:predicate`
> The predicate used to find articles to fetch. The default, 'UNSEEN UNDELETED', is probably the best choice for most people, but if you sometimes peek in your mailbox with a IMAP client and mark some articles as read (or; SEEN) you might want to set this to '1:*'. Then all articles in the mailbox is fetched, no matter what. For a complete list of predicates, see RFC 2060 section 6.4.4.

`:fetchflag`
> How to flag fetched articles on the server, the default '\Deleted' will mark them as deleted, an alternative would be '\Seen' which would simply mark them as read. These are the two most likely choices, but more flags are defined in RFC 2060 section 2.3.2.

`:dontexpunge`
> If non-nil, don't remove all articles marked as deleted in the mailbox after finishing the fetch.

> An example IMAP mail source:

```
(imap :server "mail.mycorp.com"
      :stream kerberos4
      :fetchflag "\\Seen")
```

group   Get the actual mail source from the `mail-source` group parameter, See Section 2.10 [Group Parameters], page 22.

Common Keywords
> Common keywords can be used in any type of mail source.

> Keywords:

`:plugged` If non-nil, fetch the mail even when Gnus is unplugged. If you use directory source to get mail, you can specify it as in this example:

```
(setq mail-sources
      '((directory :path "/home/pavel/.Spool/"
                   :suffix ""
                   :plugged t)))
```
> Gnus will then fetch your mail even when you are unplugged. This is useful when you use local mail and news.

6.4.4.2 Function Interface

Some of the above keywords specify a Lisp function to be executed. For each keyword `:foo`, the Lisp variable `foo` is bound to the value of the keyword while the function is executing. For example, consider the following mail-source setting:

```
(setq mail-sources '((pop :user "jrl"
                          :server "pophost" :function fetchfunc)))
```

While the function `fetchfunc` is executing, the symbol `user` is bound to "jrl", and the symbol `server` is bound to "pophost". The symbols `port`, `password`, `program`, `prescript`, `postscript`, `function`, and `authentication` are also bound (to their default values).

See above for a list of keywords for each type of mail source.

6.4.4.3 Mail Source Customization

The following is a list of variables that influence how the mail is fetched. You would normally not need to set or change any of these variables.

`mail-source-crash-box`

> File where mail will be stored while processing it. The default is
> `~/.emacs-mail-crash-box`.

`mail-source-delete-incoming`

> If non-`nil`, delete incoming files after handling them. If `t`, delete the files immediately, if `nil`, never delete any files. If a positive number, delete files older than number of days (the deletion will only happen when receiving new mail). You may also set `mail-source-delete-incoming` to `nil` and call `mail-source-delete-old-incoming` from a hook or interactively. `mail-source-delete-incoming` defaults to `10` in alpha Gnusae and `2` in released Gnusae. See Section 11.2.6 [Gnus Development], page 305.

`mail-source-delete-old-incoming-confirm`

> If non-`nil`, ask for confirmation before deleting old incoming files. This variable only applies when `mail-source-delete-incoming` is a positive number.

`mail-source-ignore-errors`

> If non-`nil`, ignore errors when reading mail from a mail source.

`mail-source-directory`

> Directory where incoming mail source files (if any) will be stored. The default is `~/Mail/`. At present, the only thing this is used for is to say where the incoming files will be stored if the variable `mail-source-delete-incoming` is `nil` or a number.

`mail-source-incoming-file-prefix`

> Prefix for file name for storing incoming mail. The default is `Incoming`, in which case files will end up with names like `Incoming30630D_` or `Incoming298602ZD`. This is really only relevant if `mail-source-delete-incoming` is `nil` or a number.

`mail-source-default-file-modes`

> All new mail files will get this file mode. The default is `#o600`.

`mail-source-movemail-program`

> If non-`nil`, name of program for fetching new mail. If `nil`, `movemail` in *exec-directory*.

6.4.4.4 Fetching Mail

The way to actually tell Gnus where to get new mail from is to set `mail-sources` to a list of mail source specifiers (see Section 6.4.4.1 [Mail Source Specifiers], page 154).

If this variable is `nil`, the mail back ends will never attempt to fetch mail by themselves.

If you want to fetch mail both from your local spool as well as a POP mail server, you'd say something like:

```
(setq mail-sources
```

```
        '((file)
          (pop :server "pop3.mail.server"
               :password "secret")))
```

Or, if you don't want to use any of the keyword defaults:

```
    (setq mail-sources
          '((file :path "/var/spool/mail/user-name")
            (pop :server "pop3.mail.server"
                 :user "user-name"
                 :port "pop3"
                 :password "secret")))
```

When you use a mail back end, Gnus will slurp all your mail from your inbox and plonk it down in your home directory. Gnus doesn't move any mail if you're not using a mail back end—you have to do a lot of magic invocations first. At the time when you have finished drawing the pentagram, lightened the candles, and sacrificed the goat, you really shouldn't be too surprised when Gnus moves your mail.

6.4.5 Mail Back End Variables

These variables are (for the most part) pertinent to all the various mail back ends.

nnmail-read-incoming-hook

> The mail back ends all call this hook after reading new mail. You can use this hook to notify any mail watch programs, if you want to.

nnmail-split-hook

> Hook run in the buffer where the mail headers of each message is kept just before the splitting based on these headers is done. The hook is free to modify the buffer contents in any way it sees fit—the buffer is discarded after the splitting has been done, and no changes performed in the buffer will show up in any files. gnus-article-decode-encoded-words is one likely function to add to this hook.

nnmail-pre-get-new-mail-hook
nnmail-post-get-new-mail-hook

> These are two useful hooks executed when treating new incoming mail—nnmail-pre-get-new-mail-hook (is called just before starting to handle the new mail) and nnmail-post-get-new-mail-hook (is called when the mail handling is done). Here's and example of using these two hooks to change the default file modes the new mail files get:

```
        (add-hook 'nnmail-pre-get-new-mail-hook
                  (lambda () (set-default-file-modes #o700)))

        (add-hook 'nnmail-post-get-new-mail-hook
                  (lambda () (set-default-file-modes #o775)))
```

nnmail-use-long-file-names

> If non-nil, the mail back ends will use long file and directory names. Groups like 'mail.misc' will end up in directories (assuming use of nnml back end) or files (assuming use of nnfolder back end) like mail.misc. If it is nil, the same group will end up in mail/misc.

`nnmail-delete-file-function`
> Function called to delete files. It is `delete-file` by default.

`nnmail-cache-accepted-message-ids`
> If non-`nil`, put the `Message-IDs` of articles imported into the back end (via `Gcc`, for instance) into the mail duplication discovery cache. The default is `nil`.

`nnmail-cache-ignore-groups`
> This can be a regular expression or a list of regular expressions. Group names that match any of the regular expressions will never be recorded in the `Message-ID` cache.
>
> This can be useful, for example, when using Fancy Splitting (see Section 6.4.6 [Fancy Mail Splitting], page 162) together with the function `nnmail-split-fancy-with-parent`.

6.4.6 Fancy Mail Splitting

If the rather simple, standard method for specifying how to split mail doesn't allow you to do what you want, you can set `nnmail-split-methods` to `nnmail-split-fancy`. Then you can play with the `nnmail-split-fancy` variable.

Let's look at an example value of this variable first:

```
;; Messages from the mailer daemon are not crossposted to any of
;; the ordinary groups.  Warnings are put in a separate group
;; from real errors.
(| ("from" mail (| ("subject" "warn.*" "mail.warning")
                   "mail.misc"))
   ;; Non-error messages are crossposted to all relevant
   ;; groups, but we don't crosspost between the group for the
   ;; (ding) list and the group for other (ding) related mail.
   (& (| (any "ding@ifi\\.uio\\.no" "ding.list")
         ("subject" "ding" "ding.misc"))
      ;; Other mailing lists...
      (any "procmail@informatik\\.rwth-aachen\\.de" "procmail.list")
      (any "SmartList@informatik\\.rwth-aachen\\.de" "SmartList.list")
      ;; Both lists below have the same suffix, so prevent
      ;; cross-posting to mkpkg.list of messages posted only to
      ;; the bugs- list, but allow cross-posting when the
      ;; message was really cross-posted.
      (any "bugs-mypackage@somewhere" "mypkg.bugs")
      (any "mypackage@somewhere" - "bugs-mypackage" "mypkg.list")
      ;; People...
      (any "larsi@ifi\\.uio\\.no" "people.Lars_Magne_Ingebrigtsen"))
   ;; Unmatched mail goes to the catch all group.
   "misc.misc")
```

This variable has the format of a *split*. A split is a (possibly) recursive structure where each split may contain other splits. Here are the possible split syntaxes:

group
> If the split is a string, that will be taken as a group name. Normal regexp match expansion will be done. See below for examples.

(`field value [- restrict [...] ] split [invert-partial]`)

The split can be a list containing at least three elements. If the first element *field* (a regexp matching a header) contains *value* (also a regexp) then store the message as specified by *split*.

If *restrict* (yet another regexp) matches some string after *field* and before the end of the matched *value*, the *split* is ignored. If none of the *restrict* clauses match, *split* is processed.

The last element *invert-partial* is optional. If it is non-nil, the match-partial-words behavior controlled by the variable `nnmail-split-fancy-match-partial-words` (see below) is be inverted. (New in Gnus 5.10.7)

(`| split ...`)

If the split is a list, and the first element is | (vertical bar), then process each *split* until one of them matches. A *split* is said to match if it will cause the mail message to be stored in one or more groups.

(`& split ...`)

If the split is a list, and the first element is &, then process all *splits* in the list.

junk

If the split is the symbol junk, then don't save (i.e., delete) this message. Use with extreme caution.

(`: function arg1 arg2 ...`)

If the split is a list, and the first element is ':', then the second element will be called as a function with *args* given as arguments. The function should return a *split*.

For instance, the following function could be used to split based on the body of the messages:

```
(defun split-on-body ()
  (save-excursion
    (save-restriction
      (widen)
      (goto-char (point-min))
      (when (re-search-forward "Some.*string" nil t)
        "string.group"))))
```

The buffer is narrowed to the header of the message in question when *function* is run. That's why `(widen)` needs to be called after `save-excursion` and `save-restriction` in the example above. Also note that with the nnimap backend, message bodies will not be downloaded by default. You need to set `nnimap-split-download-body` to t to do that (see Section 6.3.3 [Client-Side IMAP Splitting], page 150).

(`! func split`)

If the split is a list, and the first element is !, then *split* will be processed, and *func* will be called as a function with the result of *split* as argument. *func* should return a split.

nil

If the split is nil, it is ignored.

In these splits, *field* must match a complete field name.

Normally, *value* in these splits must match a complete *word* according to the fundamental mode syntax table. In other words, all *value*'s will be implicitly surrounded by `\<...\>` markers, which are word delimiters. Therefore, if you use the following split, for example,

```
(any "joe" "joemail")
```

messages sent from 'joedavis@foo.org' will normally not be filed in 'joemail'. If you want to alter this behavior, you can use any of the following three ways:

1. You can set the `nnmail-split-fancy-match-partial-words` variable to non-`nil` in order to ignore word boundaries and instead the match becomes more like a grep. This variable controls whether partial words are matched during fancy splitting. The default value is `nil`.

   Note that it influences all *value*'s in your split rules.

2. *value* beginning with `.*` ignores word boundaries in front of a word. Similarly, if *value* ends with `.*`, word boundaries in the rear of a word will be ignored. For example, the *value* `"@example\\.com"` does not match 'foo@example.com' but `".*@example\\.com"` does.

3. You can set the *invert-partial* flag in your split rules of the '(*field value* ...)' types, aforementioned in this section. If the flag is set, word boundaries on both sides of a word are ignored even if `nnmail-split-fancy-match-partial-words` is `nil`. Contrarily, if the flag is set, word boundaries are not ignored even if `nnmail-split-fancy-match-partial-words` is non-`nil`. (New in Gnus 5.10.7)

field and *value* can also be Lisp symbols, in that case they are expanded as specified by the variable `nnmail-split-abbrev-alist`. This is an alist of cons cells, where the CAR of a cell contains the key, and the CDR contains the associated value. Predefined entries in `nnmail-split-abbrev-alist` include:

from   Matches the 'From', 'Sender' and 'Resent-From' fields.

to   Matches the 'To', 'Cc', 'Apparently-To', 'Resent-To' and 'Resent-Cc' fields.

any   Is the union of the `from` and `to` entries.

`nnmail-split-fancy-syntax-table` is the syntax table in effect when all this splitting is performed.

If you want to have Gnus create groups dynamically based on some information in the headers (i.e., do `replace-match`-like substitutions in the group names), you can say things like:

```
(any "debian-\\b\\(\\w+\\)@lists.debian.org" "mail.debian.\\1")
```

In this example, messages sent to 'debian-foo@lists.debian.org' will be filed in 'mail.debian.foo'.

If the string contains the element '\\&', then the previously matched string will be substituted. Similarly, the elements '\\1' up to '\\9' will be substituted with the text matched by the groupings 1 through 9.

Where `nnmail-split-lowercase-expanded` controls whether the lowercase of the matched string should be used for the substitution. Setting it as non-`nil` is useful to avoid

the creation of multiple groups when users send to an address using different case (i.e., mailing-list@domain vs Mailing-List@Domain). The default value is `t`.

`nnmail-split-fancy-with-parent` is a function which allows you to split followups into the same groups their parents are in. Sometimes you can't make splitting rules for all your mail. For example, your boss might send you personal mail regarding different projects you are working on, and as you can't tell your boss to put a distinguishing string into the subject line, you have to resort to manually moving the messages into the right group. With this function, you only have to do it once per thread.

To use this feature, you have to set `nnmail-treat-duplicates` and `nnmail-cache-accepted-message-ids` to a non-`nil` value. And then you can include `nnmail-split-fancy-with-parent` using the colon feature, like so:

```
(setq nnmail-treat-duplicates 'warn      ; or delete
      nnmail-cache-accepted-message-ids t
      nnmail-split-fancy
      '(| (: nnmail-split-fancy-with-parent)
          ;; other splits go here
        ))
```

This feature works as follows: when `nnmail-treat-duplicates` is non-`nil`, Gnus records the message id of every message it sees in the file specified by the variable `nnmail-message-id-cache-file`, together with the group it is in (the group is omitted for non-mail messages). When mail splitting is invoked, the function `nnmail-split-fancy-with-parent` then looks at the References (and In-Reply-To) header of each message to split and searches the file specified by `nnmail-message-id-cache-file` for the message ids. When it has found a parent, it returns the corresponding group name unless the group name matches the regexp `nnmail-split-fancy-with-parent-ignore-groups`. It is recommended that you set `nnmail-message-id-cache-length` to a somewhat higher number than the default so that the message ids are still in the cache. (A value of 5000 appears to create a file some 300 kBytes in size.) When `nnmail-cache-accepted-message-ids` is non-`nil`, Gnus also records the message ids of moved articles, so that the followup messages goes into the new group.

Also see the variable `nnmail-cache-ignore-groups` if you don't want certain groups to be recorded in the cache. For example, if all outgoing messages are written to an "outgoing" group, you could set `nnmail-cache-ignore-groups` to match that group name. Otherwise, answers to all your messages would end up in the "outgoing" group.

6.4.7 Group Mail Splitting

If you subscribe to dozens of mailing lists but you don't want to maintain mail splitting rules manually, group mail splitting is for you. You just have to set `to-list` and/or `to-address` in group parameters or group customization and set `nnmail-split-methods` to `gnus-group-split`. This splitting function will scan all groups for those parameters and split mail accordingly, i.e., messages posted from or to the addresses specified in the parameters `to-list` or `to-address` of a mail group will be stored in that group.

Sometimes, mailing lists have multiple addresses, and you may want mail splitting to recognize them all: just set the `extra-aliases` group parameter to the list of additional addresses and it's done. If you'd rather use a regular expression, set `split-regexp`.

All these parameters in a group will be used to create an `nnmail-split-fancy` split, in which the *field* is 'any', the *value* is a single regular expression that matches `to-list`, `to-address`, all of `extra-aliases` and all matches of `split-regexp`, and the *split* is the name of the group. *restricts* are also supported: just set the `split-exclude` parameter to a list of regular expressions.

If you can't get the right split to be generated using all these parameters, or you just need something fancier, you can set the parameter `split-spec` to an `nnmail-split-fancy` split. In this case, all other aforementioned parameters will be ignored by `gnus-group-split`. In particular, `split-spec` may be set to `nil`, in which case the group will be ignored by `gnus-group-split`.

`gnus-group-split` will do cross-posting on all groups that match, by defining a single & fancy split containing one split for each group. If a message doesn't match any split, it will be stored in the group named in `gnus-group-split-default-catch-all-group`, unless some group has `split-spec` set to `catch-all`, in which case that group is used as the catch-all group. Even though this variable is often used just to name a group, it may also be set to an arbitrarily complex fancy split (after all, a group name is a fancy split), and this may be useful to split mail that doesn't go to any mailing list to personal mail folders. Note that this fancy split is added as the last element of a | split list that also contains a & split with the rules extracted from group parameters.

It's time for an example. Assume the following group parameters have been defined:

```
nnml:mail.bar:
((to-address . "bar@femail.com")
 (split-regexp . ".*@femail\\.com"))
nnml:mail.foo:
((to-list . "foo@nowhere.gov")
 (extra-aliases "foo@localhost" "foo-redist@home")
 (split-exclude "bugs-foo" "rambling-foo")
 (admin-address . "foo-request@nowhere.gov"))
nnml:mail.others:
((split-spec . catch-all))
```

Setting `nnmail-split-methods` to `gnus-group-split` will behave as if `nnmail-split-fancy` had been selected and variable `nnmail-split-fancy` had been set as follows:

```
(| (& (any "\\(bar@femail\\.com\\|.*@femail\\.com\\)" "mail.bar")
      (any "\\(foo@nowhere\\.gov\\|foo@localhost\\|foo-redist@home\\)"
           - "bugs-foo" - "rambling-foo" "mail.foo"))
   "mail.others")
```

If you'd rather not use group splitting for all your mail groups, you may use it for only some of them, by using `nnmail-split-fancy` splits like this:

```
(: gnus-group-split-fancy groups no-crosspost catch-all)
```

groups may be a regular expression or a list of group names whose parameters will be scanned to generate the output split. *no-crosspost* can be used to disable cross-posting; in this case, a single | split will be output. *catch-all* is the fall back fancy split, used like `gnus-group-split-default-catch-all-group`. If *catch-all* is nil, or if `split-regexp` matches the empty string in any selected group, no catch-all split will be issued. Otherwise, if some group has `split-spec` set to `catch-all`, this group will override the value of the *catch-all* argument.

Unfortunately, scanning all groups and their parameters can be quite slow, especially considering that it has to be done for every message. But don't despair! The function `gnus-group-split-setup` can be used to enable `gnus-group-split` in a much more efficient way. It sets `nnmail-split-methods` to `nnmail-split-fancy` and sets `nnmail-split-fancy` to the split produced by `gnus-group-split-fancy`. Thus, the group parameters are only scanned once, no matter how many messages are split.

However, if you change group parameters, you'd have to update `nnmail-split-fancy` manually. You can do it by running `gnus-group-split-update`. If you'd rather have it updated automatically, just tell `gnus-group-split-setup` to do it for you. For example, add to your `~/.gnus.el`:

        (gnus-group-split-setup *auto-update* *catch-all*)

If *auto-update* is non-nil, `gnus-group-split-update` will be added to `nnmail-pre-get-new-mail-hook`, so you won't ever have to worry about updating `nnmail-split-fancy` again. If you don't omit *catch-all* (it's optional, equivalent to `nil`), `gnus-group-split-default-catch-all-group` will be set to its value.

Because you may want to change `nnmail-split-fancy` after it is set by `gnus-group-split-update`, this function will run `gnus-group-split-updated-hook` just before finishing.

6.4.8 Incorporating Old Mail

Most people have lots of old mail stored in various file formats. If you have set up Gnus to read mail using one of the spiffy Gnus mail back ends, you'll probably wish to have that old mail incorporated into your mail groups.

Doing so can be quite easy.

To take an example: You're reading mail using **nnml** (see Section 6.4.13.3 [Mail Spool], page 174), and have set `nnmail-split-methods` to a satisfactory value (see Section 6.4.3 [Splitting Mail], page 152). You have an old Unix mbox file filled with important, but old, mail. You want to move it into your **nnml** groups.

Here's how:

1. Go to the group buffer.
2. Type *G f* and give the file name to the mbox file when prompted to create an **nndoc** group from the mbox file (see Section 2.9 [Foreign Groups], page 20).
3. Type *SPACE* to enter the newly created group.
4. Type *M P b* to process-mark all articles in this group's buffer (see Section 3.7.6 [Setting Process Marks], page 62).
5. Type *B r* to respool all the process-marked articles, and answer 'nnml' when prompted (see Section 3.26 [Mail Group Commands], page 107).

All the mail messages in the mbox file will now also be spread out over all your **nnml** groups. Try entering them and check whether things have gone without a glitch. If things look ok, you may consider deleting the mbox file, but I wouldn't do that unless I was absolutely sure that all the mail has ended up where it should be.

Respooling is also a handy thing to do if you're switching from one mail back end to another. Just respool all the mail in the old mail groups using the new mail back end.

6.4.9 Expiring Mail

Traditional mail readers have a tendency to remove mail articles when you mark them as read, in some way. Gnus takes a fundamentally different approach to mail reading.

Gnus basically considers mail just to be news that has been received in a rather peculiar manner. It does not think that it has the power to actually change the mail, or delete any mail messages. If you enter a mail group, and mark articles as "read", or kill them in some other fashion, the mail articles will still exist on the system. I repeat: Gnus will not delete your old, read mail. Unless you ask it to, of course.

To make Gnus get rid of your unwanted mail, you have to mark the articles as *expirable*. (With the default key bindings, this means that you have to type *E*.) This does not mean that the articles will disappear right away, however. In general, a mail article will be deleted from your system if, 1) it is marked as expirable, AND 2) it is more than one week old. If you do not mark an article as expirable, it will remain on your system until hell freezes over. This bears repeating one more time, with some spurious capitalizations: IF you do NOT mark articles as EXPIRABLE, Gnus will NEVER delete those ARTICLES.

You do not have to mark articles as expirable by hand. Gnus provides two features, called "auto-expire" and "total-expire", that can help you with this. In a nutshell, "auto-expire" means that Gnus hits *E* for you when you select an article. And "total-expire" means that Gnus considers all articles as expirable that are read. So, in addition to the articles marked 'E', also the articles marked 'r', 'R', 'O', 'K', 'Y' (and so on) are considered expirable. `gnus-auto-expirable-marks` has the full list of these marks.

When should either auto-expire or total-expire be used? Most people who are subscribed to mailing lists split each list into its own group and then turn on auto-expire or total-expire for those groups. (See Section 6.4.3 [Splitting Mail], page 152, for more information on splitting each list into its own group.)

Which one is better, auto-expire or total-expire? It's not easy to answer. Generally speaking, auto-expire is probably faster. Another advantage of auto-expire is that you get more marks to work with: for the articles that are supposed to stick around, you can still choose between tick and dormant and read marks. But with total-expire, you only have dormant and ticked to choose from. The advantage of total-expire is that it works well with adaptive scoring (see Section 7.6 [Adaptive Scoring], page 224). Auto-expire works with normal scoring but not with adaptive scoring.

Groups that match the regular expression `gnus-auto-expirable-newsgroups` will have all articles that you read marked as expirable automatically. All articles marked as expirable have an 'E' in the first column in the summary buffer.

By default, if you have auto expiry switched on, Gnus will mark all the articles you read as expirable, no matter if they were read or unread before. To avoid having articles marked as read marked as expirable automatically, you can put something like the following in your `~/.gnus.el` file:

```
(remove-hook 'gnus-mark-article-hook
             'gnus-summary-mark-read-and-unread-as-read)
(add-hook 'gnus-mark-article-hook 'gnus-summary-mark-unread-as-read)
```

Note that making a group auto-expirable doesn't mean that all read articles are expired—only the articles marked as expirable will be expired. Also note that using the *d* command won't make articles expirable—only semi-automatic marking of articles as read will mark the articles as expirable in auto-expirable groups.

Let's say you subscribe to a couple of mailing lists, and you want the articles you have read to disappear after a while:

```
(setq gnus-auto-expirable-newsgroups
      "mail.nonsense-list\\|mail.nice-list")
```

Another way to have auto-expiry happen is to have the element `auto-expire` in the group parameters of the group.

If you use adaptive scoring (see Section 7.6 [Adaptive Scoring], page 224) and auto-expiring, you'll have problems. Auto-expiring and adaptive scoring don't really mix very well.

The `nnmail-expiry-wait` variable supplies the default time an expirable article has to live. Gnus starts counting days from when the message *arrived*, not from when it was sent. The default is seven days.

Gnus also supplies a function that lets you fine-tune how long articles are to live, based on what group they are in. Let's say you want to have one month expiry period in the 'mail.private' group, a one day expiry period in the 'mail.junk' group, and a six day expiry period everywhere else:

```
(setq nnmail-expiry-wait-function
      (lambda (group)
        (cond ((string= group "mail.private")
               31)
              ((string= group "mail.junk")
               1)
              ((string= group "important")
               'never)
              (t
               6))))
```

The group names this function is fed are "unadorned" group names—no 'nnml:' prefixes and the like.

The `nnmail-expiry-wait` variable and `nnmail-expiry-wait-function` function can either be a number (not necessarily an integer) or one of the symbols `immediate` or `never`.

You can also use the `expiry-wait` group parameter to selectively change the expiry period (see Section 2.10 [Group Parameters], page 22).

The normal action taken when expiring articles is to delete them. However, in some circumstances it might make more sense to move them to other groups instead of deleting them. The variable `nnmail-expiry-target` (and the `expiry-target` group parameter) controls this. The variable supplies a default value for all groups, which can be overridden for specific groups by the group parameter. default value is `delete`, but this can also be a string (which should be the name of the group the message should be moved to), or a function (which will be called in a buffer narrowed to the message in question, and with the name of the group being moved from as its parameter) which should return a target—either a group name or `delete`.

Here's an example for specifying a group name:

```
(setq nnmail-expiry-target "nnml:expired")
```

Gnus provides a function `nnmail-fancy-expiry-target` which will expire mail to groups according to the variable `nnmail-fancy-expiry-targets`. Here's an example:

```
(setq nnmail-expiry-target 'nnmail-fancy-expiry-target
      nnmail-fancy-expiry-targets
      '((to-from "boss" "nnfolder:Work")
        ("subject" "IMPORTANT" "nnfolder:IMPORTANT.%Y.%b")
        ("from" ".*" "nnfolder:Archive-%Y")))
```

With this setup, any mail that has IMPORTANT in its Subject header and was sent in the year YYYY and month MMM, will get expired to the group `nnfolder:IMPORTANT.YYYY.MMM`. If its From or To header contains the string `boss`, it will get expired to `nnfolder:Work`. All other mail will get expired to `nnfolder:Archive-YYYY`.

If `nnmail-keep-last-article` is non-`nil`, Gnus will never expire the final article in a mail newsgroup. This is to make life easier for procmail users.

By the way: That line up there, about Gnus never expiring non-expirable articles, is a lie. If you put `total-expire` in the group parameters, articles will not be marked as expirable, but all read articles will be put through the expiry process. Use with extreme caution. Even more dangerous is the `gnus-total-expirable-newsgroups` variable. All groups that match this regexp will have all read articles put through the expiry process, which means that *all* old mail articles in the groups in question will be deleted after a while. Use with extreme caution, and don't come crying to me when you discover that the regexp you used matched the wrong group and all your important mail has disappeared. Be a *man*! Or a *woman*! Whatever you feel more comfortable with! So there!

Most people make most of their mail groups total-expirable, though.

If `gnus-inhibit-user-auto-expire` is non-`nil`, user marking commands will not mark an article as expirable, even if the group has auto-expire turned on.

The expirable marks of articles will be removed when copying or moving them to a group in which auto-expire is not turned on. This is for preventing articles from being expired unintentionally. On the other hand, to a group that has turned auto-expire on, the expirable marks of articles that are copied or moved will not be changed by default. I.e., when copying or moving to such a group, articles that were expirable will be left expirable and ones that were not expirable will not be marked as expirable. So, even though in auto-expire groups, some articles will never get expired (unless you read them again). If you don't side with that behavior that unexpirable articles may be mixed into auto-expire groups, you can set `gnus-mark-copied-or-moved-articles-as-expirable` to a non-`nil` value. In that case, articles that have been read will be marked as expirable automatically when being copied or moved to a group that has auto-expire turned on. The default value is `nil`.

6.4.10 Washing Mail

Mailers and list servers are notorious for doing all sorts of really, really stupid things with mail. "Hey, RFC 822 doesn't explicitly prohibit us from adding the string wE aRe ElItE!!!!!!1!! to the end of all lines passing through our server, so let's do that!!!!1!" Yes, but RFC 822 wasn't designed to be read by morons. Things that were considered to be self-evident were not discussed. So. Here we are.

Case in point: The German version of Microsoft Exchange adds 'AW: ' to the subjects of replies instead of 'Re: '. I could pretend to be shocked and dismayed by this, but I haven't got the energy. It is to laugh.

Gnus provides a plethora of functions for washing articles while displaying them, but it might be nicer to do the filtering before storing the mail to disk. For that purpose, we have three hooks and various functions that can be put in these hooks.

`nnmail-prepare-incoming-hook`
> This hook is called before doing anything with the mail and is meant for grand, sweeping gestures. It is called in a buffer that contains all the new, incoming mail. Functions to be used include:
>
> `nnheader-ms-strip-cr`
> > Remove trailing carriage returns from each line. This is default on Emacs running on MS machines.

`nnmail-prepare-incoming-header-hook`
> This hook is called narrowed to each header. It can be used when cleaning up the headers. Functions that can be used include:
>
> `nnmail-remove-leading-whitespace`
> > Clear leading white space that "helpful" listservs have added to the headers to make them look nice. Aaah.
> >
> > (Note that this function works on both the header on the body of all messages, so it is a potentially dangerous function to use (if a body of a message contains something that looks like a header line). So rather than fix the bug, it is of course the right solution to make it into a feature by documenting it.)
>
> `nnmail-remove-list-identifiers`
> > Some list servers add an identifier—for example, '(idm)'—to the beginning of all **Subject** headers. I'm sure that's nice for people who use stone age mail readers. This function will remove strings that match the **nnmail-list-identifiers** regexp, which can also be a list of regexp. **nnmail-list-identifiers** may not contain `\\(..\\)`.
> >
> > For instance, if you want to remove the '(idm)' and the 'nagnagnag' identifiers:
> >
> > ```
> > (setq nnmail-list-identifiers
> >       '("(idm)" "nagnagnag"))
> > ```
> >
> > This can also be done non-destructively with **gnus-list-identifiers**, See Section 3.18.3 [Article Hiding]. page 86.
>
> `nnmail-remove-tabs`
> > Translate all 'TAB' characters into 'SPACE' characters.
>
> `nnmail-ignore-broken-references`
> > Some mail user agents (e.g., Eudora and Pegasus) produce broken **References** headers, but correct **In-Reply-To** headers. This function will get rid of the **References** header if the headers contain a

line matching the regular expression `nnmail-broken-references-mailers`.

`nnmail-prepare-incoming-message-hook`
>This hook is called narrowed to each message. Functions to be used include:

>>`article-de-quoted-unreadable`
>>>Decode Quoted Readable encoding.

6.4.11 Duplicates

If you are a member of a couple of mailing lists, you will sometimes receive two copies of the same mail. This can be quite annoying, so `nnmail` checks for and treats any duplicates it might find. To do this, it keeps a cache of old `Message-IDs`: `nnmail-message-id-cache-file`, which is `~/.nnmail-cache` by default. The approximate maximum number of `Message-IDs` stored there is controlled by the `nnmail-message-id-cache-length` variable, which is 1000 by default. (So 1000 `Message-IDs` will be stored.) If all this sounds scary to you, you can set `nnmail-treat-duplicates` to `warn` (which is what it is by default), and `nnmail` won't delete duplicate mails. Instead it will insert a warning into the head of the mail saying that it thinks that this is a duplicate of a different message.

This variable can also be a function. If that's the case, the function will be called from a buffer narrowed to the message in question with the `Message-ID` as a parameter. The function must return either `nil`, `warn`, or `delete`.

You can turn this feature off completely by setting the variable to `nil`.

If you want all the duplicate mails to be put into a special *duplicates* group, you could do that using the normal mail split methods:

```
(setq nnmail-split-fancy
      '(|  ;; Messages duplicates go to a separate group.
        ("gnus-warning" "duplicat\\(e\\|ion\\) of message" "duplicate")
        ;; Message from daemons, postmaster, and the like to another.
        (any mail "mail.misc")
        ;; Other rules.
        [...] ))
```

Or something like:

```
(setq nnmail-split-methods
      '(("duplicates" "^Gnus-Warning:.*duplicate")
        ;; Other rules.
        [...]))
```

Here's a neat feature: If you know that the recipient reads her mail with Gnus, and that she has `nnmail-treat-duplicates` set to `delete`, you can send her as many insults as you like, just by using a `Message-ID` of a mail that you know that she's already received. Think of all the fun! She'll never see any of it! Whee!

6.4.12 Not Reading Mail

If you start using any of the mail back ends, they have the annoying habit of assuming that you want to read mail with them. This might not be unreasonable, but it might not be what you want.

If you set `mail-sources` and `nnmail-spool-file` to `nil`, none of the back ends will ever attempt to read incoming mail, which should help.

This might be too much, if, for instance, you are reading mail quite happily with `nnml` and just want to peek at some old (pre-Emacs 23) Rmail file you have stashed away with `nnbabyl`. All back ends have variables called back-end-`get-new-mail`. If you want to disable the `nnbabyl` mail reading, you edit the virtual server for the group to have a setting where `nnbabyl-get-new-mail` to `nil`.

All the mail back ends will call `nn*-prepare-save-mail-hook` narrowed to the article to be saved before saving it when reading incoming mail.

6.4.13 Choosing a Mail Back End

Gnus will read the mail spool when you activate a mail group. The mail file is first copied to your home directory. What happens after that depends on what format you want to store your mail in.

There are six different mail back ends in the standard Gnus, and more back ends are available separately. The mail back end most people use (because it is possibly the fastest) is `nnml` (see Section 6.4.13.3 [Mail Spool], page 174).

6.4.13.1 Unix Mail Box

The *nnmbox* back end will use the standard Un*x mbox file to store mail. `nnmbox` will add extra headers to each mail article to say which group it belongs in.

Virtual server settings:

`nnmbox-mbox-file`
> The name of the mail box in the user's home directory. Default is `~/mbox`.

`nnmbox-active-file`
> The name of the active file for the mail box. Default is `~/.mbox-active`.

`nnmbox-get-new-mail`
> If non-`nil`, `nnmbox` will read incoming mail and split it into groups. Default is `t`.

6.4.13.2 Babyl

The *nnbabyl* back end will use a Babyl mail box to store mail. `nnbabyl` will add extra headers to each mail article to say which group it belongs in.

Virtual server settings:

`nnbabyl-mbox-file`
> The name of the Babyl file. The default is `~/RMAIL`

`nnbabyl-active-file`
> The name of the active file for the Babyl file. The default is `~/.rmail-active`

`nnbabyl-get-new-mail`
> If non-`nil`, `nnbabyl` will read incoming mail. Default is `t`

6.4.13.3 Mail Spool

The *nnml* spool mail format isn't compatible with any other known format. It should be used with some caution.

If you use this back end, Gnus will split all incoming mail into files, one file for each mail, and put the articles into the corresponding directories under the directory specified by the `nnml-directory` variable. The default value is `~/Mail/`.

You do not have to create any directories beforehand; Gnus will take care of all that.

If you have a strict limit as to how many files you are allowed to store in your account, you should not use this back end. As each mail gets its own file, you might very well occupy thousands of inodes within a few weeks. If this is no problem for you, and it isn't a problem for you having your friendly systems administrator walking around, madly, shouting "Who is eating all my inodes?! Who? Who!?!", then you should know that this is probably the fastest format to use. You do not have to trudge through a big mbox file just to read your new mail.

`nnml` is probably the slowest back end when it comes to article splitting. It has to create lots of files, and it also generates NOV databases for the incoming mails. This makes it possibly the fastest back end when it comes to reading mail.

Virtual server settings:

`nnml-directory`

> All `nnml` directories will be placed under this directory. The default is the value of `message-directory` (whose default value is `~/Mail`).

`nnml-active-file`

> The active file for the `nnml` server. The default is `~/Mail/active`.

`nnml-newsgroups-file`

> The `nnml` group descriptions file. See Section 11.8.9.2 [Newsgroups File Format], page 355. The default is `~/Mail/newsgroups`.

`nnml-get-new-mail`

> If non-`nil`, `nnml` will read incoming mail. The default is `t`.

`nnml-nov-is-evil`

> If non-`nil`, this back end will ignore any NOV files. The default is `nil`.

`nnml-nov-file-name`

> The name of the NOV files. The default is `.overview`.

`nnml-prepare-save-mail-hook`

> Hook run narrowed to an article before saving.

`nnml-use-compressed-files`

> If non-`nil`, `nnml` will allow using compressed message files. This requires `auto-compression-mode` to be enabled (see Section "Compressed Files" in *The Emacs Manual*). If the value of `nnml-use-compressed-files` is a string, it is used as the file extension specifying the compression program. You can set it to '`.bz2`' if your Emacs supports it. A value of `t` is equivalent to '`.gz`'.

`nnml-compressed-files-size-threshold`

> Default size threshold for compressed message files. Message files with bodies larger than that many characters will be automatically compressed if `nnml-use-compressed-files` is non-`nil`.

If your `nnml` groups and NOV files get totally out of whack, you can do a complete update by typing *M-x nnml-generate-nov-databases*. This command will trawl through the entire `nnml` hierarchy, looking at each and every article, so it might take a while to complete. A better interface to this functionality can be found in the server buffer (see Section 6.1.2 [Server Commands], page 137).

6.4.13.4 MH Spool

`nnmh` is just like `nnml`, except that is doesn't generate NOV databases and it doesn't keep an active file or marks file. This makes `nnmh` a *much* slower back end than `nnml`, but it also makes it easier to write procmail scripts for.

Virtual server settings:

`nnmh-directory`

> All `nnmh` directories will be located under this directory. The default is the value of `message-directory` (whose default is `~/Mail`)

`nnmh-get-new-mail`

> If non-`nil`, `nnmh` will read incoming mail. The default is `t`.

`nnmh-be-safe`

> If non-`nil`, `nnmh` will go to ridiculous lengths to make sure that the articles in the folder are actually what Gnus thinks they are. It will check date stamps and stat everything in sight, so setting this to `t` will mean a serious slow-down. If you never use anything but Gnus to read the `nnmh` articles. you do not have to set this variable to `t`. The default is `nil`.

6.4.13.5 Maildir

`nnmaildir` stores mail in the maildir format, with each maildir corresponding to a group in Gnus. This format is documented here: `http://cr.yp.to/proto/maildir.html` and here: `http://www.qmail.org/man/man5/maildir.html`. `nnmaildir` also stores extra information in the `.nnmaildir/` directory within a maildir.

Maildir format was designed to allow concurrent deliveries and reading, without needing locks. With other back ends, you would have your mail delivered to a spool of some kind, and then you would configure Gnus to split mail from that spool into your groups. You can still do that with `nnmaildir`, but the more common configuration is to have your mail delivered directly to the maildirs that appear as group in Gnus.

`nnmaildir` is designed to be perfectly reliable: *C-g* will never corrupt its data in memory, and `SIGKILL` will never corrupt its data in the filesystem.

`nnmaildir` stores article marks and NOV data in each maildir. So you can copy a whole maildir from one Gnus setup to another, and you will keep your marks.

Virtual server settings:

directory

>For each of your **nnmaildir** servers (it's very unlikely that you'd need more than one), you need to create a directory and populate it with maildirs or symlinks to maildirs (and nothing else; do not choose a directory already used for other purposes). Each maildir will be represented in Gnus as a newsgroup on that server; the filename of the symlink will be the name of the group. Any filenames in the directory starting with '.' are ignored. The directory is scanned when you first start Gnus, and each time you type *g* in the group buffer; if any maildirs have been removed or added, **nnmaildir** notices at these times.
>
>The value of the **directory** parameter should be a Lisp form which is processed by **eval** and **expand-file-name** to get the path of the directory for this server. The form is **eval**ed only when the server is opened; the resulting string is used until the server is closed. (If you don't know about forms and **eval**, don't worry—a simple string will work.) This parameter is not optional; you must specify it. I don't recommend using "~/Mail" or a subdirectory of it; several other parts of Gnus use that directory by default for various things, and may get confused if **nnmaildir** uses it too. "~/.nnmaildir" is a typical value.

target-prefix

>This should be a Lisp form which is processed by **eval** and **expand-file-name**. The form is **eval**ed only when the server is opened; the resulting string is used until the server is closed.
>
>When you create a group on an **nnmaildir** server, the maildir is created with **target-prefix** prepended to its name, and a symlink pointing to that maildir is created, named with the plain group name. So if **directory** is "~/.nnmaildir" and **target-prefix** is "../maildirs/", then when you create the group foo, **nnmaildir** will create ~/.nnmaildir/../maildirs/foo as a maildir, and will create ~/.nnmaildir/foo as a symlink pointing to ../maildirs/foo.
>
>You can set **target-prefix** to a string without any slashes to create both maildirs and symlinks in the same **directory**; in this case, any maildirs found in **directory** whose names start with **target-prefix** will not be listed as groups (but the symlinks pointing to them will be).
>
>As a special case, if **target-prefix** is "" (the default), then when you create a group, the maildir will be created in **directory** without a corresponding symlink. Beware that you cannot use **gnus-group-delete-group** on such groups without the **force** argument.

directory-files

>This should be a function with the same interface as **directory-files** (such as **directory-files** itself). It is used to scan the server's **directory** for maildirs. This parameter is optional; the default is **nnheader-directory-files-safe** if **nnheader-directory-files-is-safe** is nil, and **directory-files** otherwise. (**nnheader-directory-files-is-safe** is checked only once when the server is opened; if you want to check it each time the directory is scanned, you'll have to provide your own function that does that.)

get-new-mail

> If non-nil, then after scanning for new mail in the group maildirs themselves as usual, this server will also incorporate mail the conventional Gnus way, from `mail-sources` according to `nnmail-split-methods` or `nnmail-split-fancy`. The default value is `nil`.
>
> Do *not* use the same maildir both in `mail-sources` and as an `nnmaildir` group. The results might happen to be useful, but that would be by chance, not by design, and the results might be different in the future. If your split rules create new groups, remember to supply a `create-directory` server parameter.

6.4.13.6 Group parameters

`nnmaildir` uses several group parameters. It's safe to ignore all this; the default behavior for `nnmaildir` is the same as the default behavior for other mail back ends: articles are deleted after one week, etc. Except for the expiry parameters, all this functionality is unique to `nnmaildir`, so you can ignore it if you're just trying to duplicate the behavior you already have with another back end.

If the value of any of these parameters is a vector, the first element is evaluated as a Lisp form and the result is used, rather than the original value. If the value is not a vector, the value itself is evaluated as a Lisp form. (This is why these parameters use names different from those of other, similar parameters supported by other back ends: they have different, though similar, meanings.) (For numbers, strings, `nil`, and `t`, you can ignore the `eval` business again; for other values, remember to use an extra quote and wrap the value in a vector when appropriate.)

expire-age

> An integer specifying the minimum age, in seconds, of an article before it will be expired, or the symbol **never** to specify that articles should never be expired. If this parameter is not set, `nnmaildir` falls back to the usual `nnmail-expiry-wait(-function)` variables (the `expiry-wait` group parameter overrides `nnmail-expiry-wait` and makes `nnmail-expiry-wait-function` ineffective). If you wanted a value of 3 days, you could use something like `[(* 3 24 60 60)]`; `nnmaildir` will evaluate the form and use the result. An article's age is measured starting from the article file's modification time. Normally, this is the same as the article's delivery time, but editing an article makes it younger. Moving an article (other than via expiry) may also make an article younger.

expire-group

> If this is set to a string such as a full Gnus group name, like
>
> ```
> "backend+server.address.string:group.name"
> ```
>
> and if it is not the name of the same group that the parameter belongs to, then articles will be moved to the specified group during expiry before being deleted. *If this is set to an nnmaildir group, the article will be just as old in the destination group as it was in the source group.* So be careful with expire-age in the destination group. If this is set to the name of the same group that the parameter belongs to, then the article is not expired at all. If you use the vector form, the first element is evaluated once for each article. So that form

can refer to `nnmaildir-article-file-name`, etc., to decide where to put the article. *Even if this parameter is not set,* `nnmaildir` *does not fall back to the* `expiry-target` *group parameter or the* `nnmail-expiry-target` *variable.*

read-only

> If this is set to `t`, `nnmaildir` will treat the articles in this maildir as read-only. This means: articles are not renamed from `new/` into `cur/`; articles are only found in `new/`, not `cur/`; articles are never deleted; articles cannot be edited. `new/` is expected to be a symlink to the `new/` directory of another maildir—e.g., a system-wide mailbox containing a mailing list of common interest. Everything in the maildir outside `new/` is *not* treated as read-only, so for a shared mailbox, you do still need to set up your own maildir (or have write permission to the shared mailbox); your maildir just won't contain extra copies of the articles.

directory-files

> A function with the same interface as `directory-files`. It is used to scan the directories in the maildir corresponding to this group to find articles. The default is the function specified by the server's `directory-files` parameter.

distrust-Lines:

> If non-`nil`, `nnmaildir` will always count the lines of an article, rather than use the `Lines:` header field. If `nil`, the header field will be used if present.

always-marks

> A list of mark symbols, such as `['(read expire)]`. Whenever Gnus asks `nnmaildir` for article marks, `nnmaildir` will say that all articles have these marks, regardless of whether the marks stored in the filesystem say so. This is a proof-of-concept feature that will probably be removed eventually; it ought to be done in Gnus proper, or abandoned if it's not worthwhile.

never-marks

> A list of mark symbols, such as `['(tick expire)]`. Whenever Gnus asks `nnmaildir` for article marks, `nnmaildir` will say that no articles have these marks, regardless of whether the marks stored in the filesystem say so. `never-marks` overrides `always-marks`. This is a proof-of-concept feature that will probably be removed eventually; it ought to be done in Gnus proper, or abandoned if it's not worthwhile.

nov-cache-size

> An integer specifying the size of the NOV memory cache. To speed things up, `nnmaildir` keeps NOV data in memory for a limited number of articles in each group. (This is probably not worthwhile, and will probably be removed in the future.) This parameter's value is noticed only the first time a group is seen after the server is opened—i.e., when you first start Gnus, typically. The NOV cache is never resized until the server is closed and reopened. The default is an estimate of the number of articles that would be displayed in the summary buffer: a count of articles that are either marked with `tick` or not marked with `read`, plus a little extra.

6.4.13.7 Article identification

Articles are stored in the cur/ subdirectory of each maildir. Each article file is named like uniq:info, where uniq contains no colons. nnmaildir ignores, but preserves, the :info part. (Other maildir readers typically use this part of the filename to store marks.) The uniq part uniquely identifies the article, and is used in various places in the .nnmaildir/ subdirectory of the maildir to store information about the corresponding article. The full pathname of an article is available in the variable nnmaildir-article-file-name after you request the article in the summary buffer.

6.4.13.8 NOV data

An article identified by uniq has its NOV data (used to generate lines in the summary buffer) stored in .nnmaildir/nov/uniq. There is no nnmaildir-generate-nov-databases function. (There isn't much need for it—an article's NOV data is updated automatically when the article or nnmail-extra-headers has changed.) You can force nnmaildir to regenerate the NOV data for a single article simply by deleting the corresponding NOV file, but *beware*: this will also cause nnmaildir to assign a new article number for this article, which may cause trouble with seen marks, the Agent, and the cache.

6.4.13.9 Article marks

An article identified by uniq is considered to have the mark flag when the file .nnmaildir/marks/flag/uniq exists. When Gnus asks nnmaildir for a group's marks, nnmaildir looks for such files and reports the set of marks it finds. When Gnus asks nnmaildir to store a new set of marks, nnmaildir creates and deletes the corresponding files as needed. (Actually, rather than create a new file for each mark, it just creates hard links to .nnmaildir/markfile, to save inodes.)

You can invent new marks by creating a new directory in .nnmaildir/marks/. You can tar up a maildir and remove it from your server, untar it later, and keep your marks. You can add and remove marks yourself by creating and deleting mark files. If you do this while Gnus is running and your nnmaildir server is open, it's best to exit all summary buffers for nnmaildir groups and type *s* in the group buffer first, and to type *g* or *M-g* in the group buffer afterwards. Otherwise, Gnus might not pick up the changes, and might undo them.

6.4.13.10 Mail Folders

nnfolder is a back end for storing each mail group in a separate file. Each file is in the standard Un*x mbox format. nnfolder will add extra headers to keep track of article numbers and arrival dates.

Virtual server settings:

nnfolder-directory

All the nnfolder mail boxes will be stored under this directory. The default is the value of message-directory (whose default is ~/Mail)

nnfolder-active-file

The name of the active file. The default is ~/Mail/active.

nnfolder-newsgroups-file

The name of the group descriptions file. See Section 11.8.9.2 [Newsgroups File Format], page 355. The default is ~/Mail/newsgroups `nnfolder-get-new-mail`

> If non-**nil**, **nnfolder** will read incoming mail. The default is **t**

`nnfolder-save-buffer-hook`

> Hook run before saving the folders. Note that Emacs does the normal backup renaming of files even with the **nnfolder** buffers. If you wish to switch this off, you could say something like the following in your .emacs file:

```
(defun turn-off-backup ()
  (set (make-local-variable 'backup-inhibited) t))


(add-hook 'nnfolder-save-buffer-hook 'turn-off-backup)
```

`nnfolder-delete-mail-hook`

> Hook run in a buffer narrowed to the message that is to be deleted. This function can be used to copy the message to somewhere else, or to extract some information from it before removing it.

`nnfolder-nov-is-evil`

> If non-**nil**, this back end will ignore any NOV files. The default is **nil**.

`nnfolder-nov-file-suffix`

> The extension for NOV files. The default is .nov.

`nnfolder-nov-directory`

> The directory where the NOV files should be stored. If **nil**, **nnfolder-directory** is used.

If you have lots of **nnfolder**-like files you'd like to read with **nnfolder**, you can use the *M-x nnfolder-generate-active-file* command to make **nnfolder** aware of all likely files in **nnfolder-directory**. This only works if you use long file names, though.

6.4.13.11 Comparing Mail Back Ends

First, just for terminology, the *back end* is the common word for a low-level access method—a transport, if you will, by which something is acquired. The sense is that one's mail has to come from somewhere, and so selection of a suitable back end is required in order to get that mail within spitting distance of Gnus.

The same concept exists for Usenet itself: Though access to articles is typically done by NNTP these days, once upon a midnight dreary, everyone in the world got at Usenet by running a reader on the machine where the articles lay (the machine which today we call an NNTP server), and access was by the reader stepping into the articles' directory spool area directly. One can still select between either the **nntp** or **nnspool** back ends, to select between these methods, if one happens actually to live on the server (or can see its spool directly, anyway, via NFS).

The goal in selecting a mail back end is to pick one which simultaneously represents a suitable way of dealing with the original format plus leaving mail in a form that is convenient to use in the future. Here are some high and low points on each:

`nnmbox`

> UNIX systems have historically had a single, very common, and well-defined format. All messages arrive in a single *spool file*, and they are delineated by

a line whose regular expression matches '^From_'. (My notational use of '_' is to indicate a space, to make it clear in this instance that this is not the RFC-specified 'From:' header.) Because Emacs and therefore Gnus emanate historically from the Unix environment, it is simplest if one does not mess a great deal with the original mailbox format, so if one chooses this back end, Gnus' primary activity in getting mail from the real spool area to Gnus' preferred directory is simply to copy it, with no (appreciable) format change in the process. It is the "dumbest" way to move mail into availability in the Gnus environment. This makes it fast to move into place, but slow to parse, when Gnus has to look at what's where.

nnbabyl

Once upon a time, there was the DEC-10 and DEC-20, running operating systems called TOPS and related things, and the usual (only?) mail reading environment was a thing called Babyl. I don't know what format was used for mail landing on the system, but Babyl had its own internal format to which mail was converted, primarily involving creating a spool-file-like entity with a scheme for inserting Babyl-specific headers and status bits above the top of each message in the file. Rmail was Emacs's first mail reader. it was written by Richard Stallman, and Stallman came out of that TOPS/Babyl environment, so he wrote Rmail to understand the mail files folks already had in existence. Gnus (and VM, for that matter) continue to support this format because it's perceived as having some good qualities in those mailer-specific headers/status bits stuff. Rmail itself still exists as well, of course, and is still maintained within Emacs. Since Emacs 23, it uses standard mbox format rather than Babyl.

Both of the above forms leave your mail in a single file on your file system, and they must parse that entire file each time you take a look at your mail.

nnml

nnml is the back end which smells the most as though you were actually operating with an nnspool-accessed Usenet system. (In fact, I believe nnml actually derived from nnspool code, lo these years ago.) One's mail is taken from the original spool file, and is then cut up into individual message files, 1:1. It maintains a Usenet-style active file (analogous to what one finds in an INN- or CNews-based news system in (for instance) /var/lib/news/active, or what is returned via the 'NNTP LIST' verb) and also creates *overview* files for efficient group entry, as has been defined for NNTP servers for some years now. It is slower in mail-splitting, due to the creation of lots of files, updates to the nnml active file, and additions to overview files on a per-message basis, but it is extremely fast on access because of what amounts to the indexing support provided by the active file and overviews.

nnml costs *inodes* in a big way; that is, it soaks up the resource which defines available places in the file system to put new files. Sysadmins take a dim view of heavy inode occupation within tight, shared file systems. But if you live on a personal machine where the file system is your own and space is not at a premium, nnml wins big.

It is also problematic using this back end if you are living in a FAT16-based Windows world, since much space will be wasted on all these tiny files.

nnmh

The Rand MH mail-reading system has been around UNIX systems for a very long time; it operates by splitting one's spool file of messages into individual files, but with little or no indexing support—nnmh is considered to be semantically equivalent to "nnml without active file or overviews". This is arguably the worst choice, because one gets the slowness of individual file creation married to the slowness of access parsing when learning what's new in one's groups.

nnfolder

Basically the effect of nnfolder is nnmbox (the first method described above) on a per-group basis. That is, nnmbox itself puts *all* one's mail in one file; nnfolder provides a little bit of optimization to this so that each of one's mail groups has a Unix mail box file. It's faster than nnmbox because each group can be parsed separately, and still provides the simple Unix mail box format requiring minimal effort in moving the mail around. In addition, it maintains an "active" file making it much faster for Gnus to figure out how many messages there are in each separate group.

If you have groups that are expected to have a massive amount of messages, nnfolder is not the best choice, but if you receive only a moderate amount of mail, nnfolder is probably the most friendly mail back end all over.

nnmaildir

For configuring expiry and other things, nnmaildir uses incompatible group parameters, slightly different from those of other mail back ends.

nnmaildir is largely similar to nnml, with some notable differences. Each message is stored in a separate file, but the filename is unrelated to the article number in Gnus. nnmaildir also stores the equivalent of nnml's overview files in one file per article, so it uses about twice as many inodes as nnml. (Use df -i to see how plentiful your inode supply is.) If this slows you down or takes up very much space, a non-block-structured file system.

Since maildirs don't require locking for delivery, the maildirs you use as groups can also be the maildirs your mail is directly delivered to. This means you can skip Gnus' mail splitting if your mail is already organized into different mailboxes during delivery. A directory entry in mail-sources would have a similar effect, but would require one set of mailboxes for spooling deliveries (in mbox format, thus damaging message bodies), and another set to be used as groups (in whatever format you like). A maildir has a built-in spool, in the new/ subdirectory. Beware that currently, mail moved from new/ to cur/ instead of via mail splitting will not undergo treatment such as duplicate checking.

nnmaildir stores article marks for a given group in the corresponding maildir, in a way designed so that it's easy to manipulate them from outside Gnus. You can tar up a maildir, unpack it somewhere else, and still have your marks.

nnmaildir uses a significant amount of memory to speed things up. (It keeps in memory some of the things that nnml stores in files and that nnmh repeatedly parses out of message files.) If this is a problem for you, you can set the `nov-cache-size` group parameter to something small (0 would probably not work, but 1 probably would) to make it use less memory. This caching will probably be removed in the future.

Startup is likely to be slower with `nnmaildir` than with other back ends. Everything else is likely to be faster, depending in part on your file system.

`nnmaildir` does not use `nnoo`, so you cannot use `nnoo` to write an `nnmaildir`-derived back end.

6.5 Browsing the Web

Web-based discussion forums are getting more and more popular. On many subjects, the web-based forums have become the most important forums, eclipsing the importance of mailing lists and news groups. The reason is easy to understand—they are friendly to new users; you just point and click, and there's the discussion. With mailing lists, you have to go through a cumbersome subscription procedure, and most people don't even know what a news group is.

The problem with this scenario is that web browsers are not very good at being news-readers. They do not keep track of what articles you've read; they do not allow you to score on subjects you're interested in; they do not allow off-line browsing; they require you to click around and drive you mad in the end.

So—if web browsers suck at reading discussion forums, why not use Gnus to do it instead?

Gnus has been getting a bit of a collection of back ends for providing interfaces to these sources.

The main caveat with all these web sources is that they probably won't work for a very long time. Gleaning information from the HTML data is guesswork at best, and when the layout is altered, the Gnus back end will fail. If you have reasonably new versions of these back ends, though, you should be ok.

One thing all these Web methods have in common is that the Web sources are often down, unavailable or just plain too slow to be fun. In those cases, it makes a lot of sense to let the Gnus Agent (see Section 6.9 [Gnus Unplugged], page 198) handle downloading articles, and then you can read them at leisure from your local disk. No more World Wide Wait for you.

6.5.1 Archiving Mail

Some of the back ends, notably `nnml`, `nnfolder`, and `nnmaildir`, now actually store the article marks with each group. For these servers, archiving and restoring a group while preserving marks is fairly simple.

(Preserving the group level and group parameters as well still requires ritual dancing and sacrifices to the `.newsrc.eld` deity though.)

To archive an entire `nnml`, `nnfolder`, or `nnmaildir` server, take a recursive copy of the server directory. There is no need to shut down Gnus, so archiving may be invoked by `cron` or similar. You restore the data by restoring the directory tree, and adding a server definition pointing to that directory in Gnus. The Section 3.15 [Article Backlog], page 76, Section 3.11 [Asynchronous Fetching], page 72 and other things might interfere with overwriting data, so you may want to shut down Gnus before you restore the data.

6.5.2 Web Searches

It's, like, too neat to search the Usenet for articles that match a string, but it, like, totally *sucks*, like, totally, to use one of those, like, Web browsers, and you, like, have to, rilly, like, look at the commercials, so, like, with Gnus you can do *rad*, rilly, searches without having to use a browser.

The `nnweb` back end allows an easy interface to the mighty search engine. You create an `nnweb` group, enter a search pattern, and then enter the group and read the articles like you would any normal group. The `G w` command in the group buffer (see Section 2.9 [Foreign Groups], page 20) will do this in an easy-to-use fashion.

`nnweb` groups don't really lend themselves to being solid groups—they have a very fleeting idea of article numbers. In fact, each time you enter an `nnweb` group (not even changing the search pattern), you are likely to get the articles ordered in a different manner. Not even using duplicate suppression (see Section 3.30 [Duplicate Suppression], page 113) will help, since `nnweb` doesn't even know the `Message-ID` of the articles before reading them using some search engines (Google, for instance). The only possible way to keep track of which articles you've read is by scoring on the `Date` header—mark all articles posted before the last date you read the group as read.

If the search engine changes its output substantially, `nnweb` won't be able to parse it and will fail. One could hardly fault the Web providers if they were to do this—their *raison d'être* is to make money off of advertisements, not to provide services to the community. Since `nnweb` washes the ads off all the articles, one might think that the providers might be somewhat miffed. We'll see.

Virtual server variables:

`nnweb-type`

What search engine type is being used. The currently supported types are `google`, `dejanews`, and `gmane`. Note that `dejanews` is an alias to `google`.

`nnweb-search`

The search string to feed to the search engine.

`nnweb-max-hits`

Advisory maximum number of hits per search to display. The default is 999.

`nnweb-type-definition`

Type-to-definition alist. This alist says what `nnweb` should do with the various search engine types. The following elements must be present:

`article`	Function to decode the article and provide something that Gnus understands.
`map`	Function to create an article number to message header and URL alist.
`search`	Function to send the search string to the search engine.
`address`	The address the aforementioned function should send the search string to.
`id`	Format string URL to fetch an article by `Message-ID`.

6.5.3 RSS

Some web sites have an RDF Site Summary (RSS). RSS is a format for summarizing headlines from news related sites (such as BBC or CNN). But basically anything list-like can be presented as an RSS feed: weblogs, changelogs or recent changes to a wiki (e.g., http://cliki.net/site/recent-changes).

RSS has a quite regular and nice interface, and it's possible to get the information Gnus needs to keep groups updated.

Note: you had better use Emacs which supports the utf-8 coding system because RSS uses UTF-8 for encoding non-ASCII text by default. It is also used by default for non-ASCII group names.

Use *G R* from the group buffer to subscribe to a feed—you will be prompted for the location, the title and the description of the feed. The title, which allows any characters, will be used for the group name and the name of the group data file. The description can be omitted.

An easy way to get started with nnrss is to say something like the following in the group buffer: *B nnrss RET RET y*, then subscribe to groups.

The nnrss back end saves the group data file in nnrss-directory (see below) for each nnrss group. File names containing non-ASCII characters will be encoded by the coding system specified with the nnmail-pathname-coding-system variable or other. Also See Section 2.17 [Non-ASCII Group Names], page 38, for more information.

The nnrss back end generates 'multipart/alternative' MIME articles in which each contains a 'text/plain' part and a 'text/html' part.

You can also use the following commands to import and export your subscriptions from a file in OPML format (Outline Processor Markup Language).

nnrss-opml-import *file*   [Function]
> Prompt for an OPML file, and subscribe to each feed in the file.

nnrss-opml-export   [Function]
> Write your current RSS subscriptions to a buffer in OPML format.

The following nnrss variables can be altered:

nnrss-directory
> The directory where nnrss stores its files. The default is ~/News/rss/.

nnrss-file-coding-system
> The coding system used when reading and writing the nnrss groups data files. The default is the value of mm-universal-coding-system (which defaults to emacs-mule in Emacs or escape-quoted in XEmacs).

nnrss-ignore-article-fields
> Some feeds update constantly article fields during their publications, e.g., to indicate the number of comments. However, if there is a difference between the local article and the distant one, the latter is considered to be new. To avoid this and discard some fields, set this variable to the list of fields to be ignored. The default is '(slash:comments).

`nnrss-use-local`

If you set `nnrss-use-local` to `t`, `nnrss` will read the feeds from local files in `nnrss-directory`. You can use the command `nnrss-generate-download-script` to generate a download script using `wget`.

The following code may be helpful, if you want to show the description in the summary buffer.

```
(add-to-list 'nnmail-extra-headers nnrss-description-field)
(setq gnus-summary-line-format "%U%R%z%I%(%[%4L: %-15,15f%]%) %s%uX\n")

(defun gnus-user-format-function-X (header)
  (let ((descr
         (assq nnrss-description-field (mail-header-extra header))))
    (if descr (concat "\n\t" (cdr descr)) "")))
```

The following code may be useful to open an nnrss url directly from the summary buffer.

```
(require 'browse-url)

(defun browse-nnrss-url (arg)
  (interactive "p")
  (let ((url (assq nnrss-url-field
                   (mail-header-extra
                    (gnus-data-header
                     (assq (gnus-summary-article-number)
                           gnus-newsgroup-data))))))
    (if url
        (progn
          (browse-url (cdr url))
          (gnus-summary-mark-as-read-forward 1))
      (gnus-summary-scroll-up arg))))

(eval-after-load "gnus"
  #'(define-key gnus-summary-mode-map
      (kbd "<RET>") 'browse-nnrss-url))
(add-to-list 'nnmail-extra-headers nnrss-url-field)
```

Even if you have added 'text/html' to the `mm-discouraged-alternatives` variable (see Section "Display Customization" in *The Emacs MIME Manual*) since you don't want to see HTML parts, it might be more useful especially in `nnrss` groups to display 'text/html' parts. Here's an example of setting `mm-discouraged-alternatives` as a group parameter (see Section 2.10 [Group Parameters], page 22) in order to display 'text/html' parts only in `nnrss` groups:

```
;; Set the default value of mm-discouraged-alternatives.
(eval-after-load "gnus-sum"
  '(add-to-list
    'gnus-newsgroup-variables
    '(mm-discouraged-alternatives
      . '("text/html" "image/.*"))))
```

```
;; Display 'text/html' parts in nnrss groups.
(add-to-list
 'gnus-parameters
 '("\\`nnrss:" (mm-discouraged-alternatives nil)))
```

6.6 Other Sources

Gnus can do more than just read news or mail. The methods described below allow Gnus to view directories and files as if they were newsgroups.

6.6.1 Directory Groups

If you have a directory that has lots of articles in separate files in it, you might treat it as a newsgroup. The files have to have numerical names, of course.

This might be an opportune moment to mention **ange-ftp** (and its successor **efs**), that most wonderful of all wonderful Emacs packages. When I wrote **nndir**, I didn't think much about it—a back end to read directories. Big deal.

ange-ftp changes that picture dramatically. For instance, if you enter the **ange-ftp** file name `/ftp.hpc.uh.edu:/pub/emacs/ding-list/` as the directory name, **ange-ftp** or **efs** will actually allow you to read this directory over at 'sina' as a newsgroup. Distributed news ahoy!

nndir will use NOV files if they are present.

nndir is a "read-only" back end—you can't delete or expire articles with this method. You can use **nnmh** or **nnml** for whatever you use **nndir** for, so you could switch to any of those methods if you feel the need to have a non-read-only **nndir**.

6.6.2 Anything Groups

From the **nndir** back end (which reads a single spool-like directory), it's just a hop and a skip to **nneething**, which pretends that any arbitrary directory is a newsgroup. Strange, but true.

When **nneething** is presented with a directory, it will scan this directory and assign article numbers to each file. When you enter such a group, **nneething** must create "headers" that Gnus can use. After all, Gnus is a newsreader, in case you're forgetting. **nneething** does this in a two-step process. First, it snoops each file in question. If the file looks like an article (i.e., the first few lines look like headers), it will use this as the head. If this is just some arbitrary file without a head (e.g., a C source file), **nneething** will cobble up a header out of thin air. It will use file ownership, name and date and do whatever it can with these elements.

All this should happen automatically for you, and you will be presented with something that looks very much like a newsgroup. Totally like a newsgroup, to be precise. If you select an article, it will be displayed in the article buffer, just as usual.

If you select a line that represents a directory, Gnus will pop you into a new summary buffer for this **nneething** group. And so on. You can traverse the entire disk this way, if you feel like, but remember that Gnus is not dired, really, and does not intend to be, either.

There are two overall modes to this action—ephemeral or solid. When doing the ephemeral thing (i.e., *G D* from the group buffer), Gnus will not store information on what files you have read, and what files are new, and so on. If you create a solid `nneething` group the normal way with `G m`, Gnus will store a mapping table between article numbers and file names, and you can treat this group like any other groups. When you activate a solid `nneething` group, you will be told how many unread articles it contains, etc., etc.

Some variables:

`nneething-map-file-directory`

> All the mapping files for solid `nneething` groups will be stored in this directory, which defaults to `~/.nneething/`.

`nneething-exclude-files`

> All files that match this regexp will be ignored. Nice to use to exclude auto-save files and the like, which is what it does by default.

`nneething-include-files`

> Regexp saying what files to include in the group. If this variable is non-`nil`, only files matching this regexp will be included.

`nneething-map-file`

> Name of the map files.

6.6.3 Document Groups

`nndoc` is a cute little thing that will let you read a single file as a newsgroup. Several files types are supported:

`babyl`   The Babyl format.

`mbox`   The standard Unix mbox file.

`mmdf`   The MMDF mail box format.

`news`   Several news articles appended into a file.

`rnews`   The rnews batch transport format.

`nsmail`   Netscape mail boxes.

`mime-parts`

> MIME multipart messages.

`standard-digest`

> The standard (RFC 1153) digest format.

`mime-digest`

> A MIME digest of messages.

`lanl-gov-announce`

> Announcement messages from LANL Gov Announce.

`git`   `git` commit messages.

`rfc822-forward`

> A message forwarded according to RFC822.

`outlook`   The Outlook mail box.

`oe-dbx`   The Outlook Express dbx mail box.

exim-bounce
>A bounce message from the Exim MTA.

forward   A message forwarded according to informal rules.

rfc934   An RFC934-forwarded message.

mailman   A mailman digest.

clari-briefs
>A digest of Clarinet brief news items.

slack-digest
>Non-standard digest format—matches most things, but does it badly.

mail-in-mail
>The last resort.

You can also use the special "file type" **guess**, which means that **nndoc** will try to guess what file type it is looking at. **digest** means that **nndoc** should guess what digest type the file is.

nndoc will not try to change the file or insert any extra headers into it—it will simply, like, let you use the file as the basis for a group. And that's it.

If you have some old archived articles that you want to insert into your new & spiffy Gnus mail back end, **nndoc** can probably help you with that. Say you have an old **RMAIL** file with mail that you now want to split into your new **nnml** groups. You look at that file using **nndoc** (using the *G f* command in the group buffer (see Section 2.9 [Foreign Groups], page 20)), set the process mark on all the articles in the buffer (*M P b*, for instance), and then re-spool (*B r*) using **nnml**. If all goes well, all the mail in the **RMAIL** file is now also stored in lots of **nnml** directories, and you can delete that pesky **RMAIL** file. If you have the guts!

Virtual server variables:

nndoc-article-type
>This should be one of mbox, babyl, digest, news, rnews, mmdf, forward, rfc934, rfc822-forward, mime-parts, standard-digest, slack-digest, clari-briefs, nsmail, outlook, oe-dbx, mailman, and mail-in-mail or guess.

nndoc-post-type
>This variable says whether Gnus is to consider the group a news group or a mail group. There are two valid values: mail (the default) and news.

6.6.3.1 Document Server Internals

Adding new document types to be recognized by **nndoc** isn't difficult. You just have to whip up a definition of what the document looks like, write a predicate function to recognize that document type, and then hook into **nndoc**.

First, here's an example document type definition:

```
(mmdf
 (article-begin .  "^\^A\^A\^A\^A\n")
 (body-end .  "^\^A\^A\^A\^A\n"))
```

The definition is simply a unique *name* followed by a series of regexp pseudo-variable settings. Below are the possible variables—don't be daunted by the number of variables; most document types can be defined with very few settings:

`first-article`

> If present, `nndoc` will skip past all text until it finds something that match this regexp. All text before this will be totally ignored.

`article-begin`

> This setting has to be present in all document type definitions. It says what the beginning of each article looks like. To do more complicated things that cannot be dealt with a simple regexp, you can use `article-begin-function` instead of this.

`article-begin-function`

> If present, this should be a function that moves point to the beginning of each article. This setting overrides `article-begin`.

`head-begin`

> If present, this should be a regexp that matches the head of the article. To do more complicated things that cannot be dealt with a simple regexp, you can use `head-begin-function` instead of this.

`head-begin-function`

> If present, this should be a function that moves point to the head of the article. This setting overrides `head-begin`.

`head-end` This should match the end of the head of the article. It defaults to '`^$`'—the empty line.

`body-begin`

> This should match the beginning of the body of the article. It defaults to '`^\n`'. To do more complicated things that cannot be dealt with a simple regexp, you can use `body-begin-function` instead of this.

`body-begin-function`

> If present, this function should move point to the beginning of the body of the article. This setting overrides `body-begin`.

`body-end` If present, this should match the end of the body of the article. To do more complicated things that cannot be dealt with a simple regexp, you can use `body-end-function` instead of this.

`body-end-function`

> If present, this function should move point to the end of the body of the article. This setting overrides `body-end`.

`file-begin`

> If present, this should match the beginning of the file. All text before this regexp will be totally ignored.

`file-end` If present, this should match the end of the file. All text after this regexp will be totally ignored.

So, using these variables **nndoc** is able to dissect a document file into a series of articles, each with a head and a body. However, a few more variables are needed since not all document types are all that news-like—variables needed to transform the head or the body into something that's palatable for Gnus:

prepare-body-function

> If present, this function will be called when requesting an article. It will be called with point at the start of the body, and is useful if the document has encoded some parts of its contents.

article-transform-function

> If present, this function is called when requesting an article. It's meant to be used for more wide-ranging transformation of both head and body of the article.

generate-head-function

> If present, this function is called to generate a head that Gnus can understand. It is called with the article number as a parameter, and is expected to generate a nice head for the article in question. It is called when requesting the headers of all articles.

generate-article-function

> If present, this function is called to generate an entire article that Gnus can understand. It is called with the article number as a parameter when requesting all articles.

dissection-function

> If present, this function is called to dissect a document by itself, overriding **first-article**, **article-begin**, **article-begin-function**, **head-begin**, **head-begin-function**, **head-end**, **body-begin**, **body-begin-function**, **body-end**, **body-end-function**, **file-begin**, and **file-end**.

Let's look at the most complicated example I can come up with—standard digests:

```
(standard-digest
 (first-article . ,(concat "^" (make-string 70 ?-) "\n\n+"))
 (article-begin . ,(concat "\n\n" (make-string 30 ?-) "\n\n+"))
 (prepare-body-function . nndoc-unquote-dashes)
 (body-end-function . nndoc-digest-body-end)
 (head-end . "^ ?$")
 (body-begin . "^ ?\n")
 (file-end . "^End of .*digest.*[0-9].*\n\\*\\*\\|^End of.*Digest *$")
 (subtype digest guess))
```

We see that all text before a 70-width line of dashes is ignored; all text after a line that starts with that '^**End of**' is also ignored; each article begins with a 30-width line of dashes; the line separating the head from the body may contain a single space; and that the body is run through **nndoc-unquote-dashes** before being delivered.

To hook your own document definition into **nndoc**, use the **nndoc-add-type** function. It takes two parameters—the first is the definition itself and the second (optional) parameter says where in the document type definition alist to put this definition. The alist is traversed sequentially, and **nndoc-*type*-type-p** is called for a given type *type*. So **nndoc-mmdf-type-p** is called to see whether a document is of **mmdf** type, and so on. These type predicates should return `nil` if the document is not of the correct type; `t` if it is of the correct type; and a number if the document might be of the correct type. A high number means high probability; a low number means low probability with '0' being the lowest valid number.

6.6.4 Mail-To-News Gateways

If your local `nntp` server doesn't allow posting, for some reason or other, you can post using one of the numerous mail-to-news gateways. The `nngateway` back end provides the interface.

Note that you can't read anything from this back end—it can only be used to post with.

Server variables:

`nngateway-address`

> This is the address of the mail-to-news gateway.

`nngateway-header-transformation`

> News headers often have to be transformed in some odd way or other for the mail-to-news gateway to accept it. This variable says what transformation should be called, and defaults to `nngateway-simple-header-transformation`. The function is called narrowed to the headers to be transformed and with one parameter—the gateway address.
>
> This default function just inserts a new `To` header based on the `Newsgroups` header and the gateway address. For instance, an article with this `Newsgroups` header:
>
>   Newsgroups: alt.religion.emacs
>
> will get this `To` header inserted:
>
>   To: alt-religion-emacs@GATEWAY
>
> The following pre-defined functions exist:
>
> `nngateway-simple-header-transformation`
>
> > Creates a `To` header that looks like *newsgroup*@nngateway-address.
>
> `nngateway-mail2news-header-transformation`
>
> > Creates a `To` header that looks like `nngateway-address`.

Here's an example:

```
(setq gnus-post-method
      '(nngateway
        "mail2news@replay.com"
        (nngateway-header-transformation
         nngateway-mail2news-header-transformation)))
```

So, to use this, simply say something like:

```
(setq gnus-post-method '(nngateway "GATEWAY.ADDRESS"))
```

6.6.5 The Empty Backend

`nnnil` is a backend that can be used as a placeholder if you have to specify a backend somewhere, but don't really want to. The classical example is if you don't want to have a primary select methods, but want to only use secondary ones:

```
(setq gnus-select-method '(nnnil ""))
(setq gnus-secondary-select-methods
      '((nnimap "foo")
        (nnml "")))
```

6.7 Combined Groups

Gnus allows combining a mixture of all the other group types into bigger groups.

6.7.1 Virtual Groups

An *nnvirtual group* is really nothing more than a collection of other groups.

For instance, if you are tired of reading many small groups, you can put them all in one big group, and then grow tired of reading one big, unwieldy group. The joys of computing!

You specify **nnvirtual** as the method. The address should be a regexp to match component groups.

All marks in the virtual group will stick to the articles in the component groups. So if you tick an article in a virtual group, the article will also be ticked in the component group from whence it came. (And vice versa—marks from the component groups will also be shown in the virtual group.). To create an empty virtual group, run *G V* (**gnus-group-make-empty-virtual**) in the group buffer and edit the method regexp with *M-e* (**gnus-group-edit-group-method**)

Here's an example **nnvirtual** method that collects all Andrea Dworkin newsgroups into one, big, happy newsgroup:

```
(nnvirtual "^alt\\.fan\\.andrea-dworkin$\\|^rec\\.dworkin.*")
```

The component groups can be native or foreign; everything should work smoothly, but if your computer explodes, it was probably my fault.

Collecting the same group from several servers might actually be a good idea if users have set the Distribution header to limit distribution. If you would like to read 'soc.motss' both from a server in Japan and a server in Norway, you could use the following as the group regexp:

```
"^nntp\\+server\\.jp:soc\\.motss$\\|^nntp\\+server\\.no:soc\\.motss$"
```

(Remember, though, that if you're creating the group with *G m*, you shouldn't double the backslashes, and you should leave off the quote characters at the beginning and the end of the string.)

This should work kinda smoothly—all articles from both groups should end up in this one, and there should be no duplicates. Threading (and the rest) will still work as usual, but there might be problems with the sequence of articles. Sorting on date might be an option here (see Section 2.3 [Selecting a Group], page 15).

One limitation, however—all groups included in a virtual group have to be alive (i.e., subscribed or unsubscribed). Killed or zombie groups can't be component groups for **nnvirtual** groups.

If the **nnvirtual-always-rescan** variable is non-**nil** (which is the default), **nnvirtual** will always scan groups for unread articles when entering a virtual group. If this variable is **nil** and you read articles in a component group after the virtual group has been activated, the read articles from the component group will show up when you enter the virtual group. You'll also see this effect if you have two virtual groups that have a component group in common. If that's the case, you should set this variable to t. Or you can just tap M-g on the virtual group every time before you enter it—it'll have much the same effect.

nnvirtual can have both mail and news groups as component groups. When responding to articles in nnvirtual groups, nnvirtual has to ask the back end of the component group the article comes from whether it is a news or mail back end. However, when you do a ^, there is typically no sure way for the component back end to know this, and in that case nnvirtual tells Gnus that the article came from a not-news back end. (Just to be on the safe side.)

C-c C-n in the message buffer will insert the Newsgroups line from the article you respond to in these cases.

nnvirtual groups do not inherit anything but articles and marks from component groups—group parameters, for instance, are not inherited.

6.8 Email Based Diary

This section describes a special mail back end called nndiary, and its companion library gnus-diary. It is "special" in the sense that it is not meant to be one of the standard alternatives for reading mail with Gnus. See Section 6.4.13 [Choosing a Mail Back End], page 173 for that. Instead, it is used to treat *some* of your mails in a special way, namely, as event reminders.

Here is a typical scenario:

- You've got a date with Andy Mc Dowell or Bruce Willis (select according to your sexual preference) in one month. You don't want to forget it.
- So you send a "reminder" message (actually, a diary one) to yourself.
- You forget all about it and keep on getting and reading new mail, as usual.
- From time to time, as you type 'g' in the group buffer and as the date is getting closer, the message will pop up again to remind you of your appointment, just as if it were new and unread.
- Read your "new" messages, this one included, and start dreaming again of the night you're gonna have.
- Once the date is over (you actually fell asleep just after dinner), the message will be automatically deleted if it is marked as expirable.

The Gnus Diary back end has the ability to handle regular appointments (that wouldn't ever be deleted) as well as punctual ones, operates as a real mail back end and is configurable in many ways. All of this is explained in the sections below.

6.8.1 The NNDiary Back End

nndiary is a back end very similar to nnml (see Section 6.4.13.3 [Mail Spool], page 174). Actually, it could appear as a mix of nnml and nndraft. If you know nnml, you're already familiar with the message storing scheme of nndiary: one file per message, one directory per group.

Before anything, there is one requirement to be able to run **nndiary** properly: you *must* use the group timestamp feature of Gnus. This adds a timestamp to each group's parameters. Section 2.18.3 [Group Timestamp], page 42 to see how it's done.

6.8.1.1 Diary Messages

nndiary messages are just normal ones, except for the mandatory presence of 7 special headers. These headers are of the form `X-Diary-<something>`, `<something>` being one of `Minute`, `Hour`, `Dom`, `Month`, `Year`, `Time-Zone` and `Dow`. `Dom` means "Day of Month", and `dow` means "Day of Week". These headers actually behave like crontab specifications and define the event date(s):

- For all headers except the `Time-Zone` one, a header value is either a star (meaning all possible values), or a list of fields (separated by a comma).

- A field is either an integer, or a range.

- A range is two integers separated by a dash.

- Possible integer values are 0–59 for `Minute`, 0–23 for `Hour`, 1–31 for `Dom`, 1–12 for `Month`, above 1971 for `Year` and 0–6 for `Dow` (0 meaning Sunday).

- As a special case, a star in either `Dom` or `Dow` doesn't mean "all possible values", but "use only the other field". Note that if both are star'ed, the use of either one gives the same result.

- The `Time-Zone` header is special in that it can only have one value (`GMT`, for instance). A star doesn't mean "all possible values" (because it makes no sense), but "the current local time zone". Most of the time, you'll be using a star here. However, for a list of available time zone values, see the variable **nndiary-headers**.

As a concrete example, here are the diary headers to add to your message for specifying "Each Monday and each 1st of month, at 12:00, 20:00, 21:00, 22:00, 23:00 and 24:00, from 1999 to 2010" (I'll let you find what to do then):

```
X-Diary-Minute: 0
X-Diary-Hour: 12, 20-24
X-Diary-Dom: 1
X-Diary-Month: *
X-Diary-Year: 1999-2010
X-Diary-Dow: 1
X-Diary-Time-Zone: *
```

6.8.1.2 Running NNDiary

nndiary has two modes of operation: "traditional" (the default) and "autonomous". In traditional mode, **nndiary** does not get new mail by itself. You have to move (*B m*) or copy (*B c*) mails from your primary mail back end to nndiary groups in order to handle them as diary messages. In autonomous mode, **nndiary** retrieves its own mail and handles it independently from your primary mail back end.

One should note that Gnus is not inherently designed to allow several "master" mail back ends at the same time. However, this does make sense with **nndiary**: you really want to send and receive diary messages to your diary groups directly. So, **nndiary** supports being sort of a "second primary mail back end" (to my knowledge, it is the only back end offering this feature). However, there is a limitation (which I hope to fix some day): respooling doesn't work in autonomous mode.

In order to use **nndiary** in autonomous mode, you have several things to do:

- Allow **nndiary** to retrieve new mail by itself. Put the following line in your `~/.gnus.el` file:

  ```
  (setq nndiary-get-new-mail t)
  ```

- You must arrange for diary messages (those containing `X-Diary-*` headers) to be split in a private folder *before* Gnus treat them. Again, this is needed because Gnus cannot (yet ?) properly handle multiple primary mail back ends. Getting those messages from a separate source will compensate this misfeature to some extent.

  As an example, here's my procmailrc entry to store diary files in `~/.nndiary` (the default **nndiary** mail source file):

  ```
  :0 HD :
  * ^X-Diary
  .nndiary
  ```

Once this is done, you might want to customize the following two options that affect the diary mail retrieval and splitting processes:

nndiary-mail-sources   [Variable]
> This is the diary-specific replacement for the standard **mail-sources** variable. It obeys the same syntax, and defaults to (`file :path "~/.nndiary"`).

nndiary-split-methods   [Variable]
> This is the diary-specific replacement for the standard **nnmail-split-methods** variable. It obeys the same syntax.

Finally, you may add a permanent **nndiary** virtual server (something like (**nndiary** "diary") should do) to your **gnus-secondary-select-methods**.

Hopefully, almost everything (see the TODO section in **nndiary.el**) will work as expected when you restart Gnus: in autonomous mode, typing *g* and *M-g* in the group buffer, will also get your new diary mails and split them according to your diary-specific rules, *F* will find your new diary groups etc.

6.8.1.3 Customizing NNDiary

Now that **nndiary** is up and running, it's time to customize it. The custom group is called **nndiary** (no, really ?!). You should browse it to figure out which options you'd like to tweak. The following two variables are probably the only ones you will want to change:

nndiary-reminders   [Variable]
> This is the list of times when you want to be reminded of your appointments (e.g., 3 weeks before, then 2 days before, then 1 hour before and that's it). Remember that "being reminded" means that the diary message will pop up as brand new and unread again when you get new mail.

nndiary-week-starts-on-monday   [Variable]
> Rather self-explanatory. Otherwise, Sunday is assumed (this is the default).

6.8.2 The Gnus Diary Library

Using **nndiary** manually (I mean, writing the headers by hand and so on) would be rather boring. Fortunately, there is a library called **gnus-diary** written on top of **nndiary**, that does many useful things for you.

In order to use it, add the following line to your `~/.gnus.el` file:

```
(require 'gnus-diary)
```

Also, you shouldn't use any **gnus-user-format-function-[d|D]** (see Section 3.1.1 [Summary Buffer Lines], page 44). **gnus-diary** provides both of these (sorry if you used them before).

6.8.2.1 Diary Summary Line Format

Displaying diary messages in standard summary line format (usually something like 'From Joe: Subject') is pretty useless. Most of the time, you're the one who wrote the message, and you mostly want to see the event's date.

gnus-diary provides two supplemental user formats to be used in summary line formats. D corresponds to a formatted time string for the next occurrence of the event (e.g., "Sat, Sep 22 01, 12:00"), while d corresponds to an approximate remaining time until the next occurrence of the event (e.g., "in 6 months, 1 week").

For example, here's how Joe's birthday is displayed in my **nndiary+diary:birthdays** summary buffer (note that the message is expirable, but will never be deleted, as it specifies a periodic event):

```
E  Sat, Sep 22 01, 12:00: Joe's birthday (in 6 months, 1 week)
```

In order to get something like the above, you would normally add the following line to your diary groups'parameters:

```
(gnus-summary-line-format "%U%R%z %uD: %(%s%) (%ud)\n")
```

However, **gnus-diary** does it automatically (see Section 6.8.2.4 [Diary Group Parameters], page 198). You can however customize the provided summary line format with the following user options:

gnus-diary-summary-line-format   [Variable]
> Defines the summary line format used for diary groups (see Section 3.1.1 [Summary Buffer Lines], page 44). **gnus-diary** uses it to automatically update the diary groups'parameters.

gnus-diary-time-format   [Variable]
> Defines the format to display dates in diary summary buffers. This is used by the D user format. See the docstring for details.

gnus-diary-delay-format-function   [Variable]
> Defines the format function to use for displaying delays (remaining times) in diary summary buffers. This is used by the d user format. There are currently built-in functions for English and French; you can also define your own. See the docstring for details.

6.8.2.2 Diary Articles Sorting

gnus-diary provides new sorting functions (see Section 3.10 [Sorting the Summary Buffer], page 71) called gnus-summary-sort-by-schedule, gnus-thread-sort-by-schedule and gnus-article-sort-by-schedule. These functions let you organize your diary summary buffers from the closest event to the farthest one.

gnus-diary automatically installs gnus-summary-sort-by-schedule as a menu item in the summary buffer's "sort" menu, and the two others as the primary (hence default) sorting functions in the group parameters (see Section 6.8.2.4 [Diary Group Parameters], page 198).

6.8.2.3 Diary Headers Generation

gnus-diary provides a function called gnus-diary-check-message to help you handle the X-Diary-* headers. This function ensures that the current message contains all the required diary headers, and prompts you for values or corrections if needed.

This function is hooked into the nndiary back end, so that moving or copying an article to a diary group will trigger it automatically. It is also bound to C-c C-f d in message-mode and article-edit-mode in order to ease the process of converting a usual mail to a diary one.

This function takes a prefix argument which will force prompting of all diary headers, regardless of their presence or validity. That way, you can very easily reschedule an already valid diary message, for instance.

6.8.2.4 Diary Group Parameters

When you create a new diary group, or visit one, gnus-diary automatically checks your group parameters and if needed, sets the summary line format to the diary-specific value, installs the diary-specific sorting functions, and also adds the different X-Diary-* headers to the group's posting-style. It is then easier to send a diary message, because if you use C-u a or C-u m on a diary group to prepare a message, these headers will be inserted automatically (although not filled with proper values yet).

6.8.3 Sending or Not Sending

Well, assuming you've read all of the above, here are two final notes on mail sending with nndiary:

- nndiary is a *real* mail back end. You really send real diary messages for real. This means for instance that you can give appointments to anybody (provided they use Gnus and nndiary) by sending the diary message to them as well.

- However, since nndiary also has a request-post method, you can also use C-u a instead of C-u m on a diary group and the message won't actually be sent; just stored locally in the group. This comes in very handy for private appointments.

6.9 Gnus Unplugged

In olden times (ca. February '88), people used to run their newsreaders on big machines with permanent connections to the net. News transport was dealt with by news servers, and all the newsreaders had to do was to read news. Believe it or not.

Nowadays most people read news and mail at home, and use some sort of modem to connect to the net. To avoid running up huge phone bills, it would be nice to have a way to slurp down all the news and mail, hang up the phone, read for several hours, and then upload any responses you have to make. And then you repeat the procedure.

Of course, you can use news servers for doing this as well. I've used **inn** together with **slurp**, **pop** and **sendmail** for some years, but doing that's a bore. Moving the news server functionality up to the newsreader makes sense if you're the only person reading news on a machine.

Setting up Gnus as an "offline" newsreader is quite simple. In fact, you don't have to configure anything as the agent is now enabled by default (see Section 6.9.11 [Agent Variables], page 210).

Of course, to use it as such, you have to learn a few new commands.

6.9.1 Agent Basics

First, let's get some terminology out of the way.

The Gnus Agent is said to be *unplugged* when you have severed the connection to the net (and notified the Agent that this is the case). When the connection to the net is up again (and Gnus knows this), the Agent is *plugged*.

The *local* machine is the one you're running on, and which isn't connected to the net continuously.

Downloading means fetching things from the net to your local machine. *Uploading* is doing the opposite.

You know that Gnus gives you all the opportunity you'd ever want for shooting yourself in the foot. Some people call it flexibility. Gnus is also customizable to a great extent, which means that the user has a say on how Gnus behaves. Other newsreaders might unconditionally shoot you in your foot, but with Gnus, you have a choice!

Gnus is never really in plugged or unplugged state. Rather, it applies that state to each server individually. This means that some servers can be plugged while others can be unplugged. Additionally, some servers can be ignored by the Agent altogether (which means that they're kinda like plugged always).

So when you unplug the Agent and then wonder why is Gnus opening a connection to the Net, the next step to do is to look whether all servers are agentized. If there is an unagentized server, you found the culprit.

Another thing is the *offline* state. Sometimes, servers aren't reachable. When Gnus notices this, it asks you whether you want the server to be switched to offline state. If you say yes, then the server will behave somewhat as if it was unplugged, except that Gnus will ask you whether you want to switch it back online again.

Let's take a typical Gnus session using the Agent.

- You start Gnus with **gnus-unplugged**. This brings up the Gnus Agent in a disconnected state. You can read all the news that you have already fetched while in this mode.

- You then decide to see whether any new news has arrived. You connect your machine to the net (using PPP or whatever), and then hit *J j* to make Gnus become *plugged* and use *g* to check for new mail as usual. To check for new mail in unplugged mode (see Section 6.4.4.1 [Mail Source Specifiers], page 154).

- You can then read the new news immediately, or you can download the news onto your local machine. If you want to do the latter, you press *g* to check if there are any new news and then *J s* to fetch all the eligible articles in all the groups. (To let Gnus know which articles you want to download, see Section 6.9.2 [Agent Categories], page 200).

- After fetching the articles, you press *J j* to make Gnus become unplugged again, and you shut down the PPP thing (or whatever). And then you read the news offline.

- And then you go to step 2.

Here are some things you should do the first time (or so) that you use the Agent.

- Decide which servers should be covered by the Agent. If you have a mail back end, it would probably be nonsensical to have it covered by the Agent. Go to the server buffer (^ in the group buffer) and press *J a* on the server (or servers) that you wish to have covered by the Agent (see Section 6.9.3.3 [Server Agent Commands], page 207), or *J r* on automatically added servers you do not wish to have covered by the Agent. By default, no servers are agentized.

- Decide on download policy. It's fairly simple once you decide whether you are going to use agent categories, topic parameters, and/or group parameters to implement your policy. If you're new to gnus, it is probably best to start with a category, See Section 6.9.2 [Agent Categories], page 200.

  Both topic parameters (see Section 2.16.5 [Topic Parameters], page 37) and agent categories (see Section 6.9.2 [Agent Categories], page 200) provide for setting a policy that applies to multiple groups. Which you use is entirely up to you. Topic parameters do override categories so, if you mix the two, you'll have to take that into account. If you have a few groups that deviate from your policy, you can use group parameters (see Section 2.10 [Group Parameters], page 22) to configure them.

- Uhm... that's it.

6.9.2 Agent Categories

One of the main reasons to integrate the news transport layer into the newsreader is to allow greater control over what articles to download. There's not much point in downloading huge amounts of articles, just to find out that you're not interested in reading any of them. It's better to be somewhat more conservative in choosing what to download, and then mark the articles for downloading manually if it should turn out that you're interested in the articles anyway.

One of the more effective methods for controlling what is to be downloaded is to create a *category* and then assign some (or all) groups to this category. Groups that do not belong in any other category belong to the `default` category. Gnus has its own buffer for creating and managing categories.

If you prefer, you can also use group parameters (see Section 2.10 [Group Parameters], page 22) and topic parameters (see Section 2.16.5 [Topic Parameters], page 37) for an alternative approach to controlling the agent. The only real difference is that categories are specific to the agent (so there is less to learn) while group and topic parameters include the kitchen sink.

Since you can set agent parameters in several different places we have a rule to decide which source to believe. This rule specifies that the parameter sources are checked in the following order: group parameters, topic parameters, agent category, and finally customizable variables. So you can mix all of these sources to produce a wide range of behavior, just don't blame me if you don't remember where you put your settings.

6.9.2.1 Category Syntax

A category consists of a name, the list of groups belonging to the category, and a number of optional parameters that override the customizable variables. The complete list of agent parameters are listed below.

`agent-groups`

> The list of groups that are in this category.

`agent-predicate`

> A predicate which (generally) gives a rough outline of which articles are eligible for downloading; and

`agent-score`

> a score rule which (generally) gives you a finer granularity when deciding what articles to download. (Note that this *download score* is not necessarily related to normal scores.)

`agent-enable-expiration`

> a boolean indicating whether the agent should expire old articles in this group. Most groups should be expired to conserve disk space. In fact, its probably safe to say that the gnus.* hierarchy contains the only groups that should not be expired.

`agent-days-until-old`

> an integer indicating the number of days that the agent should wait before deciding that a read article is safe to expire.

`agent-low-score`

> an integer that overrides the value of **gnus-agent-low-score**.

`agent-high-score`

> an integer that overrides the value of **gnus-agent-high-score**.

`agent-short-article`

> an integer that overrides the value of **gnus-agent-short-article**.

`agent-long-article`

> an integer that overrides the value of **gnus-agent-long-article**.

`agent-enable-undownloaded-faces`

> a symbol indicating whether the summary buffer should display undownloaded articles using the **gnus-summary-*-undownloaded-face** faces. Any symbol other than **nil** will enable the use of undownloaded faces.

The name of a category can not be changed once the category has been created.

Each category maintains a list of groups that are exclusive members of that category. The exclusivity rule is automatically enforced, add a group to a new category and it is automatically removed from its old category.

A predicate in its simplest form can be a single predicate such as **true** or **false**. These two will download every available article or nothing respectively. In the case of these two special predicates an additional score rule is superfluous.

Predicates of **high** or **low** download articles in respect of their scores in relationship to **gnus-agent-high-score** and **gnus-agent-low-score** as described below.

To gain even finer control of what is to be regarded eligible for download a predicate can consist of a number of predicates with logical operators sprinkled in between.

Perhaps some examples are in order.

Here's a simple predicate. (It's the default predicate, in fact, used for all groups that don't belong to any other category.)

```
short
```

Quite simple, eh? This predicate is true if and only if the article is short (for some value of "short").

Here's a more complex predicate:

```
(or high
    (and
     (not low)
     (not long)))
```

This means that an article should be downloaded if it has a high score, or if the score is not low and the article is not long. You get the drift.

The available logical operators are **or**, **and** and **not**. (If you prefer, you can use the more "C"-ish operators '|', & and ! instead.)

The following predicates are pre-defined, but if none of these fit what you want to do, you can write your own.

When evaluating each of these predicates, the named constant will be bound to the value determined by calling **gnus-agent-find-parameter** on the appropriate parameter. For example, gnus-agent-short-article will be bound to (**gnus-agent-find-parameter** group 'agent-short-article). This means that you can specify a predicate in your category then tune that predicate to individual groups.

short   True if the article is shorter than **gnus-agent-short-article** lines; default 100.

long   True if the article is longer than **gnus-agent-long-article** lines; default 200.

low   True if the article has a download score less than **gnus-agent-low-score**; default 0.

high   True if the article has a download score greater than **gnus-agent-high-score**; default 0.

spam   True if the Gnus Agent guesses that the article is spam. The heuristics may change over time, but at present it just computes a checksum and sees whether articles match.

true   Always true.

false   Always false.

If you want to create your own predicate function, here's what you have to know: The functions are called with no parameters, but the **gnus-headers** and **gnus-score** dynamic variables are bound to useful values.

For example, you could decide that you don't want to download articles that were posted more than a certain number of days ago (e.g., posted more than **gnus-agent-expire-days** ago) you might write a function something along the lines of the following:

```
(defun my-article-old-p ()
  "Say whether an article is old."
  (< (time-to-days (date-to-time (mail-header-date gnus-headers)))
     (- (time-to-days (current-time)) gnus-agent-expire-days)))
```

with the predicate then defined as:

```
(not my-article-old-p)
```

or you could append your predicate to the predefined **gnus-category-predicate-alist** in your `~/.gnus.el` or wherever.

```
(require 'gnus-agent)
(setq  gnus-category-predicate-alist
  (append gnus-category-predicate-alist
        '((old . my-article-old-p))))
```

and simply specify your predicate as:

```
(not old)
```

If/when using something like the above, be aware that there are many misconfigured systems/mailers out there and so an article's date is not always a reliable indication of when it was posted. Hell, some people just don't give a damn.

The above predicates apply to *all* the groups which belong to the category. However, if you wish to have a specific predicate for an individual group within a category, or you're just too lazy to set up a new category, you can enter a group's individual predicate in its group parameters like so:

```
(agent-predicate . short)
```

This is the group/topic parameter equivalent of the agent category default. Note that when specifying a single word predicate like this, the **agent-predicate** specification must be in dotted pair notation.

The equivalent of the longer example from above would be:

```
(agent-predicate or high (and (not low) (not long)))
```

The outer parenthesis required in the category specification are not entered here as, not being in dotted pair notation, the value of the predicate is assumed to be a list.

Now, the syntax of the download score is the same as the syntax of normal score files, except that all elements that require actually seeing the article itself are verboten. This means that only the following headers can be scored on: **Subject**, **From**, **Date**, **Message-ID**, **References**, **Chars**, **Lines**, and **Xref**.

As with predicates, the specification of the **download score rule** to use in respect of a group can be in either the category definition if it's to be applicable to all groups in therein, or a group's parameters if it's to be specific to that group.

In both of these places the **download score rule** can take one of three forms:

1. Score rule

   This has the same syntax as a normal Gnus score file except only a subset of scoring keywords are available as mentioned above.

   example:

   - Category specification

     ```
     (("from"
             ("Lars Ingebrigtsen" 1000000 nil s))
      ("lines"
             (500 -100 nil <)))
     ```

   - Group/Topic Parameter specification

     ```
     (agent-score ("from"
                         ("Lars Ingebrigtsen" 1000000 nil s))
                   ("lines"
                         (500 -100 nil <)))
     ```

     Again, note the omission of the outermost parenthesis here.

2. Agent score file

   These score files must *only* contain the permitted scoring keywords stated above.

   example:

   - Category specification

     ```
     ("~/News/agent.SCORE")
     ```

     or perhaps

     ```
     ("~/News/agent.SCORE" "~/News/agent.group.SCORE")
     ```

   - Group Parameter specification

     ```
     (agent-score "~/News/agent.SCORE")
     ```

     Additional score files can be specified as above. Need I say anything about parenthesis?

3. Use **normal** score files

   If you don't want to maintain two sets of scoring rules for a group, and your desired **downloading** criteria for a group are the same as your **reading** criteria then you can tell the agent to refer to your **normal** score files when deciding what to download.

   These directives in either the category definition or a group's parameters will cause the agent to read in all the applicable score files for a group, *filtering out* those sections that do not relate to one of the permitted subset of scoring keywords.

   - Category Specification

     ```
     file
     ```

   - Group Parameter specification

     ```
     (agent-score . file)
     ```

6.9.2.2 Category Buffer

You'd normally do all category maintenance from the category buffer. When you enter it for the first time (with the *J c* command from the group buffer), you'll only see the **default** category.

The following commands are available in this buffer:

q	Return to the group buffer (**gnus-category-exit**).
e	Use a customization buffer to set all of the selected category's parameters at one time (**gnus-category-customize-category**).
k	Kill the current category (**gnus-category-kill**).
c	Copy the current category (**gnus-category-copy**).
a	Add a new category (**gnus-category-add**).
p	Edit the predicate of the current category (**gnus-category-edit-predicate**).
g	Edit the list of groups belonging to the current category (**gnus-category-edit-groups**).
s	Edit the download score rule of the current category (**gnus-category-edit-score**).
l	List all the categories (**gnus-category-list**).

6.9.2.3 Category Variables

gnus-category-mode-hook
> Hook run in category buffers.

gnus-category-line-format
> Format of the lines in the category buffer (see Section 9.4 [Formatting Variables], page 250). Valid elements are:

> | | |
> |---|---|
> | 'c' | The name of the category. |
> | 'g' | The number of groups in the category. |

gnus-category-mode-line-format
> Format of the category mode line (see Section 9.4.2 [Mode Line Formatting], page 251).

gnus-agent-short-article
> Articles that have fewer lines than this are short. Default 100.

gnus-agent-long-article
> Articles that have more lines than this are long. Default 200.

gnus-agent-low-score
> Articles that have a score lower than this have a low score. Default 0.

gnus-agent-high-score
> Articles that have a score higher than this have a high score. Default 0.

gnus-agent-expire-days
> The number of days that a 'read' article must stay in the agent's local disk before becoming eligible for expiration (While the name is the same, this doesn't mean expiring the article on the server. It just means deleting the local copy of the article). What is also important to understand is that the counter starts with the time the article was written to the local disk and not the time the article was read. Default 7.

`gnus-agent-enable-expiration`

> Determines whether articles in a group are, by default, expired or retained indefinitely. The default is `ENABLE` which means that you'll have to disable expiration when desired. On the other hand, you could set this to `DISABLE`. In that case, you would then have to enable expiration in selected groups.

6.9.3 Agent Commands

All the Gnus Agent commands are on the *J* submap. The *J j* (`gnus-agent-toggle-plugged`) command works in all modes, and toggles the plugged/unplugged state of the Gnus Agent.

6.9.3.1 Group Agent Commands

J u   Fetch all eligible articles in the current group (`gnus-agent-fetch-groups`).

J c   Enter the Agent category buffer (`gnus-enter-category-buffer`).

J s   Fetch all eligible articles in all groups (`gnus-agent-fetch-session`).

J S   Send all sendable messages in the queue group (`gnus-group-send-queue`). See Section 5.7 [Drafts], page 133.

J a   Add the current group to an Agent category (`gnus-agent-add-group`). This command understands the process/prefix convention (see Section 9.1 [Process/Prefix], page 249).

J r   Remove the current group from its category, if any (`gnus-agent-remove-group`). This command understands the process/prefix convention (see Section 9.1 [Process/Prefix], page 249).

J Y   Synchronize flags changed while unplugged with remote server, if any.

6.9.3.2 Summary Agent Commands

J #   Mark the article for downloading (`gnus-agent-mark-article`).

J M-#   Remove the downloading mark from the article (`gnus-agent-unmark-article`).

@   Toggle whether to download the article (`gnus-agent-toggle-mark`). The download mark is '%' by default.

J c   Mark all articles as read (`gnus-agent-catchup`) that are neither cached, downloaded, nor downloadable.

J S   Download all eligible (see Section 6.9.2 [Agent Categories], page 200) articles in this group. (`gnus-agent-fetch-group`).

J s   Download all processable articles in this group. (`gnus-agent-summary-fetch-series`).

J u   Download all downloadable articles in the current group (`gnus-agent-summary-fetch-group`).

6.9.3.3 Server Agent Commands

J a   Add the current server to the list of servers covered by the Gnus Agent (`gnus-agent-add-server`).

J r   Remove the current server from the list of servers covered by the Gnus Agent (`gnus-agent-remove-server`).

6.9.4 Agent Visuals

If you open a summary while unplugged and, Gnus knows from the group's active range that there are more articles than the headers currently stored in the Agent, you may see some articles whose subject looks something like '`[Undownloaded article #####]`'. These are placeholders for the missing headers. Aside from setting a mark, there is not much that can be done with one of these placeholders. When Gnus finally gets a chance to fetch the group's headers, the placeholders will automatically be replaced by the actual headers. You can configure the summary buffer's maneuvering to skip over the placeholders if you care (See `gnus-auto-goto-ignores`).

While it may be obvious to all, the only headers and articles available while unplugged are those headers and articles that were fetched into the Agent while previously plugged. To put it another way, "If you forget to fetch something while plugged, you might have a less than satisfying unplugged session". For this reason, the Agent adds two visual effects to your summary buffer. These effects display the download status of each article so that you always know which articles will be available when unplugged.

The first visual effect is the '`%O`' spec. If you customize `gnus-summary-line-format` to include this specifier, you will add a single character field that indicates an article's download status. Articles that have been fetched into either the Agent or the Cache, will display `gnus-downloaded-mark` (defaults to '`+`'). All other articles will display `gnus-undownloaded-mark` (defaults to '`-`'). If you open a group that has not been agentized, a space (' ') will be displayed.

The second visual effect are the undownloaded faces. The faces, there are three indicating the article's score (low, normal, high), seem to result in a love/hate response from many Gnus users. The problem is that the face selection is controlled by a list of condition tests and face names (See `gnus-summary-highlight`). Each condition is tested in the order in which it appears in the list so early conditions have precedence over later conditions. All of this means that, if you tick an undownloaded article, the article will continue to be displayed in the undownloaded face rather than the ticked face.

If you use the Agent as a cache (to avoid downloading the same article each time you visit it or to minimize your connection time), the undownloaded face will probably seem like a good idea. The reason being that you do all of our work (marking, reading, deleting) with downloaded articles so the normal faces always appear. For those users using the agent to improve online performance by caching the NOV database (most users since 5.10.2), the undownloaded faces may appear to be an absolutely horrible idea. The issue being that, since none of their articles have been fetched into the Agent, all of the normal faces will be obscured by the undownloaded faces.

If you would like to use the undownloaded faces, you must enable the undownloaded faces by setting the `agent-enable-undownloaded-faces` group parameter to `t`. This parameter, like all other agent parameters, may be set on an Agent Category (see Section 6.9.2 [Agent

Categories], page 200), a Group Topic (see Section 2.16.5 [Topic Parameters], page 37), or an individual group (see Section 2.10 [Group Parameters], page 22).

The one problem common to all users using the agent is how quickly it can consume disk space. If you using the agent on many groups, it is even more difficult to effectively recover disk space. One solution is the '%F' format available in gnus-group-line-format. This format will display the actual disk space used by articles fetched into both the agent and cache. By knowing which groups use the most space, users know where to focus their efforts when "agent expiring" articles.

6.9.5 Agent as Cache

When Gnus is plugged, it is not efficient to download headers or articles from the server again, if they are already stored in the Agent. So, Gnus normally only downloads headers once, and stores them in the Agent. These headers are later used when generating the summary buffer, regardless of whether you are plugged or unplugged. Articles are not cached in the Agent by default though (that would potentially consume lots of disk space), but if you have already downloaded an article into the Agent, Gnus will not download the article from the server again but use the locally stored copy instead.

If you so desire, you can configure the agent (see gnus-agent-cache see Section 6.9.11 [Agent Variables], page 210) to always download headers and articles while plugged. Gnus will almost certainly be slower, but it will be kept synchronized with the server. That last point probably won't make any sense if you are using a nntp or nnimap back end.

6.9.6 Agent Expiry

The Agent back end, nnagent, doesn't handle expiry. Well, at least it doesn't handle it like other back ends. Instead, there are special gnus-agent-expire and gnus-agent-expire-group commands that will expire all read articles that are older than gnus-agent-expire-days days. They can be run whenever you feel that you're running out of space. Neither are particularly fast or efficient, and it's not a particularly good idea to interrupt them (with C-g or anything else) once you've started one of them.

Note that other functions might run gnus-agent-expire for you to keep the agent synchronized with the group.

The agent parameter agent-enable-expiration may be used to prevent expiration in selected groups.

If gnus-agent-expire-all is non-nil, the agent expiration commands will expire all articles—unread, read, ticked and dormant. If nil (which is the default), only read articles are eligible for expiry, and unread, ticked and dormant articles will be kept indefinitely.

If you find that some articles eligible for expiry are never expired, perhaps some Gnus Agent files are corrupted. There's are special commands, gnus-agent-regenerate and gnus-agent-regenerate-group, to fix possible problems.

6.9.7 Agent Regeneration

The local data structures used by nnagent may become corrupted due to certain exceptional conditions. When this happens, nnagent functionality may degrade or even fail. The solution to this problem is to repair the local data structures by removing all internal inconsistencies.

For example, if your connection to your server is lost while downloaded articles into the agent, the local data structures will not know about articles successfully downloaded prior to the connection failure. Running `gnus-agent-regenerate` or `gnus-agent-regenerate-group` will update the data structures such that you don't need to download these articles a second time.

The command `gnus-agent-regenerate` will perform `gnus-agent-regenerate-group` on every agentized group. While you can run `gnus-agent-regenerate` in any buffer, it is strongly recommended that you first close all summary buffers.

The command `gnus-agent-regenerate-group` uses the local copies of individual articles to repair the local NOV(header) database. It then updates the internal data structures that document which articles are stored locally. An optional argument will mark articles in the agent as unread.

6.9.8 Agent and flags

The Agent works with any Gnus back end including those, such as nnimap, that store flags (read, ticked, etc.) on the server. Sadly, the Agent does not actually know which backends keep their flags in the backend server rather than in `.newsrc`. This means that the Agent, while unplugged or disconnected, will always record all changes to the flags in its own files.

When you plug back in, Gnus will then check to see if you have any changed any flags and ask if you wish to synchronize these with the server. This behavior is customizable by `gnus-agent-synchronize-flags`.

If `gnus-agent-synchronize-flags` is `nil`, the Agent will never automatically synchronize flags. If it is `ask`, which is the default, the Agent will check if you made any changes and if so ask if you wish to synchronize these when you re-connect. If it has any other value, all flags will be synchronized automatically.

If you do not wish to synchronize flags automatically when you re-connect, you can do it manually with the `gnus-agent-synchronize-flags` command that is bound to *J Y* in the group buffer.

Technical note: the synchronization algorithm does not work by "pushing" all local flags to the server, but rather by incrementally updated the server view of flags by changing only those flags that were changed by the user. Thus, if you set one flag on an article, quit the group then re-select the group and remove the flag; the flag will be set and removed from the server when you "synchronize". The queued flag operations can be found in the per-server `flags` file in the Agent directory. It's emptied when you synchronize flags.

6.9.9 Agent and IMAP

The Agent works with any Gnus back end, including nnimap. However, since there are some conceptual differences between NNTP and IMAP, this section (should) provide you with some information to make Gnus Agent work smoother as a IMAP Disconnected Mode client.

Some things are currently not implemented in the Agent that you'd might expect from a disconnected IMAP client, including:

- Copying/moving articles into nnimap groups when unplugged.
- Creating/deleting nnimap groups when unplugged.

6.9.10 Outgoing Messages

By default, when Gnus is unplugged, all outgoing messages (both mail and news) are stored in the draft group "queue" (see Section 5.7 [Drafts], page 133). You can view them there after posting, and edit them at will.

You can control the circumstances under which outgoing mail is queued (see `gnus-agent-queue-mail`, see Section 6.9.11 [Agent Variables], page 210). Outgoing news is always queued when Gnus is unplugged, and never otherwise.

You can send the messages either from the draft group with the special commands available there, or you can use the *J S* command in the group buffer to send all the sendable messages in the draft group. Posting news will only work when Gnus is plugged, but you can send mail at any time.

If sending mail while unplugged does not work for you and you worry about hitting *J S* by accident when unplugged, you can have Gnus ask you to confirm your action (see `gnus-agent-prompt-send-queue`, see Section 6.9.11 [Agent Variables], page 210).

6.9.11 Agent Variables

`gnus-agent`

> Is the agent enabled? The default is **t**. When first enabled, the agent will use `gnus-agent-auto-agentize-methods` to automatically mark some back ends as agentized. You may change which back ends are agentized using the agent commands in the server buffer.
>
> To enter the server buffer, use the ^ (`gnus-group-enter-server-mode`) command in the group buffer.

`gnus-agent-directory`

> Where the Gnus Agent will store its files. The default is `~/News/agent/`.

`gnus-agent-handle-level`

> Groups on levels (see Section 2.6 [Group Levels], page 17) higher than this variable will be ignored by the Agent. The default is `gnus-level-subscribed`, which means that only subscribed group will be considered by the Agent by default.

`gnus-agent-plugged-hook`

> Hook run when connecting to the network.

`gnus-agent-unplugged-hook`

> Hook run when disconnecting from the network.

`gnus-agent-fetched-hook`

> Hook run when finished fetching articles.

`gnus-agent-cache`

> Variable to control whether use the locally stored NOV and articles when plugged, e.g., essentially using the Agent as a cache. The default is non-**nil**, which means to use the Agent as a cache.

`gnus-agent-go-online`

> If `gnus-agent-go-online` is **nil**, the Agent will never automatically switch offline servers into online status. If it is **ask**, the default, the Agent will ask if

you wish to switch offline servers into online status when you re-connect. If it
has any other value, all offline servers will be automatically switched into online
status.

`gnus-agent-mark-unread-after-downloaded`

> If `gnus-agent-mark-unread-after-downloaded` is non-`nil`, mark articles as
> unread after downloading. This is usually a safe thing to do as the newly
> downloaded article has obviously not been read. The default is `t`.

`gnus-agent-synchronize-flags`

> If `gnus-agent-synchronize-flags` is `nil`, the Agent will never automatically
> synchronize flags. If it is `ask`, which is the default, the Agent will check if you
> made any changes and if so ask if you wish to synchronize these when you re-
> connect. If it has any other value, all flags will be synchronized automatically.

`gnus-agent-consider-all-articles`

> If `gnus-agent-consider-all-articles` is non-`nil`, the agent will let the agent
> predicate decide whether articles need to be downloaded or not, for all articles.
> When `nil`, the default, the agent will only let the predicate decide whether
> unread articles are downloaded or not. If you enable this, you may also want
> to look into the agent expiry settings (see Section 6.9.2.3 [Category Variables],
> page 205), so that the agent doesn't download articles which the agent will later
> expire, over and over again.

`gnus-agent-max-fetch-size`

> The agent fetches articles into a temporary buffer prior to parsing them into
> individual files. To avoid exceeding the max. buffer size, the agent alternates
> between fetching and parsing until all articles have been fetched. `gnus-agent-`
> `max-fetch-size` provides a size limit to control how often the cycling occurs.
> A large value improves performance. A small value minimizes the time lost
> should the connection be lost while fetching (You may need to run `gnus-agent-`
> `regenerate-group` to update the group's state. However, all articles parsed
> prior to losing the connection will be available while unplugged). The default
> is 10M so it is unusual to see any cycling.

`gnus-server-unopen-status`

> Perhaps not an Agent variable, but closely related to the Agent, this variable
> says what will happen if Gnus cannot open a server. If the Agent is enabled, the
> default, `nil`, makes Gnus ask the user whether to deny the server or whether
> to unplug the agent. If the Agent is disabled, Gnus always simply deny the
> server. Other choices for this variable include `denied` and `offline` the latter
> is only valid if the Agent is used.

`gnus-auto-goto-ignores`

> Another variable that isn't an Agent variable, yet so closely related that most
> will look for it here, this variable tells the summary buffer how to maneuver
> around undownloaded (only headers stored in the agent) and unfetched (neither
> article nor headers stored) articles.
>
> The valid values are `nil` (maneuver to any article), `undownloaded`
> (maneuvering while unplugged ignores articles that have not been fetched),

> always-undownloaded (maneuvering always ignores articles that have not
> been fetched), unfetched (maneuvering ignores articles whose headers have
> not been fetched).

gnus-agent-queue-mail

> When gnus-agent-queue-mail is always, Gnus will always queue mail rather
> than sending it straight away. When t, Gnus will queue mail when unplugged
> only. When nil, never queue mail. The default is t.

gnus-agent-prompt-send-queue

> When gnus-agent-prompt-send-queue is non-nil Gnus will prompt you to
> confirm that you really wish to proceed if you hit J S while unplugged. The
> default is nil.

gnus-agent-auto-agentize-methods

> If you have never used the Agent before (or more technically, if
> ~/News/agent/lib/servers does not exist), Gnus will automatically agentize
> a few servers for you. This variable control which back ends should be
> auto-agentized. It is typically only useful to agentize remote back ends.
> The auto-agentizing has the same effect as running J a on the servers (see
> Section 6.9.3.3 [Server Agent Commands], page 207). If the file exist, you
> must manage the servers manually by adding or removing them, this variable
> is only applicable the first time you start Gnus. The default is 'nil'.

6.9.12 Example Setup

If you don't want to read this manual, and you have a fairly standard setup, you may be
able to use something like the following as your ~/.gnus.el file to get started.

```
;; Define how Gnus is to fetch news.  We do this over NNTP
;; from your ISP's server.
(setq gnus-select-method '(nntp "news.your-isp.com"))

;; Define how Gnus is to read your mail.  We read mail from
;; your ISP's POP server.
(setq mail-sources '((pop :server "pop.your-isp.com")))

;; Say how Gnus is to store the mail.  We use nnml groups.
(setq gnus-secondary-select-methods '((nnml "")))

;; Make Gnus into an offline newsreader.
;; (gnus-agentize) ; The obsolete setting.
;; (setq gnus-agent t) ; Now the default.
```

That should be it, basically. Put that in your ~/.gnus.el file, edit to suit your needs,
start up PPP (or whatever), and type M-x gnus.

If this is the first time you've run Gnus, you will be subscribed automatically to a few
default newsgroups. You'll probably want to subscribe to more groups, and to do that, you
have to query the NNTP server for a complete list of groups with the A A command. This
usually takes quite a while, but you only have to do it once.

After reading and parsing a while, you'll be presented with a list of groups. Subscribe to the ones you want to read with the u command. l to make all the killed groups disappear after you've subscribe to all the groups you want to read. (A k will bring back all the killed groups.)

You can now read the groups at once, or you can download the articles with the J s command. And then read the rest of this manual to find out which of the other gazillion things you want to customize.

6.9.13 Batching Agents

Having the Gnus Agent fetch articles (and post whatever messages you've written) is quite easy once you've gotten things set up properly. The following shell script will do everything that is necessary:

You can run a complete batch command from the command line with the following incantation:

```
#!/bin/sh
emacs -batch -l ~/.emacs -l ~/.gnus.el -f gnus-agent-batch >/dev/null 2>&1
```

6.9.14 Agent Caveats

The Gnus Agent doesn't seem to work like most other offline newsreaders. Here are some common questions that some imaginary people may ask:

If I read an article while plugged, do they get entered into the Agent?

> **No.** If you want this behavior, add `gnus-agent-fetch-selected-article` to `gnus-select-article-hook`.

If I read an article while plugged, and the article already exists in
> the Agent, will it get downloaded once more?

> **No**, unless `gnus-agent-cache` is `nil`.

In short, when Gnus is unplugged, it only looks into the locally stored articles; when it's plugged, it talks to your ISP and may also use the locally stored articles.

7 Scoring

Other people use *kill files*, but we here at Gnus Towers like scoring better than killing, so we'd rather switch than fight. They do something completely different as well, so sit up straight and pay attention!

All articles have a default score (`gnus-summary-default-score`), which is 0 by default. This score may be raised or lowered either interactively or by score files. Articles that have a score lower than `gnus-summary-mark-below` are marked as read.

Gnus will read any *score files* that apply to the current group before generating the summary buffer.

There are several commands in the summary buffer that insert score entries based on the current article. You can, for instance, ask Gnus to lower or increase the score of all articles with a certain subject.

There are two sorts of scoring entries: Permanent and temporary. Temporary score entries are self-expiring entries. Any entries that are temporary and have not been used for, say, a week, will be removed silently to help keep the sizes of the score files down.

7.1 Summary Score Commands

The score commands that alter score entries do not actually modify real score files. That would be too inefficient. Gnus maintains a cache of previously loaded score files, one of which is considered the *current score file alist*. The score commands simply insert entries into this list, and upon group exit, this list is saved.

The current score file is by default the group's local score file, even if no such score file actually exists. To insert score commands into some other score file (e.g., `all.SCORE`), you must first make this score file the current one.

General score commands that don't actually change the score file:

V s   Set the score of the current article (`gnus-summary-set-score`).

V S   Display the score of the current article (`gnus-summary-current-score`).

V t   Display all score rules that have been used on the current article (`gnus-score-find-trace`). In the *Score Trace* buffer, you may type *e* to edit score file corresponding to the score rule on current line and *f* to format (`gnus-score-pretty-print`) the score file and edit it.

V w   List words used in scoring (`gnus-score-find-favourite-words`).

V R   Run the current summary through the scoring process (`gnus-summary-rescore`). This might be useful if you're playing around with your score files behind Gnus' back and want to see the effect you're having.

V c   Make a different score file the current (`gnus-score-change-score-file`).

V e   Edit the current score file (`gnus-score-edit-current-scores`). You will be popped into a `gnus-score-mode` buffer (see Section 7.5 [Score File Editing], page 223).

V f   Edit a score file and make this score file the current one (`gnus-score-edit-file`).

V F   Flush the score cache (`gnus-score-flush-cache`). This is useful after editing
               score files.

V C   Customize a score file in a visually pleasing manner (`gnus-score-customize`).

    The rest of these commands modify the local score file.

V m   Prompt for a score, and mark all articles with a score below this as read
               (`gnus-score-set-mark-below`).

V x   Prompt for a score, and add a score rule to the current score file to expunge all
               articles below this score (`gnus-score-set-expunge-below`).

    The keystrokes for actually making score entries follow a very regular pattern, so there's
no need to list all the commands. (Hundreds of them.)

1. The first key is either *I* (upper case i) for increasing the score or *L* for lowering the
   score.

2. The second key says what header you want to score on. The following keys are available:

   `a`   Score on the author name.

   `s`   Score on the subject line.

   `x`   Score on the `Xref` line—i.e., the cross-posting line.

   `r`   Score on the `References` line.

   `d`   Score on the date.

   `l`   Score on the number of lines.

   `i`   Score on the `Message-ID` header.

   `e`   Score on an "extra" header, that is, one of those in gnus-extra-headers, if
               your NNTP server tracks additional header data in overviews.

   `f`   Score on followups—this matches the author name, and adds scores to the
               followups to this author. (Using this key leads to the creation of `ADAPT`
               files.)

   `b`   Score on the body.

   `h`   Score on the head.

   `t`   Score on thread. (Using this key leads to the creation of `ADAPT` files.)

3. The third key is the match type. Which match types are valid depends on what headers
   you are scoring on.

   `strings`

           `e`   Exact matching.

           `s`   Substring matching.

           `f`   Fuzzy matching (see Section 9.15 [Fuzzy Matching], page 267).

           `r`   Regexp matching

   `date`

b	Before date.
a	After date.
n	This date.

`number`

<	Less than number.
=	Equal to number.
>	Greater than number.

4. The fourth and usually final key says whether this is a temporary (i.e., expiring) score entry, or a permanent (i.e., non-expiring) score entry, or whether it is to be done immediately, without adding to the score file.

t	Temporary score entry.
p	Permanent score entry.
i	Immediately scoring.

5. If you are scoring on 'e' (extra) headers, you will then be prompted for the header name on which you wish to score. This must be a header named in gnus-extra-headers, and 'TAB' completion is available.

So, let's say you want to increase the score on the current author with exact matching permanently: *I a e p*. If you want to lower the score based on the subject line, using substring matching, and make a temporary score entry: *L s s t*. Pretty easy.

To make things a bit more complicated, there are shortcuts. If you use a capital letter on either the second or third keys, Gnus will use defaults for the remaining one or two keystrokes. The defaults are "substring" and "temporary". So *I A* is the same as *I a s t*, and *I a R* is the same as *I a r t*.

These functions take both the numerical prefix and the symbolic prefix (see Section 9.3 [Symbolic Prefixes], page 250). A numerical prefix says how much to lower (or increase) the score of the article. A symbolic prefix of **a** says to use the **all.SCORE** file for the command instead of the current score file.

The **gnus-score-mimic-keymap** says whether these commands will pretend they are keymaps or not.

7.2 Group Score Commands

There aren't many of these as yet, I'm afraid.

W e	Edit the apply-to-all-groups all.SCORE file. You will be popped into a **gnus-score-mode** buffer (see Section 7.5 [Score File Editing], page 223).
W f	Gnus maintains a cache of score alists to avoid having to reload them all the time. This command will flush the cache (**gnus-score-flush-cache**).

You can do scoring from the command line by saying something like:

```
$ emacs -batch -l ~/.emacs -l ~/.gnus.el -f gnus-batch-score
```

7.3 Score Variables

gnus-use-scoring

> If nil, Gnus will not check for score files, and will not, in general, do any score-related work. This is t by default.

gnus-kill-killed

> If this variable is nil, Gnus will never apply score files to articles that have already been through the kill process. While this may save you lots of time, it also means that if you apply a kill file to a group, and then change the kill file and want to run it over you group again to kill more articles, it won't work. You have to set this variable to t to do that. (It is t by default.)

gnus-kill-files-directory

> All kill and score files will be stored in this directory, which is initialized from the SAVEDIR environment variable by default. This is ~/News/ by default.

gnus-score-file-suffix

> Suffix to add to the group name to arrive at the score file name (SCORE by default.)

gnus-score-uncacheable-files

> All score files are normally cached to avoid excessive re-loading of score files. However, this might make your Emacs grow big and bloated, so this regexp can be used to weed out score files unlikely to be needed again. It would be a bad idea to deny caching of all.SCORE, while it might be a good idea to not cache comp.infosystems.www.authoring.misc.ADAPT. In fact, this variable is 'ADAPT$' by default, so no adaptive score files will be cached.

gnus-save-score

> If you have really complicated score files, and do lots of batch scoring, then you might set this variable to t. This will make Gnus save the scores into the .newsrc.eld file.

> If you do not set this to t, then manual scores (like those set with V s (gnus-summary-set-score)) will not be preserved across group visits.

gnus-score-interactive-default-score

> Score used by all the interactive raise/lower commands to raise/lower score with. Default is 1000, which may seem excessive, but this is to ensure that the adaptive scoring scheme gets enough room to play with. We don't want the small changes from the adaptive scoring to overwrite manually entered data.

gnus-summary-default-score

> Default score of an article, which is 0 by default.

gnus-summary-expunge-below

> Don't display the summary lines of articles that have scores lower than this variable. This is nil by default, which means that no articles will be hidden. This variable is local to the summary buffers, and has to be set from gnus-summary-mode-hook.

`gnus-score-over-mark`

> Mark (in the third column) used for articles with a score over the default. Default is '+'.

`gnus-score-below-mark`

> Mark (in the third column) used for articles with a score below the default. Default is '-'.

`gnus-score-find-score-files-function`

> Function used to find score files for the current group. This function is called with the name of the group as the argument.
>
> Predefined functions available are:
>
> `gnus-score-find-single`
>
>> Only apply the group's own score file.
>
> `gnus-score-find-bnews`
>
>> Apply all score files that match, using bnews syntax. This is the default. If the current group is 'gnu.emacs.gnus', for instance, `all.emacs.all.SCORE`, `not.alt.all.SCORE` and `gnu.all.SCORE` would all apply. In short, the instances of 'all' in the score file names are translated into '.*', and then a regexp match is done.
>>
>> This means that if you have some score entries that you want to apply to all groups, then you put those entries in the `all.SCORE` file.
>>
>> The score files are applied in a semi-random order, although Gnus will try to apply the more general score files before the more specific score files. It does this by looking at the number of elements in the score file names—discarding the 'all' elements.
>
> `gnus-score-find-hierarchical`
>
>> Apply all score files from all the parent groups. This means that you can't have score files like `all.SCORE`, but you can have `SCORE`, `comp.SCORE` and `comp.emacs.SCORE` for each server.
>
> This variable can also be a list of functions. In that case, all these functions will be called with the group name as argument, and all the returned lists of score files will be applied. These functions can also return lists of lists of score alists directly. In that case, the functions that return these non-file score alists should probably be placed before the "real" score file functions, to ensure that the last score file returned is the local score file. Phu.
>
> For example, to do hierarchical scoring but use a non-server-specific overall score file, you could use the value
>
>> ```
>> (list (lambda (group) ("all.SCORE"))
>>       'gnus-score-find-hierarchical)
>> ```

`gnus-score-expiry-days`

> This variable says how many days should pass before an unused score file entry is expired. If this variable is `nil`, no score file entries are expired. It's 7 by default.

`gnus-update-score-entry-dates`
> If this variable is non-`nil`, temporary score entries that have been triggered (matched) will have their dates updated. (This is how Gnus controls expiry—all non-matched-entries will become too old while matched entries will stay fresh and young.) However, if you set this variable to `nil`, even matched entries will grow old and will have to face that oh-so grim reaper.

`gnus-score-after-write-file-function`
> Function called with the name of the score file just written.

`gnus-score-thread-simplify`
> If this variable is non-`nil`, article subjects will be simplified for subject scoring purposes in the same manner as with threading—according to the current value of `gnus-simplify-subject-functions`. If the scoring entry uses `substring` or `exact` matching, the match will also be simplified in this manner.

7.4 Score File Format

A score file is an `emacs-lisp` file that normally contains just a single form. Casual users are not expected to edit these files; everything can be changed from the summary buffer.

Anyway, if you'd like to dig into it yourself, here's an example:

```
(("from"
  ("Lars Ingebrigtsen" -10000)
  ("Per Abrahamsen")
  ("larsi\\|lmi" -50000 nil R))
 ("subject"
  ("Ding is Badd" nil 728373))
 ("xref"
  ("alt.politics" -1000 728372 s))
 ("lines"
  (2 -100 nil <))
 (mark 0)
 (expunge -1000)
 (mark-and-expunge -10)
 (read-only nil)
 (orphan -10)
 (adapt t)
 (files "/hom/larsi/News/gnu.SCORE")
 (exclude-files "all.SCORE")
 (local (gnus-newsgroup-auto-expire t)
        (gnus-summary-make-false-root empty))
 (eval (ding)))
```

This example demonstrates most score file elements. See Section 7.15 [Advanced Scoring], page 231, for a different approach.

Even though this looks much like Lisp code, nothing here is actually `evaled`. The Lisp reader is used to read this form, though, so it has to be valid syntactically, if not semantically.

Six keys are supported by this alist:

STRING   If the key is a string, it is the name of the header to perform the match on. Scoring can only be performed on these eight headers: From, Subject, References, Message-ID, Xref, Lines, Chars and Date. In addition to these headers, there are three strings to tell Gnus to fetch the entire article and do the match on larger parts of the article: Body will perform the match on the body of the article, Head will perform the match on the head of the article, and All will perform the match on the entire article. Note that using any of these last three keys will slow down group entry *considerably*. The final "header" you can score on is Followup. These score entries will result in new score entries being added for all follow-ups to articles that matches these score entries.

Following this key is an arbitrary number of score entries, where each score entry has one to four elements.

1. The first element is the *match element*. On most headers this will be a string, but on the Lines and Chars headers, this must be an integer.

2. If the second element is present, it should be a number—the *score element*. This number should be an integer in the neginf to posinf interval. This number is added to the score of the article if the match is successful. If this element is not present, the gnus-score-interactive-default-score number will be used instead. This is 1000 by default.

3. If the third element is present, it should be a number—the *date element*. This date says when the last time this score entry matched, which provides a mechanism for expiring the score entries. It this element is not present, the score entry is permanent. The date is represented by the number of days since December 31, 1 BCE.

4. If the fourth element is present, it should be a symbol—the *type element*. This element specifies what function should be used to see whether this score entry matches the article. What match types that can be used depends on what header you wish to perform the match on.

From, Subject, References, Xref, Message-ID
For most header types, there are the r and R (regexp), as well as s and S (substring) types, and e and E (exact match), and w (word match) types. If this element is not present, Gnus will assume that substring matching should be used. R, S, and E differ from the others in that the matches will be done in a case-sensitive manner. All these one-letter types are really just abbreviations for the regexp, string, exact, and word types, which you can use instead, if you feel like.

Extra   Just as for the standard string overview headers, if you are using gnus-extra-headers, you can score on these headers' values. In this case, there is a 5th element in the score entry, being the name of the header to be scored. The following entry is useful in your all.SCORE file in case of spam attacks from a single origin host, if your NNTP server tracks 'NNTP-Posting-Host' in overviews:

("111.222.333.444" -1000 nil s

```
                "NNTP-Posting-Host")
```

Lines, Chars

These two headers use different match types: `<`, `>`, `=`, `>=` and `<=`.

These predicates are true if

```
(PREDICATE HEADER MATCH)
```

evaluates to non-`nil`. For instance, the advanced match (`"lines" 4 <`) (see Section 7.15 [Advanced Scoring], page 231) will result in the following form:

```
(< header-value 4)
```

Or to put it another way: When using `<` on `Lines` with 4 as the match, we get the score added if the article has less than 4 lines. (It's easy to get confused and think it's the other way around. But it's not. I think.)

When matching on `Lines`, be careful because some back ends (like `nndir`) do not generate `Lines` header, so every article ends up being marked as having 0 lines. This can lead to strange results if you happen to lower score of the articles with few lines.

Date

For the Date header we have three kinda silly match types: `before`, `at` and `after`. I can't really imagine this ever being useful, but, like, it would feel kinda silly not to provide this function. Just in case. You never know. Better safe than sorry. Once burnt, twice shy. Don't judge a book by its cover. Never not have sex on a first date. (I have been told that at least one person, and I quote, "found this function indispensable", however.)

A more useful match type is `regexp`. With it, you can match the date string using a regular expression. The date is normalized to ISO8601 compact format first—*YYYYMMDDTHHMMSS*. If you want to match all articles that have been posted on April 1st in every year, you could use '`....0401.........`' as a match string, for instance. (Note that the date is kept in its original time zone, so this will match articles that were posted when it was April 1st where the article was posted from. Time zones are such wholesome fun for the whole family, eh?)

Head, Body, All

These three match keys use the same match types as the `From` (etc.) header uses.

Followup

This match key is somewhat special, in that it will match the `From` header, and affect the score of not only the matching articles, but also all followups to the matching articles. This allows you to increase the score of followups to your own articles, or decrease the score of followups to the articles of some known trouble-maker. Uses the same match types as the From header uses. (Using this match key will lead to creation of ADAPT files.)

Thread This match key works along the same lines as the Followup match key. If you say that you want to score on a (sub-)thread started by an article with a Message-ID x, then you add a 'thread' match. This will add a new 'thread' match for each article that has x in its References header. (These new 'thread' matches will use the Message-IDs of these matching articles.) This will ensure that you can raise/lower the score of an entire thread, even though some articles in the thread may not have complete References headers. Note that using this may lead to nondeterministic scores of the articles in the thread. (Using this match key will lead to creation of ADAPT files.)

mark The value of this entry should be a number. Any articles with a score lower than this number will be marked as read.

expunge The value of this entry should be a number. Any articles with a score lower than this number will be removed from the summary buffer.

mark-and-expunge The value of this entry should be a number. Any articles with a score lower than this number will be marked as read and removed from the summary buffer.

thread-mark-and-expunge The value of this entry should be a number. All articles that belong to a thread that has a total score below this number will be marked as read and removed from the summary buffer. gnus-thread-score-function says how to compute the total score for a thread.

files The value of this entry should be any number of file names. These files are assumed to be score files as well, and will be loaded the same way this one was.

exclude-files The clue of this entry should be any number of files. These files will not be loaded, even though they would normally be so, for some reason or other.

eval The value of this entry will be evaled. This element will be ignored when handling global score files.

read-only Read-only score files will not be updated or saved. Global score files should feature this atom (see Section 7.12 [Global Score Files], page 229). (Note: *Global* here really means *global*; not your personal apply-to-all-groups score files.)

orphan The value of this entry should be a number. Articles that do not have parents will get this number added to their scores. Imagine you follow some high-volume newsgroup, like 'comp.lang.c'. Most likely you will only follow a few of the threads, also want to see any new threads.

You can do this with the following two score file entries:

```
(orphan -500)
(mark-and-expunge -100)
```

When you enter the group the first time, you will only see the new threads. You then raise the score of the threads that you find interesting (with *I T* or *I S*), and ignore (*c y*) the rest. Next time you enter the group, you will see new articles in the interesting threads, plus any new threads.

I.e., the orphan score atom is for high-volume groups where a few interesting threads which can't be found automatically by ordinary scoring rules exist.

adapt   This entry controls the adaptive scoring. If it is **t**, the default adaptive scoring rules will be used. If it is **ignore**, no adaptive scoring will be performed on this group. If it is a list, this list will be used as the adaptive scoring rules. If it isn't present, or is something other than **t** or **ignore**, the default adaptive scoring rules will be used. If you want to use adaptive scoring on most groups, you'd set **gnus-use-adaptive-scoring** to **t**, and insert an (**adapt ignore**) in the groups where you do not want adaptive scoring. If you only want adaptive scoring in a few groups, you'd set **gnus-use-adaptive-scoring** to **nil**, and insert (**adapt t**) in the score files of the groups where you want it.

adapt-file
            All adaptive score entries will go to the file named by this entry. It will also be applied when entering the group. This atom might be handy if you want to adapt on several groups at once, using the same adaptive file for a number of groups.

local   The value of this entry should be a list of (*var value*) pairs. Each *var* will be made buffer-local to the current summary buffer, and set to the value specified. This is a convenient, if somewhat strange, way of setting variables in some groups if you don't like hooks much. Note that the *value* won't be evaluated.

7.5 Score File Editing

You normally enter all scoring commands from the summary buffer, but you might feel the urge to edit them by hand as well, so we've supplied you with a mode for that.

It's simply a slightly customized **emacs-lisp** mode, with these additional commands:

C-c C-c   Save the changes you have made and return to the summary buffer (**gnus-score-edit-exit**).

C-c C-d   Insert the current date in numerical format (**gnus-score-edit-insert-date**). This is really the day number, if you were wondering.

C-c C-p   The adaptive score files are saved in an unformatted fashion. If you intend to read one of these files, you want to *pretty print* it first. This command (**gnus-score-pretty-print**) does that for you.

Type *M-x gnus-score-mode* to use this mode.

`gnus-score-menu-hook` is run in score mode buffers.

In the summary buffer you can use commands like *V f*, *V e* and *V t* to begin editing score files.

7.6 Adaptive Scoring

If all this scoring is getting you down, Gnus has a way of making it all happen automatically—as if by magic. Or rather, as if by artificial stupidity, to be precise.

When you read an article, or mark an article as read, or kill an article, you leave marks behind. On exit from the group, Gnus can sniff these marks and add score elements depending on what marks it finds. You turn on this ability by setting `gnus-use-adaptive-scoring` to t or (`line`). If you want score adaptively on separate words appearing in the subjects, you should set this variable to (`word`). If you want to use both adaptive methods, set this variable to (`word line`).

To give you complete control over the scoring process, you can customize the `gnus-default-adaptive-score-alist` variable. For instance, it might look something like this:

```
(setq gnus-default-adaptive-score-alist
  '((gnus-unread-mark)
    (gnus-ticked-mark (from 4))
    (gnus-dormant-mark (from 5))
    (gnus-del-mark (from -4) (subject -1))
    (gnus-read-mark (from 4) (subject 2))
    (gnus-expirable-mark (from -1) (subject -1))
    (gnus-killed-mark (from -1) (subject -3))
    (gnus-kill-file-mark)
    (gnus-ancient-mark)
    (gnus-low-score-mark)
    (gnus-catchup-mark (from -1) (subject -1))))
```

As you see, each element in this alist has a mark as a key (either a variable name or a "real" mark—a character). Following this key is a arbitrary number of header/score pairs. If there are no header/score pairs following the key, no adaptive scoring will be done on articles that have that key as the article mark. For instance, articles with `gnus-unread-mark` in the example above will not get adaptive score entries.

Each article can have only one mark, so just a single of these rules will be applied to each article.

To take `gnus-del-mark` as an example—this alist says that all articles that have that mark (i.e., are marked with 'e') will have a score entry added to lower based on the `From` header by -4, and lowered by `Subject` by -1. Change this to fit your prejudices.

If you have marked 10 articles with the same subject with `gnus-del-mark`, the rule for that mark will be applied ten times. That means that that subject will get a score of ten times -1, which should be, unless I'm much mistaken, -10.

If you have auto-expirable (mail) groups (see Section 6.4.9 [Expiring Mail], page 168), all the read articles will be marked with the 'E' mark. This'll probably make adaptive scoring slightly impossible, so auto-expiring and adaptive scoring doesn't really mix very well.

The headers you can score on are `from`, `subject`, `message-id`, `references`, `xref`, `lines`, `chars` and `date`. In addition, you can score on `followup`, which will create an adaptive score entry that matches on the `References` header using the `Message-ID` of the current article, thereby matching the following thread.

If you use this scheme, you should set the score file atom `mark` to something small—like -300, perhaps, to avoid having small random changes result in articles getting marked as read.

After using adaptive scoring for a week or so, Gnus should start to become properly trained and enhance the authors you like best, and kill the authors you like least, without you having to say so explicitly.

You can control what groups the adaptive scoring is to be performed on by using the score files (see Section 7.4 [Score File Format], page 219). This will also let you use different rules in different groups.

The adaptive score entries will be put into a file where the name is the group name with `gnus-adaptive-file-suffix` appended. The default is `ADAPT`.

Adaptive score files can get huge and are not meant to be edited by human hands. If `gnus-adaptive-pretty-print` is `nil` (the default) those files will not be written in a human readable way.

When doing adaptive scoring, substring or fuzzy matching would probably give you the best results in most cases. However, if the header one matches is short, the possibility for false positives is great, so if the length of the match is less than `gnus-score-exact-adapt-limit`, exact matching will be used. If this variable is `nil`, exact matching will always be used to avoid this problem.

As mentioned above, you can adapt either on individual words or entire headers. If you adapt on words, the `gnus-default-adaptive-word-score-alist` variable says what score each instance of a word should add given a mark.

```
(setq gnus-default-adaptive-word-score-alist
      '((,gnus-read-mark . 30)
        (,gnus-catchup-mark . -10)
        (,gnus-killed-mark . -20)
        (,gnus-del-mark . -15)))
```

This is the default value. If you have adaption on words enabled, every word that appears in subjects of articles marked with `gnus-read-mark` will result in a score rule that increase the score with 30 points.

Words that appear in the `gnus-default-ignored-adaptive-words` list will be ignored. If you wish to add more words to be ignored, use the `gnus-ignored-adaptive-words` list instead.

Some may feel that short words shouldn't count when doing adaptive scoring. If so, you may set `gnus-adaptive-word-length-limit` to an integer. Words shorter than this number will be ignored. This variable defaults to `nil`.

When the scoring is done, `gnus-adaptive-word-syntax-table` is the syntax table in effect. It is similar to the standard syntax table, but it considers numbers to be non-word-constituent characters.

If `gnus-adaptive-word-minimum` is set to a number, the adaptive word scoring process will never bring down the score of an article to below this number. The default is `nil`.

If `gnus-adaptive-word-no-group-words` is set to `t`, gnus won't adaptively word score any of the words in the group name. Useful for groups like 'comp.editors.emacs', where most of the subject lines contain the word 'emacs'.

After using this scheme for a while, it might be nice to write a **gnus-psychoanalyze-user** command to go through the rules and see what words you like and what words you don't like. Or perhaps not.

Note that the adaptive word scoring thing is highly experimental and is likely to change in the future. Initial impressions seem to indicate that it's totally useless as it stands. Some more work (involving more rigorous statistical methods) will have to be done to make this useful.

7.7 Home Score File

The score file where new score file entries will go is called the *home score file*. This is normally (and by default) the score file for the group itself. For instance, the home score file for 'gnu.emacs.gnus' is `gnu.emacs.gnus.SCORE`.

However, this may not be what you want. It is often convenient to share a common home score file among many groups—all 'emacs' groups could perhaps use the same home score file.

The variable that controls this is `gnus-home-score-file`. It can be:

1. A string. Then this file will be used as the home score file for all groups.
2. A function. The result of this function will be used as the home score file. The function will be called with the name of the group as the parameter.
3. A list. The elements in this list can be:
   1. (*regexp file-name*). If the *regexp* matches the group name, the *file-name* will be used as the home score file.
   2. A function. If the function returns non-`nil`, the result will be used as the home score file. The function will be called with the name of the group as the parameter.
   3. A string. Use the string as the home score file.

The list will be traversed from the beginning towards the end looking for matches.

So, if you want to use just a single score file, you could say:

```
(setq gnus-home-score-file
      "my-total-score-file.SCORE")
```

If you want to use `gnu.SCORE` for all 'gnu' groups and `rec.SCORE` for all 'rec' groups (and so on), you can say:

```
(setq gnus-home-score-file
      'gnus-hierarchial-home-score-file)
```

This is a ready-made function provided for your convenience. Other functions include

`gnus-current-home-score-file`

Return the "current" regular score file. This will make scoring commands add entry to the "innermost" matching score file.

If you want to have one score file for the 'emacs' groups and another for the 'comp' groups, while letting all other groups use their own home score files:

```
(setq gnus-home-score-file
      ;; All groups that match the regexp "\\.emacs"
      '(("\\.emacs" "emacs.SCORE")
        ;; All the comp groups in one score file
        ("^comp" "comp.SCORE")))
```

`gnus-home-adapt-file` works exactly the same way as `gnus-home-score-file`, but says what the home adaptive score file is instead. All new adaptive file entries will go into the file specified by this variable, and the same syntax is allowed.

In addition to using `gnus-home-score-file` and `gnus-home-adapt-file`, you can also use group parameters (see Section 2.10 [Group Parameters], page 22) and topic parameters (see Section 2.16.5 [Topic Parameters], page 37) to achieve much the same. Group and topic parameters take precedence over this variable.

7.8 Followups To Yourself

Gnus offers two commands for picking out the `Message-ID` header in the current buffer. Gnus will then add a score rule that scores using this `Message-ID` on the `References` header of other articles. This will, in effect, increase the score of all articles that respond to the article in the current buffer. Quite useful if you want to easily note when people answer what you've said.

`gnus-score-followup-article`
> This will add a score to articles that directly follow up your own article.

`gnus-score-followup-thread`
> This will add a score to all articles that appear in a thread "below" your own article.

These two functions are both primarily meant to be used in hooks like `message-sent-hook`, like this:

```
(add-hook 'message-sent-hook 'gnus-score-followup-thread)
```

If you look closely at your own `Message-ID`, you'll notice that the first two or three characters are always the same. Here's two of mine:

```
<x6u3u47icf.fsf@eyesore.no>
<x6sp9o7ibw.fsf@eyesore.no>
```

So "my" ident on this machine is 'x6'. This can be exploited—the following rule will raise the score on all followups to myself:

```
("references"
 ("<x6[0-9a-z]+\\.fsf\\(_-_\\)?@.*eyesore\\.no>"
  1000 nil r))
```

Whether it's the first two or first three characters that are "yours" is system-dependent.

7.9 Scoring On Other Headers

Gnus is quite fast when scoring the "traditional" headers—'From', 'Subject' and so on. However, scoring other headers requires writing a `head` scoring rule, which means that Gnus has to request every single article from the back end to find matches. This takes a long time in big groups.

You can inhibit this slow scoring on headers or body by setting the variable `gnus-inhibit-slow-scoring`. If `gnus-inhibit-slow-scoring` is regexp, slow scoring is inhibited if the group matches the regexp. If it is `t`, slow scoring on it is inhibited for all groups.

Now, there's not much you can do about the slowness for news groups, but for mail groups, you have greater control. In Section 3.1.2 [To From Newsgroups], page 47, it's explained in greater detail what this mechanism does, but here's a cookbook example for `nnml` on how to allow scoring on the 'To' and 'Cc' headers.

Put the following in your `~/.gnus.el` file.

```
(setq gnus-extra-headers '(To Cc Newsgroups Keywords)
      nnmail-extra-headers gnus-extra-headers)
```

Restart Gnus and rebuild your `nnml` overview files with the *M-x nnml-generate-nov-databases* command. This will take a long time if you have much mail.

Now you can score on 'To' and 'Cc' as "extra headers" like so: *I e s p To RET <your name> RET*.

See? Simple.

7.10 Scoring Tips

Crossposts

If you want to lower the score of crossposts, the line to match on is the `Xref` header.

```
("xref" (" talk.politics.misc:" -1000))
```

Multiple crossposts

If you want to lower the score of articles that have been crossposted to more than, say, 3 groups:

```
("xref"
  ("[^:\n]+:[0-9]+ +[^:\n]+:[0-9]+ +[^:\n]+:[0-9]+"
   -1000 nil r))
```

Matching on the body

This is generally not a very good idea—it takes a very long time. Gnus actually has to fetch each individual article from the server. But you might want to anyway, I guess. Even though there are three match keys (`Head`, `Body` and `All`), you should choose one and stick with it in each score file. If you use any two, each article will be fetched *twice*. If you want to match a bit on the `Head` and a bit on the `Body`, just use `All` for all the matches.

Marking as read

> You will probably want to mark articles that have scores below a certain number as read. This is most easily achieved by putting the following in your `all.SCORE` file:

> ```
> ((mark -100))
> ```

> You may also consider doing something similar with `expunge`.

Negated character classes

> If you say stuff like `[^abcd]*`, you may get unexpected results. That will match newlines, which might lead to, well, The Unknown. Say `[^abcd\n]*` instead.

7.11 Reverse Scoring

If you want to keep just articles that have 'Sex with Emacs' in the subject header, and expunge all other articles, you could put something like this in your score file:

```
(("subject"
  ("Sex with Emacs" 2))
 (mark 1)
 (expunge 1))
```

So, you raise all articles that match 'Sex with Emacs' and mark the rest as read, and expunge them to boot.

7.12 Global Score Files

Sure, other newsreaders have "global kill files". These are usually nothing more than a single kill file that applies to all groups, stored in the user's home directory. Bah! Puny, weak newsreaders!

What I'm talking about here are Global Score Files. Score files from all over the world, from users everywhere, uniting all nations in one big, happy score file union! Ange-score! New and untested!

All you have to do to use other people's score files is to set the `gnus-global-score-files` variable. One entry for each score file, or each score file directory. Gnus will decide by itself what score files are applicable to which group.

To use the score file `/ftp@ftp.gnus.org:/pub/larsi/ding/score/soc.motss.SCORE` and all score files in the `/ftp@ftp.some-where:/pub/score` directory, say this:

```
(setq gnus-global-score-files
      '("/ftp@ftp.gnus.org:/pub/larsi/ding/score/soc.motss.SCORE"
        "/ftp@ftp.some-where:/pub/score/"))
```

Simple, eh? Directory names must end with a '/'. These directories are typically scanned only once during each Gnus session. If you feel the need to manually re-scan the remote directories, you can use the `gnus-score-search-global-directories` command.

Note that, at present, using this option will slow down group entry somewhat. (That is—a lot.)

If you want to start maintaining score files for other people to use, just put your score file up for anonymous ftp and announce it to the world. Become a retro-moderator! Participate in the retro-moderator wars sure to ensue, where retro-moderators battle it out for the sympathy of the people, luring them to use their score files on false premises! Yay! The net is saved!

Here are some tips for the would-be retro-moderator, off the top of my head:

- Articles heavily crossposted are probably junk.
- To lower a single inappropriate article, lower by `Message-ID`.
- Particularly brilliant authors can be raised on a permanent basis.
- Authors that repeatedly post off-charter for the group can safely be lowered out of existence.
- Set the `mark` and `expunge` atoms to obliterate the nastiest articles completely.
- Use expiring score entries to keep the size of the file down. You should probably have a long expiry period, though, as some sites keep old articles for a long time.

. . . I wonder whether other newsreaders will support global score files in the future. *Snicker*. Yup, any day now, newsreaders like Blue Wave, xrn and 1stReader are bound to implement scoring. Should we start holding our breath yet?

7.13 Kill Files

Gnus still supports those pesky old kill files. In fact, the kill file entries can now be expiring, which is something I wrote before Daniel Quinlan thought of doing score files, so I've left the code in there.

In short, kill processing is a lot slower (and I do mean *a lot*) than score processing, so it might be a good idea to rewrite your kill files into score files.

Anyway, a kill file is a normal `emacs-lisp` file. You can put any forms into this file, which means that you can use kill files as some sort of primitive hook function to be run on group entry, even though that isn't a very good idea.

Normal kill files look like this:

```
(gnus-kill "From" "Lars Ingebrigtsen")
(gnus-kill "Subject" "ding")
(gnus-expunge "X")
```

This will mark every article written by me as read, and remove the marked articles from the summary buffer. Very useful, you'll agree.

Other programs use a totally different kill file syntax. If Gnus encounters what looks like a **rn** kill file, it will take a stab at interpreting it.

Two summary functions for editing a GNUS kill file:

M-k   Edit this group's kill file (**gnus-summary-edit-local-kill**).

M-K   Edit the general kill file (**gnus-summary-edit-global-kill**).

Two group mode functions for editing the kill files:

M-k   Edit this group's kill file (**gnus-group-edit-local-kill**).

M-K   Edit the general kill file (**gnus-group-edit-global-kill**).

Kill file variables:

gnus-kill-file-name

> A kill file for the group 'soc.motss' is normally called soc.motss.KILL. The suffix appended to the group name to get this file name is detailed by the gnus-kill-file-name variable. The "global" kill file (not in the score file sense of "global", of course) is just called KILL.

gnus-kill-save-kill-file

> If this variable is non-nil, Gnus will save the kill file after processing, which is necessary if you use expiring kills.

gnus-apply-kill-hook

> A hook called to apply kill files to a group. It is (gnus-apply-kill-file) by default. If you want to ignore the kill file if you have a score file for the same group, you can set this hook to (gnus-apply-kill-file-unless-scored). If you don't want kill files to be processed, you should set this variable to nil.

gnus-kill-file-mode-hook

> A hook called in kill-file mode buffers.

7.14 Converting Kill Files

If you have loads of old kill files, you may want to convert them into score files. If they are "regular", you can use the gnus-kill-to-score.el package; if not, you'll have to do it by hand.

The kill to score conversion package isn't included in Emacs by default. You can fetch it from the contrib directory of the Gnus distribution or from http://heim.ifi.uio.no/~larsi/ding-various/gnus-kill-to-score.el.

If your old kill files are very complex—if they contain more non-gnus-kill forms than not, you'll have to convert them by hand. Or just let them be as they are. Gnus will still use them as before.

7.15 Advanced Scoring

Scoring on Subjects and From headers is nice enough, but what if you're really interested in what a person has to say only when she's talking about a particular subject? Or what if you really don't want to read what person A has to say when she's following up to person B, but want to read what she says when she's following up to person C?

By using advanced scoring rules you may create arbitrarily complex scoring patterns.

7.15.1 Advanced Scoring Syntax

Ordinary scoring rules have a string as the first element in the rule. Advanced scoring rules have a list as the first element. The second element is the score to be applied if the first element evaluated to a non-nil value.

These lists may consist of three logical operators, one redirection operator, and various match operators.

Logical operators:

&
and   This logical operator will evaluate each of its arguments until it finds one that
        evaluates to `false`, and then it'll stop. If all arguments evaluate to `true` values,
        then this operator will return `true`.

|
or   This logical operator will evaluate each of its arguments until it finds one that
        evaluates to `true`. If no arguments are `true`, then this operator will return
        `false`.

!
not
        This logical operator only takes a single argument. It returns the logical nega-
        tion of the value of its argument.

There is an *indirection operator* that will make its arguments apply to the ancestors of
the current article being scored. For instance, `1-` will make score rules apply to the parent
of the current article. `2-` will make score rules apply to the grandparent of the current
article. Alternatively, you can write `^^`, where the number of `^`s (carets) says how far back
into the ancestry you want to go.

Finally, we have the match operators. These are the ones that do the real work. Match
operators are header name strings followed by a match and a match type. A typical match
operator looks like '`("from" "Lars Ingebrigtsen" s)`'. The header names are the same as
when using simple scoring, and the match types are also the same.

7.15.2 Advanced Scoring Examples

Please note that the following examples are score file rules. To make a complete score file
from them, surround them with another pair of parentheses.

Let's say you want to increase the score of articles written by Lars when he's talking
about Gnus:

```
((&
  ("from" "Lars Ingebrigtsen")
  ("subject" "Gnus"))
 1000)
```

Quite simple, huh?

When he writes long articles, he sometimes has something nice to say:

```
((&
  ("from" "Lars Ingebrigtsen")
  (|
   ("subject" "Gnus")
   ("lines" 100 >)))
 1000)
```

However, when he responds to things written by Reig Eigil Logge, you really don't want
to read what he's written:

```
((&
  ("from" "Lars Ingebrigtsen")
  (1- ("from" "Reig Eigil Logge")))
```

```
    -100000)
```
Everybody that follows up Redmondo when he writes about disappearing socks should have their scores raised, but only when they talk about white socks. However, when Lars talks about socks, it's usually not very interesting:

```
((&
  (1-
   (&
    ("from" "redmondo@.*no" r)
    ("body" "disappearing.*socks" t)))
   (! ("from" "Lars Ingebrigtsen"))
   ("body" "white.*socks"))
  1000)
```

Suppose you're reading a high volume group and you're only interested in replies. The plan is to score down all articles that don't have subject that begin with "Re:", "Fw:" or "Fwd:" and then score up all parents of articles that have subjects that begin with reply marks.

```
((! ("subject" "re:\\|fwd?:" r))
  -200)
((1- ("subject" "re:\\|fwd?:" r))
  200)
```

The possibilities are endless.

7.15.3 Advanced Scoring Tips

The & and | logical operators do short-circuit logic. That is, they stop processing their arguments when it's clear what the result of the operation will be. For instance, if one of the arguments of an & evaluates to **false**, there's no point in evaluating the rest of the arguments. This means that you should put slow matches ('body', 'header') last and quick matches ('from', 'subject') first.

The indirection arguments (1- and so on) will make their arguments work on previous generations of the thread. If you say something like:

```
...
(1-
 (1-
  ("from" "lars")))
...
```

Then that means "score on the from header of the grandparent of the current article". An indirection is quite fast, but it's better to say:

```
(1-
 (&
  ("from" "Lars")
  ("subject" "Gnus")))
```

than it is to say:

```
(&
 (1- ("from" "Lars"))
 (1- ("subject" "Gnus")))
```

7.16 Score Decays

You may find that your scores have a tendency to grow without bounds, especially if you're using adaptive scoring. If scores get too big, they lose all meaning—they simply max out and it's difficult to use them in any sensible way.

Gnus provides a mechanism for decaying scores to help with this problem. When score files are loaded and **gnus-decay-scores** is non-**nil**, Gnus will run the score files through the decaying mechanism thereby lowering the scores of all non-permanent score rules. If **gnus-decay-scores** is a regexp, only score files matching this regexp are treated. E.g., you may set it to '\\.ADAPT\\'' if only *adaptive* score files should be decayed. The decay itself if performed by the **gnus-decay-score-function** function, which is **gnus-decay-score** by default. Here's the definition of that function:

```
(defun gnus-decay-score (score)
  "Decay SCORE according to 'gnus-score-decay-constant'
and 'gnus-score-decay-scale'."
  (let ((n (- score
              (* (if (< score 0) -1 1)
                 (min (abs score)
                      (max gnus-score-decay-constant
                           (* (abs score)
                              gnus-score-decay-scale)))))))
    (if (and (featurep 'xemacs)
             ;; XEmacs's floor can handle only the floating point
             ;; number below the half of the maximum integer.
             (> (abs n) (lsh -1 -2)))
        (string-to-number
         (car (split-string (number-to-string n) "\\.")))
      (floor n))))
```

gnus-score-decay-constant is 3 by default and **gnus-score-decay-scale** is 0.05. This should cause the following:

1. Scores between -3 and 3 will be set to 0 when this function is called.

2. Scores with magnitudes between 3 and 60 will be shrunk by 3.

3. Scores with magnitudes greater than 60 will be shrunk by 5% of the score.

If you don't like this decay function, write your own. It is called with the score to be decayed as its only parameter, and it should return the new score, which should be an integer.

Gnus will try to decay scores once a day. If you haven't run Gnus for four days, Gnus will decay the scores four times, for instance.

8 Searching

FIXME: Add a brief overview of Gnus search capabilities. A brief comparison of nnir, nnmairix, contrib/gnus-namazu would be nice as well.

This chapter describes tools for searching groups and servers for articles matching a query and then retrieving those articles. Gnus provides a simpler mechanism for searching through articles in a summary buffer to find those matching a pattern. See Section 3.27.2 [Searching for Articles], page 110.

8.1 nnir

This section describes how to use **nnir** to search for articles within gnus.

8.1.1 What is nnir?

nnir is a Gnus interface to a number of tools for searching through mail and news repositories. Different backends (like **nnimap** and **nntp**) work with different tools (called *engines* in **nnir** lingo), but all use the same basic search interface.

The **nnimap** and **gmane** search engines should work with no configuration. Other engines require a local index that needs to be created and maintained outside of Gnus.

8.1.2 Basic Usage

In the group buffer typing *G G* will search the group on the current line by calling **gnus-group-make-nnir-group**. This prompts for a query string, creates an ephemeral **nnir** group containing the articles that match this query, and takes you to a summary buffer showing these articles. Articles may then be read, moved and deleted using the usual commands.

The **nnir** group made in this way is an **ephemeral** group, and some changes are not permanent: aside from reading, moving, and deleting, you can't act on the original article. But there is an alternative: you can *warp* (i.e., jump) to the original group for the article on the current line with *A W*, aka **gnus-warp-to-article**. Even better, the function **gnus-summary-refer-thread**, bound by default in summary buffers to *A T*, will first warp to the original group before it works its magic and includes all the articles in the thread. From here you can read, move and delete articles, but also copy them, alter article marks, whatever. Go nuts.

You say you want to search more than just the group on the current line? No problem: just process-mark the groups you want to search. You want even more? Calling for an nnir search with the cursor on a topic heading will search all the groups under that heading.

Still not enough? OK, in the server buffer **gnus-group-make-nnir-group** (now bound to *G*) will search all groups from the server on the current line. Too much? Want to ignore certain groups when searching, like spam groups? Just customize **nnir-ignored-newsgroups**.

One more thing: individual search engines may have special search features. You can access these special features by giving a prefix-arg to **gnus-group-make-nnir-group**. If you are searching multiple groups with different search engines you will be prompted for the special search features for each engine separately.

8.1.3 Setting up nnir

To set up nnir you may need to do some prep work. Firstly, you may need to configure the search engines you plan to use. Some of them, like `imap` and `gmane`, need no special configuration. Others, like `namazu` and `swish`, require configuration as described below. Secondly, you need to associate a search engine with a server or a backend.

If you just want to use the `imap` engine to search `nnimap` servers, and the `gmane` engine to search `gmane` then you don't have to do anything. But you might want to read the details of the query language anyway.

8.1.3.1 Associating Engines

When searching a group, `nnir` needs to know which search engine to use. You can configure a given server to use a particular engine by setting the server variable `nnir-search-engine` to the engine name. For example to use the `namazu` engine to search the server named `home` you can use

```
(setq gnus-secondary-select-methods
      '((nnml "home"
          (nnimap-address "localhost")
          (nnir-search-engine namazu))))
```

Alternatively you might want to use a particular engine for all servers with a given backend. For example, you might want to use the `imap` engine for all servers using the `nnimap` backend. In this case you can customize the variable `nnir-method-default-engines`. This is an alist of pairs of the form (`backend` . `engine`). By default this variable is set to use the `imap` engine for all servers using the `nnimap` backend, and the `gmane` backend for `nntp` servers. (Don't worry, the `gmane` search engine won't actually try to search non-gmane `nntp` servers.) But if you wanted to use `namazu` for all your servers with an `nnimap` backend you could change this to

```
'((nnimap . namazu)
  (nntp . gmane))
```

8.1.3.2 The imap Engine

The `imap` engine requires no configuration.

Queries using the `imap` engine follow a simple query language. The search is always case-insensitive and supports the following features (inspired by the Google search input language):

'Boolean query operators'

AND, OR, and NOT are supported, and parentheses can be used to control operator precedence, e.g., (emacs OR xemacs) AND linux. Note that operators must be written with all capital letters to be recognized. Also preceding a term with a − sign is equivalent to NOT term.

'Automatic AND queries'

If you specify multiple words then they will be treated as an AND expression intended to match all components.

'Phrase searches'
>If you wrap your query in double-quotes then it will be treated as a literal string.

By default the whole message will be searched. The query can be limited to a specific part of a message by using a prefix-arg. After inputting the query this will prompt (with completion) for a message part. Choices include "Whole message", "Subject", "From", and "To". Any unrecognized input is interpreted as a header name. For example, typing *Message-ID* in response to this prompt will limit the query to the Message-ID header.

Finally selecting "Imap" will interpret the query as a raw IMAP search query. The format of such queries can be found in RFC3501.

If you don't like the default of searching whole messages you can customize **nnir-imap-default-search-key**. For example to use IMAP queries by default

```
(setq nnir-imap-default-search-key "Imap")
```

8.1.3.3 The gmane Engine

The **gmane** engine requires no configuration.

Gmane queries follow a simple query language:

'Boolean query operators'
>AND, OR, NOT (or AND NOT), and XOR are supported. and brackets can be used to control operator precedence, e.g., (emacs OR xemacs) AND linux. Note that operators must be written with all capital letters to be recognized.

'Required and excluded terms'
>+ and − can be used to require or exclude terms, e.g., football −american

'Unicode handling'
>The search engine converts all text to utf-8, so searching should work in any language.

'Stopwords'
>Common English words (like 'the' and 'a') are ignored by default. You can override this by prefixing such words with a + (e.g., +the) or enclosing the word in quotes (e.g., "the").

The query can be limited to articles by a specific author using a prefix-arg. After inputting the query this will prompt for an author name (or part of a name) to match.

8.1.3.4 The swish++ Engine

FIXME: Say something more here.

Documentation for swish++ may be found at the swish++ sourceforge page: http://swishplusplus.sourceforge.net

nnir-swish++-program
>The name of the swish++ executable. Defaults to **search**

nnir-swish++-additional-switches
>A list of strings to be given as additional arguments to swish++. **nil** by default.

```
nnir-swish++-remove-prefix
```
> The prefix to remove from each file name returned by swish++ in order to get a group name. By default this is `$HOME/Mail`.

8.1.3.5 The swish-e Engine

FIXME: Say something more here.

Documentation for swish-e may be found at the swish-e homepage `http://swish-e.org`

```
nnir-swish-e-program
```
> The name of the swish-e search program. Defaults to `swish-e`.

```
nnir-swish-e-additional-switches
```
> A list of strings to be given as additional arguments to swish-e. `nil` by default.

```
nnir-swish-e-remove-prefix
```
> The prefix to remove from each file name returned by swish-e in order to get a group name. By default this is `$HOME/Mail`.

8.1.3.6 The namazu Engine

Using the namazu engine requires creating and maintaining index files. One directory should contain all the index files, and nnir must be told where to find them by setting the **nnir-namazu-index-directory** variable.

To work correctly the **nnir-namazu-remove-prefix** variable must also be correct. This is the prefix to remove from each file name returned by Namazu in order to get a proper group name (albeit with '/' instead of '.').

For example, suppose that Namazu returns file names such as '`/home/john/Mail/mail/misc/42`'. For this example, use the following setting: (setq nnir-namazu-remove-prefix "/home/john/Mail/") Note the trailing slash. Removing this prefix from the directory gives '`mail/misc/42`'. nnir knows to remove the '/42' and to replace '/' with '.' to arrive at the correct group name '`mail.misc`'.

Extra switches may be passed to the namazu search command by setting the variable **nnir-namazu-additional-switches**. It is particularly important not to pass any any switches to namazu that will change the output format. Good switches to use include '–sort', '–ascending', '–early' and '–late'. Refer to the Namazu documentation for further information on valid switches.

Mail must first be indexed with the 'mknmz' program. Read the documentation for namazu to create a configuration file. Here is an example:

```
package conf;  # Don't remove this line!

# Paths which will not be indexed. Don't use '^' or '$' anchors.
$EXCLUDE_PATH = "spam|sent";

# Header fields which should be searchable. case-insensitive
$REMAIN_HEADER = "from|date|message-id|subject";

# Searchable fields. case-insensitive
$SEARCH_FIELD = "from|date|message-id|subject";

# The max length of a word.
$WORD_LENG_MAX = 128;

# The max length of a field.
$MAX_FIELD_LENGTH = 256;
```

For this example, mail is stored in the directories '~/Mail/mail/', '~/Mail/lists/' and '~/Mail/archive/', so to index them go to the index directory set in **nnir-namazu-index-directory** and issue the following command:

    mknmz --mailnews ~/Mail/archive/ ~/Mail/mail/ ~/Mail/lists/

For maximum searching efficiency you might want to have a cron job run this command periodically, say every four hours.

8.1.3.7 The notmuch Engine

nnir-notmuch-program
> The name of the notmuch search executable. Defaults to 'notmuch'.

nnir-notmuch-additional-switches
> A list of strings, to be given as additional arguments to notmuch.

nnir-notmuch-remove-prefix
> The prefix to remove from each file name returned by notmuch in order to get a group name (albeit with '/' instead of '.'). This is a regular expression.

8.1.3.8 The hyrex Engine

This engine is obsolete.

8.1.3.9 Customizations

nnir-method-default-engines
> Alist of pairs of server backends and search engines. The default associations are
>
>   (nnimap . imap)
>   (nntp . gmane)

nnir-ignored-newsgroups
> A regexp to match newsgroups in the active file that should be skipped when searching all groups on a server.

`nnir-summary-line-format`

> The format specification to be used for lines in an nnir summary buffer. All the items from 'gnus-summary-line-format' are available, along with three items unique to nnir summary buffers:
>
> | | |
> |---|---|
> | %Z | Search retrieval score value (integer) |
> | %G | Article original full group name (string) |
> | %g | Article original short group name (string) |
>
> If `nil` (the default) this will use `gnus-summary-line-format`.

`nnir-retrieve-headers-override-function`

> If non-`nil`, a function that retrieves article headers rather than using the gnus built-in function. This function takes an article list and group as arguments and populates the 'nntp-server-buffer' with the retrieved headers. It should then return either 'nov or 'headers indicating the retrieved header format. Failure to retrieve headers should return `nil`.
>
> If this variable is `nil`, or if the provided function returns `nil` for a search result, `gnus-retrieve-headers` will be called instead."

8.2 nnmairix

This paragraph describes how to set up mairix and the back end `nnmairix` for indexing and searching your mail from within Gnus. Additionally, you can create permanent "smart" groups which are bound to mairix searches and are automatically updated.

8.2.1 About mairix

Mairix is a tool for indexing and searching words in locally stored mail. It was written by Richard Curnow and is licensed under the GPL. Mairix comes with most popular GNU/Linux distributions, but it also runs under Windows (with cygwin), Mac OS X and Solaris. The homepage can be found at `http://www.rpcurnow.force9.co.uk/mairix/index.html`

Though mairix might not be as flexible as other search tools like swish++ or namazu, which you can use via the `nnir` back end, it has the prime advantage of being incredibly fast. On current systems, it can easily search through headers and message bodies of thousands and thousands of mails in well under a second. Building the database necessary for searching might take a minute or two, but only has to be done once fully. Afterwards, the updates are done incrementally and therefore are really fast, too. Additionally, mairix is very easy to set up.

For maximum speed though, mairix should be used with mails stored in `Maildir` or `MH` format (this includes the `nnml` back end), although it also works with mbox. Mairix presents the search results by populating a *virtual* maildir/MH folder with symlinks which point to the "real" message files (if mbox is used, copies are made). Since mairix already presents search results in such a virtual mail folder, it is very well suited for using it as an external program for creating *smart* mail folders, which represent certain mail searches.

8.2.2 nnmairix requirements

Mairix searches local mail—that means, mairix absolutely must have direct access to your mail folders. If your mail resides on another server (e.g., an IMAP server) and you happen to have shell access, **nnmairix** supports running mairix remotely, e.g., via ssh.

Additionally, **nnmairix** only supports the following Gnus back ends: **nnml**, **nnmaildir**, and **nnimap**. You must use one of these back ends for using **nnmairix**. Other back ends, like **nnmbox**, **nnfolder** or **nnmh**, won't work.

If you absolutely must use mbox and still want to use **nnmairix**, you can set up a local IMAP server, which you then access via **nnimap**. This is a rather massive setup for accessing some mbox files, so just change to MH or Maildir already... However, if you're really, really passionate about using mbox, you might want to look into the package **mairix.el**, which comes with Emacs 23.

8.2.3 What nnmairix does

The back end **nnmairix** enables you to call mairix from within Gnus, either to query mairix with a search term or to update the database. While visiting a message in the summary buffer, you can use several pre-defined shortcuts for calling mairix, e.g., to quickly search for all mails from the sender of the current message or to display the whole thread associated with the message, even if the mails are in different folders.

Additionally, you can create permanent **nnmairix** groups which are bound to certain mairix searches. This way, you can easily create a group containing mails from a certain sender, with a certain subject line or even for one specific thread based on the Message-ID. If you check for new mail in these folders (e.g., by pressing *g* or *M-g*), they automatically update themselves by calling mairix.

You might ask why you need **nnmairix** at all, since mairix already creates the group, populates it with links to the mails so that you can then access it with Gnus, right? Well, this *might* work, but often does not—at least not without problems. Most probably you will get strange article counts, and sometimes you might see mails which Gnus claims have already been canceled and are inaccessible. This is due to the fact that Gnus isn't really amused when things are happening behind its back. Another problem can be the mail back end itself, e.g., if you use mairix with an IMAP server (I had Dovecot complaining about corrupt index files when mairix changed the contents of the search group). Using **nnmairix** should circumvent these problems.

nnmairix is not really a mail back end—it's actually more like a wrapper, sitting between a "real" mail back end where mairix stores the searches and the Gnus front end. You can choose between three different mail back ends for the mairix folders: **nnml**, **nnmaildir** or **nnimap**. **nnmairix** will call the mairix binary so that the search results are stored in folders named **zz_mairix-<NAME>-<NUMBER>** on this mail back end, but it will present these folders in the Gnus front end only with **<NAME>**. You can use an existing mail back end where you already store your mail, but if you're uncomfortable with **nnmairix** creating new mail groups alongside your other mail, you can also create, e.g., a new **nnmaildir** or **nnml** server exclusively for mairix, but then make sure those servers do not accidentally receive your new mail (see Section 8.2.9 [nnmairix caveats], page 247). A special case exists if you want to use mairix remotely on an IMAP server with **nnimap**—here the mairix folders and your other mail must be on the same **nnimap** back end.

8.2.4 Setting up mairix

First: create a backup of your mail folders (see Section 8.2.9 [nnmairix caveats], page 247).

Setting up mairix is easy: simply create a `.mairixrc` file with (at least) the following entries:

```
# Your Maildir/MH base folder
base=~/Maildir
```

This is the base folder for your mails. All the following directories are relative to this base folder. If you want to use **nnmairix** with **nnimap**, this base directory has to point to the mail directory where the IMAP server stores the mail folders!

```
maildir= ... your maildir folders which should be indexed ...
mh= ... your nnml/mh folders which should be indexed ...
mbox = ... your mbox files which should be indexed ...
```

This specifies all your mail folders and mbox files (relative to the base directory!) you want to index with mairix. Note that the **nnml** back end saves mails in MH format, so you have to put those directories in the **mh** line. See the example at the end of this section and mairixrc's man-page for further details.

```
omit=zz_mairix-*
```

This should make sure that you don't accidentally index the mairix search results. You can change the prefix of these folders with the variable **nnmairix-group-prefix**.

```
mformat= ... 'maildir' or 'mh' ...
database= ... location of database file ...
```

The **format** setting specifies the output format for the mairix search folder. Set this to **mh** if you want to access search results with **nnml**. Otherwise choose **maildir**.

To summarize, here is my shortened `.mairixrc` file as an example:

```
base=~/Maildir
maildir=.personal:.work:.logcheck:.sent
mh=../Mail/nnml/*...
mbox=../mboxmail/mailarchive_year*
mformat=maildir
omit=zz_mairix-*
database=~/.mairixdatabase
```

In this case, the base directory is `~/Maildir`, where all my Maildir folders are stored. As you can see, the folders are separated by colons. If you wonder why every folder begins with a dot: this is because I use Dovecot as IMAP server, which again uses **Maildir++** folders. For testing nnmairix, I also have some **nnml** mail, which is saved in `~/Mail/nnml`. Since this has to be specified relative to the **base** directory, the `../Mail` notation is needed. Note that the line ends in `*...`, which means to recursively scan all files under this directory. Without the three dots, the wildcard `*` will not work recursively. I also have some old mbox files with archived mail lying around in `~/mboxmail`. The other lines should be obvious.

See the man page for **mairixrc** for details and further options, especially regarding wildcard usage, which may be a little different than you are used to.

Now simply call **mairix** to create the index for the first time. Note that this may take a few minutes, but every following index will do the updates incrementally and hence is very fast.

8.2.5 Configuring nnmairix

In group mode, type *G b c* (nnmairix-create-server-and-default-group). This will ask you for all necessary information and create a **nnmairix** server as a foreign server. You will have to specify the following:

- The **name** of the nnmairix server—choose whatever you want.

- The name of the **back end server** where mairix should store its searches. This must be a full server name, like nnml:mymail. Just hit *TAB* to see the available servers. Currently, servers which are accessed through nnmaildir, nnimap and nnml are supported. As explained above, for locally stored mails, this can be an existing server where you store your mails. However, you can also create, e.g., a new nnmaildir or nnml server exclusively for nnmairix in your secondary select methods (see Section 1.1 [Finding the News], page 2). If you use a secondary nnml server just for mairix, make sure that you explicitly set the server variable **nnml-get-new-mail** to **nil**, or you might lose mail (see Section 8.2.9 [nnmairix caveats], page 247). If you want to use mairix remotely on an IMAP server, you have to choose the corresponding nnimap server here.

- The **command** to call the mairix binary. This will usually just be **mairix**, but you can also choose something like **ssh SERVER mairix** if you want to call mairix remotely, e.g., on your IMAP server. If you want to add some default options to mairix, you could do this here, but better use the variable **nnmairix-mairix-search-options** instead.

- The name of the **default search group**. This will be the group where all temporary mairix searches are stored, i.e., all searches which are not bound to permanent nnmairix groups. Choose whatever you like.

- If the mail back end is nnimap or nnmaildir, you will be asked if you work with **Maildir++**, i.e., with hidden maildir folders (=beginning with a dot). For example, you have to answer 'yes' here if you work with the Dovecot IMAP server. Otherwise, you should answer 'no' here.

8.2.6 nnmairix keyboard shortcuts

In group mode:

G b c   Creates **nnmairix** server and default search group for this server (nnmairix-create-server-and-default-group). You should have done this by now (see Section 8.2.5 [Configuring nnmairix], page 243).

G b s   Prompts for query which is then sent to the mairix binary. Search results are put into the default search group which is automatically displayed (nnmairix-search).

G b m   Allows you to create a mairix search or a permanent group more comfortably using graphical widgets, similar to a customization group. Just try it to see how it works (nnmairix-widget-search).

G b i   Another command for creating a mairix query more comfortably, but uses only the minibuffer (nnmairix-search-interactive).

G b g   Creates a permanent group which is associated with a search query (nnmairix-create-search-group). The **nnmairix** back end automatically calls mairix when you update this group with *g* or *M-g*.

G b q   Changes the search query for the **nnmairix** group under cursor (**nnmairix-group-change-query-this-group**).

G b t   Toggles the 'threads' parameter for the **nnmairix** group under cursor, i.e., if you want see the whole threads of the found messages (**nnmairix-group-toggle-threads-this-group**).

G b u   Calls mairix binary for updating the database (**nnmairix-update-database**). The default parameters are **-F** and **-Q** for making this as fast as possible (see variable **nnmairix-mairix-update-options** for defining these default options).

G b r   Keep articles in this **nnmairix** group always read or unread, or leave the marks unchanged (**nnmairix-group-toggle-readmarks-this-group**).

G b d   Recreate **nnmairix** group on the "real" mail back end (**nnmairix-group-delete-recreate-this-group**). You can do this if you always get wrong article counts with a **nnmairix** group.

G b a   Toggles the **allow-fast** parameters for group under cursor (**nnmairix-group-toggle-allowfast-this-group**). The default behavior of **nnmairix** is to do a mairix search every time you update or enter the group. With the **allow-fast** parameter set, mairix will only be called when you explicitly update the group, but not upon entering. This makes entering the group faster, but it may also lead to dangling symlinks if something changed between updating and entering the group which is not yet in the mairix database.

G b p   Toggle marks propagation for this group (**nnmairix-group-toggle-propmarks-this-group**). (see Section 8.2.7 [Propagating marks], page 245).

G b o   Manually propagate marks (**nnmairix-propagate-marks**); needed only when **nnmairix-propagate-marks-upon-close** is set to **nil**.

In summary mode:

$ m   Allows you to create a mairix query or group based on the current message using graphical widgets (same as **nnmairix-widget-search**) (**nnmairix-widget-search-from-this-article**).

$ g   Interactively creates a new search group with query based on the current message, but uses the minibuffer instead of graphical widgets (**nnmairix-create-search-group-from-message**).

$ t   Searches thread for the current article (**nnmairix-search-thread-this-article**). This is effectively a shortcut for calling **nnmairix-search** with 'm:msgid' of the current article and enabled threads.

$ f   Searches all messages from sender of the current article (**nnmairix-search-from-this-article**). This is a shortcut for calling **nnmairix-search** with 'f:From'.

$ o   (Only in **nnmairix** groups!) Tries determine the group this article originally came from and displays the article in this group, so that, e.g., replying to this article the correct posting styles/group parameters are applied (**nnmairix-goto-original-article**). This function will use the registry if available, but can also parse the article file name as a fallback method.

$ u   Remove possibly existing tick mark from original article (`nnmairix-remove-tick-mark-original-article`). (see Section 8.2.8 [nnmairix tips and tricks], page 246).

8.2.7 Propagating marks

First of: you really need a patched mairix binary for using the marks propagation feature efficiently. Otherwise, you would have to update the mairix database all the time. You can get the patch at

`http://www.randomsample.de/mairix-maildir-patch.tar`

You need the mairix v0.21 source code for this patch; everything else is explained in the accompanied readme file. If you don't want to use marks propagation, you don't have to apply these patches, but they also fix some annoyances regarding changing maildir flags, so it might still be useful to you.

With the patched mairix binary, you can use **nnmairix** as an alternative to mail splitting (see Section 6.4.6 [Fancy Mail Splitting], page 162). For example, instead of splitting all mails from 'david@foobar.com' into a group, you can simply create a search group with the query 'f:david@foobar.com'. This is actually what "smart folders" are all about: simply put everything in one mail folder and dynamically create searches instead of splitting. This is more flexible, since you can dynamically change your folders any time you want to. This also implies that you will usually read your mails in the **nnmairix** groups instead of your "real" mail groups.

There is one problem, though: say you got a new mail from 'david@foobar.com'; it will now show up in two groups, the "real" group (your INBOX, for example) and in the **nnmairix** search group (provided you have updated the mairix database). Now you enter the **nnmairix** group and read the mail. The mail will be marked as read, but only in the **nnmairix** group—in the "real" mail group it will be still shown as unread.

You could now catch up the mail group (see Section 2.5 [Group Data], page 17), but this is tedious and error prone, since you may overlook mails you don't have created **nnmairix** groups for. Of course, you could first use **nnmairix-goto-criginal-article** (see Section 8.2.6 [nnmairix keyboard shortcuts], page 243) and then read the mail in the original group, but that's even more cumbersome.

Clearly, the easiest way would be if marks could somehow be automatically set for the original article. This is exactly what *marks propagation* is about.

Marks propagation is inactive by default. You can activate it for a certain **nnmairix** group with **nnmairix-group-toggle-propmarks-this-group** (bound to *G b p*). This function will warn you if you try to use it with your default search group; the reason is that the default search group is used for temporary searches, and it's easy to accidentally propagate marks from this group. However, you can ignore this warning if you really want to.

With marks propagation enabled, all the marks you set in a **nnmairix** group should now be propagated to the original article. For example, you can now tick an article (by default with *!*) and this mark should magically be set for the original article, too.

A few more remarks which you may or may not want to know:

Marks will not be set immediately, but only upon closing a group. This not only makes marks propagation faster, it also avoids problems with dangling symlinks when dealing with maildir files (since changing flags will change the file name). You can also control when to propagate marks via `nnmairix-propagate-marks-upon-close` (see the doc-string for details).

Obviously, `nnmairix` will have to look up the original group for every article you want to set marks for. If available, `nnmairix` will first use the registry for determining the original group. The registry is very fast, hence you should really, really enable the registry when using marks propagation. If you don't have to worry about RAM and disc space, set `gnus-registry-max-entries` to a large enough value; to be on the safe side, choose roughly the amount of mails you index with mairix.

If you don't want to use the registry or the registry hasn't seen the original article yet, `nnmairix` will use an additional mairix search for determining the file name of the article. This, of course, is way slower than the registry—if you set hundreds or even thousands of marks this way, it might take some time. You can avoid this situation by setting `nnmairix-only-use-registry` to t.

Maybe you also want to propagate marks the other way round, i.e., if you tick an article in a "real" mail group, you'd like to have the same article in a `nnmairix` group ticked, too. For several good reasons, this can only be done efficiently if you use maildir. To immediately contradict myself, let me mention that it WON'T work with `nnmaildir`, since `nnmaildir` stores the marks externally and not in the file name. Therefore, propagating marks to `nnmairix` groups will usually only work if you use an IMAP server which uses maildir as its file format.

If you work with this setup, just set `nnmairix-propagate-marks-to-nnmairix-groups` to t and see what happens. If you don't like what you see, just set it to `nil` again. One problem might be that you get a wrong number of unread articles; this usually happens when you delete or expire articles in the original groups. When this happens, you can recreate the `nnmairix` group on the back end using *G b d*.

8.2.8 nnmairix tips and tricks

- Checking Mail

  I put all my important mail groups at group level 1. The mairix groups have group level 5, so they do not get checked at start up (see Section 2.6 [Group Levels], page 17).

  I use the following to check for mails:

  ```
  (defun my-check-mail-mairix-update (level)
    (interactive "P")
    ;; if no prefix given, set level=1
    (gnus-group-get-new-news (or level 1))
    (nnmairix-update-groups "mairixsearch" t t)
    (gnus-group-list-groups))

  (define-key gnus-group-mode-map "g" 'my-check-mail-mairix-update)
  ```

  Instead of '`"mairixsearch"`' use the name of your `nnmairix` server. See the doc string for `nnmairix-update-groups` for details.

- Example: search group for ticked articles

  For example, you can create a group for all ticked articles, where the articles always stay unread:

Hit *G b g*, enter group name (e.g., 'important'), use 'F:f' as query and do not include threads.

Now activate marks propagation for this group by using *G b p*. Then activate the always-unread feature by using *G b r* twice.

So far so good—but how do you remove the tick marks in the **nnmairix** group? There are two options: You may simply use **nnmairix-remove-tick-mark-original-article** (bound to *$ u*) to remove tick marks from the original article. The other possibility is to set **nnmairix-propagate-marks-to-nnmairix-groups** to **t**, but see the above comments about this option. If it works for you, the tick marks should also exist in the **nnmairix** group and you can remove them as usual, e.g., by marking an article as read.

When you have removed a tick mark from the original article, this article should vanish from the **nnmairix** group after you have updated the mairix database and updated the group. Fortunately, there is a function for doing exactly that: **nnmairix-update-groups**. See the previous code snippet and the doc string for details.

- Dealing with auto-subscription of mail groups

  As described before, all **nnmairix** groups are in fact stored on the mail back end in the form 'zz_mairix-<NAME>-<NUMBER>'. You can see them when you enter the back end server in the server buffer. You should not subscribe these groups! Unfortunately, these groups will usually get *auto-subscribed* when you use **nnmaildir** or **nnml**, i.e., you will suddenly see groups of the form 'zz_mairix*' pop up in your group buffer. If this happens to you, simply kill these groups with C-k. For avoiding this, turn off auto-subscription completely by setting the variable **gnus-auto-subscribed-groups** to **nil** (see Section 1.4.3 [Filtering New Groups], page 5), or if you like to keep this feature use the following kludge for turning it off for all groups beginning with 'zz_':

  ```
  (setq gnus-auto-subscribed-groups
        "^\\(nnml\\|nnfolder\\|nnmbox\\|nnmh\\|nnbabyl\\|nnmaildir\\).*:\\([^z]\\|z$
  ```

8.2.9 nnmairix caveats

- You can create a secondary **nnml** server just for nnmairix, but then you have to explicitly set the corresponding server variable **nnml-get-new-mail** to **nil**. Otherwise, new mail might get put into this secondary server (and would never show up again). Here's an example server definition:

  ```
  (nnml "mairix" (nnml-directory "mairix") (nnml-get-new-mail nil))
  ```

  (The **nnmaildir** back end also has a server variable **get-new-mail**, but its default value is **nil**, so you don't have to explicitly set it if you use a **nnmaildir** server just for mairix.)

- If you use the Gnus registry: don't use the registry with **nnmairix** groups (put them in **gnus-registry-unfollowed-groups**; this is the default). Be *extra careful* if you use **gnus-registry-split-fancy-with-parent**; mails which are split into **nnmairix** groups are usually gone for good as soon as you check the group for new mail (yes, it has happened to me...).

- Therefore: *Never ever* put "real" mails into **nnmairix** groups (you shouldn't be able to, anyway).

- If you use the Gnus agent (see Section 6.9 [Gnus Unplugged], page 198): don't agentize `nnmairix` groups (though I have no idea what happens if you do).

- mairix does only support us-ascii characters.

- `nnmairix` uses a rather brute force method to force Gnus to completely reread the group on the mail back end after mairix was called—it simply deletes and re-creates the group on the mail back end. So far, this has worked for me without any problems, and I don't see how `nnmairix` could delete other mail groups than its own, but anyway: you really should have a backup of your mail folders.

- All necessary information is stored in the group parameters (see Section 2.10 [Group Parameters], page 22). This has the advantage that no active file is needed, but also implies that when you kill a `nnmairix` group, it is gone for good.

- If you create and kill a lot of `nnmairix` groups, the "zz_mairix-*" groups will accumulate on the mail back end server. To delete old groups which are no longer needed, call `nnmairix-purge-old-groups`. Note that this assumes that you don't save any "real" mail in folders of the form `zz_mairix-<NAME>-<NUMBER>`. You can change the prefix of `nnmairix` groups by changing the variable `nnmairix-group-prefix`.

- The following only applies if you *don't* use the mentioned patch for mairix (see Section 8.2.7 [Propagating marks], page 245):

  A problem can occur when using `nnmairix` with maildir folders and comes with the fact that maildir stores mail flags like 'Seen' or 'Replied' by appending chars 'S' and 'R' to the message file name, respectively. This implies that currently you would have to update the mairix database not only when new mail arrives, but also when mail flags are changing. The same applies to new mails which are indexed while they are still in the 'new' folder but then get moved to 'cur' when Gnus has seen the mail. If you don't update the database after this has happened, a mairix query can lead to symlinks pointing to non-existing files. In Gnus, these messages will usually appear with "(none)" entries in the header and can't be accessed. If this happens to you, using *G b u* and updating the group will usually fix this.

9 Various

9.1 Process/Prefix

Many functions, among them functions for moving, decoding and saving articles, use what is known as the *Process/Prefix convention*.

This is a method for figuring out what articles the user wants the command to be performed on.

It goes like this:

If the numeric prefix is N, perform the operation on the next N articles, starting with the current one. If the numeric prefix is negative, perform the operation on the previous N articles, starting with the current one.

If `transient-mark-mode` in non-`nil` and the region is active, all articles in the region will be worked upon.

If there is no numeric prefix, but some articles are marked with the process mark, perform the operation on the articles marked with the process mark.

If there is neither a numeric prefix nor any articles marked with the process mark, just perform the operation on the current article.

Quite simple, really, but it needs to be made clear so that surprises are avoided.

Commands that react to the process mark will push the current list of process marked articles onto a stack and will then clear all process marked articles. You can restore the previous configuration with the *M P y* command (see Section 3.7.6 [Setting Process Marks], page 62).

One thing that seems to shock & horrify lots of people is that, for instance, *3 d* does exactly the same as *d d d*. Since each *d* (which marks the current article as read) by default goes to the next unread article after marking, this means that *3 d* will mark the next three unread articles as read, no matter what the summary buffer looks like. Set `gnus-summary-goto-unread` to `nil` for a more straightforward action.

Many commands do not use the process/prefix convention. All commands that do explicitly say so in this manual. To apply the process/prefix convention to commands that do not use it, you can use the *M-&* command. For instance, to mark all the articles in the group as expirable, you could say *M P b M-& E*.

9.2 Interactive

`gnus-novice-user`

If this variable is non-`nil`, you are either a newcomer to the World of Usenet, or you are very cautious, which is a nice thing to be, really. You will be given questions of the type "Are you sure you want to do this?" before doing anything dangerous. This is `t` by default.

`gnus-expert-user`

If this variable is non-`nil`, you will seldom be asked any questions by Gnus. It will simply assume you know what you're doing, no matter how strange. For example, quitting Gnus, exiting a group without an update, catching up with a group, deleting expired articles, and replying by mail to a news message will not require confirmation.

`gnus-interactive-catchup`

> Require confirmation before catching up a group if non-`nil`. It is **t** by default.

`gnus-interactive-exit`

> If non-`nil`, require a confirmation when exiting Gnus. If `quiet`, update any active summary buffers automatically without querying. The default value is **t**.

9.3 Symbolic Prefixes

Quite a lot of Emacs commands react to the (numeric) prefix. For instance, *C-u 4 C-f* moves point four characters forward, and *C-u 9 0 0 I s s p* adds a permanent `Subject` substring score rule of 900 to the current article.

This is all nice and well, but what if you want to give a command some additional information? Well, what most commands do is interpret the "raw" prefix in some special way. *C-u 0 C-x C-s* means that one doesn't want a backup file to be created when saving the current buffer, for instance. But what if you want to save without making a backup file, and you want Emacs to flash lights and play a nice tune at the same time? You can't, and you're probably perfectly happy that way.

I'm not, so I've added a second prefix—the *symbolic prefix*. The prefix key is *M-i* (`gnus-symbolic-argument`), and the next character typed in is the value. You can stack as many *M-i* prefixes as you want. *M-i a C-M-u* means "feed the *C-M-u* command the symbolic prefix **a**". *M-i a M-i b C-M-u* means "feed the *C-M-u* command the symbolic prefixes **a** and **b**". You get the drift.

Typing in symbolic prefixes to commands that don't accept them doesn't hurt, but it doesn't do any good either. Currently not many Gnus functions make use of the symbolic prefix.

If you're interested in how Gnus implements this, see Section 11.8.7 [Extended Interactive], page 353.

9.4 Formatting Variables

Throughout this manual you've probably noticed lots of variables called things like `gnus-group-line-format` and `gnus-summary-mode-line-format`. These control how Gnus is to output lines in the various buffers. There's quite a lot of them. Fortunately, they all use the same syntax, so there's not that much to be annoyed by.

Here's an example format spec (from the group buffer): '`%M%S%5y: %(%g%)\n`'. We see that it is indeed extremely ugly, and that there are lots of percentages everywhere.

Currently Gnus uses the following formatting variables: `gnus-group-line-format`, `gnus-summary-line-format`, `gnus-server-line-format`, `gnus-topic-line-format`, `gnus-group-mode-line-format`, `gnus-summary-mode-line-format`, `gnus-article-mode-line-format`, `gnus-server-mode-line-format`, and `gnus-summary-pick-line-format`.

All these format variables can also be arbitrary elisp forms. In that case, they will be `eval`ed to insert the required lines.

Gnus includes a command to help you while creating your own format specs. *M-x gnus-update-format* will `eval` the current form, update the spec in question and pop you to a buffer where you can examine the resulting Lisp code to be run to generate the line.

9.4.1 Formatting Basics

Each '%' element will be replaced by some string or other when the buffer in question is generated. '%5y' means "insert the 'y' spec, and pad with spaces to get a 5-character field".

As with normal C and Emacs Lisp formatting strings, the numerical modifier between the '%' and the formatting type character will *pad* the output so that it is always at least that long. '%5y' will make the field always (at least) five characters wide by padding with spaces to the left. If you say '%-5y', it will pad to the right instead.

You may also wish to limit the length of the field to protect against particularly wide values. For that you can say '%4,6y', which means that the field will never be more than 6 characters wide and never less than 4 characters wide.

Also Gnus supports some extended format specifications, such as '%&user-date;'.

9.4.2 Mode Line Formatting

Mode line formatting variables (e.g., `gnus-summary-mode-line-format`) follow the same rules as other, buffer line oriented formatting variables (see Section 9.4.1 [Formatting Basics], page 251) with the following two differences:

1. There must be no newline ('\n') at the end.

2. The special '%%b' spec can be used to display the buffer name. Well. it's no spec at all, really—'%%' is just a way to quote '%' to allow it to pass through the formatting machinery unmangled, so that Emacs receives '%b', which is something the Emacs mode line display interprets to mean "show the buffer name". For a full list of mode line specs Emacs understands, see the documentation of the `mode-line-format` variable.

9.4.3 Advanced Formatting

It is frequently useful to post-process the fields in some way. Padding, limiting, cutting off parts and suppressing certain values can be achieved by using *tilde modifiers*. A typical tilde spec might look like '%~(cut 3)~(ignore "0")y'.

These are the valid modifiers:

pad
pad-left   Pad the field to the left with spaces until it reaches the required length.

pad-right
            Pad the field to the right with spaces until it reaches the required length.

max
max-left   Cut off characters from the left until it reaches the specified length.

max-right
            Cut off characters from the right until it reaches the specified length.

cut
cut-left   Cut off the specified number of characters from the left.

cut-right
:   Cut off the specified number of characters from the right.

ignore
:   Return an empty string if the field is equal to the specified value.

form
:   Use the specified form as the field value when the '@' spec is used.

    Here's an example:

    ```
    "~(form (current-time-string))@"
    ```

Let's take an example. The '%o' spec in the summary mode lines will return a date in compact ISO8601 format—'19960809T230410'. This is quite a mouthful, so we want to shave off the century number and the time, leaving us with a six-character date. That would be '%~(cut-left 2)~(max-right 6)~(pad 6)o'. (Cutting is done before maxing, and we need the padding to ensure that the date is never less than 6 characters to make it look nice in columns.)

Ignoring is done first; then cutting; then maxing; and then as the very last operation, padding.

9.4.4 User-Defined Specs

All the specs allow for inserting user defined specifiers—'u'. The next character in the format string should be a letter. Gnus will call the function **gnus-user-format-function-**'X', where 'X' is the letter following '%u'. The function will be passed a single parameter—what the parameter means depends on what buffer it's being called from. The function should return a string, which will be inserted into the buffer just like information from any other specifier. This function may also be called with dummy values, so it should protect against that.

Also Gnus supports extended user-defined specs, such as '%u&foo;'. Gnus will call the function **gnus-user-format-function-**'foo'.

You can also use tilde modifiers (see Section 9.4.3 [Advanced Formatting], page 251 to achieve much the same without defining new functions. Here's an example: '%~(form (count-lines (point-min) (point)))@'. The form given here will be evaluated to yield the current line number, and then inserted.

9.4.5 Formatting Fonts

There are specs for highlighting, and these are shared by all the format variables. Text inside the '%(' and '%)' specifiers will get the special **mouse-face** property set, which means that it will be highlighted (with **gnus-mouse-face**) when you put the mouse pointer over it.

Text inside the '%{' and '%}' specifiers will have their normal faces set using **gnus-face-**0, which is **bold** by default. If you say '%1{', you'll get **gnus-face-1** instead, and so on. Create as many faces as you wish. The same goes for the **mouse-face** specs—you can say '%3(hello%)' to have 'hello' mouse-highlighted with **gnus-mouse-face-3**.

Text inside the '%<<' and '%>>' specifiers will get the special **balloon-help** property set to **gnus-balloon-face-0**. If you say '%1<<', you'll get **gnus-balloon-face-1** and so on. The **gnus-balloon-face-*** variables should be either strings or symbols naming functions that return a string. When the mouse passes over text with this property set, a balloon window will appear and display the string. Please refer to Section "Tooltips" in

The Emacs Manual, (in Emacs) or the doc string of `balloon-help-mode` (in XEmacs) for more information on this. (For technical reasons, the guillemets have been approximated as '<<' and '>>' in this paragraph.)

Here's an alternative recipe for the group buffer:

```
;; Create three face types.
(setq gnus-face-1 'bold)
(setq gnus-face-3 'italic)

;; We want the article count to be in
;; a bold and green face.  So we create
;; a new face called my-green-bold.
(copy-face 'bold 'my-green-bold)
;; Set the color.
(set-face-foreground 'my-green-bold "ForestGreen")
(setq gnus-face-2 'my-green-bold)

;; Set the new & fancy format.
(setq gnus-group-line-format
      "%M%S%3{%5y%}%2[:%] %(%1{%g%}%)\n")
```

I'm sure you'll be able to use this scheme to create totally unreadable and extremely vulgar displays. Have fun!

Note that the '%(' specs (and friends) do not make any sense on the mode-line variables.

9.4.6 Positioning Point

Gnus usually moves point to a pre-defined place on each line in most buffers. By default, point move to the first colon character on the line. You can customize this behavior in three different ways.

You can move the colon character to somewhere else on the line.

You can redefine the function that moves the point to the colon. The function is called `gnus-goto-colon`.

But perhaps the most convenient way to deal with this, if you don't want to have a colon in your line, is to use the '%*' specifier. If you put a '%*' somewhere in your format line definition, Gnus will place point there.

9.4.7 Tabulation

You can usually line up your displays by padding and cutting your strings. However, when combining various strings of different size, it can often be more convenient to just output the strings, and then worry about lining up the following text afterwards.

To do that, Gnus supplies tabulator specs—'%='. There are two different types—*hard tabulators* and *soft tabulators*.

'%50=' will insert space characters to pad the line up to column 50. If the text is already past column 50, nothing will be inserted. This is the soft tabulator.

'%-50=' will insert space characters to pad the line up to column 50. If the text is already past column 50, the excess text past column 50 will be removed. This is the hard tabulator.

9.4.8 Wide Characters

Fixed width fonts in most countries have characters of the same width. Some countries, however, use Latin characters mixed with wider characters—most notable East Asian countries.

The problem is that when formatting, Gnus assumes that if a string is 10 characters wide, it'll be 10 Latin characters wide on the screen. In these countries, that's not true.

To help fix this, you can set `gnus-use-correct-string-widths` to `t`. This makes buffer generation slower, but the results will be prettier. The default value under XEmacs is `t` but `nil` for Emacs.

9.5 Window Layout

No, there's nothing here about X, so be quiet.

If `gnus-use-full-window` non-`nil`, Gnus will delete all other windows and occupy the entire Emacs screen by itself. It is `t` by default.

Setting this variable to `nil` kinda works, but there are glitches. Use at your own peril.

`gnus-buffer-configuration` describes how much space each Gnus buffer should be given. Here's an excerpt of this variable:

```
((group (vertical 1.0 (group 1.0 point)))
 (article (vertical 1.0 (summary 0.25 point)
                        (article 1.0))))
```

This is an alist. The *key* is a symbol that names some action or other. For instance, when displaying the group buffer, the window configuration function will use `group` as the key. A full list of possible names is listed below.

The *value* (i.e., the *split*) says how much space each buffer should occupy. To take the `article` split as an example:

```
(article (vertical 1.0 (summary 0.25 point)
                       (article 1.0)))
```

This *split* says that the summary buffer should occupy 25% of upper half of the screen, and that it is placed over the article buffer. As you may have noticed, 100% + 25% is actually 125% (yup, I saw y'all reaching for that calculator there). However, the special number `1.0` is used to signal that this buffer should soak up all the rest of the space available after the rest of the buffers have taken whatever they need. There should be only one buffer with the `1.0` size spec per split.

Point will be put in the buffer that has the optional third element `point`. In a `frame` split, the last subsplit having a leaf split where the tag `frame-focus` is a member (i.e., is the third or fourth element in the list, depending on whether the `point` tag is present) gets focus.

Here's a more complicated example:

```
(article (vertical 1.0 (group 4)
                       (summary 0.25 point)
                       (article 1.0)))
```

If the size spec is an integer instead of a floating point number, then that number will be used to say how many lines a buffer should occupy, not a percentage.

If the *split* looks like something that can be `evaled` (to be precise—if the `car` of the split is a function or a subr), this split will be `evaled`. If the result is non-`nil`, it will be used as a split.

Not complicated enough for you? Well, try this on for size:

```
(article (horizontal 1.0
             (vertical 0.5
                (group 1.0))
             (vertical 1.0
                (summary 0.25 point)
                (article 1.0))))
```

Whoops. Two buffers with the mystery 100% tag. And what's that `horizontal` thingie?

If the first element in one of the split is `horizontal`, Gnus will split the window horizontally, giving you two windows side-by-side. Inside each of these strips you may carry on all you like in the normal fashion. The number following `horizontal` says what percentage of the screen is to be given to this strip.

For each split, there *must* be one element that has the 100% tag. The splitting is never accurate, and this buffer will eat any leftover lines from the splits.

To be slightly more formal, here's a definition of what a valid split may look like:

```
split      = frame | horizontal | vertical | buffer | form
frame      = "(frame " size *split ")"
horizontal = "(horizontal " size *split ")"
vertical   = "(vertical " size *split ")"
buffer     = "(" buf-name " " size *[ "point" ] *[ "frame-focus"] ")"
size       = number | frame-params
buf-name   = group | article | summary ...
```

The limitations are that the `frame` split can only appear as the top-level split. *form* should be an Emacs Lisp form that should return a valid split. We see that each split is fully recursive, and may contain any number of `vertical` and `horizontal` splits.

Finding the right sizes can be a bit complicated. No window may be less than `gnus-window-min-height` (default 1) characters high, and all windows must be at least `gnus-window-min-width` (default 1) characters wide. Gnus will try to enforce this before applying the splits. If you want to use the normal Emacs window width/height limit, you can just set these two variables to `nil`.

If you're not familiar with Emacs terminology, `horizontal` and `vertical` splits may work the opposite way of what you'd expect. Windows inside a `horizontal` split are shown side-by-side, and windows within a `vertical` split are shown above each other.

If you want to experiment with window placement, a good tip is to call `gnus-configure-frame` directly with a split. This is the function that does all the real work when splitting buffers. Below is a pretty nonsensical configuration with 5 windows; two for the group buffer and three for the article buffer. (I said it was nonsensical.) If you `eval` the statement below, you can get an idea of how that would look straight away, without going through the normal Gnus channels. Play with it until you're satisfied, and then use `gnus-add-configuration` to add your new creation to the buffer configuration list.

```
(gnus-configure-frame
```

```
'(horizontal 1.0
   (vertical 10
      (group 1.0)
      (article 0.3 point))
   (vertical 1.0
      (article 1.0)
      (horizontal 4
         (group 1.0)
         (article 10)))))
```

You might want to have several frames as well. No prob—just use the **frame** split:

```
(gnus-configure-frame
 '(frame 1.0
         (vertical 1.0
                   (summary 0.25 point frame-focus)
                   (article 1.0))
         (vertical ((height . 5) (width . 15)
                    (user-position . t)
                    (left . -1) (top . 1))
                   (picon 1.0))))
```

This split will result in the familiar summary/article window configuration in the first (or "main") frame, while a small additional frame will be created where picons will be shown. As you can see, instead of the normal 1.0 top-level spec, each additional split should have a frame parameter alist as the size spec. See Section "Frame Parameters" in *The GNU Emacs Lisp Reference Manual*. Under XEmacs, a frame property list will be accepted, too—for instance, (**height 5 width 15 left -1 top 1**) is such a plist. The list of all possible keys for **gnus-buffer-configuration** can be found in its default value.

Note that the **message** key is used for both **gnus-group-mail** and **gnus-summary-mail-other-window**. If it is desirable to distinguish between the two, something like this might be used:

```
(message (horizontal 1.0
                     (vertical 1.0 (message 1.0 point))
                     (vertical 0.24
                               (if (buffer-live-p gnus-summary-buffer)
                                   '(summary 0.5))
                               (group 1.0))))
```

One common desire for a multiple frame split is to have a separate frame for composing mail and news while leaving the original frame intact. To accomplish that, something like the following can be done:

```
(message
 (frame 1.0
        (if (not (buffer-live-p gnus-summary-buffer))
            (car (cdr (assoc 'group gnus-buffer-configuration)))
          (car (cdr (assoc 'summary gnus-buffer-configuration))))
        (vertical ((user-position . t) (top . 1) (left . 1)
```

```
                                 (name . "Message"))
                                 (message 1.0 point))))
```

Since the `gnus-buffer-configuration` variable is so long and complicated, there's a function you can use to ease changing the config of a single setting: `gnus-add-configuration`. If, for instance, you want to change the `article` setting, you could say:

```
(gnus-add-configuration
 '(article (vertical 1.0
            (group 4)
            (summary .25 point)
            (article 1.0))))
```

You'd typically stick these `gnus-add-configuration` calls in your `~/.gnus.el` file or in some startup hook—they should be run after Gnus has been loaded.

If all windows mentioned in the configuration are already visible, Gnus won't change the window configuration. If you always want to force the "right" window configuration, you can set `gnus-always-force-window-configuration` to non-`nil`.

If you're using tree displays (see Section 3.25 [Tree Display], page 105), and the tree window is displayed vertically next to another window, you may also want to fiddle with `gnus-tree-minimize-window` to avoid having the windows resized.

9.5.1 Window Configuration Names

Here's a list of most of the currently known window configurations, and when they're used:

`group`   The group buffer.

`summary` Entering a group and showing only the summary.

`article` Selecting an article.

`server`   The server buffer.

`browse`   Browsing groups from the server buffer.

`message` Composing a (new) message.

`only-article`
           Showing only the article buffer.

`edit-article`
           Editing an article.

`edit-form`
           Editing group parameters and the like.

`edit-score`
           Editing a server definition.

`post`   Composing a news message.

`reply`   Replying or following up an article without yanking the text.

`forward` Forwarding a message.

`reply-yank`
> Replying or following up an article with yanking the text.

`mail-bound`
> Bouncing a message.

`pipe`   Sending an article to an external process.

`bug`   Sending a bug report.

`score-trace`
> Displaying the score trace.

`score-words`
> Displaying the score words.

`split-trace`
> Displaying the split trace.

`compose-bounce`
> Composing a bounce message.

`mml-preview`
> Previewing a MIME part.

9.5.2 Example Window Configurations

- Narrow left hand side occupied by group buffer. Right hand side split between summary buffer (top one-sixth) and article buffer (bottom).

```
(gnus-add-configuration
 '(article
   (horizontal 1.0
               (vertical 25 (group 1.0))
               (vertical 1.0
                         (summary 0.16 point)
                         (article 1.0)))))

(gnus-add-configuration
 '(summary
   (horizontal 1.0
               (vertical 25 (group 1.0))
               (vertical 1.0 (summary 1.0 point)))))
```

9.6 Faces and Fonts

Fiddling with fonts and faces used to be very difficult, but these days it is very simple. You simply say *M-x customize-face*, pick out the face you want to alter, and alter it via the standard Customize interface.

9.7 Mode Lines

`gnus-updated-mode-lines` says what buffers should keep their mode lines updated. It is a list of symbols. Supported symbols include **group**, **article**, **summary**, **server**, **browse**, and `tree`. If the corresponding symbol is present, Gnus will keep that mode line updated with information that may be pertinent. If this variable is `nil`, screen refresh may be quicker.

By default, Gnus displays information on the current article in the mode lines of the summary and article buffers. The information Gnus wishes to display (e.g., the subject of the article) is often longer than the mode lines, and therefore have to be cut off at some point. The `gnus-mode-non-string-length` variable says how long the other elements on the line is (i.e., the non-info part). If you put additional elements on the mode line (e.g., a clock), you should modify this variable:

```
(add-hook 'display-time-hook
          (lambda () (setq gnus-mode-non-string-length
                       (+ 21
                          (if line-number-mode 5 0)
                          (if column-number-mode 4 0)
                          (length display-time-string)))))
```

If this variable is `nil` (which is the default), the mode line strings won't be chopped off, and they won't be padded either. Note that the default is unlikely to be desirable, as even the percentage complete in the buffer may be crowded off the mode line; the user should configure this variable appropriately for her configuration.

9.8 Highlighting and Menus

The `gnus-visual` variable controls most of the Gnus-prettifying aspects. If `nil`, Gnus won't attempt to create menus or use fancy colors or fonts. This will also inhibit loading the `gnus-vis.el` file.

This variable can be a list of visual properties that are enabled. The following elements are valid, and are all included by default:

`group-highlight`
> Do highlights in the group buffer.

`summary-highlight`
> Do highlights in the summary buffer.

`article-highlight`
> Do highlights in the article buffer.

`highlight`
> Turn on highlighting in all buffers.

`group-menu`
> Create menus in the group buffer.

`summary-menu`
> Create menus in the summary buffers.

`article-menu`
> Create menus in the article buffer.

`browse-menu`
> Create menus in the browse buffer.

`server-menu`
>   Create menus in the server buffer.

`score-menu`
>   Create menus in the score buffers.

`menu`   Create menus in all buffers.

So if you only want highlighting in the article buffer and menus in all buffers, you could say something like:

>   `(setq gnus-visual '(article-highlight menu))`

If you want highlighting only and no menus whatsoever, you'd say:

>   `(setq gnus-visual '(highlight))`

If `gnus-visual` is `t`, highlighting and menus will be used in all Gnus buffers.

Other general variables that influence the look of all buffers include:

`gnus-mouse-face`
>   This is the face (i.e., font) used for mouse highlighting in Gnus. No mouse highlights will be done if `gnus-visual` is `nil`.

There are hooks associated with the creation of all the different menus:

`gnus-article-menu-hook`
>   Hook called after creating the article mode menu.

`gnus-group-menu-hook`
>   Hook called after creating the group mode menu.

`gnus-summary-menu-hook`
>   Hook called after creating the summary mode menu.

`gnus-server-menu-hook`
>   Hook called after creating the server mode menu.

`gnus-browse-menu-hook`
>   Hook called after creating the browse mode menu.

`gnus-score-menu-hook`
>   Hook called after creating the score mode menu.

9.9 Daemons

Gnus, being larger than any program ever written (allegedly), does lots of strange stuff that you may wish to have done while you're not present. For instance, you may want it to check for new mail once in a while. Or you may want it to close down all connections to all servers when you leave Emacs idle. And stuff like that.

Gnus will let you do stuff like that by defining various *handlers*. Each handler consists of three elements: A *function*, a *time*, and an *idle* parameter.

Here's an example of a handler that closes connections when Emacs has been idle for thirty minutes:

>   `(gnus-demon-close-connections nil 30)`

Here's a handler that scans for PGP headers every hour when Emacs is idle:

```
(gnus-demon-scan-pgp 60 t)
```

This *time* parameter and that *idle* parameter work together in a strange, but wonderful fashion. Basically, if *idle* is `nil`, then the function will be called every *time* minutes.

If *idle* is `t`, then the function will be called after *time* minutes only if Emacs is idle. So if Emacs is never idle, the function will never be called. But once Emacs goes idle, the function will be called every *time* minutes.

If *idle* is a number and *time* is a number, the function will be called every *time* minutes only when Emacs has been idle for *idle* minutes.

If *idle* is a number and *time* is `nil`, the function will be called once every time Emacs has been idle for *idle* minutes.

And if *time* is a string, it should look like '`07:31`', and the function will then be called once every day somewhere near that time. Modified by the *idle* parameter, of course.

(When I say "minute" here, I really mean **gnus-demon-timestep** seconds. This is 60 by default. If you change that variable, all the timings in the handlers will be affected.)

So, if you want to add a handler, you could put something like this in your `~/.gnus.el` file:

```
(gnus-demon-add-handler 'gnus-demon-close-connections 30 t)
```

Some ready-made functions to do this have been created: **gnus-demon-add-disconnection**, **gnus-demon-add-nntp-close-connection**, **gnus-demon-add-scan-timestamps**, **gnus-demon-add-rescan**, and **gnus-demon-add-scanmail**. Just put those functions in your `~/.gnus.el` if you want those abilities.

If you add handlers to **gnus-demon-handlers** directly, you should run **gnus-demon-init** to make the changes take hold. To cancel all daemons, you can use the **gnus-demon-cancel** function.

Note that adding daemons can be pretty naughty if you over do it. Adding functions that scan all news and mail from all servers every two seconds is a sure-fire way of getting booted off any respectable system. So behave.

9.10 Undo

It is very useful to be able to undo actions one has done. In normal Emacs buffers, it's easy enough—you just push the **undo** button. In Gnus buffers, however, it isn't that simple.

The things Gnus displays in its buffer is of no value whatsoever to Gnus—it's all just data designed to look nice to the user. Killing a group in the group buffer with `C-k` makes the line disappear, but that's just a side-effect of the real action—the removal of the group in question from the internal Gnus structures. Undoing something like that can't be done by the normal Emacs **undo** function.

Gnus tries to remedy this somewhat by keeping track of what the user does and coming up with actions that would reverse the actions the user takes. When the user then presses the **undo** key, Gnus will run the code to reverse the previous action, or the previous actions. However, not all actions are easily reversible, so Gnus currently offers a few key functions to be undoable. These include killing groups, yanking groups, and changing the list of read articles of groups. That's it, really. More functions may be added in the future, but each added function means an increase in data to be stored, so Gnus will never be totally undoable.

The undoability is provided by the `gnus-undo-mode` minor mode. It is used if `gnus-use-undo` is non-`nil`, which is the default. The `C-M-_` key performs the `gnus-undo` command, which should feel kinda like the normal Emacs `undo` command.

9.11 Predicate Specifiers

Some Gnus variables are *predicate specifiers*. This is a special form that allows flexible specification of predicates without having to type all that much.

These specifiers are lists consisting of functions, symbols and lists.

Here's an example:

```
(or gnus-article-unseen-p
    gnus-article-unread-p)
```

The available symbols are `or`, `and` and `not`. The functions all take one parameter.

Internally, Gnus calls `gnus-make-predicate` on these specifiers to create a function that can be called. This input parameter to this function will be passed along to all the functions in the predicate specifier.

9.12 Moderation

If you are a moderator, you can use the `gnus-mdrtn.el` package. It is not included in the standard Gnus package. Write a mail to 'larsi@gnus.org' and state what group you moderate, and you'll get a copy.

The moderation package is implemented as a minor mode for summary buffers. Put

```
(add-hook 'gnus-summary-mode-hook 'gnus-moderate)
```

in your ~/.gnus.el file.

If you are the moderator of 'rec.zoofle', this is how it's supposed to work:

1. You split your incoming mail by matching on 'Newsgroups:.*rec.zoofle', which will put all the to-be-posted articles in some mail group—for instance, 'nnml:rec.zoofle'.

2. You enter that group once in a while and post articles using the `e` (edit-and-post) or `s` (just send unedited) commands.

3. If, while reading the 'rec.zoofle' newsgroup, you happen upon some articles that weren't approved by you, you can cancel them with the `c` command.

To use moderation mode in these two groups, say:

```
(setq gnus-moderated-list
      "^nnml:rec.zoofle$\\|^rec.zoofle$")
```

9.13 Fetching a Group

It is sometimes convenient to be able to just say "I want to read this group and I don't care whether Gnus has been started or not". This is perhaps more useful for people who write code than for users, but the command `gnus-fetch-group` provides this functionality in any case. It takes the group name as a parameter.

9.14 Image Enhancements

XEmacs, as well as Emacs 21[1] and up, are able to display pictures and stuff, so Gnus has taken advantage of that.

9.14.1 X-Face

`X-Face` headers describe a 48x48 pixel black-and-white (1 bit depth) image that's supposed to represent the author of the message. It seems to be supported by an ever-growing number of mail and news readers.

Viewing an `X-Face` header either requires an Emacs that has 'compface' support (which most XEmacs versions have), or that you have suitable conversion or display programs installed. If your Emacs has image support the default action is to display the face before the `From` header. If there's no native `X-Face` support, Gnus will try to convert the `X-Face` header using external programs from the `pbmplus` package and friends, see below. For XEmacs it's faster if XEmacs has been compiled with `X-Face` support. The default action under Emacs without image support is to fork off the `display` program.

On a GNU/Linux system, the `display` program is included in the ImageMagick package. For external conversion programs look for packages with names like `netpbm`, `libgr-progs` and `compface`. On Windows, you may use the packages `netpbm` and `compface` from `http://gnuwin32.sourceforge.net`. You need to add the `bin` directory to your `PATH` environment variable.

The variable `gnus-article-x-face-command` controls which programs are used to display the `X-Face` header. If this variable is a string, this string will be executed in a subshell. If it is a function, this function will be called with the face as the argument. If `gnus-article-x-face-too-ugly` (which is a regexp) matches the `From` header, the face will not be shown.

(Note: `x-face` is used in the variable/function names, not `xface`).

Face and variable:

`gnus-x-face`

Face to show X-Face. The colors from this face are used as the foreground and background colors of the displayed X-Faces. The default colors are black and white.

`gnus-face-properties-alist`

Alist of image types and properties applied to Face (see Section 9.14.2 [Face], page 264) and X-Face images. The default value is `((pbm . (:face gnus-x-face)) (png . nil))` for Emacs or `((xface . (:face gnus-x-face)))` for XEmacs. Here are examples:

```
;; Specify the altitude of Face and X-Face images in the From header.
(setq gnus-face-properties-alist
      '((pbm . (:face gnus-x-face :ascent 80))
        (png . (:ascent 80))))

;; Show Face and X-Face images as pressed buttons.
```

[1] Emacs 21 on MS Windows doesn't support images, Emacs 22 does.

```
(setq gnus-face-properties-alist
      '((pbm . (:face gnus-x-face :relief -2))
        (png . (:relief -2))))
```

see Section "Image Descriptors" in *The Emacs Lisp Reference Manual* for the valid properties for various image types. Currently, `pbm` is used for X-Face images and `png` is used for Face images in Emacs. Only the `:face` property is effective on the `xface` image type in XEmacs if it is built with the 'libcompface' library.

If you use posting styles, you can use an `x-face-file` entry in `gnus-posting-styles`, See Section 5.6 [Posting Styles], page 131. If you don't, Gnus provides a few convenience functions and variables to allow easier insertion of X-Face headers in outgoing messages. You also need the above mentioned ImageMagick, netpbm or other image conversion packages (depending the values of the variables below) for these functions.

`gnus-random-x-face` goes through all the 'pbm' files in `gnus-x-face-directory` and picks one at random, and then converts it to the X-Face format by using the `gnus-convert-pbm-to-x-face-command` shell command. The 'pbm' files should be 48x48 pixels big. It returns the X-Face header data as a string.

`gnus-insert-random-x-face-header` calls `gnus-random-x-face` and inserts a 'X-Face' header with the randomly generated data.

`gnus-x-face-from-file` takes a GIF file as the parameter, and then converts the file to X-Face format by using the `gnus-convert-image-to-x-face-command` shell command.

Here's how you would typically use the first function. Put something like the following in your `~/.gnus.el` file:

```
(setq message-required-news-headers
      (nconc message-required-news-headers
             (list '(X-Face . gnus-random-x-face))))
```

Using the last function would be something like this:

```
(setq message-required-news-headers
      (nconc message-required-news-headers
             (list '(X-Face . (lambda ()
                                (gnus-x-face-from-file
                                 "~/My-face.gif"))))))
```

9.14.2 Face

`Face` headers are essentially a funkier version of `X-Face` ones. They describe a 48x48 pixel colored image that's supposed to represent the author of the message.

The contents of a `Face` header must be a base64 encoded PNG image. See http://quimby.gnus.org/circus/face/ for the precise specifications.

The `gnus-face-properties-alist` variable affects the appearance of displayed Face images. See Section 9.14.1 [X-Face], page 263.

Viewing a `Face` header requires an Emacs that is able to display PNG images.

Gnus provides a few convenience functions and variables to allow easier insertion of Face headers in outgoing messages.

`gnus-convert-png-to-face` takes a 48x48 PNG image, no longer than 726 bytes long, and converts it to a face.

`gnus-face-from-file` takes a JPEG file as the parameter, and then converts the file to Face format by using the `gnus-convert-image-to-face-command` shell command.

Here's how you would typically use this function. Put something like the following in your `~/.gnus.el` file:

```
(setq message-required-news-headers
      (nconc message-required-news-headers
             (list '(Face . (lambda ()
                              (gnus-face-from-file "~/face.jpg"))))))
```

9.14.3 Smileys

Smiley is a package separate from Gnus, but since Gnus is currently the only package that uses Smiley, it is documented here.

In short—to use Smiley in Gnus, put the following in your `~/.gnus.el` file:

```
(setq gnus-treat-display-smileys t)
```

Smiley maps text smiley faces—':-)', '8-)', ':-(' and the like—to pictures and displays those instead of the text smiley faces. The conversion is controlled by a list of regexps that matches text and maps that to file names.

The alist used is specified by the `smiley-regexp-alist` variable. The first item in each element is the regexp to be matched; the second element is the regexp match group that is to be replaced by the picture; and the third element is the name of the file to be displayed.

The following variables customize the appearance of the smileys:

`smiley-style`

        Specifies the smiley style. Predefined smiley styles include `low-color` (small 13x14 pixel, three-color images), `medium` (more colorful images, 16x16 pixel), and `grayscale` (grayscale images, 14x14 pixel). The default depends on the height of the default face.

`smiley-data-directory`

        Where Smiley will look for smiley faces files. You shouldn't set this variable anymore. Customize `smiley-style` instead.

`gnus-smiley-file-types`

        List of suffixes on smiley file names to try.

9.14.4 Picons

So... You want to slow down your news reader even more! This is a good way to do so. It's also a great way to impress people staring over your shoulder as you read news.

What are Picons? To quote directly from the Picons Web site:

        Picons is short for "personal icons". They're small, constrained images used to represent users and domains on the net, organized into databases so that the appropriate image for a given e-mail address can be found. Besides users and domains, there are picon databases for Usenet newsgroups and weather forecasts. The picons are in either monochrome `XBM` format or color `XPM` and `GIF` formats.

For instructions on obtaining and installing the picons databases, point your Web browser at `http://www.cs.indiana.edu/picons/ftp/index.html`.

If you are using Debian GNU/Linux, saying '`apt-get install picons.*`' will install the picons where Gnus can find them.

To enable displaying picons, simply make sure that `gnus-picon-databases` points to the directory containing the Picons databases.

The variable `gnus-picon-style` controls how picons are displayed. If `inline`, the textual representation is replaced. If `right`, picons are added right to the textual representation.

The value of the variable `gnus-picon-properties` is a list of properties applied to picons.

The following variables offer control over where things are located.

`gnus-picon-databases`
> The location of the picons database. This is a list of directories containing the `news`, `domains`, `users` (and so on) subdirectories. Defaults to (`"/usr/lib/picon"` `"/usr/local/faces"`).

`gnus-picon-news-directories`
> List of subdirectories to search in `gnus-picon-databases` for newsgroups faces. (`"news"`) is the default.

`gnus-picon-user-directories`
> List of subdirectories to search in `gnus-picon-databases` for user faces. (`"users"` `"usenix"` `"local"` `"misc"`) is the default.

`gnus-picon-domain-directories`
> List of subdirectories to search in `gnus-picon-databases` for domain name faces. Defaults to (`"domains"`). Some people may want to add '`"unknown"`' to this list.

`gnus-picon-file-types`
> Ordered list of suffixes on picon file names to try. Defaults to (`"xpm"` `"gif"` `"xbm"`) minus those not built-in your Emacs.

`gnus-picon-inhibit-top-level-domains`
> If non-`nil` (which is the default), don't display picons for things like '`.net`' and '`.de`', which aren't usually very interesting.

9.14.5 Gravatars

A gravatar is an image registered to an e-mail address.

You can submit yours on-line at `http://www.gravatar.com`.

The following variables offer control over how things are displayed.

`gnus-gravatar-size`
> The size in pixels of gravatars. Gravatars are always square, so one number for the size is enough.

`gnus-gravatar-properties`
> List of image properties applied to Gravatar images.

`gnus-gravatar-too-ugly`
> Regexp that matches mail addresses or names of people of which avatars should not be displayed, or `nil`. It default to the value of `gnus-article-x-face-too-ugly` (see Section 9.14.1 [X-Face], page 263).

If you want to see them in the From field, set:

    (setq gnus-treat-from-gravatar 'head)

If you want to see them in the Cc and To fields, set:

    (setq gnus-treat-mail-gravatar 'head)

9.14.6 Various XEmacs Variables

`gnus-xmas-glyph-directory`
> This is where Gnus will look for pictures. Gnus will normally auto-detect this directory, but you may set it manually if you have an unusual directory structure.

`gnus-xmas-modeline-glyph`
> A glyph displayed in all Gnus mode lines. It is a tiny gnu head by default.

9.14.6.1 Toolbar

`gnus-use-toolbar`
> This variable specifies the position to display the toolbar. If `nil`, don't display toolbars. If it is non-`nil`, it should be one of the symbols `default`, `top`, `bottom`, `right`, and `left`. `default` means to use the default toolbar, the rest mean to display the toolbar on the place which those names show. The default is `default`.

`gnus-toolbar-thickness`
> Cons of the height and the width specifying the thickness of a toolbar. The height is used for the toolbar displayed on the top or the bottom, the width is used for the toolbar displayed on the right or the left. The default is that of the default toolbar.

`gnus-group-toolbar`
> The toolbar in the group buffer.

`gnus-summary-toolbar`
> The toolbar in the summary buffer.

`gnus-summary-mail-toolbar`
> The toolbar in the summary buffer of mail groups.

9.15 Fuzzy Matching

Gnus provides *fuzzy matching* of `Subject` lines when doing things like scoring, thread gathering and thread comparison.

As opposed to regular expression matching, fuzzy matching is very fuzzy. It's so fuzzy that there's not even a definition of what *fuzziness* means, and the implementation has changed over time.

Basically, it tries to remove all noise from lines before comparing. 'Re: ', parenthetical remarks, white space, and so on, are filtered out of the strings before comparing the results. This often leads to adequate results—even when faced with strings generated by text manglers masquerading as newsreaders.

9.16 Thwarting Email Spam

In these last days of the Usenet, commercial vultures are hanging about and grepping through news like crazy to find email addresses they can foist off their scams and products to. As a reaction to this, many people have started putting nonsense addresses into their `From` lines. I think this is counterproductive—it makes it difficult for people to send you legitimate mail in response to things you write, as well as making it difficult to see who wrote what. This rewriting may perhaps be a bigger menace than the unsolicited commercial email itself in the end.

The biggest problem I have with email spam is that it comes in under false pretenses. I press *g* and Gnus merrily informs me that I have 10 new emails. I say "Golly gee! Happy is me!" and select the mail group, only to find two pyramid schemes, seven advertisements ("New! Miracle tonic for growing full, lustrous hair on your toes!") and one mail asking me to repent and find some god.

This is annoying. Here's what you can do about it.

9.16.1 The problem of spam

First, some background on spam.

If you have access to e-mail, you are familiar with spam (technically termed UCE, Unsolicited Commercial E-mail). Simply put, it exists because e-mail delivery is very cheap compared to paper mail, so only a very small percentage of people need to respond to an UCE to make it worthwhile to the advertiser. Ironically, one of the most common spams is the one offering a database of e-mail addresses for further spamming. Senders of spam are usually called *spammers*, but terms like *vermin*, *scum*, *sociopaths*, and *morons* are in common use as well.

Spam comes from a wide variety of sources. It is simply impossible to dispose of all spam without discarding useful messages. A good example is the TMDA system, which requires senders unknown to you to confirm themselves as legitimate senders before their e-mail can reach you. Without getting into the technical side of TMDA, a downside is clearly that e-mail from legitimate sources may be discarded if those sources can't or won't confirm themselves through the TMDA system. Another problem with TMDA is that it requires its users to have a basic understanding of e-mail delivery and processing.

The simplest approach to filtering spam is filtering, at the mail server or when you sort through incoming mail. If you get 200 spam messages per day from 'random-address@vmadmin.com', you block 'vmadmin.com'. If you get 200 messages about 'VIAGRA', you discard all messages with 'VIAGRA' in the message. If you get lots of spam from Bulgaria, for example, you try to filter all mail from Bulgarian IPs.

This, unfortunately, is a great way to discard legitimate e-mail. The risks of blocking a whole country (Bulgaria, Norway, Nigeria, China, etc.) or even a continent (Asia, Africa, Europe, etc.) from contacting you should be obvious, so don't do it if you have the choice.

In another instance, the very informative and useful RISKS digest has been blocked by overzealous mail filters because it **contained** words that were common in spam messages. Nevertheless, in isolated cases, with great care, direct filtering of mail can be useful.

Another approach to filtering e-mail is the distributed spam processing, for instance DCC implements such a system. In essence, N systems around the world agree that a machine X in Ghana, Estonia, or California is sending out spam e-mail, and these N systems enter X or the spam e-mail from X into a database. The criteria for spam detection vary—it may be the number of messages sent, the content of the messages, and so on. When a user of the distributed processing system wants to find out if a message is spam, he consults one of those N systems.

Distributed spam processing works very well against spammers that send a large number of messages at once, but it requires the user to set up fairly complicated checks. There are commercial and free distributed spam processing systems. Distributed spam processing has its risks as well. For instance legitimate e-mail senders have been accused of sending spam, and their web sites and mailing lists have been shut down for some time because of the incident.

The statistical approach to spam filtering is also popular. It is based on a statistical analysis of previous spam messages. Usually the analysis is a simple word frequency count, with perhaps pairs of words or 3-word combinations thrown into the mix. Statistical analysis of spam works very well in most of the cases, but it can classify legitimate e-mail as spam in some cases. It takes time to run the analysis, the full message must be analyzed, and the user has to store the database of spam analysis. Statistical analysis on the server is gaining popularity. This has the advantage of letting the user Just Read Mail, but has the disadvantage that it's harder to tell the server that it has misclassified mail.

Fighting spam is not easy, no matter what anyone says. There is no magic switch that will distinguish Viagra ads from Mom's e-mails. Even people are having a hard time telling spam apart from non-spam, because spammers are actively looking to fool us into thinking they are Mom, essentially. Spamming is irritating, irresponsible, and idiotic behavior from a bunch of people who think the world owes them a favor. We hope the following sections will help you in fighting the spam plague.

9.16.2 Anti-Spam Basics

One way of dealing with spam is having Gnus split out all spam into a 'spam' mail group (see Section 6.4.3 [Splitting Mail], page 152).

First, pick one (1) valid mail address that you can be reached at, and put it in your From header of all your news articles. (I've chosen 'larsi@trym.ifi.uio.no', but for many addresses on the form 'larsi+usenet@ifi.uio.no' will be a better choice. Ask your sysadmin whether your sendmail installation accepts keywords in the local part of the mail address.)

```
(setq message-default-news-headers
      "From: Lars Magne Ingebrigtsen <larsi@trym.ifi.uio.no>\n")
```

Then put the following split rule in `nnmail-split-fancy` (see Section 6.4.6 [Fancy Mail Splitting], page 162):

```
(...
 (to "larsi@trym.ifi.uio.no"
     (| ("subject" "re:.*" "misc")
        ("references" ".*@.*" "misc")
        "spam"))
 ...)
```

This says that all mail to this address is suspect, but if it has a `Subject` that starts with a 'Re:' or has a `References` header, it's probably ok. All the rest goes to the 'spam' group. (This idea probably comes from Tim Pierce.)

In addition, many mail spammers talk directly to your SMTP server and do not include your email address explicitly in the `To` header. Why they do this is unknown—perhaps it's to thwart this thwarting scheme? In any case, this is trivial to deal with—you just put anything not addressed to you in the 'spam' group by ending your fancy split rule in this way:

```
(
 ...
 (to "larsi" "misc")
 "spam")
```

In my experience, this will sort virtually everything into the right group. You still have to check the 'spam' group from time to time to check for legitimate mail, though. If you feel like being a good net citizen, you can even send off complaints to the proper authorities on each unsolicited commercial email—at your leisure.

This works for me. It allows people an easy way to contact me (they can just press `r` in the usual way), and I'm not bothered at all with spam. It's a win-win situation. Forging `From` headers to point to non-existent domains is yucky, in my opinion.

Be careful with this approach. Spammers are wise to it.

9.16.3 SpamAssassin, Vipul's Razor, DCC, etc

The days where the hints in the previous section were sufficient in avoiding spam are coming to an end. There are many tools out there that claim to reduce the amount of spam you get. This section could easily become outdated fast, as new products replace old, but fortunately most of these tools seem to have similar interfaces. Even though this section will use SpamAssassin as an example, it should be easy to adapt it to most other tools.

Note that this section does not involve the `spam.el` package, which is discussed in the next section. If you don't care for all the features of `spam.el`, you can make do with these simple recipes.

If the tool you are using is not installed on the mail server, you need to invoke it yourself. Ideas on how to use the `:postscript` mail source parameter (see Section 6.4.4.1 [Mail Source Specifiers], page 154) follow.

```
(setq mail-sources
      '((file :prescript "formail -bs spamassassin < /var/mail/%u")
        (pop :user "jrl"
```

```
:server "pophost"
:postscript
"mv %t /tmp/foo; formail -bs spamc < /tmp/foo > %t")))
```

Once you manage to process your incoming spool somehow, thus making the mail contain, e.g., a header indicating it is spam, you are ready to filter it out. Using normal split methods (see Section 6.4.3 [Splitting Mail], page 152):

```
(setq nnmail-split-methods '(("spam"  "^X-Spam-Flag: YES")
                            ...))
```

Or using fancy split methods (see Section 6.4.6 [Fancy Mail Splitting], page 162):

```
(setq nnmail-split-methods 'nnmail-split-fancy
      nnmail-split-fancy '(| ("X-Spam-Flag" "YES" "spam")
                           ...))
```

Some people might not like the idea of piping the mail through various programs using a :prescript (if some program is buggy, you might lose all mail). If you are one of them, another solution is to call the external tools during splitting. Example fancy split method:

```
(setq nnmail-split-fancy '(| (: kevin-spamassassin)
                           ...))
(defun kevin-spamassassin ()
  (save-excursion
    (save-restriction
      (widen)
      (if (eq 1 (call-process-region (point-min) (point-max)
                                     "spamc" nil nil nil "-c"))
          "spam")))))
```

Note that with the nnimap back end, message bodies will not be downloaded by default. You need to set nnimap-split-download-body to t to do that (see Section 6.3.3 [Client-Side IMAP Splitting], page 150).

That is about it. As some spam is likely to get through anyway, you might want to have a nifty function to call when you happen to read spam. And here is the nifty function:

```
(defun my-gnus-raze-spam ()
  "Submit SPAM to Vipul's Razor, then mark it as expirable."
  (interactive)
  (gnus-summary-save-in-pipe "razor-report -f -d" t)
  (gnus-summary-mark-as-expirable 1))
```

9.16.4 Hashcash

A novel technique to fight spam is to require senders to do something costly and demonstrably unique for each message they send. This has the obvious drawback that you cannot rely on everyone in the world using this technique, since it is not part of the Internet standards, but it may be useful in smaller communities.

While the tools in the previous section work well in practice, they work only because the tools are constantly maintained and updated as new form of spam appears. This means that a small percentage of spam will always get through. It also means that somewhere, someone needs to read lots of spam to update these tools. Hashcash avoids that, but instead prefers that everyone you contact through e-mail supports the scheme. You can view the two approaches as pragmatic vs dogmatic. The approaches have their own advantages and disadvantages, but as often in the real world, a combination of them is stronger than either one of them separately.

The "something costly" is to burn CPU time, more specifically to compute a hash collision up to a certain number of bits. The resulting hashcash cookie is inserted in a 'X-Hashcash:' header. For more details, and for the external application `hashcash` you need to install to use this feature, see `http://www.hashcash.org/`. Even more information can be found at `http://www.camram.org/`.

If you wish to generate hashcash for each message you send, you can customize `message-generate-hashcash` (see Section "Mail Headers" in *The Message Manual*), as in:

    (setq message-generate-hashcash t)

You will need to set up some additional variables as well:

`hashcash-default-payment`
> This variable indicates the default number of bits the hash collision should consist of. By default this is 20. Suggested useful values include 17 to 29.

`hashcash-payment-alist`
> Some receivers may require you to spend burn more CPU time than the default. This variable contains a list of '(*addr amount*)' cells, where *addr* is the receiver (email address or newsgroup) and *amount* is the number of bits in the collision that is needed. It can also contain '(*addr string amount*)' cells, where the *string* is the string to use (normally the email address or newsgroup name is used).

`hashcash-path`
> Where the `hashcash` binary is installed. This variable should be automatically set by `executable-find`, but if it's `nil` (usually because the `hashcash` binary is not in your path) you'll get a warning when you check hashcash payments and an error when you generate hashcash payments.

Gnus can verify hashcash cookies, although this can also be done by hand customized mail filtering scripts. To verify a hashcash cookie in a message, use the `mail-check-payment` function in the `hashcash.el` library. You can also use the `spam.el` package with the `spam-use-hashcash` back end to validate hashcash cookies in incoming mail and filter mail accordingly (see Section 9.17.6.4 [Anti-spam Hashcash Payments], page 283).

9.17 Spam Package

The Spam package provides Gnus with a centralized mechanism for detecting and filtering spam. It filters new mail, and processes messages according to whether they are spam or ham. (*Ham* is the name used throughout this manual to indicate non-spam messages.)

9.17.1 Spam Package Introduction

You must read this section to understand how the Spam package works. Do not skip, speed-read, or glance through this section.

Make sure you read the section on the `spam.el` sequence of events. See See Section 9.17.7 [Extending the Spam package], page 289.

To use the Spam package, you **must** first run the function `spam-initialize`:

```
(spam-initialize)
```

This autoloads `spam.el` and installs the various hooks necessary to let the Spam package do its job. In order to make use of the Spam package, you have to set up certain group parameters and variables, which we will describe below. All of the variables controlling the Spam package can be found in the 'spam' customization group.

There are two "contact points" between the Spam package and the rest of Gnus: checking new mail for spam, and leaving a group.

Checking new mail for spam is done in one of two ways: while splitting incoming mail, or when you enter a group.

The first way, checking for spam while splitting incoming mail, is suited to mail back ends such as `nnml` or `nnimap`, where new mail appears in a single spool file. The Spam package processes incoming mail, and sends mail considered to be spam to a designated "spam" group. See Section 9.17.2 [Filtering Incoming Mail], page 274.

The second way is suited to back ends such as `nntp`, which have no incoming mail spool, or back ends where the server is in charge of splitting incoming mail. In this case, when you enter a Gnus group, the unseen or unread messages in that group are checked for spam. Detected spam messages are marked as spam. See Section 9.17.3 [Detecting Spam in Groups], page 276.

In either case, you have to tell the Spam package what method to use to detect spam messages. There are several methods, or *spam back ends* (not to be confused with Gnus back ends!) to choose from: spam "blacklists" and "whitelists", dictionary-based filters, and so forth. See Section 9.17.6 [Spam Back Ends], page 281.

In the Gnus summary buffer, messages that have been identified as spam always appear with a '$' symbol.

The Spam package divides Gnus groups into three categories: ham groups, spam groups, and unclassified groups. You should mark each of the groups you subscribe to as either a ham group or a spam group, using the **spam-contents** group parameter (see Section 2.10 [Group Parameters], page 22). Spam groups have a special property: when you enter a spam group, all unseen articles are marked as spam. Thus, mail split into a spam group is automatically marked as spam.

Identifying spam messages is only half of the Spam package's job. The second half comes into play whenever you exit a group buffer. At this point, the Spam package does several things:

First, it calls *spam and ham processors* to process the articles according to whether they are spam or ham. There is a pair of spam and ham processors associated with each spam back end, and what the processors do depends on the back end. At present, the main role of spam and ham processors is for dictionary-based spam filters: they add the contents of the messages in the group to the filter's dictionary, to improve its ability to detect future spam. The **spam-process** group parameter specifies what spam processors to use. See Section 9.17.4 [Spam and Ham Processors], page 276.

If the spam filter failed to mark a spam message, you can mark it yourself, so that the message is processed as spam when you exit the group:

$

M-d

M s x

S x   Mark current article as spam, showing it with the '$' mark (gnus-summary-mark-as-spam).

Similarly, you can unmark an article if it has been erroneously marked as spam. See Section 3.7.4 [Setting Marks], page 60.

Normally, a ham message found in a non-ham group is not processed as ham—the rationale is that it should be moved into a ham group for further processing (see below). However, you can force these articles to be processed as ham by setting spam-process-ham-in-spam-groups and spam-process-ham-in-nonham-groups.

The second thing that the Spam package does when you exit a group is to move ham articles out of spam groups, and spam articles out of ham groups. Ham in a spam group is moved to the group specified by the variable gnus-ham-process-destinations, or the group parameter ham-process-destination. Spam in a ham group is moved to the group specified by the variable gnus-spam-process-destinations, or the group parameter spam-process-destination. If these variables are not set, the articles are left in their current group. If an article cannot be moved (e.g., with a read-only backend such as NNTP), it is copied.

If an article is moved to another group, it is processed again when you visit the new group. Normally, this is not a problem, but if you want each article to be processed only once, load the gnus-registry.el package and set the variable spam-log-to-registry to t. See Section 9.17.5 [Spam Package Configuration Examples], page 278.

Normally, spam groups ignore gnus-spam-process-destinations. However, if you set spam-move-spam-nonspam-groups-only to nil, spam will also be moved out of spam groups, depending on the spam-process-destination parameter.

The final thing the Spam package does is to mark spam articles as expired, which is usually the right thing to do.

If all this seems confusing, don't worry. Soon it will be as natural as typing Lisp one-liners on a neural interface... err, sorry, that's 50 years in the future yet. Just trust us, it's not so bad.

9.17.2 Filtering Incoming Mail

To use the Spam package to filter incoming mail, you must first set up fancy mail splitting. See Section 6.4.6 [Fancy Mail Splitting], page 162. The Spam package defines a special splitting function that you can add to your fancy split variable (either nnmail-split-fancy or nnimap-split-fancy, depending on your mail back end):

        (: spam-split)

The spam-split function scans incoming mail according to your chosen spam back end(s), and sends messages identified as spam to a spam group. By default, the spam group is a group named 'spam', but you can change this by customizing spam-split-group. Make sure the contents of spam-split-group are an unqualified group name. For instance, in an nnimap server 'your-server', the value 'spam' means 'nnimap+your-server:spam'. The value 'nnimap+server:spam' is therefore wrong—it gives the group 'nnimap+your-server:nnimap+server:spam'.

`spam-split` does not modify the contents of messages in any way.

Note for IMAP users: if you use the `spam-check-bogofilter`, `spam-check-ifile`, and `spam-check-stat` spam back ends, you should also set the variable `nnimap-split-download-body` to `t`. These spam back ends are most useful when they can "scan" the full message body. By default, the nnimap back end only retrieves the message headers; `nnimap-split-download-body` tells it to retrieve the message bodies as well. We don't set this by default because it will slow IMAP down, and that is not an appropriate decision to make on behalf of the user. See Section 6.3.3 [Client-Side IMAP Splitting], page 150.

You have to specify one or more spam back ends for `spam-split` to use, by setting the `spam-use-*` variables. See Section 9.17.6 [Spam Back Ends], page 281. Normally, `spam-split` simply uses all the spam back ends you enabled in this way. However, you can tell `spam-split` to use only some of them. Why this is useful? Suppose you are using the `spam-use-regex-headers` and `spam-use-blackholes` spam back ends, and the following split rule:

```
nnimap-split-fancy '(|
                    (any "ding" "ding")
                    (: spam-split)
                    ;; default mailbox
                    "mail")
```

The problem is that you want all ding messages to make it to the ding folder. But that will let obvious spam (for example, spam detected by SpamAssassin, and `spam-use-regex-headers`) through, when it's sent to the ding list. On the other hand, some messages to the ding list are from a mail server in the blackhole list, so the invocation of `spam-split` can't be before the ding rule.

The solution is to let SpamAssassin headers supersede ding rules, and perform the other `spam-split` rules (including a second invocation of the regex-headers check) after the ding rule. This is done by passing a parameter to `spam-split`:

```
nnimap-split-fancy
        '(|
          ;; spam detected by spam-use-regex-headers goes to 'regex-spam'
          (: spam-split "regex-spam" 'spam-use-regex-headers)
          (any "ding" "ding")
          ;; all other spam detected by spam-split goes to spam-split-group
          (: spam-split)
          ;; default mailbox
          "mail")
```

This lets you invoke specific `spam-split` checks depending on your particular needs, and target the results of those checks to a particular spam group. You don't have to throw all mail into all the spam tests. Another reason why this is nice is that messages to mailing lists you have rules for don't have to have resource-intensive blackhole checks performed on them. You could also specify different spam checks for your nnmail split vs. your nnimap split. Go crazy.

You should set the `spam-use-*` variables for whatever spam back ends you intend to use. The reason is that when loading `spam.el`, some conditional loading is done depending on what `spam-use-xyz` variables you have set. See Section 9.17.6 [Spam Back Ends], page 281.

9.17.3 Detecting Spam in Groups

To detect spam when visiting a group, set the group's `spam-autodetect` and `spam-autodetect-methods` group parameters. These are accessible with `G c` or `G p`, as usual (see Section 2.10 [Group Parameters], page 22).

You should set the `spam-use-*` variables for whatever spam back ends you intend to use. The reason is that when loading `spam.el`, some conditional loading is done depending on what `spam-use-xyz` variables you have set.

By default, only unseen articles are processed for spam. You can force Gnus to recheck all messages in the group by setting the variable `spam-autodetect-recheck-messages` to t.

If you use the `spam-autodetect` method of checking for spam, you can specify different spam detection methods for different groups. For instance, the 'ding' group may have `spam-use-BBDB` as the autodetection method, while the 'suspect' group may have the `spam-use-blacklist` and `spam-use-bogofilter` methods enabled. Unlike with `spam-split`, you don't have any control over the *sequence* of checks, but this is probably unimportant.

9.17.4 Spam and Ham Processors

Spam and ham processors specify special actions to take when you exit a group buffer. Spam processors act on spam messages, and ham processors on ham messages. At present, the main role of these processors is to update the dictionaries of dictionary-based spam back ends such as Bogofilter (see Section 9.17.6.7 [Bogofilter], page 284) and the Spam Statistics package (see Section 9.17.6.10 [Spam Statistics Filtering], page 287).

The spam and ham processors that apply to each group are determined by the group's `spam-process` group parameter. If this group parameter is not defined, they are determined by the variable `gnus-spam-process-newsgroups`.

Gnus learns from the spam you get. You have to collect your spam in one or more spam groups, and set or customize the variable `spam-junk-mailgroups` as appropriate. You can also declare groups to contain spam by setting their group parameter `spam-contents` to `gnus-group-spam-classification-spam`, or by customizing the corresponding variable `gnus-spam-newsgroup-contents`. The `spam-contents` group parameter and the `gnus-spam-newsgroup-contents` variable can also be used to declare groups as *ham* groups if you set their classification to `gnus-group-spam-classification-ham`. If groups are not classified by means of `spam-junk-mailgroups`, `spam-contents`, or `gnus-spam-newsgroup-contents`, they are considered *unclassified*. All groups are unclassified by default.

In spam groups, all messages are considered to be spam by default: they get the '$' mark (`gnus-spam-mark`) when you enter the group. If you have seen a message, had it marked as spam, then unmarked it, it won't be marked as spam when you enter the group thereafter. You can disable that behavior, so all unread messages will get the '$' mark, if you set the `spam-mark-only-unseen-as-spam` parameter to `nil`. You should remove the '$' mark when you are in the group summary buffer for every message that is not spam after all. To remove the '$' mark, you can use `M-u` to "unread" the article, or `d` for declaring it read the non-spam way. When you leave a group, all spam-marked ('$') articles are sent to a spam processor which will study them as spam samples.

Messages may also be deleted in various other ways, and unless `ham-marks` group parameter gets overridden below, marks 'R' and 'r' for default read or explicit delete, marks 'X' and 'K' for automatic or explicit kills, as well as mark 'Y' for low scores, are all considered to be associated with articles which are not spam. This assumption might be false, in particular if you use kill files or score files as means for detecting genuine spam, you should then adjust the `ham-marks` group parameter.

`ham-marks`   [Variable]
> You can customize this group or topic parameter to be the list of marks you want to consider ham. By default, the list contains the deleted, read, killed, kill-filed, and low-score marks (the idea is that these articles have been read, but are not spam). It can be useful to also include the tick mark in the ham marks. It is not recommended to make the unread mark a ham mark, because it normally indicates a lack of classification. But you can do it, and we'll be happy for you.

`spam-marks`   [Variable]
> You can customize this group or topic parameter to be the list of marks you want to consider spam. By default, the list contains only the spam mark. It is not recommended to change that, but you can if you really want to.

When you leave *any* group, regardless of its `spam-contents` classification, all spam-marked articles are sent to a spam processor, which will study these as spam samples. If you explicit kill a lot, you might sometimes end up with articles marked 'X' which you never saw, and which might accidentally contain spam. Best is to make sure that real spam is marked with '$', and nothing else.

When you leave a *spam* group, all spam-marked articles are marked as expired after processing with the spam processor. This is not done for *unclassified* or *ham* groups. Also, any **ham** articles in a spam group will be moved to a location determined by either the `ham-process-destination` group parameter or a match in the `gnus-ham-process-destinations` variable, which is a list of regular expressions matched with group names (it's easiest to customize this variable with *M-x customize-variable RET gnus-ham-process-destinations*). Each group name list is a standard Lisp list, if you prefer to customize the variable manually. If the `ham-process-destination` parameter is not set, ham articles are left in place. If the `spam-mark-ham-unread-before-move-from-spam-group` parameter is set, the ham articles are marked as unread before being moved.

If ham can not be moved—because of a read-only back end such as NNTP, for example, it will be copied.

Note that you can use multiples destinations per group or regular expression! This enables you to send your ham to a regular mail group and to a *ham training* group.

When you leave a *ham* group, all ham-marked articles are sent to a ham processor, which will study these as non-spam samples.

By default the variable `spam-process-ham-in-spam-groups` is `nil`. Set it to `t` if you want ham found in spam groups to be processed. Normally this is not done, you are expected instead to send your ham to a ham group and process it there.

By default the variable `spam-process-ham-in-nonham-groups` is `nil`. Set it to `t` if you want ham found in non-ham (spam or unclassified) groups to be processed. Normally this is not done, you are expected instead to send your ham to a ham group and process it there.

When you leave a *ham* or *unclassified* group, all **spam** articles are moved to a location determined by either the `spam-process-destination` group parameter or a match in the `gnus-spam-process-destinations` variable, which is a list of regular expressions matched with group names (it's easiest to customize this variable with *M-x customize-variable RET gnus-spam-process-destinations*). Each group name list is a standard Lisp list, if you prefer to customize the variable manually. If the `spam-process-destination` parameter is not set, the spam articles are only expired. The group name is fully qualified, meaning that if you see 'nntp:servername' before the group name in the group buffer then you need it here as well.

If spam can not be moved—because of a read-only back end such as NNTP, for example, it will be copied.

Note that you can use multiples destinations per group or regular expression! This enables you to send your spam to multiple *spam training* groups.

The problem with processing ham and spam is that Gnus doesn't track this processing by default. Enable the `spam-log-to-registry` variable so `spam.el` will use `gnus-registry.el` to track what articles have been processed, and avoid processing articles multiple times. Keep in mind that if you limit the number of registry entries, this won't work as well as it does without a limit.

Set this variable if you want only unseen articles in spam groups to be marked as spam. By default, it is set. If you set it to `nil`, unread articles will also be marked as spam.

Set this variable if you want ham to be unmarked before it is moved out of the spam group. This is very useful when you use something like the tick mark '!' to mark ham—the article will be placed in your `ham-process-destination`, unmarked as if it came fresh from the mail server.

When autodetecting spam, this variable tells `spam.el` whether only unseen articles or all unread articles should be checked for spam. It is recommended that you leave it off.

9.17.5 Spam Package Configuration Examples

Ted's setup

From Ted Zlatanov <tzz@lifelogs.com>.

```
;; for gnus-registry-split-fancy-with-parent and spam autodetection
;; see gnus-registry.el for more information
(gnus-registry-initialize)
(spam-initialize)

(setq
 spam-log-to-registry t        ; for spam autodetection
 spam-use-BBDB t
 spam-use-regex-headers t    ; catch X-Spam-Flag (SpamAssassin)
 ;; all groups with 'spam' in the name contain spam
 gnus-spam-newsgroup-contents
   '(("spam" gnus-group-spam-classification-spam))
 ;; see documentation for these
 spam-move-spam-nonspam-groups-only nil
```

```
spam-mark-only-unseen-as-spam t
spam-mark-ham-unread-before-move-from-spam-group t
;; understand what this does before you copy it to your own setup!
;; for nnimap you'll probably want to set nnimap-split-methods, see the manual
nnimap-split-fancy '(|
                           ;; trace references to parents and put in their group
                           (: gnus-registry-split-fancy-with-parent)
                           ;; this will catch server-side SpamAssassin tags
                           (: spam-split 'spam-use-regex-headers)
                           (any "ding" "ding")
                           ;; note that spam by default will go to 'spam'
                           (: spam-split)
                           ;; default mailbox
                           "mail"))
```

;; my parameters, set with *G p*

;; all nnml groups, and all nnimap groups except
;; 'nnimap+mail.lifelogs.com:train' and
;; 'nnimap+mail.lifelogs.com:spam': any spam goes to nnimap training,
;; because it must have been detected manually

```
((spam-process-destination . "nnimap+mail.lifelogs.com:train"))
```

;; all NNTP groups
;; autodetect spam with the blacklist and ham with the BBDB
```
((spam-autodetect-methods spam-use-blacklist spam-use-BBDB)
```
;; send all spam to the training group
```
 (spam-process-destination . "nnimap+mail.lifelogs.com:train"))
```

;; only some NNTP groups, where I want to autodetect spam
```
((spam-autodetect . t))
```

;; my nnimap 'nnimap+mail.lifelogs.com:spam' group

;; this is a spam group
```
((spam-contents gnus-group-spam-classification-spam)
```

;; any spam (which happens when I enter for all unseen messages,
;; because of the **gnus-spam-newsgroup-contents** setting above), goes to
;; 'nnimap+mail.lifelogs.com:train' unless I mark it as ham

```
(spam-process-destination "nnimap+mail.lifelogs.com:train")
```

;; any ham goes to my 'nnimap+mail.lifelogs.com:mail' folder, but
;; also to my 'nnimap+mail.lifelogs.com:trainham' folder for training

```
(ham-process-destination "nnimap+mail.lifelogs.com:mail"
                         "nnimap+mail.lifelogs.com:trainham")
;; in this group, only '!' marks are ham
(ham-marks
 (gnus-ticked-mark))
;; remembers senders in the blacklist on the way out—this is
;; definitely not needed, it just makes me feel better
(spam-process (gnus-group-spam-exit-processor-blacklist)))


;; Later, on the IMAP server I use the 'train' group for training
;; SpamAssassin to recognize spam, and the 'trainham' group fora
;; recognizing ham—but Gnus has nothing to do with it.
```

Using `spam.el` on an IMAP server with a statistical filter on the server

From Reiner Steib <reiner.steib@gmx.de>.

My provider has set up bogofilter (in combination with DCC) on the mail server (IMAP). Recognized spam goes to 'spam.detected', the rest goes through the normal filter rules, i.e., to 'some.folder' or to 'INBOX'. Training on false positives or negatives is done by copying or moving the article to 'training.ham' or 'training.spam' respectively. A cron job on the server feeds those to bogofilter with the suitable ham or spam options and deletes them from the 'training.ham' and 'training.spam' folders.

With the following entries in `gnus-parameters`, `spam.el` does most of the job for me:

```
("nnimap:spam\\.detected"
 (gnus-article-sort-functions '(gnus-article-sort-by-chars))
 (ham-process-destination "nnimap:INBOX" "nnimap:training.ham")
 (spam-contents gnus-group-spam-classification-spam))
("nnimap:\\(INBOX\\|other-folders\\)"
 (spam-process-destination . "nnimap:training.spam")
 (spam-contents gnus-group-spam-classification-ham))
```

- **The Spam folder:**

  In the folder 'spam.detected', I have to check for false positives (i.e., legitimate mails, that were wrongly judged as spam by bogofilter or DCC).

  Because of the `gnus-group-spam-classification-spam` entry, all messages are marked as spam (with $). When I find a false positive, I mark the message with some other ham mark (`ham-marks`, Section 9.17.4 [Spam and Ham Processors], page 276). On group exit, those messages are copied to both groups, 'INBOX' (where I want to have the article) and 'training.ham' (for training bogofilter) and deleted from the 'spam.detected' folder.

  The `gnus-article-sort-by-chars` entry simplifies detection of false positives for me. I receive lots of worms (sweN, ...), that all have a similar size. Grouping them by size (i.e., chars) makes finding other false positives easier. (Of course worms aren't *spam* (UCE, UBE) strictly speaking. Anyhow, bogofilter is an excellent tool for filtering those unwanted mails for me.)

- **Ham folders:**

  In my ham folders, I just hit *S x* (gnus-summary-mark-as-spam) whenever I see an unrecognized spam mail (false negative). On group exit, those messages are moved to 'training.spam'.

Reporting spam articles in Gmane groups with spam-report.el

From Reiner Steib <reiner.steib@gmx.de>.

With following entry in **gnus-parameters**, *S x* (gnus-summary-mark-as-spam) marks articles in **gmane.*** groups as spam and reports the to Gmane at group exit:

```
("^gmane\\."
    (spam-process (gnus-group-spam-exit-processor-report-gmane)))
```

Additionally, I use (setq spam-report-gmane-use-article-number nil) because I don't read the groups directly from news.gmane.org, but through my local news server (leafnode). I.e., the article numbers are not the same as on news.gmane.org, thus **spam-report.el** has to check the X-Report-Spam header to find the correct number.

9.17.6 Spam Back Ends

The spam package offers a variety of back ends for detecting spam. Each back end defines a set of methods for detecting spam (see Section 9.17.2 [Filtering Incoming Mail], page 274, see Section 9.17.3 [Detecting Spam in Groups], page 276), and a pair of spam and ham processors (see Section 9.17.4 [Spam and Ham Processors], page 276).

9.17.6.1 Blacklists and Whitelists

spam-use-blacklist   [Variable]

Set this variable to **t** if you want to use blacklists when splitting incoming mail. Messages whose senders are in the blacklist will be sent to the **spam-split-group**. This is an explicit filter, meaning that it acts only on mail senders *declared* to be spammers.

spam-use-whitelist   [Variable]

Set this variable to **t** if you want to use whitelists when splitting incoming mail. Messages whose senders are not in the whitelist will be sent to the next spam-split rule. This is an explicit filter, meaning that unless someone is in the whitelist, their messages are not assumed to be spam or ham.

spam-use-whitelist-exclusive   [Variable]

Set this variable to **t** if you want to use whitelists as an implicit filter, meaning that every message will be considered spam unless the sender is in the whitelist. Use with care.

gnus-group-spam-exit-processor-blacklist   [Variable]

Add this symbol to a group's **spam-process** parameter by customizing the group parameters or the **gnus-spam-process-newsgroups** variable. When this symbol is added to a group's **spam-process** parameter, the senders of spam-marked articles will be added to the blacklist.

WARNING

Instead of the obsolete `gnus-group-spam-exit-processor-blacklist`, it is recommended that you use `(spam spam-use-blacklist)`. Everything will work the same way, we promise.

`gnus-group-ham-exit-processor-whitelist`   [Variable]

Add this symbol to a group's `spam-process` parameter by customizing the group parameters or the `gnus-spam-process-newsgroups` variable. When this symbol is added to a group's `spam-process` parameter, the senders of ham-marked articles in *ham* groups will be added to the whitelist.

WARNING

Instead of the obsolete `gnus-group-ham-exit-processor-whitelist`, it is recommended that you use `(ham spam-use-whitelist)`. Everything will work the same way, we promise.

Blacklists are lists of regular expressions matching addresses you consider to be spam senders. For instance, to block mail from any sender at 'vmadmin.com', you can put 'vmadmin.com' in your blacklist. You start out with an empty blacklist. Blacklist entries use the Emacs regular expression syntax.

Conversely, whitelists tell Gnus what addresses are considered legitimate. All messages from whitelisted addresses are considered non-spam. Also see Section 9.17.6.2 [BBDB Whitelists], page 282. Whitelist entries use the Emacs regular expression syntax.

The blacklist and whitelist file locations can be customized with the `spam-directory` variable (`~/News/spam` by default), or the `spam-whitelist` and `spam-blacklist` variables directly. The whitelist and blacklist files will by default be in the `spam-directory` directory, named `whitelist` and `blacklist` respectively.

9.17.6.2 BBDB Whitelists

`spam-use-BBDB`   [Variable]

Analogous to `spam-use-whitelist` (see Section 9.17.6.1 [Blacklists and Whitelists], page 281), but uses the BBDB as the source of whitelisted addresses, without regular expressions. You must have the BBDB loaded for `spam-use-BBDB` to work properly. Messages whose senders are not in the BBDB will be sent to the next spam-split rule. This is an explicit filter, meaning that unless someone is in the BBDB, their messages are not assumed to be spam or ham.

`spam-use-BBDB-exclusive`   [Variable]

Set this variable to `t` if you want to use the BBDB as an implicit filter, meaning that every message will be considered spam unless the sender is in the BBDB. Use with care. Only sender addresses in the BBDB will be allowed through; all others will be classified as spammers.

While `spam-use-BBDB-exclusive` *can* be used as an alias for `spam-use-BBDB` as far as `spam.el` is concerned, it is *not* a separate back end. If you set `spam-use-BBDB-exclusive` to `t`, *all* your BBDB splitting will be exclusive.

`gnus-group-ham-exit-processor-BBDB`   [Variable]

Add this symbol to a group's `spam-process` parameter by customizing the group parameters or the `gnus-spam-process-newsgroups` variable. When this symbol is added to a group's `spam-process` parameter, the senders of ham-marked articles in *ham* groups will be added to the BBDB.

WARNING

Instead of the obsolete `gnus-group-ham-exit-processor-BBDB`, it is recommended that you use (ham spam-use-BBDB). Everything will work the same way, we promise.

9.17.6.3 Gmane Spam Reporting

`gnus-group-spam-exit-processor-report-gmane`   [Variable]

Add this symbol to a group's `spam-process` parameter by customizing the group parameters or the `gnus-spam-process-newsgroups` variable. When this symbol is added to a group's `spam-process` parameter, the spam-marked articles groups will be reported to the Gmane administrators via a HTTP request.

Gmane can be found at `http://gmane.org`.

WARNING

Instead of the obsolete `gnus-group-spam-exit-processor-report-gmane`, it is recommended that you use (spam spam-use-gmane). Everything will work the same way, we promise.

`spam-report-gmane-use-article-number`   [Variable]

This variable is `t` by default. Set it to `nil` if you are running your own news server, for instance, and the local article numbers don't correspond to the Gmane article numbers. When `spam-report-gmane-use-article-number` is `nil`, `spam-report.el` will fetch the number from the article headers.

`spam-report-user-mail-address`   [Variable]

Mail address exposed in the User-Agent spam reports to Gmane. It allows the Gmane administrators to contact you in case of misreports. The default is `user-mail-address`.

9.17.6.4 Anti-spam Hashcash Payments

`spam-use-hashcash`   [Variable]

Similar to `spam-use-whitelist` (see Section 9.17.6.1 [Blacklists and Whitelists], page 281), but uses hashcash tokens for whitelisting messages instead of the sender address. Messages without a hashcash payment token will be sent to the next spam-split rule. This is an explicit filter, meaning that unless a hashcash token is found, the messages are not assumed to be spam or ham.

9.17.6.5 Blackholes

`spam-use-blackholes`   [Variable]

This option is disabled by default. You can let Gnus consult the blackhole-type distributed spam processing systems (DCC, for instance) when you set this option. The variable `spam-blackhole-servers` holds the list of blackhole servers Gnus will consult. The current list is fairly comprehensive, but make sure to let us know if it contains outdated servers.

The blackhole check uses the `dig.el` package, but you can tell `spam.el` to use `dns.el` instead for better performance if you set `spam-use-dig` to `nil`. It is not recommended at this time to set `spam-use-dig` to `nil` despite the possible performance improvements, because some users may be unable to use it, but you can try it and see if it works for you.

`spam-blackhole-servers`   [Variable]
> The list of servers to consult for blackhole checks.

`spam-blackhole-good-server-regex`   [Variable]
> A regular expression for IPs that should not be checked against the blackhole server list. When set to `nil`, it has no effect.

`spam-use-dig`   [Variable]
> Use the `dig.el` package instead of the `dns.el` package. The default setting of `t` is recommended.

Blackhole checks are done only on incoming mail. There is no spam or ham processor for blackholes.

9.17.6.6 Regular Expressions Header Matching

`spam-use-regex-headers`   [Variable]
> This option is disabled by default. You can let Gnus check the message headers against lists of regular expressions when you set this option. The variables `spam-regex-headers-spam` and `spam-regex-headers-ham` hold the list of regular expressions. Gnus will check against the message headers to determine if the message is spam or ham, respectively.

`spam-regex-headers-spam`   [Variable]
> The list of regular expressions that, when matched in the headers of the message, positively identify it as spam.

`spam-regex-headers-ham`   [Variable]
> The list of regular expressions that, when matched in the headers of the message, positively identify it as ham.

Regular expression header checks are done only on incoming mail. There is no specific spam or ham processor for regular expressions.

9.17.6.7 Bogofilter

`spam-use-bogofilter`   [Variable]
> Set this variable if you want `spam-split` to use Eric Raymond's speedy Bogofilter.
>
> With a minimum of care for associating the '`$`' mark for spam articles only, Bogofilter training all gets fairly automatic. You should do this until you get a few hundreds of articles in each category, spam or not. The command `S t` in summary mode, either for debugging or for curiosity, shows the *spamicity* score of the current article (between 0.0 and 1.0).

Bogofilter determines if a message is spam based on a specific threshold. That threshold can be customized, consult the Bogofilter documentation.

If the `bogofilter` executable is not in your path, Bogofilter processing will be turned off.

You should not enable this if you use `spam-use-bogofilter-headers`.

M s t

S t   Get the Bogofilter spamicity score (`spam-bogofilter-score`).

`spam-use-bogofilter-headers`   [Variable]
> Set this variable if you want `spam-split` to use Eric Raymond's speedy Bogofilter, looking only at the message headers. It works similarly to `spam-use-bogofilter`, but the `X-Bogosity` header must be in the message already. Normally you would do this with a procmail recipe or something similar; consult the Bogofilter installation documents for details.
>
> You should not enable this if you use `spam-use-bogofilter`.

`gnus-group-spam-exit-processor-bogofilter`   [Variable]
> Add this symbol to a group's `spam-process` parameter by customizing the group parameters or the `gnus-spam-process-newsgroups` variable. When this symbol is added to a group's `spam-process` parameter, spam-marked articles will be added to the Bogofilter spam database.
>
> *WARNING*
>
> Instead of the obsolete `gnus-group-spam-exit-processor-bogofilter`, it is recommended that you use (`spam spam-use-bogofilter`). Everything will work the same way, we promise.

`gnus-group-ham-exit-processor-bogofilter`   [Variable]
> Add this symbol to a group's `spam-process` parameter by customizing the group parameters or the `gnus-spam-process-newsgroups` variable. When this symbol is added to a group's `spam-process` parameter, the ham-marked articles in *ham* groups will be added to the Bogofilter database of non-spam messages.
>
> *WARNING*
>
> Instead of the obsolete `gnus-group-ham-exit-processor-bogofilter`, it is recommended that you use (`ham spam-use-bogofilter`). Everything will work the same way, we promise.

`spam-bogofilter-database-directory`   [Variable]
> This is the directory where Bogofilter will store its databases. It is not specified by default, so Bogofilter will use its own default database directory.

The Bogofilter mail classifier is similar to `ifile` in intent and purpose. A ham and a spam processor are provided, plus the `spam-use-bogofilter` and `spam-use-bogofilter-headers` variables to indicate to spam-split that Bogofilter should either be used, or has already been used on the article. The 0.9.2.1 version of Bogofilter was used to test this functionality.

9.17.6.8 SpamAssassin back end

`spam-use-spamassassin`   [Variable]

> Set this variable if you want `spam-split` to use SpamAssassin.
>
> SpamAssassin assigns a score to each article based on a set of rules and tests, including a Bayesian filter. The Bayesian filter can be trained by associating the '$' mark for spam articles. The spam score can be viewed by using the command $S t$ in summary mode.
>
> If you set this variable, each article will be processed by SpamAssassin when `spam-split` is called. If your mail is preprocessed by SpamAssassin, and you want to just use the SpamAssassin headers, set `spam-use-spamassassin-headers` instead.
>
> You should not enable this if you use `spam-use-spamassassin-headers`.

`spam-use-spamassassin-headers`   [Variable]

> Set this variable if your mail is preprocessed by SpamAssassin and want `spam-split` to split based on the SpamAssassin headers.
>
> You should not enable this if you use `spam-use-spamassassin`.

`spam-spamassassin-program`   [Variable]

> This variable points to the SpamAssassin executable. If you have `spamd` running, you can set this variable to the `spamc` executable for faster processing. See the SpamAssassin documentation for more information on `spamd`/`spamc`.

SpamAssassin is a powerful and flexible spam filter that uses a wide variety of tests to identify spam. A ham and a spam processors are provided, plus the `spam-use-spamassassin` and `spam-use-spamassassin-headers` variables to indicate to spam-split that SpamAssassin should be either used, or has already been used on the article. The 2.63 version of SpamAssassin was used to test this functionality.

9.17.6.9 ifile spam filtering

`spam-use-ifile`   [Variable]

> Enable this variable if you want `spam-split` to use `ifile`, a statistical analyzer similar to Bogofilter.

`spam-ifile-all-categories`   [Variable]

> Enable this variable if you want `spam-use-ifile` to give you all the ifile categories, not just spam/non-spam. If you use this, make sure you train ifile as described in its documentation.

`spam-ifile-spam-category`   [Variable]

> This is the category of spam messages as far as ifile is concerned. The actual string used is irrelevant, but you probably want to leave the default value of 'spam'.

`spam-ifile-database`   [Variable]

> This is the filename for the ifile database. It is not specified by default, so ifile will use its own default database name.

The ifile mail classifier is similar to Bogofilter in intent and purpose. A ham and a spam processor are provided, plus the `spam-use-ifile` variable to indicate to spam-split that ifile should be used. The 1.2.1 version of ifile was used to test this functionality.

9.17.6.10 Spam Statistics Filtering

This back end uses the Spam Statistics Emacs Lisp package to perform statistics-based filtering (see Section 9.17.8 [Spam Statistics Package], page 290). Before using this, you may want to perform some additional steps to initialize your Spam Statistics dictionary. See Section 9.17.8.1 [Creating a spam-stat dictionary], page 291.

`spam-use-stat`   [Variable]

`gnus-group-spam-exit-processor-stat`   [Variable]

> Add this symbol to a group's `spam-process` parameter by customizing the group parameters or the `gnus-spam-process-newsgroups` variable. When this symbol is added to a group's `spam-process` parameter, the spam-marked articles will be added to the spam-stat database of spam messages.
>
> *WARNING*
>
> Instead of the obsolete `gnus-group-spam-exit-processor-stat`, it is recommended that you use `(spam spam-use-stat)`. Everything will work the same way, we promise.

`gnus-group-ham-exit-processor-stat`   [Variable]

> Add this symbol to a group's `spam-process` parameter by customizing the group parameters or the `gnus-spam-process-newsgroups` variable. When this symbol is added to a group's `spam-process` parameter, the ham-marked articles in *ham* groups will be added to the spam-stat database of non-spam messages.
>
> *WARNING*
>
> Instead of the obsolete `gnus-group-ham-exit-processor-stat`, it is recommended that you use `(ham spam-use-stat)`. Everything will work the same way, we promise.

This enables `spam.el` to cooperate with `spam-stat.el`. `spam-stat.el` provides an internal (Lisp-only) spam database, which unlike ifile or Bogofilter does not require external programs. A spam and a ham processor, and the `spam-use-stat` variable for `spam-split` are provided.

9.17.6.11 Using SpamOracle with Gnus

An easy way to filter out spam is to use SpamOracle. SpamOracle is an statistical mail filtering tool written by Xavier Leroy and needs to be installed separately.

There are several ways to use SpamOracle with Gnus. In all cases, your mail is piped through SpamOracle in its *mark* mode. SpamOracle will then enter an 'X-Spam' header indicating whether it regards the mail as a spam mail or not.

One possibility is to run SpamOracle as a `:prescript` from the See Section 6.4.4.1 [Mail Source Specifiers], page 154, (see Section 9.16.3 [SpamAssassin], page 270). This method has the advantage that the user can see the *X-Spam* headers.

The easiest method is to make `spam.el` (see Section 9.17 [Spam Package], page 272) call SpamOracle.

To enable SpamOracle usage by `spam.el`, set the variable `spam-use-spamoracle` to `t` and configure the `nnmail-split-fancy` or `nnimap-split-fancy`. See Section 9.17 [Spam Package], page 272. In this example the 'INBOX' of an nnimap server is filtered using SpamOracle. Mails recognized as spam mails will be moved to `spam-split-group`, 'Junk' in this case. Ham messages stay in 'INBOX':

```
(setq spam-use-spamoracle t
      spam-split-group "Junk"
      ;; for nnimap you'll probably want to set nnimap-split-methods, see the manual
      nnimap-split-inbox '("INBOX")
      nnimap-split-fancy '(| (: spam-split) "INBOX"))
```

`spam-use-spamoracle`   [Variable]

> Set to `t` if you want Gnus to enable spam filtering using SpamOracle.

`spam-spamoracle-binary`   [Variable]

> Gnus uses the SpamOracle binary called `spamoracle` found in the user's PATH. Using the variable `spam-spamoracle-binary`, this can be customized.

`spam-spamoracle-database`   [Variable]

> By default, SpamOracle uses the file `~/.spamoracle.db` as a database to store its analysis. This is controlled by the variable `spam-spamoracle-database` which defaults to `nil`. That means the default SpamOracle database will be used. In case you want your database to live somewhere special, set `spam-spamoracle-database` to this path.

SpamOracle employs a statistical algorithm to determine whether a message is spam or ham. In order to get good results, meaning few false hits or misses, SpamOracle needs training. SpamOracle learns the characteristics of your spam mails. Using the *add* mode (training mode) one has to feed good (ham) and spam mails to SpamOracle. This can be done by pressing | in the Summary buffer and pipe the mail to a SpamOracle process or using `spam.el`'s spam- and ham-processors, which is much more convenient. For a detailed description of spam- and ham-processors, See Section 9.17 [Spam Package], page 272.

`gnus-group-spam-exit-processor-spamoracle`   [Variable]

> Add this symbol to a group's `spam-process` parameter by customizing the group parameter or the `gnus-spam-process-newsgroups` variable. When this symbol is added to a group's `spam-process` parameter, spam-marked articles will be sent to SpamOracle as spam samples.
>
> *WARNING*
>
> Instead of the obsolete `gnus-group-spam-exit-processor-spamoracle`, it is recommended that you use `(spam spam-use-spamoracle)`. Everything will work the same way, we promise.

`gnus-group-ham-exit-processor-spamoracle`   [Variable]

> Add this symbol to a group's `spam-process` parameter by customizing the group parameter or the `gnus-spam-process-newsgroups` variable. When this symbol is added to a group's `spam-process` parameter, the ham-marked articles in *ham* groups will be sent to the SpamOracle as samples of ham messages.
>
> *WARNING*
>
> Instead of the obsolete `gnus-group-ham-exit-processor-spamoracle`, it is recommended that you use `(ham spam-use-spamoracle)`. Everything will work the same way, we promise.

Example: These are the Group Parameters of a group that has been classified as a ham group, meaning that it should only contain ham messages.

```
((spam-contents gnus-group-spam-classification-ham)
 (spam-process ((ham spam-use-spamoracle)
                (spam spam-use-spamoracle))))
```

For this group the `spam-use-spamoracle` is installed for both ham and spam processing. If the group contains spam message (e.g., because SpamOracle has not had enough sample messages yet) and the user marks some messages as spam messages, these messages will be processed by SpamOracle. The processor sends the messages to SpamOracle as new samples for spam.

9.17.7 Extending the Spam package

Say you want to add a new back end called blackbox. For filtering incoming mail, provide the following:

1. Code

    ```
    (defvar spam-use-blackbox nil
      "True if blackbox should be used.")
    ```

    Write `spam-check-blackbox` if Blackbox can check incoming mail.

    Write `spam-blackbox-register-routine` and `spam-blackbox-unregister-routine` using the bogofilter register/unregister routines as a start, or other register/unregister routines more appropriate to Blackbox, if Blackbox can register/unregister spam and ham.

2. Functionality

    The `spam-check-blackbox` function should return 'nil' or `spam-split-group`, observing the other conventions. See the existing `spam-check-*` functions for examples of what you can do, and stick to the template unless you fully understand the reasons why you aren't.

For processing spam and ham messages, provide the following:

1. Code

    Note you don't have to provide a spam or a ham processor. Only provide them if Blackbox supports spam or ham processing.

    Also, ham and spam processors are being phased out as single variables. Instead the form (spam spam-use-blackbox) or (ham spam-use-blackbox) is favored. For now, spam/ham processor variables are still around but they won't be for long.

    ```
    (defvar gnus-group-spam-exit-processor-blackbox "blackbox-spam"
      "The Blackbox summary exit spam processor.
    Only applicable to spam groups.")

    (defvar gnus-group-ham-exit-processor-blackbox "blackbox-ham"
      "The whitelist summary exit ham processor.
    Only applicable to non-spam (unclassified and ham) groups.")
    ```

2. Gnus parameters
    Add

```
(const :tag "Spam: Blackbox" (spam spam-use-blackbox))
(const :tag "Ham: Blackbox"  (ham spam-use-blackbox))
```

to the `spam-process` group parameter in `gnus.el`. Make sure you do it twice, once for the parameter and once for the variable customization.

Add

```
(variable-item spam-use-blackbox)
```

to the `spam-autodetect-methods` group parameter in `gnus.el` if Blackbox can check incoming mail for spam contents.

Finally, use the appropriate `spam-install-*-backend` function in `spam.el`. Here are the available functions.

1. `spam-install-backend-alias`

   This function will simply install an alias for a back end that does everything like the original back end. It is currently only used to make `spam-use-BBDB-exclusive` act like `spam-use-BBDB`.

2. `spam-install-nocheck-backend`

   This function installs a back end that has no check function, but can register/unregister ham or spam. The `spam-use-gmane` back end is such a back end.

3. `spam-install-checkonly-backend`

   This function will install a back end that can only check incoming mail for spam contents. It can't register or unregister messages. `spam-use-blackholes` and `spam-use-hashcash` are such back ends.

4. `spam-install-statistical-checkonly-backend`

   This function installs a statistical back end (one which requires the full body of a message to check it) that can only check incoming mail for contents. `spam-use-regex-body` is such a filter.

5. `spam-install-statistical-backend`

   This function install a statistical back end with incoming checks and registration/unregistration routines. `spam-use-bogofilter` is set up this way.

6. `spam-install-backend`

   This is the most normal back end installation, where a back end that can check and register/unregister messages is set up without statistical abilities. The `spam-use-BBDB` is such a back end.

7. `spam-install-mover-backend`

   Mover back ends are internal to `spam.el` and specifically move articles around when the summary is exited. You will very probably never install such a back end.

9.17.8 Spam Statistics Package

Paul Graham has written an excellent essay about spam filtering using statistics: A Plan for Spam. In it he describes the inherent deficiency of rule-based filtering as used by SpamAssassin, for example: Somebody has to write the rules, and everybody else has to install these rules. You are always late. It would be much better, he argues, to filter mail based on whether it somehow resembles spam or non-spam. One way to measure this is word distribution. He then goes on to describe a solution that checks whether a new mail resembles any of your other spam mails or not.

The basic idea is this: Create a two collections of your mail, one with spam, one with non-spam. Count how often each word appears in either collection, weight this by the total number of mails in the collections, and store this information in a dictionary. For every word in a new mail, determine its probability to belong to a spam or a non-spam mail. Use the 15 most conspicuous words, compute the total probability of the mail being spam. If this probability is higher than a certain threshold, the mail is considered to be spam.

The Spam Statistics package adds support to Gnus for this kind of filtering. It can be used as one of the back ends of the Spam package (see Section 9.17 [Spam Package], page 272), or by itself.

Before using the Spam Statistics package, you need to set it up. First, you need two collections of your mail, one with spam, one with non-spam. Then you need to create a dictionary using these two collections, and save it. And last but not least, you need to use this dictionary in your fancy mail splitting rules.

9.17.8.1 Creating a spam-stat dictionary

Before you can begin to filter spam based on statistics, you must create these statistics based on two mail collections, one with spam, one with non-spam. These statistics are then stored in a dictionary for later use. In order for these statistics to be meaningful, you need several hundred emails in both collections.

Gnus currently supports only the nnml back end for automated dictionary creation. The nnml back end stores all mails in a directory, one file per mail. Use the following:

spam-stat-process-spam-directory   [Function]
    Create spam statistics for every file in this directory. Every file is treated as one spam
    mail.

spam-stat-process-non-spam-directory   [Function]
    Create non-spam statistics for every file in this directory. Every file is treated as one
    non-spam mail.

Usually you would call spam-stat-process-spam-directory on a directory such as ~/Mail/mail/spam (this usually corresponds to the group 'nnml:mail.spam'), and you would call spam-stat-process-non-spam-directory on a directory such as ~/Mail/mail/misc (this usually corresponds to the group 'nnml:mail.misc').

When you are using IMAP, you won't have the mails available locally, so that will not work. One solution is to use the Gnus Agent to cache the articles. Then you can use directories such as "~/News/agent/nnimap/mail.yourisp.com/personal_spam" for spam-stat-process-spam-directory. See Section 6.9.5 [Agent as Cache], page 208.

spam-stat   [Variable]
    This variable holds the hash-table with all the statistics—the dictionary we have been
    talking about. For every word in either collection, this hash-table stores a vector
    describing how often the word appeared in spam and often it appeared in non-spam
    mails.

If you want to regenerate the statistics from scratch, you need to reset the dictionary.

spam-stat-reset   [Function]
>   Reset the `spam-stat` hash-table, deleting all the statistics.

When you are done, you must save the dictionary. The dictionary may be rather large. If you will not update the dictionary incrementally (instead, you will recreate it once a month, for example), then you can reduce the size of the dictionary by deleting all words that did not appear often enough or that do not clearly belong to only spam or only non-spam mails.

spam-stat-reduce-size   [Function]
>   Reduce the size of the dictionary. Use this only if you do not want to update the dictionary incrementally.

spam-stat-save   [Function]
>   Save the dictionary.

spam-stat-file   [Variable]
>   The filename used to store the dictionary. This defaults to `~/.spam-stat.el`.

9.17.8.2 Splitting mail using spam-stat

This section describes how to use the Spam statistics *independently* of the See Section 9.17 [Spam Package], page 272.

First, add the following to your `~/.gnus.el` file:

```
(require 'spam-stat)
(spam-stat-load)
```

This will load the necessary Gnus code, and the dictionary you created.

Next, you need to adapt your fancy splitting rules: You need to determine how to use `spam-stat`. The following examples are for the nnml back end. Using the nnimap back end works just as well. Just use `nnimap-split-fancy` instead of `nnmail-split-fancy`.

In the simplest case, you only have two groups, 'mail.misc' and 'mail.spam'. The following expression says that mail is either spam or it should go into 'mail.misc'. If it is spam, then `spam-stat-split-fancy` will return 'mail.spam'.

```
(setq nnmail-split-fancy
      '(| (: spam-stat-split-fancy)
          "mail.misc"))
```

spam-stat-split-fancy-spam-group   [Variable]
>   The group to use for spam. Default is 'mail.spam'.

If you also filter mail with specific subjects into other groups, use the following expression. Only mails not matching the regular expression are considered potential spam.

```
(setq nnmail-split-fancy
      '(| ("Subject" "\\bspam-stat\\b" "mail.emacs")
          (: spam-stat-split-fancy)
          "mail.misc"))
```

If you want to filter for spam first, then you must be careful when creating the dictionary. Note that `spam-stat-split-fancy` must consider both mails in 'mail.emacs' and in 'mail.misc' as non-spam, therefore both should be in your collection of non-spam mails, when creating the dictionary!

```
(setq nnmail-split-fancy
      '(| (: spam-stat-split-fancy)
          ("Subject" "\\bspam-stat\\b" "mail.emacs")
          "mail.misc"))
```

You can combine this with traditional filtering. Here, we move all HTML-only mails into the 'mail.spam.filtered' group. Note that since spam-stat-split-fancy will never see them, the mails in 'mail.spam.filtered' should be neither in your collection of spam mails, nor in your collection of non-spam mails, when creating the dictionary!

```
(setq nnmail-split-fancy
      '(| ("Content-Type" "text/html" "mail.spam.filtered")
          (: spam-stat-split-fancy)
          ("Subject" "\\bspam-stat\\b" "mail.emacs")
          "mail.misc"))
```

9.17.8.3 Low-level interface to the spam-stat dictionary

The main interface to using spam-stat, are the following functions:

spam-stat-buffer-is-spam [Function]
Called in a buffer, that buffer is considered to be a new spam mail. Use this for new mail that has not been processed before.

spam-stat-buffer-is-no-spam [Function]
Called in a buffer, that buffer is considered to be a new non-spam mail. Use this for new mail that has not been processed before.

spam-stat-buffer-change-to-spam [Function]
Called in a buffer, that buffer is no longer considered to be normal mail but spam. Use this to change the status of a mail that has already been processed as non-spam.

spam-stat-buffer-change-to-non-spam [Function]
Called in a buffer, that buffer is no longer considered to be spam but normal mail. Use this to change the status of a mail that has already been processed as spam.

spam-stat-save [Function]
Save the hash table to the file. The filename used is stored in the variable spam-stat-file.

spam-stat-load [Function]
Load the hash table from a file. The filename used is stored in the variable spam-stat-file.

spam-stat-score-word [Function]
Return the spam score for a word.

spam-stat-score-buffer [Function]
Return the spam score for a buffer.

spam-stat-split-fancy [Function]
Use this function for fancy mail splitting. Add the rule '(: spam-stat-split-fancy)' to nnmail-split-fancy

Make sure you load the dictionary before using it. This requires the following in your
`~/.gnus.el` file:

```
(require 'spam-stat)
(spam-stat-load)
```

Typical test will involve calls to the following functions:

```
Reset: (setq spam-stat (make-hash-table :test 'equal))
Learn spam: (spam-stat-process-spam-directory "~/Mail/mail/spam")
Learn non-spam: (spam-stat-process-non-spam-directory "~/Mail/mail/misc")
Save table: (spam-stat-save)
File size: (nth 7 (file-attributes spam-stat-file))
Number of words: (hash-table-count spam-stat)
Test spam: (spam-stat-test-directory "~/Mail/mail/spam")
Test non-spam: (spam-stat-test-directory "~/Mail/mail/misc")
Reduce table size: (spam-stat-reduce-size)
Save table: (spam-stat-save)
File size: (nth 7 (file-attributes spam-stat-file))
Number of words: (hash-table-count spam-stat)
Test spam: (spam-stat-test-directory "~/Mail/mail/spam")
Test non-spam: (spam-stat-test-directory "~/Mail/mail/misc")
```

Here is how you would create your dictionary:

```
Reset: (setq spam-stat (make-hash-table :test 'equal))
Learn spam: (spam-stat-process-spam-directory "~/Mail/mail/spam")
Learn non-spam: (spam-stat-process-non-spam-directory "~/Mail/mail/misc")
Repeat for any other non-spam group you need...
Reduce table size: (spam-stat-reduce-size)
Save table: (spam-stat-save)
```

9.18 The Gnus Registry

The Gnus registry is a package that tracks messages by their Message-ID across all backends.
This allows Gnus users to do several cool things, be the envy of the locals, get free haircuts,
and be experts on world issues. Well, maybe not all of those, but the features are pretty
cool.

Although they will be explained in detail shortly, here's a quick list of said features in
case your attention span is... never mind.

1. Split messages to their parent

   This keeps discussions in the same group. You can use the subject and the sender in
   addition to the Message-ID. Several strategies are available.

2. Refer to messages by ID

   Commands like **gnus-summary-refer-parent-article** can take advantage of the registry to jump to the referred article, regardless of the group the message is in.

3. Store custom flags and keywords

   The registry can store custom flags and keywords for a message. For instance, you can
   mark a message "To-Do" this way and the flag will persist whether the message is in
   the nnimap, nnml, nnmaildir, etc. backends.

4. Store arbitrary data

   Through a simple ELisp API, the registry can remember any data for a message. A
   built-in inverse map, when activated, allows quick lookups of all messages matching a
   particular set of criteria.

9.18.1 Gnus Registry Setup

Fortunately, setting up the Gnus registry is pretty easy:

```
(setq gnus-registry-max-entries 2500)

(gnus-registry-initialize)
```

This adds registry saves to Gnus newsrc saves (which happen on exit and when you press *s* from the *Group* buffer. It also adds registry calls to article actions in Gnus (copy, move, etc.) so it's not easy to undo the initialization. See **gnus-registry-initialize** for the gory details.

Here are other settings used by the author of the registry (understand what they do before you copy them blindly).

```
(setq
 gnus-registry-split-strategy 'majority
 gnus-registry-ignored-groups '(("nntp" t)
                                ("nnrss" t)
                                ("spam" t)
                                ("train" t))
 gnus-registry-max-entries 500000
 ;; this is the default
 gnus-registry-track-extra '(sender subject))
```

They say: keep a lot of messages around, track messages by sender and subject (not just parent Message-ID), and when the registry splits incoming mail, use a majority rule to decide where messages should go if there's more than one possibility. In addition, the registry should ignore messages in groups that match "nntp", "nnrss", "spam", or "train."

You are doubtless impressed by all this, but you ask: "I am a Gnus user, I customize to live. Give me more." Here you go, these are the general settings.

gnus-registry-unfollowed-groups   [Variable]
> The groups that will not be followed by **gnus-registry-split-fancy-with-parent**. They will still be remembered by the registry. This is a list of regular expressions. By default any group name that ends with "delayed", "drafts", "queue", or "INBOX", belongs to the nnmairix backend, or contains the word "archive" is not followed.

gnus-registry-max-entries   [Variable]
> The number (an integer or **nil** for unlimited) of entries the registry will keep.

gnus-registry-max-pruned-entries   [Variable]
> The maximum number (an integer or **nil** for unlimited) of entries the registry will keep after pruning.

gnus-registry-cache-file   [Variable]
> The file where the registry will be stored between Gnus sessions. By default the file name is **.gnus.registry.eioio** in the same directory as your **.newsrc.eld**.

9.18.2 Fetching by `Message-ID` Using the Registry

The registry knows how to map each `Message-ID` to the group it's in. This can be leveraged to enhance the "article refer method", the thing that tells Gnus how to look up an article given its Message-ID (see Section 3.23 [Finding the Parent], page 102).

The `nnregistry` refer method does exactly that. It has the advantage that an article may be found regardless of the group it's in—provided its `Message-ID` is known to the registry. It can be enabled by augmenting the start-up file with something along these lines:

```
;; Keep enough entries to have a good hit rate when referring to an
;; article using the registry.  Use long group names so that Gnus
;; knows where the article is.
(setq gnus-registry-max-entries 2500)

(gnus-registry-initialize)

(setq gnus-refer-article-method
      '(current
        (nnregistry)
        (nnweb "gmane" (nnweb-type gmane)))))
```

The example above instructs Gnus to first look up the article in the current group, or, alternatively, using the registry, and finally, if all else fails, using Gmane.

9.18.3 Fancy splitting to parent

Simply put, this lets you put followup e-mail where it belongs.

Every message has a Message-ID, which is unique, and the registry remembers it. When the message is moved or copied, the registry will notice this and offer the new group as a choice to the splitting strategy.

When a followup is made, usually it mentions the original message's Message-ID in the headers. The registry knows this and uses that mention to find the group where the original message lives. You only have to put a rule like this:

```
(setq nnimap-my-split-fancy '(|

    ;; split to parent: you need this
    (: gnus-registry-split-fancy-with-parent)

    ;; other rules, as an example
    (: spam-split)
    ;; default mailbox
    "mail")
```

in your fancy split setup. In addition, you may want to customize the following variables.

`gnus-registry-track-extra`   [Variable]
> This is a list of symbols, so it's best to change it from the Customize interface. By default it's (`subject sender recipient`), which may work for you. It can be annoying if your mail flow is large and people don't stick to the same groups.

When you decide to stop tracking any of those extra data, you can use the command `gnus-registry-remove-extra-data` to purge it from the existing registry entries.

`gnus-registry-split-strategy`   [Variable]
> This is a symbol, so it's best to change it from the Customize interface. By default it's `nil`, but you may want to set it to `majority` or `first` to split by sender or subject based on the majority of matches or on the first found. I find `majority` works best.

9.18.4 Store custom flags and keywords

The registry lets you set custom flags and keywords per message. You can use the Gnus->Registry Marks menu or the *M M x* keyboard shortcuts, where *x* is the first letter of the mark's name.

`gnus-registry-marks`   [Variable]
> The custom marks that the registry can use. You can modify the default list, if you like. If you do, you'll have to exit Emacs before they take effect (you can also unload the registry and reload it or evaluate the specific macros you'll need, but you probably don't want to bother). Use the Customize interface to modify the list.
>
> By default this list has the `Important`, `Work`, `Personal`, `To-Do`, and `Later` marks. They all have keyboard shortcuts like *M M i* for Important, using the first letter.

`gnus-registry-mark-article`   [Function]
> Call this function to mark an article with a custom registry mark. It will offer the available marks for completion.

You can use `defalias` to install a summary line formatting function that will show the registry marks. There are two flavors of this function, either showing the marks as single characters, using their `:char` property, or showing the marks as full strings.

```
;; show the marks as single characters (see the :char property in
;; 'gnus-registry-marks'):
;; (defalias 'gnus-user-format-function-M 'gnus-registry-article-marks-to-chars)

;; show the marks by name (see 'gnus-registry-marks'):
;; (defalias 'gnus-user-format-function-M 'gnus-registry-article-marks-to-names)
```

9.18.5 Store arbitrary data

The registry has a simple API that uses a Message-ID as the key to store arbitrary data (as long as it can be converted to a list for storage).

`gnus-registry-set-id-key` (*id key value*)   [Function]
> Store `value` under `key` for message `id`.

`gnus-registry-get-id-key` (*id key*)   [Function]
> Get the data under `key` for message `id`.

`gnus-registry-extra-entries-precious`   [Variable]
> If any extra entries are precious, their presence will make the registry keep the whole entry forever, even if there are no groups for the Message-ID and if the size limit of the registry is reached. By default this is just (`marks`) so the custom registry marks are precious.

9.19 Interaction with other modes

9.19.1 Dired

`gnus-dired-minor-mode` provides some useful functions for dired buffers. It is enabled with

    (add-hook 'dired-mode-hook 'turn-on-gnus-dired-mode)

C-c C-m C-a

> Send dired's marked files as an attachment (**gnus-dired-attach**). You will be prompted for a message buffer.

C-c C-m C-l

> Visit a file according to the appropriate mailcap entry (**gnus-dired-find-file-mailcap**). With prefix, open file in a new buffer.

C-c C-m C-p

> Print file according to the mailcap entry (**gnus-dired-print**). If there is no print command, print in a PostScript image.

9.20 Various Various

`gnus-home-directory`

> All Gnus file and directory variables will be initialized from this variable, which defaults to ~/.

`gnus-directory`

> Most Gnus storage file and directory variables will be initialized from this variable, which defaults to the **SAVEDIR** environment variable, or ~/News/ if that variable isn't set.
>
> Note that Gnus is mostly loaded when the ~/.gnus.el file is read. This means that other directory variables that are initialized from this variable won't be set properly if you set this variable in ~/.gnus.el. Set this variable in .emacs instead.

`gnus-default-directory`

> Not related to the above variable at all—this variable says what the default directory of all Gnus buffers should be. If you issue commands like *C-x C-f*, the prompt you'll get starts in the current buffer's default directory. If this variable is **nil** (which is the default), the default directory will be the default directory of the buffer you were in when you started Gnus.

`gnus-verbose`

> This variable is an integer between zero and ten. The higher the value, the more messages will be displayed. If this variable is zero, Gnus will never flash any messages, if it is seven (which is the default), most important messages will be shown, and if it is ten, Gnus won't ever shut up, but will flash so many messages it will make your head swim.

`gnus-verbose-backends`

> This variable works the same way as **gnus-verbose**, but it applies to the Gnus back ends instead of Gnus proper.

`gnus-add-timestamp-to-message`

> This variable controls whether to add timestamps to messages that are controlled by `gnus-verbose` and `gnus-verbose-backends` and are issued. The default value is `nil` which means never to add timestamp. If it is `log`, add timestamps to only the messages that go into the *Messages* buffer (in XEmacs, it is the *Message-Log* buffer). If it is neither `nil` nor `log`, add timestamps not only to log messages but also to the ones displayed in the echo area.

`nnheader-max-head-length`

> When the back ends read straight heads of articles, they all try to read as little as possible. This variable (default 8192) specifies the absolute max length the back ends will try to read before giving up on finding a separator line between the head and the body. If this variable is `nil`, there is no upper read bound. If it is `t`, the back ends won't try to read the articles piece by piece, but read the entire articles. This makes sense with some versions of `ange-ftp` or `efs`.

`nnheader-head-chop-length`

> This variable (default 2048) says how big a piece of each article to read when doing the operation described above.

`nnheader-file-name-translation-alist`

> This is an alist that says how to translate characters in file names. For instance, if ':' is invalid as a file character in file names on your system (you OS/2 user you), you could say something like:

```
(setq nnheader-file-name-translation-alist
      '((?: . ?_)))
```

> In fact, this is the default value for this variable on OS/2 and MS Windows (phooey) systems.

`gnus-hidden-properties`

> This is a list of properties to use to hide "invisible" text. It is (`invisible t intangible t`) by default on most systems, which makes invisible text invisible and intangible.

`gnus-parse-headers-hook`

> A hook called before parsing headers. It can be used, for instance, to gather statistics on the headers fetched, or perhaps you'd like to prune some headers. I don't see why you'd want that, though.

`gnus-shell-command-separator`

> String used to separate two shell commands. The default is ';'.

`gnus-invalid-group-regexp`

> Regexp to match "invalid" group names when querying user for a group name. The default value catches some **really** invalid group names who could possibly mess up Gnus internally (like allowing ':' in a group name, which is normally used to delimit method and group).
>
> IMAP users might want to allow '/' in group names though.

`gnus-safe-html-newsgroups`

> Groups in which links in html articles are considered all safe. The value may be a regexp matching those groups, a list of group names, or `nil`. This over-

rides `mm-w3m-safe-url-regexp`. The default value is `"\\`nnrss[+:]"`. This is effective only when emacs-w3m renders html articles, i.e., in the case `mm-text-html-renderer` is set to `w3m`. See Section "Display Customization" in *The Emacs MIME Manual*.

10 The End

Well, that's the manual—you can get on with your life now. Keep in touch. Say hello to your cats from me.

My **ghod**—I just can't stand goodbyes. Sniffle.

Ol' Charles Reznikoff said it pretty well, so I leave the floor to him:

Te Deum

Not because of victories
I sing,
having none,
but for the common sunshine,
the breeze,
the largess of the spring.

Not for victory
but for the day's work done
as well as I was able;
not for a seat upon the dais
but at the common table.

11 Appendices

11.1 XEmacs

XEmacs is distributed as a collection of packages. You should install whatever packages the Gnus XEmacs package requires. The current requirements are 'gnus', 'mail-lib', 'xemacs-base', 'eterm', 'sh-script', 'net-utils', 'os-utils', 'dired', 'mh-e', 'sieve', 'ps-print', 'pgg', 'mailcrypt', 'ecrypto', and 'sasl'.

11.2 History

GNUS was written by Masanobu UMEDA. When autumn crept up in '94, Lars Magne Ingebrigtsen grew bored and decided to rewrite Gnus.

If you want to investigate the person responsible for this outrage, you can point your (feh!) web browser to http://quimby.gnus.org/. This is also the primary distribution point for the new and spiffy versions of Gnus, and is known as The Site That Destroys Newsrcs And Drives People Mad.

During the first extended alpha period of development, the new Gnus was called "(ding) Gnus". *(ding)* is, of course, short for *ding is not Gnus*, which is a total and utter lie, but who cares? (Besides, the "Gnus" in this abbreviation should probably be pronounced "news" as UMEDA intended, which makes it a more appropriate name, don't you think?)

In any case, after spending all that energy on coming up with a new and spunky name, we decided that the name was *too* spunky, so we renamed it back again to "Gnus". But in mixed case. "Gnus" vs. "GNUS". New vs. old.

11.2.1 Gnus Versions

The first "proper" release of Gnus 5 was done in November 1995 when it was included in the Emacs 19.30 distribution (132 (ding) Gnus releases plus 15 Gnus 5.0 releases).

In May 1996 the next Gnus generation (aka. "September Gnus" (after 99 releases)) was released under the name "Gnus 5.2" (40 releases).

On July 28th 1996 work on Red Gnus was begun, and it was released on January 25th 1997 (after 84 releases) as "Gnus 5.4" (67 releases).

On September 13th 1997, Quassia Gnus was started and lasted 37 releases. It was released as "Gnus 5.6" on March 8th 1998 (46 releases).

Gnus 5.6 begat Pterodactyl Gnus on August 29th 1998 and was released as "Gnus 5.8" (after 99 releases and a CVS repository) on December 3rd 1999.

On the 26th of October 2000, Oort Gnus was begun and was released as Gnus 5.10 on May 1st 2003 (24 releases).

On the January 4th 2004, No Gnus was begun.

On April 19, 2010 Gnus development was moved to Git. See http://git.gnus.org for details (http://www.gnus.org will be updated with the information when possible).

On the January 31th 2012, Ma Gnus was begun.

If you happen upon a version of Gnus that has a prefixed name—"(ding) Gnus", "September Gnus", "Red Gnus", "Quassia Gnus", "Pterodactyl Gnus", "Oort Gnus", "No

Gnus", "Ma Gnus"—don't panic. Don't let it know that you're frightened. Back away. Slowly. Whatever you do, don't run. Walk away, calmly, until you're out of its reach. Find a proper released version of Gnus and snuggle up to that instead.

11.2.2 Why?

What's the point of Gnus?

I want to provide a "rad", "happening", "way cool" and "hep" newsreader, that lets you do anything you can think of. That was my original motivation, but while working on Gnus, it has become clear to me that this generation of newsreaders really belong in the stone age. Newsreaders haven't developed much since the infancy of the net. If the volume continues to rise with the current rate of increase, all current newsreaders will be pretty much useless. How do you deal with newsgroups that have thousands of new articles each day? How do you keep track of millions of people who post?

Gnus offers no real solutions to these questions, but I would very much like to see Gnus being used as a testing ground for new methods of reading and fetching news. Expanding on UMEDA-san's wise decision to separate the newsreader from the back ends, Gnus now offers a simple interface for anybody who wants to write new back ends for fetching mail and news from different sources. I have added hooks for customizations everywhere I could imagine it being useful. By doing so, I'm inviting every one of you to explore and invent.

May Gnus never be complete. *C-u 100 M-x all-hail-emacs* and *C-u 100 M-x all-hail-xemacs*.

11.2.3 Compatibility

Gnus was designed to be fully compatible with GNUS. Almost all key bindings have been kept. More key bindings have been added, of course, but only in one or two obscure cases have old bindings been changed.

Our motto is:

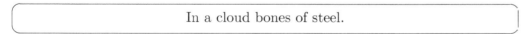

In a cloud bones of steel.

All commands have kept their names. Some internal functions have changed their names.

The **gnus-uu** package has changed drastically. See Section 3.17 [Decoding Articles], page 80.

One major compatibility question is the presence of several summary buffers. All variables relevant while reading a group are buffer-local to the summary buffer they belong in. Although many important variables have their values copied into their global counterparts whenever a command is executed in the summary buffer, this change might lead to incorrect values being used unless you are careful.

All code that relies on knowledge of GNUS internals will probably fail. To take two examples: Sorting **gnus-newsrc-alist** (or changing it in any way, as a matter of fact) is strictly verboten. Gnus maintains a hash table that points to the entries in this alist (which speeds up many functions), and changing the alist directly will lead to peculiar results.

Old hilit19 code does not work at all. In fact, you should probably remove all hilit code from all Gnus hooks (**gnus-group-prepare-hook** and **gnus-summary-prepare-hook**). Gnus provides various integrated functions for highlighting. These are faster and more accurate. To make life easier for everybody, Gnus will by default remove all hilit calls from all hilit hooks. Uncleanliness! Away!

Packages like `expire-kill` will no longer work. As a matter of fact, you should probably remove all old GNUS packages (and other code) when you start using Gnus. More likely than not, Gnus already does what you have written code to make GNUS do. (Snicker.)

Even though old methods of doing things are still supported, only the new methods are documented in this manual. If you detect a new method of doing something while reading this manual, that does not mean you have to stop doing it the old way.

Gnus understands all GNUS startup files.

Overall, a casual user who hasn't written much code that depends on GNUS internals should suffer no problems. If problems occur, please let me know by issuing that magic command *M-x gnus-bug*.

If you are in the habit of sending bug reports *very* often, you may find the helpful help buffer annoying after a while. If so, set `gnus-bug-create-help-buffer` to `nil` to avoid having it pop up at you.

11.2.4 Conformity

No rebels without a clue here, ma'am. We conform to all standards known to (wo)man. Except for those standards and/or conventions we disagree with, of course.

RFC (2)822
> There are no known breaches of this standard.

RFC 1036   There are no known breaches of this standard, either.

Son-of-RFC 1036
> We do have some breaches to this one.
>
> > *X-Newsreader*
> > *User-Agent*
> > > These are considered to be "vanity headers", while I consider them to be consumer information. After seeing so many badly formatted articles coming from `tin` and `Netscape` I know not to use either of those for posting articles. I would not have known that if it wasn't for the `X-Newsreader` header.

USEFOR   USEFOR is an IETF working group writing a successor to RFC 1036, based on Son-of-RFC 1036. They have produced a number of drafts proposing various changes to the format of news articles. The Gnus towers will look into implementing the changes when the draft is accepted as an RFC.

MIME—RFC 2045–2049 etc
> All the various MIME RFCs are supported.

Disposition Notifications—RFC 2298
> Message Mode is able to request notifications from the receiver.

PGP—RFC 1991 and RFC 2440
> RFC 1991 is the original PGP message specification, published as an informational RFC. RFC 2440 was the follow-up, now called Open PGP, and put on

the Standards Track. Both document a non-MIME aware PGP format. Gnus supports both encoding (signing and encryption) and decoding (verification and decryption).

PGP/MIME—RFC 2015/3156

RFC 2015 (superseded by 3156 which references RFC 2440 instead of RFC 1991) describes the MIME-wrapping around the RFC 1991/2440 format. Gnus supports both encoding and decoding.

S/MIME—RFC 2633

RFC 2633 describes the S/MIME format.

IMAP—RFC 1730/2060, RFC 2195, RFC 2086, RFC 2359, RFC 2595, RFC 1731

RFC 1730 is IMAP version 4, updated somewhat by RFC 2060 (IMAP 4 revision 1). RFC 2195 describes CRAM-MD5 authentication for IMAP. RFC 2086 describes access control lists (ACLs) for IMAP. RFC 2359 describes a IMAP protocol enhancement. RFC 2595 describes the proper TLS integration (STARTTLS) with IMAP. RFC 1731 describes the GSSAPI/Kerberos4 mechanisms for IMAP.

If you ever notice Gnus acting non-compliant with regards to the texts mentioned above, don't hesitate to drop a note to Gnus Towers and let us know.

11.2.5 Emacsen

This version of Gnus should work on:

- Emacs 23.1 and up.
- XEmacs 21.4 and up.

This Gnus version will absolutely not work on any Emacsen older than that. Not reliably, at least. Older versions of Gnus may work on older Emacs versions. Particularly, Gnus 5.10.8 should also work on Emacs 20.7 and XEmacs 21.1.

11.2.6 Gnus Development

Gnus is developed in a two-phased cycle. The first phase involves much discussion on the development mailing list 'ding@gnus.org', where people propose changes and new features, post patches and new back ends. This phase is called the *alpha* phase, since the Gnusae released in this phase are *alpha releases*, or (perhaps more commonly in other circles) *snapshots*. During this phase, Gnus is assumed to be unstable and should not be used by casual users. Gnus alpha releases have names like "Oort Gnus" and "No Gnus". See Section 11.2.1 [Gnus Versions], page 302.

After futzing around for 10–100 alpha releases, Gnus is declared *frozen*, and only bug fixes are applied. Gnus loses the prefix, and is called things like "Gnus 5.10.1" instead. Normal people are supposed to be able to use these, and these are mostly discussed on the 'gnu.emacs.gnus' newsgroup. This newgroup is mirrored to the mailing list 'info-gnus-english@gnu.org' which is carried on Gmane as 'gmane.emacs.gnus.user'. These releases are finally integrated in Emacs.

Some variable defaults differ between alpha Gnusae and released Gnusae, in particular, `mail-source-delete-incoming`. This is to prevent lossage of mail if an alpha release hiccups while handling the mail. See Section 6.4.4.3 [Mail Source Customization], page 160.

The division of discussion between the ding mailing list and the Gnus newsgroup is not purely based on publicity concerns. It's true that having people write about the horrible things that an alpha Gnus release can do (sometimes) in a public forum may scare people off, but more importantly, talking about new experimental features that have been introduced may confuse casual users. New features are frequently introduced, fiddled with, and judged to be found wanting, and then either discarded or totally rewritten. People reading the mailing list usually keep up with these rapid changes, while people on the newsgroup can't be assumed to do so.

So if you have problems with or questions about the alpha versions, direct those to the ding mailing list 'ding@gnus.org'. This list is also available on Gmane as 'gmane.emacs.gnus.general'.

Some variable defaults differ between alpha Gnusae and released Gnusae, in particular, `mail-source-delete-incoming`. This is to prevent lossage of mail if an alpha release hiccups while handling the mail. See Section 6.4.4.3 [Mail Source Customization], page 160.

11.2.7 Contributors

The new Gnus version couldn't have been done without the help of all the people on the (ding) mailing list. Every day for over a year I have gotten billions of nice bug reports from them, filling me with joy, every single one of them. Smooches. The people on the list have been tried beyond endurance, what with my "oh, that's a neat idea <type type>, yup, I'll release it right away <ship off> no wait, that doesn't work at all <type type>, yup, I'll ship that one off right away <ship off> no, wait, that absolutely does not work" policy for releases. Micro$oft—bah. Amateurs. I'm *much* worse. (Or is that "worser"? "much worser"? "worsest"?)

I would like to take this opportunity to thank the Academy for... oops, wrong show.

- Masanobu UMEDA—the writer of the original GNUS.
- Shenghuo Zhu—uudecode.el, mm-uu.el, rfc1843.el, nnwarchive and many, many other things connected with MIME and other types of en/decoding, as well as general bug fixing, new functionality and stuff.
- Per Abrahamsen—custom, scoring, highlighting and SOUP code (as well as numerous other things).
- Luis Fernandes—design and graphics.
- Joe Reiss—creator of the smiley faces.
- Justin Sheehy—the FAQ maintainer.
- Erik Naggum—help, ideas, support, code and stuff.
- Wes Hardaker—`gnus-picon.el` and the manual section on *picons* (see Section 9.14.4 [Picons], page 265).
- Kim-Minh Kaplan—further work on the picon code.
- Brad Miller—`gnus-gl.el` and the GroupLens manual section.
- Sudish Joseph—innumerable bug fixes.
- Ilja Weis—`gnus-topic.el`.
- Steven L. Baur—lots and lots and lots of bug detection and fixes.
- Vladimir Alexiev—the refcard and reference booklets.

- Felix Lee & Jamie Zawinski—I stole some pieces from the XGnus distribution by Felix Lee and JWZ.

- Scott Byer—`nnfolder.el` enhancements & rewrite.

- Peter Mutsaers—orphan article scoring code.

- Ken Raeburn—POP mail support.

- Hallvard B Furuseth—various bits and pieces, especially dealing with .newsrc files.

- Brian Edmonds—`gnus-bbdb.el`.

- David Moore—rewrite of `nnvirtual.el` and many other things.

- Kevin Davidson—came up with the name *ding*, so blame him.

- François Pinard—many, many interesting and thorough bug reports, as well as autoconf support.

This manual was proof-read by Adrian Aichner, with Ricardo Nassif, Mark Borges, and Jost Krieger proof-reading parts of the manual.

The following people have contributed many patches and suggestions:

Christopher Davis, Andrew Eskilsson, Kai Grossjohann, Kevin Greiner, Jesper Harder, Paul Jarc, Simon Josefsson, David Kågedal, Richard Pieri, Fabrice Popineau, Daniel Quinlan, Michael Shields, Reiner Steib, Jason L. Tibbitts, III, Jack Vinson, Katsumi Yamaoka, and Teodor Zlatanov.

Also thanks to the following for patches and stuff:

Jari Aalto, Adrian Aichner, Vladimir Alexiev, Russ Allbery, Peter Arius, Matt Armstrong, Marc Auslander, Miles Bader, Alexei V. Barantsev, Frank Bennett, Robert Bihlmeyer, Chris Bone, Mark Borges, Mark Boyns, Lance A. Brown, Rob Browning, Kees de Bruin, Martin Buchholz, Joe Buehler, Kevin Buhr, Alastair Burt, Joao Cachopo, Zlatko Calusic, Massimo Campostrini, Castor, David Charlap, Dan Christensen, Kevin Christian, Jae-you Chung, James H. Cloos, Jr., Laura Conrad, Michael R. Cook, Glenn Coombs, Andrew J. Cosgriff, Neil Crellin, Frank D. Cringle, Geoffrey T. Dairiki, Andre Deparade, Ulrik Dickow, Dave Disser, Rui-Tao Dong, Joev Dubach, Michael Welsh Duggan, Dave Edmondson, Paul Eggert, Mark W. Eichin, Karl Eichwalder, Enami Tsugutomo, Michael Ernst, Luc Van Eycken, Sam Falkner, Nelson Jose dos Santos Ferreira, Sigbjorn Finne, Sven Fischer, Paul Fisher, Decklin Foster, Gary D. Foster, Paul Franklin, Guy Geens, Arne Georg Gleditsch, David S. Goldberg, Michelangelo Grigni, Dale Hagglund, D. Hall, Magnus Hammerin, Kenichi Handa, Raja R. Harinath, Yoshiki Hayashi, P. E. Jareth Hein, Hisashige Kenji, Scott Hofmann, Tassilo Horn, Marc Horowitz, Gunnar Horrigmo, Richard Hoskins, Brad Howes, Miguel de Icaza, François Felix Ingrand, Tatsuya Ichikawa, Ishikawa Ichiro, Lee Iverson, Iwamuro Motonori, Rajappa Iyer, Andreas Jaeger, Adam P. Jenkins, Randell Jesup, Fred Johansen, Gareth Jones, Greg Klanderman, Karl Kleinpaste, Michael Klingbeil, Peter Skov Knudsen, Shuhei Kobayashi, Petr Konecny, Koseki Yoshinori, Thor Kristoffersen, Jens Lautenbacher, Martin Larose, Seokchan Lee, Joerg Lenneis, Carsten Leonhardt, James LewisMoss, Christian Limpach, Markus Linnala, Dave Love, Mike McEwan, Tonny Madsen, Shlomo Mahlab, Nat Makarevitch, Istvan Marko, David Martin, Jason R. Mastaler, Gordon Matzigkeit, Timo Metzemakers, Richard Mlynarik, Lantz Moore, Morioka Tomohiko, Erik Toubro Nielsen, Hrvoje Niksic, Andy Norman, Fred Oberhauser, C. R. Oldham, Alexandre Oliva, Ken Olstad, Masaharu Onishi, Hideki Ono, Ettore Perazzoli, William Perry, Stephen Peters, Jens-Ulrik Holger Petersen, Ulrich

Pfeifer, Matt Pharr, Andy Piper, John McClary Prevost, Bill Pringlemeir, Mike Pullen, Jim Radford, Colin Rafferty, Lasse Rasinen, Lars Balker Rasmussen, Joe Reiss, Renaud Rioboo, Roland B. Roberts, Bart Robinson, Christian von Roques, Markus Rost, Jason Rumney, Wolfgang Rupprecht, Jay Sachs, Dewey M. Sasser, Conrad Sauerwald, Loren Schall, Dan Schmidt, Ralph Schleicher, Philippe Schnoebelen, Andreas Schwab, Randal L. Schwartz, Danny Siu, Matt Simmons, Paul D. Smith, Jeff Sparkes, Toby Speight, Michael Sperber, Darren Stalder, Richard Stallman, Greg Stark, Sam Steingold, Paul Stevenson, Jonas Steverud, Paul Stodghill, Kiyokazu Suto, Kurt Swanson, Samuel Tardieu, Teddy, Chuck Thompson, Tozawa Akihiko, Philippe Troin, James Troup, Trung Tran-Duc, Jack Twilley, Aaron M. Ucko, Aki Vehtari, Didier Verna, Vladimir Volovich, Jan Vroonhof, Stefan Waldherr, Pete Ware, Barry A. Warsaw, Christoph Wedler, Joe Wells, Lee Willis, and Lloyd Zusman.

For a full overview of what each person has done, the ChangeLogs included in the Gnus alpha distributions should give ample reading (550kB and counting).

Apologies to everybody that I've forgotten, of which there are many, I'm sure.

Gee, that's quite a list of people. I guess that must mean that there actually are people who are using Gnus. Who'd'a thunk it!

11.2.8 New Features

These lists are, of course, just *short* overviews of the *most* important new features. No, really. There are tons more. Yes, we have feeping creaturism in full effect.

11.2.8.1 (ding) Gnus

New features in Gnus 5.0/5.1:

- The look of all buffers can be changed by setting format-like variables (see Section 2.1 [Group Buffer Format], page 11 and see Section 3.1 [Summary Buffer Format], page 44).
- Local spool and several NNTP servers can be used at once (see Chapter 6 [Select Methods], page 136).
- You can combine groups into virtual groups (see Section 6.7.1 [Virtual Groups], page 193).
- You can read a number of different mail formats (see Section 6.4 [Getting Mail], page 150). All the mail back ends implement a convenient mail expiry scheme (see Section 6.4.9 [Expiring Mail], page 168).
- Gnus can use various strategies for gathering threads that have lost their roots (thereby gathering loose sub-threads into one thread) or it can go back and retrieve enough headers to build a complete thread (see Section 3.9.1 [Customizing Threading], page 65).
- Killed groups can be displayed in the group buffer, and you can read them as well (see Section 2.11 [Listing Groups], page 29).
- Gnus can do partial group updates—you do not have to retrieve the entire active file just to check for new articles in a few groups (see Section 1.8 [The Active File], page 8).
- Gnus implements a sliding scale of subscribedness to groups (see Section 2.6 [Group Levels], page 17).
- You can score articles according to any number of criteria (see Chapter 7 [Scoring], page 214). You can even get Gnus to find out how to score articles for you (see Section 7.6 [Adaptive Scoring], page 224).

- Gnus maintains a dribble buffer that is auto-saved the normal Emacs manner, so it should be difficult to lose much data on what you have read if your machine should go down (see Section 1.7 [Auto Save], page 8).

- Gnus now has its own startup file (`~/.gnus.el`) to avoid cluttering up the `.emacs` file.

- You can set the process mark on both groups and articles and perform operations on all the marked items (see Section 9.1 [Process/Prefix], page 249).

- You can list subsets of groups according to, well, anything (see Section 2.11 [Listing Groups], page 29).

- You can browse foreign servers and subscribe to groups from those servers (see Section 2.14 [Browse Foreign Server], page 32).

- Gnus can fetch articles, asynchronously, on a second connection to the server (see Section 3.11 [Asynchronous Fetching], page 72).

- You can cache articles locally (see Section 3.12 [Article Caching], page 74).

- The uudecode functions have been expanded and generalized (see Section 3.17 [Decoding Articles], page 80).

- You can still post uuencoded articles, which was a little-known feature of GNUS' past (see Section 3.17.5.3 [Uuencoding and Posting], page 83).

- Fetching parents (and other articles) now actually works without glitches (see Section 3.23 [Finding the Parent], page 102).

- Gnus can fetch FAQs and group descriptions (see Section 2.18.2 [Group Information], page 41).

- Digests (and other files) can be used as the basis for groups (see Section 6.6.3 [Document Groups], page 188).

- Articles can be highlighted and customized (see Section 4.4 [Customizing Articles], page 120).

- URLs and other external references can be buttonized (see Section 3.18.6 [Article Buttons], page 92).

- You can do lots of strange stuff with the Gnus window & frame configuration (see Section 9.5 [Window Layout], page 254).

11.2.8.2 September Gnus

New features in Gnus 5.2/5.3:

- A new message composition mode is used. All old customization variables for `mail-mode`, `rnews-reply-mode` and `gnus-msg` are now obsolete.

- Gnus is now able to generate *sparse* threads—threads where missing articles are represented by empty nodes (see Section 3.9.1 [Customizing Threading], page 65).

    ```
    (setq gnus-build-sparse-threads 'some)
    ```

- Outgoing articles are stored on a special archive server (see Section 5.5 [Archived Messages], page 128).

- Partial thread regeneration now happens when articles are referred.

- Gnus can make use of GroupLens predictions.

- Picons (personal icons) can be displayed under XEmacs (see Section 9.14.4 [Picons], page 265).

- A `trn`-like tree buffer can be displayed (see Section 3.25 [Tree Display], page 105).

    `(setq gnus-use-trees t)`

- An `nn`-like pick-and-read minor mode is available for the summary buffers (see Section 3.24.1 [Pick and Read], page 103).

    `(add-hook 'gnus-summary-mode-hook 'gnus-pick-mode)`

- In binary groups you can use a special binary minor mode (see Section 3.24.2 [Binary Groups], page 104).

- Groups can be grouped in a folding topic hierarchy (see Section 2.16 [Group Topics], page 33).

    `(add-hook 'gnus-group-mode-hook 'gnus-topic-mode)`

- Gnus can re-send and bounce mail (see Section 3.5.1 [Summary Mail Commands], page 53).

- Groups can now have a score, and bubbling based on entry frequency is possible (see Section 2.7 [Group Score], page 19).

    `(add-hook 'gnus-summary-exit-hook 'gnus-summary-bubble-group)`

- Groups can be process-marked, and commands can be performed on groups of groups (see Section 2.8 [Marking Groups], page 19).

- Caching is possible in virtual groups.

- `nndoc` now understands all kinds of digests, mail boxes, rnews news batches, ClariNet briefs collections, and just about everything else (see Section 6.6.3 [Document Groups], page 188).

- Gnus has a new back end (`nnsoup`) to create/read SOUP packets.

- The Gnus cache is much faster.

- Groups can be sorted according to many criteria (see Section 2.12 [Sorting Groups], page 30).

- New group parameters have been introduced to set list-addresses and expiry times (see Section 2.10 [Group Parameters], page 22).

- All formatting specs allow specifying faces to be used (see Section 9.4.5 [Formatting Fonts], page 252).

- There are several more commands for setting/removing/acting on process marked articles on the `M P` submap (see Section 3.7.6 [Setting Process Marks], page 62).

- The summary buffer can be limited to show parts of the available articles based on a wide range of criteria. These commands have been bound to keys on the `/` submap (see Section 3.8 [Limiting], page 63).

- Articles can be made persistent with the `*` command (see Section 3.13 [Persistent Articles], page 75).

- All functions for hiding article elements are now toggles.

- Article headers can be buttonized (see Section 3.18.4 [Article Washing], page 88).

- All mail back ends support fetching articles by `Message-ID`.

- Duplicate mail can now be treated properly (see Section 6.4.11 [Duplicates], page 172).

- All summary mode commands are available directly from the article buffer (see Section 4.5 [Article Keymap], page 123).

- Frames can be part of `gnus-buffer-configuration` (see Section 9.5 [Window Layout], page 254).

- Mail can be re-scanned by a daemonic process (see Section 9.9 [Daemons], page 260).

- Groups can be made permanently visible (see Section 2.11 [Listing Groups], page 29).

  `(setq gnus-permanently-visible-groups "^nnml:")`

- Many new hooks have been introduced to make customizing easier.

- Gnus respects the `Mail-Copies-To` header.

- Threads can be gathered by looking at the `References` header (see Section 3.9.1 [Customizing Threading], page 65).

  ```
  (setq gnus-summary-thread-gathering-function
        'gnus-gather-threads-by-references)
  ```

- Read articles can be stored in a special backlog buffer to avoid refetching (see Section 3.15 [Article Backlog], page 76).

  `(setq gnus-keep-backlog 50)`

- A clean copy of the current article is always stored in a separate buffer to allow easier treatment.

- Gnus can suggest where to save articles (see Section 3.16 [Saving Articles], page 76).

- Gnus doesn't have to do as much prompting when saving (see Section 3.16 [Saving Articles], page 76).

  `(setq gnus-prompt-before-saving t)`

- `gnus-uu` can view decoded files asynchronously while fetching articles (see Section 3.17.5.2 [Other Decode Variables], page 82).

  `(setq gnus-uu-grabbed-file-functions 'gnus-uu-grab-view)`

- Filling in the article buffer now works properly on cited text (see Section 3.18.4 [Article Washing], page 88).

- Hiding cited text adds buttons to toggle hiding, and how much cited text to hide is now customizable (see Section 3.18.3 [Article Hiding], page 86).

  `(setq gnus-cited-lines-visible 2)`

- Boring headers can be hidden (see Section 3.18.3 [Article Hiding], page 86).

- Default scoring values can now be set from the menu bar.

- Further syntax checking of outgoing articles have been added.

11.2.8.3 Red Gnus

New features in Gnus 5.4/5.5:

- `nntp.el` has been totally rewritten in an asynchronous fashion.

- Article prefetching functionality has been moved up into Gnus (see Section 3.11 [Asynchronous Fetching], page 72).

- Scoring can now be performed with logical operators like **and**, **or**, **not**, and parent redirection (see Section 7.15 [Advanced Scoring], page 231).

- Article washing status can be displayed in the article mode line (see Section 4.6 [Misc Article], page 124).

- `gnus.el` has been split into many smaller files.

- Suppression of duplicate articles based on Message-ID can be done (see Section 3.30 [Duplicate Suppression], page 113).

    `(setq gnus-suppress-duplicates t)`

- New variables for specifying what score and adapt files are to be considered home score and adapt files (see Section 7.7 [Home Score File], page 226) have been added.

- `nndoc` was rewritten to be easily extensible (see Section 6.6.3.1 [Document Server Internals], page 189).

- Groups can inherit group parameters from parent topics (see Section 2.16.5 [Topic Parameters], page 37).

- Article editing has been revamped and is now actually usable.

- Signatures can be recognized in more intelligent fashions (see Section 3.18.10 [Article Signature], page 96).

- Summary pick mode has been made to look more **nn**-like. Line numbers are displayed and the . command can be used to pick articles (**Pick and Read**).

- Commands for moving the `.newsrc.eld` from one server to another have been added (see Section 1.5 [Changing Servers], page 6).

- There's a way now to specify that "uninteresting" fields be suppressed when generating lines in buffers (see Section 9.4.3 [Advanced Formatting], page 251).

- Several commands in the group buffer can be undone with `C-M-_` (see Section 9.10 [Undo], page 261).

- Scoring can be done on words using the new score type `w` (see Section 7.4 [Score File Format], page 219).

- Adaptive scoring can be done on a Subject word-by-word basis (see Section 7.6 [Adaptive Scoring], page 224).

    `(setq gnus-use-adaptive-scoring '(word))`

- Scores can be decayed (see Section 7.16 [Score Decays], page 234).

    `(setq gnus-decay-scores t)`

- Scoring can be performed using a regexp on the Date header. The Date is normalized to compact ISO 8601 format first (see Section 7.4 [Score File Format], page 219).

- A new command has been added to remove all data on articles from the native server (see Section 1.5 [Changing Servers], page 6).

- A new command for reading collections of documents (`nndoc` with `nnvirtual` on top) has been added—`C-M-d` (see Section 3.27.4 [Really Various Summary Commands], page 110).

- Process mark sets can be pushed and popped (see Section 3.7.6 [Setting Process Marks], page 62).

- A new mail-to-news back end makes it possible to post even when the NNTP server doesn't allow posting (see Section 6.6.4 [Mail-To-News Gateways], page 192).

- A new back end for reading searches from Web search engines (*DejaNews*, *Alta Vista*, *InReference*) has been added (see Section 6.5.2 [Web Searches], page 184).

- Groups inside topics can now be sorted using the standard sorting functions, and each topic can be sorted independently (see Section 2.16.3 [Topic Sorting], page 36).

- Subsets of the groups can be sorted independently (**Sorting Groups**).

- Cached articles can be pulled into the groups (see Section 3.27.3 [Summary Generation Commands], page 110).

- Score files are now applied in a more reliable order (see Section 7.3 [Score Variables], page 217).

- Reports on where mail messages end up can be generated (see Section 6.4.3 [Splitting Mail], page 152).

- More hooks and functions have been added to remove junk from incoming mail before saving the mail (see Section 6.4.10 [Washing Mail], page 170).

- Emphasized text can be properly fontisized:

11.2.8.4 Quassia Gnus

New features in Gnus 5.6:

- New functionality for using Gnus as an offline newsreader has been added. A plethora of new commands and modes have been added. See Section 6.9 [Gnus Unplugged], page 198, for the full story.

- The **nndraft** back end has returned, but works differently than before. All Message buffers are now also articles in the **nndraft** group, which is created automatically.

- **gnus-alter-header-function** can now be used to alter header values.

- **gnus-summary-goto-article** now accept Message-IDs.

- A new Message command for deleting text in the body of a message outside the region: *C-c C-v*.

- You can now post to component group in **nnvirtual** groups with *C-u C-c C-c*.

- **nntp-rlogin-program**—new variable to ease customization.

- *C-u C-c C-c* in **gnus-article-edit-mode** will now inhibit re-highlighting of the article buffer.

- New element in **gnus-boring-article-headers**—**long-to**.

- *M-i* symbolic prefix command. See Section 9.3 [Symbolic Prefixes], page 250, for details.

- *L* and *I* in the summary buffer now take the symbolic prefix **a** to add the score rule to the **all.SCORE** file.

- **gnus-simplify-subject-functions** variable to allow greater control over simplification.

- *A T*—new command for fetching the current thread.

- */ T*—new command for including the current thread in the limit.

- *M-RET* is a new Message command for breaking cited text.

- '\\1'-expressions are now valid in **nnmail-split-methods**.

- The **custom-face-lookup** function has been removed. If you used this function in your initialization files, you must rewrite them to use **face-spec-set** instead.

- Canceling now uses the current select method. Symbolic prefix **a** forces normal posting method.

- New command to translate M******** sm*rtq**t*s into proper text—**W d**.
- For easier debugging of **nntp**, you can set **nntp-record-commands** to a non-**nil** value.
- **nntp** now uses **~/.authinfo**, a **.netrc**-like file, for controlling where and how to send AUTHINFO to NNTP servers.
- A command for editing group parameters from the summary buffer has been added.
- A history of where mails have been split is available.
- A new article date command has been added—**article-date-iso8601**.
- Subjects can be simplified when threading by setting **gnus-score-thread-simplify**.
- A new function for citing in Message has been added—**message-cite-original-without-signature**.
- **article-strip-all-blank-lines**—new article command.
- A new Message command to kill to the end of the article has been added.
- A minimum adaptive score can be specified by using the **gnus-adaptive-word-minimum** variable.
- The "lapsed date" article header can be kept continually updated by the **gnus-start-date-timer** command.
- Web listserv archives can be read with the **nnlistserv** back end.
- Old dejanews archives can now be read by **nnweb**.

11.2.8.5 Pterodactyl Gnus

New features in Gnus 5.8:

- The mail-fetching functions have changed. See the manual for the many details. In particular, all procmail fetching variables are gone.

  If you used procmail like in

  ```
  (setq nnmail-use-procmail t)
  (setq nnmail-spool-file 'procmail)
  (setq nnmail-procmail-directory "~/mail/incoming/")
  (setq nnmail-procmail-suffix "\\.in")
  ```

  this now has changed to

  ```
  (setq mail-sources
        '((directory :path "~/mail/incoming/"
                     :suffix ".in")))
  ```

  See Section 6.4.4.1 [Mail Source Specifiers], page 154.
- Gnus is now a MIME-capable reader. This affects many parts of Gnus, and adds a slew of new commands. See the manual for details.
- Gnus has also been multilingualized. This also affects too many parts of Gnus to summarize here, and adds many new variables.
- **gnus-auto-select-first** can now be a function to be called to position point.
- The user can now decide which extra headers should be included in summary buffers and NOV files.
- **gnus-article-display-hook** has been removed. Instead, a number of variables starting with **gnus-treat-** have been added.

- The Gnus posting styles have been redone again and now works in a subtly different manner.

- New web-based back ends have been added: `nnslashdot`, `nnwarchive` and `nnultimate`. nnweb has been revamped, again, to keep up with ever-changing layouts.

- Gnus can now read IMAP mail via `nnimap`.

11.2.8.6 Oort Gnus

New features in Gnus 5.10:

- Installation changes

  - Upgrading from previous (stable) version if you have used Oort.

    If you have tried Oort (the unstable Gnus branch leading to this release) but went back to a stable version, be careful when upgrading to this version. In particular, you will probably want to remove all `.marks` (nnml) and `.mrk` (nnfolder) files, so that flags are read from your `.newsrc.eld` instead of from the `.marks`/`.mrk` file where this release store flags. See a later entry for more information about marks. Note that downgrading isn't save in general.

  - Lisp files are now installed in `.../site-lisp/gnus/` by default. It defaulted to `.../site-lisp/` formerly. In addition to this, the new installer issues a warning if other Gnus installations which will shadow the latest one are detected. You can then remove those shadows manually or remove them using `make remove-installed-shadows`.

  - New `make.bat` for compiling and installing Gnus under MS Windows

    Use `make.bat` if you want to install Gnus under MS Windows, the first argument to the batch-program should be the directory where `xemacs.exe` respectively `emacs.exe` is located, if you want to install Gnus after compiling it, give `make.bat /copy` as the second parameter.

    `make.bat` has been rewritten from scratch, it now features automatic recognition of XEmacs and Emacs, generates `gnus-load.el`, checks if errors occur while compilation and generation of info files and reports them at the end of the build process. It now uses `makeinfo` if it is available and falls back to `infohack.el` otherwise. `make.bat` should now install all files which are necessary to run Gnus and be generally a complete replacement for the `configure; make; make install` cycle used under Unix systems.

    The new `make.bat` makes `make-x.bat` and `xemacs.mak` superfluous, so they have been removed.

  - `~/News/overview/` not used.

    As a result of the following change, the `~/News/overview/` directory is not used any more. You can safely delete the entire hierarchy.

  - (require 'gnus-load)

    If you use a stand-alone Gnus distribution, you'd better add `(require 'gnus-load)` into your `~/.emacs` after adding the Gnus lisp directory into load-path.

    File `gnus-load.el` contains autoload commands, functions and variables, some of which may not be included in distributions of Emacsen.

- New packages and libraries within Gnus
  - The revised Gnus FAQ is included in the manual, See Section 11.10 [Frequently Asked Questions], page 358.
  - TLS wrapper shipped with Gnus

    TLS/SSL is now supported in IMAP and NNTP via `tls.el` and GnuTLS.
  - Improved anti-spam features.

    Gnus is now able to take out spam from your mail and news streams using a wide variety of programs and filter rules. Among the supported methods are RBL blocklists, bogofilter and white/blacklists. Hooks for easy use of external packages such as SpamAssassin and Hashcash are also new. Section 9.16 [Thwarting Email Spam], page 268 and Section 9.17 [Spam Package], page 272.
  - Gnus supports server-side mail filtering using Sieve.

    Sieve rules can be added as Group Parameters for groups, and the complete Sieve script is generated using *D g* from the Group buffer, and then uploaded to the server using *C-c C-l* in the generated Sieve buffer. See Section 2.18.5 [Sieve Commands], page 43, and the new Sieve manual *Emacs Sieve*.
- Changes in group mode
  - `gnus-group-read-ephemeral-group` can be called interactively, using *G M*.
  - Retrieval of charters and control messages

    There are new commands for fetching newsgroup charters (*H c*) and control messages (*H C*).
  - The new variable `gnus-parameters` can be used to set group parameters.

    Earlier this was done only via *G p* (or *G c*), which stored the parameters in `~/.newsrc.eld`, but via this variable you can enjoy the powers of customize, and simplified backups since you set the variable in `~/.gnus.el` instead of `~/.newsrc.eld`. The variable maps regular expressions matching group names to group parameters, a'la:

    ```
    (setq gnus-parameters
          '(("mail\\..*"
             (gnus-show-threads nil)
             (gnus-use-scoring nil))
            ("^nnimap:\\(foo.bar\\)$"
             (to-group . "\\1"))))
    ```
  - Unread count correct in nnimap groups.

    The estimated number of unread articles in the group buffer should now be correct for nnimap groups. This is achieved by calling **nnimap-fixup-unread-after-getting-new-news** from the **gnus-setup-news-hook** (called on startup) and **gnus-after-getting-new-news-hook** (called after getting new mail). If you have modified those variables from the default, you may want to add **nnimap-fixup-unread-after-getting-new-news** again. If you were happy with the estimate and want to save some (minimal) time when getting new mail, remove the function.

- Group names are treated as UTF-8 by default.

  This is supposedly what USEFOR wanted to migrate to. See `gnus-group-name-charset-group-alist` and `gnus-group-name-charset-method-alist` for customization.

- `gnus-group-charset-alist` and `gnus-group-ignored-charsets-alist`.

  The regexps in these variables are compared with full group names instead of real group names in 5.8. Users who customize these variables should change those regexps accordingly. For example:

  ```
  ("^han\\>" euc-kr) -> ("\\(^\\|:\\)han\\>" euc-kr)
  ```

- Old intermediate incoming mail files (`Incoming*`) are deleted after a couple of days, not immediately. See Section 6.4.4.3 [Mail Source Customization], page 160. (New in Gnus 5.10.10 / Emacs 22.2)

- Changes in summary and article mode

  - *F* (`gnus-article-followup-with-original`) and *R* (`gnus-article-reply-with-original`) only yank the text in the region if the region is active.

  - In draft groups, *e* is now bound to `gnus-draft-edit-message`. Use *B w* for `gnus-summary-edit-article` instead.

  - Article Buttons

    More buttons for URLs, mail addresses, Message-IDs, Info links, man pages and Emacs or Gnus related references. See Section 3.18.6 [Article Buttons], page 92. The variables `gnus-button-*-level` can be used to control the appearance of all article buttons. See Section 3.18.7 [Article Button Levels], page 94.

  - Single-part yenc encoded attachments can be decoded.

  - Picons

    The picons code has been reimplemented to work in GNU Emacs—some of the previous options have been removed or renamed.

    Picons are small "personal icons" representing users, domain and newsgroups, which can be displayed in the Article buffer. See Section 9.14.4 [Picons], page 265.

  - If the new option `gnus-treat-body-boundary` is non-`nil`, a boundary line is drawn at the end of the headers.

  - Signed article headers (X-PGP-Sig) can be verified with *W p*.

  - The Summary Buffer uses an arrow in the fringe to indicate the current article. Use `(setq gnus-summary-display-arrow nil)` to disable it.

  - Warn about email replies to news

    Do you often find yourself replying to news by email by mistake? Then the new option `gnus-confirm-mail-reply-to-news` is just the thing for you.

  - If the new option `gnus-summary-display-while-building` is non-`nil`, the summary buffer is shown and updated as it's being built.

  - Gnus supports RFC 2369 mailing list headers, and adds a number of related commands in mailing list groups. See Section 3.32 [Mailing List], page 115.

  - The Date header can be displayed in a format that can be read aloud in English. See Section 3.18.8 [Article Date], page 94.

- diffs are automatically highlighted in groups matching `mm-uu-diff-groups-regexp`

- Better handling of Microsoft citation styles

  Gnus now tries to recognize the mangled header block that some Microsoft mailers use to indicate that the rest of the message is a citation, even though it is not quoted in any way. The variable `gnus-cite-unsightly-citation-regexp` matches the start of these citations.

  The new command `W Y f` (`gnus-article-outlook-deuglify-article`) allows deuglifying broken Outlook (Express) articles.

- `gnus-article-skip-boring`

  If you set `gnus-article-skip-boring` to `t`, then Gnus will not scroll down to show you a page that contains only boring text, which by default means cited text and signature. You can customize what is skippable using `gnus-article-boring-faces`.

  This feature is especially useful if you read many articles that consist of a little new content at the top with a long, untrimmed message cited below.

- Smileys (':-)', ';-)' etc.) are now displayed graphically in Emacs too.

  Put (`setq gnus-treat-display-smileys nil`) in `~/.gnus.el` to disable it.

- Face headers handling. See Section 9.14.2 [Face], page 264.

- In the summary buffer, the new command `/ N` inserts new messages and `/ o` inserts old messages.

- Gnus decodes morse encoded messages if you press `W m`.

- `gnus-summary-line-format`

  The default value changed to '`%U%R%z%I%(%[%4L: %-23,23f%]%) %s\n`'. Moreover `gnus-extra-headers`, `nnmail-extra-headers` and `gnus-ignored-from-addresses` changed their default so that the users name will be replaced by the recipient's name or the group name posting to for NNTP groups.

- Deleting of attachments.

  The command `gnus-mime-save-part-and-strip` (bound to `C-o` on MIME buttons) saves a part and replaces the part with an external one. `gnus-mime-delete-part` (bound to `d` on MIME buttons) removes a part. It works only on back ends that support editing.

- `gnus-default-charset`

  The default value is determined from the `current-language-environment` variable, instead of `iso-8859-1`. Also the '`.*`' item in `gnus-group-charset-alist` is removed.

- Printing capabilities are enhanced.

  Gnus supports Muttprint natively with `O P` from the Summary and Article buffers. Also, each individual MIME part can be printed using `p` on the MIME button.

- Extended format specs.

  Format spec '`%&user-date;`' is added into `gnus-summary-line-format-alist`. Also, user defined extended format specs are supported. The extended format specs look like '`%u&foo;`', which invokes function `gnus-user-format-function-foo`. Because '`&`' is used as the escape character, old user defined format '`%u&`' is no longer supported.

- `/ *` (`gnus-summary-limit-include-cached`) is rewritten.

  It was aliased to `Y c` (`gnus-summary-insert-cached-articles`). The new function filters out other articles.

- Some limiting commands accept a `C-u` prefix to negate the match.

  If `C-u` is used on subject, author or extra headers, i.e., `/ s`, `/ a`, and `/ x` (`gnus-summary-limit-to-{subject,author,extra}`) respectively, the result will be to display all articles that do not match the expression.

- Gnus inlines external parts (message/external).

- Changes in Message mode and related Gnus features

  - Delayed articles

    You can delay the sending of a message with `C-c C-j` in the Message buffer. The messages are delivered at specified time. This is useful for sending yourself reminders. See Section 3.6 [Delayed Articles], page 56.

  - If the new option `nnml-use-compressed-files` is non-`nil`, the nnml back end allows compressed message files.

  - The new option `gnus-gcc-mark-as-read` automatically marks Gcc articles as read.

  - Externalizing of attachments

    If `gnus-gcc-externalize-attachments` or `message-fcc-externalize-attachments` is non-`nil`, attach local files as external parts.

  - The envelope sender address can be customized when using Sendmail. See Section "Mail Variables" in *Message Manual*.

  - Gnus no longer generate the Sender: header automatically.

    Earlier it was generated when the user configurable email address was different from the Gnus guessed default user address. As the guessing algorithm is rarely correct these days, and (more controversially) the only use of the Sender: header was to check if you are entitled to cancel/supersede news (which is now solved by Cancel Locks instead, see another entry), generation of the header has been disabled by default. See the variables `message-required-headers`, `message-required-news-headers`, and `message-required-mail-headers`.

  - Features from third party `message-utils.el` added to `message.el`.

    Message now asks if you wish to remove '`(was: <old subject>)`' from subject lines (see `message-subject-trailing-was-query`). `C-c M-m` and `C-c M-f` inserts markers indicating included text. `C-c C-f a` adds a X-No-Archive: header. `C-c C-f x` inserts appropriate headers and a note in the body for cross-postings and followups (see the variables `message-cross-post-*`).

  - References and X-Draft-From headers are no longer generated when you start composing messages and `message-generate-headers-first` is `nil`.

  - Easy inclusion of X-Faces headers. See Section 9.14.1 [X-Face], page 263.

- Group Carbon Copy (GCC) quoting

  To support groups that contains SPC and other weird characters, groups are quoted before they are placed in the Gcc: header. This means variables such as **gnus-message-archive-group** should no longer contain quote characters to make groups containing SPC work. Also, if you are using the string 'nnml:foo, nnml:bar' (indicating Gcc into two groups) you must change it to return the list ("nnml:foo" "nnml:bar"), otherwise the Gcc: line will be quoted incorrectly. Note that returning the string 'nnml:foo, nnml:bar' was incorrect earlier, it just didn't generate any problems since it was inserted directly.

- `message-insinuate-rmail`

  Adding (`message-insinuate-rmail`) and (`setq mail-user-agent 'gnus-user-agent`) in .emacs convinces Rmail to compose, reply and forward messages in message-mode, where you can enjoy the power of MML.

- `message-minibuffer-local-map`

  The line below enables BBDB in resending a message:

  ```
  (define-key message-minibuffer-local-map [(tab)]
    'bbdb-complete-name)
  ```

- `gnus-posting-styles`

  Add a new format of match like

  ```
  ((header "to" "larsi.*org")
   (Organization "Somewhere, Inc."))
  ```

  The old format like the lines below is obsolete, but still accepted.

  ```
  (header "to" "larsi.*org"
          (Organization "Somewhere, Inc."))
  ```

- `message-ignored-news-headers` and `message-ignored-mail-headers`

  'X-Draft-From' and 'X-Gnus-Agent-Meta-Information' have been added into these two variables. If you customized those, perhaps you need add those two headers too.

- Gnus supports the "format=flowed" (RFC 2646) parameter. On composing messages, it is enabled by **use-hard-newlines**. Decoding format=flowed was present but not documented in earlier versions.

- The option **mm-fill-flowed** can be used to disable treatment of "format=flowed" messages. Also, flowed text is disabled when sending inline PGP signed messages. See Section "Flowed text" in *The Emacs MIME Manual*. (New in Gnus 5.10.7)

- Gnus supports the generation of RFC 2298 Disposition Notification requests.

  This is invoked with the *C-c M-n* key binding from message mode.

- Message supports the Importance: (RFC 2156) header.

  In the message buffer, *C-c C-f C-i* or *C-c C-u* cycles through the valid values.

- Gnus supports Cancel Locks in News.

  This means a header 'Cancel-Lock' is inserted in news posting. It is used to determine if you wrote an article or not (for canceling and superseding). Gnus generates a random password string the first time you post a message, and saves it in your `~/.emacs` using the Custom system. While the variable is called `canlock-password`, it is not security sensitive data. Publishing your canlock string on the web will not allow anyone to be able to anything she could not already do. The behavior can be changed by customizing `message-insert-canlock`.

- Gnus supports PGP (RFC 1991/2440), PGP/MIME (RFC 2015/3156) and S/MIME (RFC 2630–2633).

  It needs an external S/MIME and OpenPGP implementation, but no additional Lisp libraries. This add several menu items to the Attachments menu, and `C-c RET` key bindings, when composing messages. This also obsoletes `gnus-article-hide-pgp-hook`.

- MML (Mime compose) prefix changed from `M-m` to `C-c C-m`.

  This change was made to avoid conflict with the standard binding of `back-to-indentation`, which is also useful in message mode.

- The default for `message-forward-show-mml` changed to the symbol `best`.

  The behavior for the `best` value is to show MML (i.e., convert to MIME) when appropriate. MML will not be used when forwarding signed or encrypted messages, as the conversion invalidate the digital signature.

- If `auto-compression-mode` is enabled, attachments are automatically decompressed when activated.

- Support for non-ASCII domain names

  Message supports non-ASCII domain names in From:, To: and Cc: and will query you whether to perform encoding when you try to send a message. The variable `message-use-idna` controls this. Gnus will also decode non-ASCII domain names in From:, To: and Cc: when you view a message. The variable `gnus-use-idna` controls this.

- You can now drag and drop attachments to the Message buffer. See `mml-dnd-protocol-alist` and `mml-dnd-attach-options`. See Section "MIME" in *Message Manual*.

- `auto-fill-mode` is enabled by default in Message mode. See `message-fill-column`. See Section "Message Headers" in *Message Manual*.

- Changes in back ends

  - Gnus can display RSS newsfeeds as a newsgroup. See Section 6.5.3 [RSS], page 185.

  - The nndoc back end now supports mailman digests and exim bounces.

  - Gnus supports Maildir groups.

    Gnus includes a new back end `nnmaildir.el`. See Section 6.4.13.5 [Maildir], page 175.

  - The nnml and nnfolder back ends store marks for each groups.

    This makes it possible to take backup of nnml/nnfolder servers/groups separately of `~/.newsrc.eld`, while preserving marks. It also makes it possible to share articles and marks between users (without sharing the `~/.newsrc.eld` file) within, e.g., a department. It works by storing the marks stored in `~/.newsrc.eld` in a per-group file `.marks` (for nnml) and *groupname*`.mrk` (for nnfolder, named *group-name*). If the nnml/nnfolder is moved to another machine, Gnus will automatically use the `.marks` or `.mrk` file instead of the information in `~/.newsrc.eld`. The new server variables `nnml-marks-is-evil` and `nnfolder-marks-is-evil` can be used to disable this feature.

- Appearance

  - The menu bar item (in Group and Summary buffer) named "Misc" has been re-named to "Gnus".

  - The menu bar item (in Message mode) named "MML" has been renamed to "Attachments". Note that this menu also contains security related stuff, like signing and encryption (see Section "Security" in *Message Manual*).

  - The tool bars have been updated to use GNOME icons in Group, Summary and Message mode. You can also customize the tool bars: *M-x customize-apropos RET -tool-bar$* should get you started. This is a new feature in Gnus 5.10.10. (Only for Emacs, not in XEmacs.)

  - The tool bar icons are now (de)activated correctly in the group buffer, see the variable `gnus-group-update-tool-bar`. Its default value depends on your Emacs version. This is a new feature in Gnus 5.10.9.

- Miscellaneous changes

  - `gnus-agent`

    The Gnus Agent has seen a major updated and is now enabled by default, and all nntp and nnimap servers from `gnus-select-method` and `gnus-secondary-select-method` are agentized by default. Earlier only the server in `gnus-select-method` was agentized by the default, and the agent was disabled by default. When the agent is enabled, headers are now also retrieved from the Agent cache instead of the back ends when possible. Earlier this only happened in the unplugged state. You can enroll or remove servers with *J a* and *J r* in the server buffer. Gnus will not download articles into the Agent cache, unless you instruct it to do so, though, by using *J u* or *J s* from the Group buffer. You revert to the old behavior of having the Agent disabled with (setq `gnus-agent` nil). Note that putting (`gnus-agentize`) in `~/.gnus.el` is not needed any more.

  - Gnus reads the NOV and articles in the Agent if plugged.

    If one reads an article while plugged, and the article already exists in the Agent, it won't get downloaded once more. (setq `gnus-agent-cache` nil) reverts to the old behavior.

  - Dired integration

    `gnus-dired-minor-mode` (see Section 9.19 [Other modes], page 298) installs key bindings in dired buffers to send a file as an attachment, open a file using the appropriate mailcap entry, and print a file using the mailcap entry.

  - The format spec %C for positioning point has changed to %*.

  - `gnus-slave-unplugged`

    A new command which starts Gnus offline in slave mode.

11.2.8.7 No Gnus

New features in No Gnus:

- Supported Emacs versions The following Emacs versions are supported by No Gnus:
    - Emacs 22 and up
    - XEmacs 21.4
    - XEmacs 21.5
    - SXEmacs
- Installation changes
    - Upgrading from previous (stable) version if you have used No Gnus.

      If you have tried No Gnus (the unstable Gnus branch leading to this release) but went back to a stable version, be careful when upgrading to this version. In particular, you will probably want to remove the `~/News/marks` directory (perhaps selectively), so that flags are read from your `~/.newsrc.eld` instead of from the stale marks file, where this release will store flags for nntp. See a later entry for more information about nntp marks. Note that downgrading isn't safe in general.

    - Incompatibility when switching from Emacs 23 to Emacs 22 In Emacs 23, Gnus uses Emacs's new internal coding system `utf-8-emacs` for saving articles drafts and `~/.newsrc.eld`. These files may not be read correctly in Emacs 22 and below. If you want to use Gnus across different Emacs versions, you may set `mm-auto-save-coding-system` to `emacs-mule`.

    - Lisp files are now installed in `.../site-lisp/gnus/` by default. It defaulted to `.../site-lisp/` formerly. In addition to this, the new installer issues a warning if other Gnus installations which will shadow the latest one are detected. You can then remove those shadows manually or remove them using `make remove-installed-shadows`.

    - The installation directory name is allowed to have spaces and/or tabs.
- New packages and libraries within Gnus
    - New version of `nnimap`

      `nnimap` has been reimplemented in a mostly-compatible way. See the Gnus manual for a description of the new interface. In particular, `nnimap-inbox` and the client side split method has changed.

    - Gnus includes the Emacs Lisp SASL library.

      This provides a clean API to SASL mechanisms from within Emacs. The user visible aspects of this, compared to the earlier situation, include support for DIGEST-MD5 and NTLM. See Section "Emacs SASL" in *Emacs SASL*.

    - ManageSieve connections uses the SASL library by default.

      The primary change this brings is support for DIGEST-MD5 and NTLM, when the server supports it.

    - Gnus includes a password cache mechanism in password.el.

      It is enabled by default (see `password-cache`), with a short timeout of 16 seconds (see `password-cache-expiry`). If PGG is used as the PGP back end, the PGP passphrase is managed by this mechanism. Passwords for ManageSieve connections are managed by this mechanism, after querying the user about whether to do so.

- Using EasyPG with Gnus When EasyPG, is available, Gnus will use it instead of PGG. EasyPG is an Emacs user interface to GNU Privacy Guard. See Section "EasyPG Assistant user's manual" in *EasyPG Assistant user's manual*. EasyPG is included in Emacs 23 and available separately as well.

- Changes in group mode
  - Symbols like `gcc-self` now have the same precedence rules in `gnus-parameters` as other "real" variables: The last match wins instead of the first match.
  - Old intermediate incoming mail files (`Incoming*`) are deleted after a couple of days, not immediately. See Section 6.4.4.3 [Mail Source Customization], page 160. (New in Gnus 5.10.10 / No Gnus 0.8)

- Changes in summary and article mode
  - There's now only one variable that determines how HTML is rendered: `mm-text-html-renderer`.
  - Gnus now supports sticky article buffers. Those are article buffers that are not reused when you select another article. See Section 3.14 [Sticky Articles], page 75.
  - Gnus can selectively display 'text/html' articles with a WWW browser with *K H*. See Section 3.19 [MIME Commands], page 96.
  - International host names (IDNA) can now be decoded inside article bodies using *W i* (`gnus-summary-idna-message`). This requires that GNU Libidn (`http://www.gnu.org/software/libidn/`) has been installed.
  - The non-ASCII group names handling has been much improved. The back ends that fully support non-ASCII group names are now `nntp`, `nnml`, and `nnrss`. Also the agent, the cache, and the marks features work with those back ends. See Section 2.17 [Non-ASCII Group Names], page 38.
  - Gnus now displays DNS master files sent as text/dns using dns-mode.
  - Gnus supports new limiting commands in the Summary buffer: */r* (`gnus-summary-limit-to-replied`) and */R* (`gnus-summary-limit-to-recipient`). See Section 3.8 [Limiting], page 63.
  - You can now fetch all ticked articles from the server using *Y t* (`gnus-summary-insert-ticked-articles`). See Section 3.27.3 [Summary Generation Commands], page 110.
  - Gnus supports a new sort command in the Summary buffer: *C-c C-s C-t* (`gnus-summary-sort-by-recipient`). See Section 3.22 [Summary Sorting], page 101.
  - S/MIME now features LDAP user certificate searches. You need to configure the server in `smime-ldap-host-list`.
  - URLs inside OpenPGP headers are retrieved and imported to your PGP key ring when you click on them.
  - Picons can be displayed right from the textual address, see `gnus-picon-style`. See Section 9.14.4 [Picons], page 265.
  - ANSI SGR control sequences can be transformed using *W A*.

    ANSI sequences are used in some Chinese hierarchies for highlighting articles (`gnus-article-treat-ansi-sequences`).

- Gnus now MIME decodes articles even when they lack "MIME-Version" header. This changes the default of `gnus-article-loose-mime`.

- `gnus-decay-scores` can be a regexp matching score files. For example, set it to '`\\.ADAPT\\`'' and only adaptive score files will be decayed. See Section 7.16 [Score Decays], page 234.

- Strings prefixing to the `To` and `Newsgroup` headers in summary lines when using `gnus-ignored-from-addresses` can be customized with `gnus-summary-to-prefix` and `gnus-summary-newsgroup-prefix`. See Section 3.1.2 [To From Newsgroups], page 47.

- You can replace MIME parts with external bodies. See `gnus-mime-replace-part` and `gnus-article-replace-part`. See Section 3.19 [MIME Commands], page 96, Section 4.2 [Using MIME], page 117.

- The option `mm-fill-flowed` can be used to disable treatment of format=flowed messages. Also, flowed text is disabled when sending inline PGP signed messages. See Section "Flowed text" in *The Emacs MIME Manual*. (New in Gnus 5.10.7)

- Now the new command `S W` (`gnus-article-wide-reply-with-original`) for a wide reply in the article buffer yanks a text that is in the active region, if it is set, as well as the `R` (`gnus-article-reply-with-original`) command. Note that the `R` command in the article buffer no longer accepts a prefix argument, which was used to make it do a wide reply. See Section 4.5 [Article Keymap], page 123.

- The new command `C-h b` (`gnus-article-describe-bindings`) used in the article buffer now shows not only the article commands but also the real summary commands that are accessible from the article buffer.

- Changes in Message mode
  - Gnus now defaults to saving all outgoing messages in per-month nnfolder archives.

  - Gnus now supports the "hashcash" client puzzle anti-spam mechanism. Use (`setq message-generate-hashcash t`) to enable. See Section 9.16.4 [Hashcash], page 271.

  - You can now drag and drop attachments to the Message buffer. See `mml-dnd-protocol-alist` and `mml-dnd-attach-options`. See Section "MIME" in *Message Manual*.

  - The option `message-yank-empty-prefix` now controls how empty lines are prefixed in cited text. See Section "Insertion Variables" in *Message Manual*.

  - Gnus uses narrowing to hide headers in Message buffers. The `References` header is hidden by default. To make all headers visible, use (`setq message-hidden-headers nil`). See Section "Message Headers" in *Message Manual*.

  - You can highlight different levels of citations like in the article buffer. See `gnus-message-highlight-citation`.

  - `auto-fill-mode` is enabled by default in Message mode. See `message-fill-column`. See Section "Message Headers" in *Message Manual*.

  - You can now store signature files in a special directory named `message-signature-directory`.

- The option `message-citation-line-format` controls the format of the "Whomever writes:" line. You need to set `message-citation-line-function` to `message-insert-formatted-citation-line` as well.

- Changes in Browse Server mode
  - Gnus' sophisticated subscription methods are now available in Browse Server buffers as well using the variable `gnus-browse-subscribe-newsgroup-method`.

- Changes in back ends
  - The nntp back end stores article marks in `~/News/marks`.

    The directory can be changed using the (customizable) variable `nntp-marks-directory`, and marks can be disabled using the (back end) variable `nntp-marks-is-evil`. The advantage of this is that you can copy `~/News/marks` (using rsync, scp or whatever) to another Gnus installation, and it will realize what articles you have read and marked. The data in `~/News/marks` has priority over the same data in `~/.newsrc.eld`.

  - You can import and export your RSS subscriptions from OPML files. See Section 6.5.3 [RSS], page 185.

  - IMAP identity (RFC 2971) is supported.

    By default, Gnus does not send any information about itself, but you can customize it using the variable `nnimap-id`.

  - The `nnrss` back end now supports multilingual text. Non-ASCII group names for the `nnrss` groups are also supported. See Section 6.5.3 [RSS], page 185.

  - Retrieving mail with POP3 is supported over SSL/TLS and with StartTLS.

  - The nnml back end allows other compression programs beside `gzip` for compressed message files. See Section 6.4.13.3 [Mail Spool], page 174.

  - The nnml back end supports group compaction.

    This feature, accessible via the functions `gnus-group-compact-group` (*G z* in the group buffer) and `gnus-server-compact-server` (*z* in the server buffer) renumbers all articles in a group, starting from 1 and removing gaps. As a consequence, you get a correct total article count (until messages are deleted again).

- Appearance
  - The tool bar has been updated to use GNOME icons. You can also customize the tool bars: *M-x customize-apropos RET -tool-bar$* should get you started. (Only for Emacs, not in XEmacs.)

  - The tool bar icons are now (de)activated correctly in the group buffer, see the variable `gnus-group-update-tool-bar`. Its default value depends on your Emacs version.

  - You can change the location of XEmacs's toolbars in Gnus buffers. See `gnus-use-toolbar` and `message-use-toolbar`.

- Miscellaneous changes
  - Having edited the select-method for the foreign server in the server buffer is immediately reflected to the subscription of the groups which use the server in question. For instance, if you change `nntp-via-address` into 'bar.example.com' from

'foo.example.com', Gnus will connect to the news host by way of the intermediate host 'bar.example.com' from next time.

- The all.SCORE file can be edited from the group buffer using W e.

- You can set gnus-mark-copied-or-moved-articles-as-expirable to a non-nil value so that articles that have been read may be marked as expirable automatically when copying or moving them to a group that has auto-expire turned on. The default is nil and copying and moving of articles behave as before; i.e., the expirable marks will be unchanged except that the marks will be removed when copying or moving articles to a group that has not turned auto-expire on. See Section 6.4.9 [Expiring Mail], page 168.

- NoCeM support has been removed.

- Carpal mode has been removed.

11.2.8.8 Ma Gnus

I'm sure there will be lots of text here. It's really spelled Gnus.

New features in Ma Gnus:

- Installation changes
  - Lisp source files and info files to be installed will be compressed by gzip by default.

    If you don't want those files to be compressed, use the configure option '--without-compress-install'. Lisp source files that don't have the compiled elc version in the installation directory will not be compressed.

- Changes in summary and article mode
  - By default, MIME part buttons for attachments (if any) will appear in the end of the article header in addition to the bottom of the article body, so you can easily find them without scrolling the article again and again. See Section 3.19 [MIME Commands], page 96.

- Changes in Message mode and related Gnus features
  - The new hooks gnus-gcc-pre-body-encode-hook and gnus-gcc-post-body-encode-hook are run before/after encoding the message body of the Gcc copy of a sent message. See See Section 5.5 [Archived Messages], page 128.

11.3 The Manual

This manual was generated from a TeXinfo file and then run through either `texi2dvi` to get what you hold in your hands now.

The following conventions have been used:

1. This is a 'string'
2. This is a *keystroke*
3. This is a `file`
4. This is a `symbol`

So if I were to say "set `flargnoze` to 'yes'", that would mean:

```
(setq flargnoze "yes")
```

If I say "set `flumphel` to yes", that would mean:

```
(setq flumphel 'yes)
```

'yes' and yes are two *very* different things—don't ever get them confused.

11.4 On Writing Manuals

I guess most manuals are written after-the-fact; documenting a program that's already there. This is not how this manual is written. When implementing something, I write the manual entry for that something straight away. I then see that it's difficult to explain the functionality, so I write how it's supposed to be, and then I change the implementation. Writing the documentation and writing the code go hand in hand.

This, of course, means that this manual has no, or little, flow. It documents absolutely everything in Gnus, but often not where you're looking for it. It is a reference manual, and not a guide to how to get started with Gnus.

That would be a totally different book, that should be written using the reference manual as source material. It would look quite different.

11.5 Terminology

news   This is what you are supposed to use this thing for—reading news. News is generally fetched from a nearby NNTP server, and is generally publicly available to everybody. If you post news, the entire world is likely to read just what you have written, and they'll all snigger mischievously. Behind your back.

mail   Everything that's delivered to you personally is mail. Some news/mail readers (like Gnus) blur the distinction between mail and news, but there is a difference. Mail is private. News is public. Mailing is not posting, and replying is not following up.

reply   Send a mail to the person who has written what you are reading.

follow up   Post an article to the current newsgroup responding to the article you are reading.

back end   Gnus considers mail and news to be mostly the same, really. The only difference is how to access the actual articles. News articles are commonly fetched via the protocol NNTP, whereas mail messages could be read from a file on the local disk. The internal architecture of Gnus thus comprises a "front end" and a number of "back ends". Internally, when you enter a group (by hitting `RET`, say), you thereby invoke a function in the front end in Gnus. The front end then "talks" to a back end and says things like "Give me the list of articles in the foo group" or "Show me article number 4711".

So a back end mainly defines either a protocol (the `nntp` back end accesses news via NNTP, the `nnimap` back end accesses mail via IMAP) or a file format and directory layout (the `nnspool` back end accesses news via the common "spool directory" format, the `nnml` back end access mail via a file format and directory layout that's quite similar).

Gnus does not handle the underlying media, so to speak—this is all done by the back ends. A back end is a collection of functions to access the articles.

However, sometimes the term "back end" is also used where "server" would have been more appropriate. And then there is the term "select method" which can mean either. The Gnus terminology can be quite confusing.

native   Gnus will always use one method (and back end) as the *native*, or default, way of getting news. Groups from the native select method have names like 'gnu.emacs.gnus'.

foreign   You can also have any number of foreign groups active at the same time. These are groups that use non-native non-secondary back ends for getting news. Foreign groups have names like 'nntp+news.gmane.org:gmane.emacs.gnus.devel'.

secondary   Secondary back ends are somewhere half-way between being native and being foreign, but they mostly act like they are native, but they, too have names like 'nntp+news.gmane.org:gmane.emacs.gnus.devel'.

article   A message that has been posted as news.

mail message
  A message that has been mailed.

message   A mail message or news article

head   The top part of a message, where administrative information (etc.) is put.

body   The rest of an article. Everything not in the head is in the body.

header   A line from the head of an article.

headers   A collection of such lines, or a collection of heads. Or even a collection of NOV lines.

NOV   NOV stands for News OverView, which is a type of news server header which provide datas containing the condensed header information of articles. They are produced by the server itself; in the `nntp` back end Gnus uses the ones that the NNTP server makes, but Gnus makes them by itself for some backends (in particular, `nnml`).

          When Gnus enters a group, it asks the back end for the headers of all unread articles in the group. Most servers support the News OverView format, which is more compact and much faster to read and parse than the normal HEAD format.

          The NOV data consist of one or more text lines (see Section "Motion by Text Lines" in The Emacs Lisp Reference Manual) where each line has the header information of one article. The header information is a tab-separated series of the header's contents including an article number, a subject, an author, a date, a message-id, references, etc.

          Those data enable Gnus to generate summary lines quickly. However, if the server does not support NOV or you disable it purposely or for some reason, Gnus will try to generate the header information by parsing each article's headers one by one. It will take time. Therefore, it is not usually a good idea to set nn*-nov-is-evil (see Section 11.6.1 [Slow/Expensive Connection], page 332) to a non-`nil` value unless you know that the server makes wrong NOV data.

level   Each group is subscribed at some level or other (1–9). The ones that have a lower level are "more" subscribed than the groups with a higher level. In fact, groups on levels 1–5 are considered subscribed; 6–7 are unsubscribed; 8 are zombies; and 9 are killed. Commands for listing groups and scanning for new articles will all use the numeric prefix as working level.

killed groups
  No information on killed groups is stored or updated, which makes killed groups much easier to handle than subscribed groups.

zombie groups
  Just like killed groups, only slightly less dead.

active file The news server has to keep track of what articles it carries, and what groups exist. All this information in stored in the active file, which is rather large, as you might surmise.

bogus groups

> A group that exists in the `.newsrc` file, but isn't known to the server (i.e., it isn't in the active file), is a *bogus group*. This means that the group probably doesn't exist (any more).

activating   The act of asking the server for info on a group and computing the number of unread articles is called *activating the group*. Un-activated groups are listed with '*' in the group buffer.

spool   News servers store their articles locally in one fashion or other. One old-fashioned storage method is to have just one file per article. That's called a "traditional spool".

server   A machine one can connect to and get news (or mail) from.

select method

> A structure that specifies the back end, the server and the virtual server settings.

virtual server

> A named select method. Since a select method defines all there is to know about connecting to a (physical) server, taking the thing as a whole is a virtual server.

washing   Taking a buffer and running it through a filter of some sort. The result will (more often than not) be cleaner and more pleasing than the original.

ephemeral groups

> Most groups store data on what articles you have read. *Ephemeral* groups are groups that will have no data stored—when you exit the group, it'll disappear into the aether.

solid groups

> This is the opposite of ephemeral groups. All groups listed in the group buffer are solid groups.

sparse articles

> These are article placeholders shown in the summary buffer when `gnus-build-sparse-threads` has been switched on.

threading   To put responses to articles directly after the articles they respond to—in a hierarchical fashion.

root   The first article in a thread is the root. It is the ancestor of all articles in the thread.

parent   An article that has responses.

child   An article that responds to a different article—its parent.

digest   A collection of messages in one file. The most common digest format is specified by RFC 1153.

splitting   The action of sorting your emails according to certain rules. Sometimes incorrectly called mail filtering.

11.6 Customization

All variables are properly documented elsewhere in this manual. This section is designed to give general pointers on how to customize Gnus for some quite common situations.

11.6.1 Slow/Expensive Connection

If you run Emacs on a machine locally, and get your news from a machine over some very thin strings, you want to cut down on the amount of data Gnus has to get from the server.

`gnus-read-active-file`

> Set this to `nil`, which will inhibit Gnus from requesting the entire active file from the server. This file is often very large. You also have to set `gnus-check-new-newsgroups` and `gnus-check-bogus-newsgroups` to `nil` to make sure that Gnus doesn't suddenly decide to fetch the active file anyway.

`gnus-nov-is-evil`

> Usually this one must *always* be `nil` (which is the default). If, for example, you wish to not use NOV (see Section 11.5 [Terminology], page 329) with the `nntp` back end (see Section 3.29 [Crosspost Handling], page 112), set `nntp-nov-is-evil` to a non-`nil` value instead of setting this. But you normally do not need to set `nntp-nov-is-evil` since Gnus by itself will detect whether the NNTP server supports NOV. Anyway, grabbing article headers from the NNTP server will not be very fast if you tell Gnus not to use NOV.
>
> As the variables for the other back ends, there are `nndiary-nov-is-evil`, `nndir-nov-is-evil`, `nnfolder-nov-is-evil`, `nnimap-nov-is-evil`, `nnml-nov-is-evil`, and `nnspool-nov-is-evil`. Note that a non-`nil` value for `gnus-nov-is-evil` overrides all those variables.

11.6.2 Slow Terminal Connection

Let's say you use your home computer for dialing up the system that runs Emacs and Gnus. If your modem is slow, you want to reduce (as much as possible) the amount of data sent over the wires.

`gnus-auto-center-summary`

> Set this to `nil` to inhibit Gnus from re-centering the summary buffer all the time. If it is `vertical`, do only vertical re-centering. If it is neither `nil` nor `vertical`, do both horizontal and vertical recentering.

`gnus-visible-headers`

> Cut down on the headers included in the articles to the minimum. You can, in fact, make do without them altogether—most of the useful data is in the summary buffer, anyway. Set this variable to '^NEVVVVER' or 'From:', or whatever you feel you need.
>
> Use the following to enable all the available hiding features:

```
(setq gnus-treat-hide-headers 'head
      gnus-treat-hide-signature t
      gnus-treat-hide-citation t)
```

`gnus-use-full-window`

> By setting this to `nil`, you can make all the windows smaller. While this doesn't really cut down much generally, it means that you have to see smaller portions of articles before deciding that you didn't want to read them anyway.

`gnus-thread-hide-subtree`

> If this is non-`nil`, all threads in the summary buffer will be hidden initially.

`gnus-updated-mode-lines`

> If this is `nil`, Gnus will not put information in the buffer mode lines, which might save some time.

11.6.3 Little Disk Space

The startup files can get rather large, so you may want to cut their sizes a bit if you are running out of space.

`gnus-save-newsrc-file`

> If this is `nil`, Gnus will never save `.newsrc`—it will only save `.newsrc.eld`. This means that you will not be able to use any other newsreaders than Gnus. This variable is `t` by default.

`gnus-read-newsrc-file`

> If this is `nil`, Gnus will never read `.newsrc`—it will only read `.newsrc.eld`. This means that you will not be able to use any other newsreaders than Gnus. This variable is `t` by default.

`gnus-save-killed-list`

> If this is `nil`, Gnus will not save the list of dead groups. You should also set `gnus-check-new-newsgroups` to `ask-server` and `gnus-check-bogus-newsgroups` to `nil` if you set this variable to `nil`. This variable is `t` by default.

11.6.4 Slow Machine

If you have a slow machine, or are just really impatient, there are a few things you can do to make Gnus run faster.

Set `gnus-check-new-newsgroups` and `gnus-check-bogus-newsgroups` to `nil` to make startup faster.

Set `gnus-show-threads`, `gnus-use-cross-reference` and `gnus-nov-is-evil` to `nil` to make entering and exiting the summary buffer faster. Also see Section 11.6.1 [Slow/Expensive Connection], page 332.

11.7 Troubleshooting

Gnus works *so* well straight out of the box—I can't imagine any problems, really.

Ahem.

1. Make sure your computer is switched on.

2. Make sure that you really load the current Gnus version. If you have been running GNUS, you need to exit Emacs and start it up again before Gnus will work.

3. Try doing an *M-x gnus-version*. If you get something that looks like 'Ma Gnus v0.12' you have the right files loaded. Otherwise you have some old .el files lying around. Delete these.

4. Read the help group (*G h* in the group buffer) for a FAQ and a how-to.

5. Gnus works on many recursive structures, and in some extreme (and very rare) cases Gnus may recurse down "too deeply" and Emacs will beep at you. If this happens to you, set `max-lisp-eval-depth` to 500 or something like that.

If all else fails, report the problem as a bug.

If you find a bug in Gnus, you can report it with the *M-x gnus-bug* command. *M-x set-variable RET debug-on-error RET t RET*, and send me the backtrace. I will fix bugs, but I can only fix them if you send me a precise description as to how to reproduce the bug.

You really can never be too detailed in a bug report. Always use the *M-x gnus-bug* command when you make bug reports, even if it creates a 10Kb mail each time you use it, and even if you have sent me your environment 500 times before. I don't care. I want the full info each time.

It is also important to remember that I have no memory whatsoever. If you send a bug report, and I send you a reply, and then you just send back "No, it's not! Moron!", I will have no idea what you are insulting me about. Always over-explain everything. It's much easier for all of us—if I don't have all the information I need, I will just mail you and ask for more info, and everything takes more time.

If the problem you're seeing is very visual, and you can't quite explain it, copy the Emacs window to a file (with `xwd`, for instance), put it somewhere it can be reached, and include the URL of the picture in the bug report.

If you would like to contribute a patch to fix bugs or make improvements, please produce the patch using 'diff -u'.

If you want to debug your problem further before reporting, possibly in order to solve the problem yourself and send a patch, you can use edebug. Debugging Lisp code is documented in the Elisp manual (see Section "Debugging Lisp Programs" in *The GNU Emacs Lisp Reference Manual*). To get you started with edebug, consider if you discover some weird behavior when pressing *c*, the first step is to do *C-h k c* and click on the hyperlink (Emacs only) in the documentation buffer that leads you to the function definition, then press *M-x edebug-defun RET* with point inside that function, return to Gnus and press *c* to invoke the code. You will be placed in the lisp buffer and can single step using *SPC* and evaluate expressions using *M-:* or inspect variables using *C-h v*, abort execution with *q*, and resume execution with *c* or *g*.

Sometimes, a problem do not directly generate an elisp error but manifests itself by causing Gnus to be very slow. In these cases, you can use *M-x toggle-debug-on-quit* and press *C-g* when things are slow, and then try to analyze the backtrace (repeating the procedure helps isolating the real problem areas).

A fancier approach is to use the elisp profiler, ELP. The profiler is (or should be) fully documented elsewhere, but to get you started there are a few steps that need to be followed. First, instrument the part of Gnus you are interested in for profiling, e.g., *M-x elp-instrument-package RET gnus* or *M-x elp-instrument-package RET message*. Then perform the operation that is slow and press *M-x elp-results*. You will then see which operations that takes time, and can debug them further. If the entire operation takes much longer than the time spent in the slowest function in the profiler output, you probably profiled the wrong part of Gnus. To reset profiling statistics, use *M-x elp-reset-all*. *M-x elp-restore-all* is supposed to remove profiling, but given the complexities and dynamic code generation in Gnus, it might not always work perfectly.

If you just need help, you are better off asking on '**gnu.emacs.gnus**'. I'm not very helpful. You can also ask on the ding mailing list. Write to ding-request@gnus.org to subscribe.

11.8 Gnus Reference Guide

It is my hope that other people will figure out smart stuff that Gnus can do, and that other people will write those smart things as well. To facilitate that I thought it would be a good idea to describe the inner workings of Gnus. And some of the not-so-inner workings, while I'm at it.

You can never expect the internals of a program not to change, but I will be defining (in some details) the interface between Gnus and its back ends (this is written in stone), the format of the score files (ditto), data structures (some are less likely to change than others) and general methods of operation.

11.8.1 Gnus Utility Functions

When writing small functions to be run from hooks (and stuff), it's vital to have access to the Gnus internal functions and variables. Below is a list of the most common ones.

`gnus-newsgroup-name`
> This variable holds the name of the current newsgroup.

`gnus-find-method-for-group`
> A function that returns the select method for *group*.

`gnus-group-real-name`
> Takes a full (prefixed) Gnus group name, and returns the unprefixed name.

`gnus-group-prefixed-name`
> Takes an unprefixed group name and a select method, and returns the full (prefixed) Gnus group name.

`gnus-get-info`
> Returns the group info list for *group* (see Section 11.8.6 [Group Info], page 352).

`gnus-group-unread`
> The number of unread articles in *group*, or t if that is unknown.

`gnus-active`
> The active entry (i.e., a cons cell containing the lowest and highest article numbers) for *group*.

`gnus-set-active`
> Set the active entry for *group*.

`gnus-add-current-to-buffer-list`
> Adds the current buffer to the list of buffers to be killed on Gnus exit.

`gnus-continuum-version`
> Takes a Gnus version string as a parameter and returns a floating point number. Earlier versions will always get a lower number than later versions.

`gnus-group-read-only-p`
> Says whether *group* is read-only or not.

`gnus-news-group-p`
> Says whether *group* came from a news back end.

`gnus-ephemeral-group-p`
>   Says whether *group* is ephemeral or not.

`gnus-server-to-method`
>   Returns the select method corresponding to *server*.

`gnus-server-equal`
>   Says whether two virtual servers are essentially equal. For instance, two virtual servers may have server parameters in different order, but this function will consider them equal.

`gnus-group-native-p`
>   Says whether *group* is native or not.

`gnus-group-secondary-p`
>   Says whether *group* is secondary or not.

`gnus-group-foreign-p`
>   Says whether *group* is foreign or not.

`gnus-group-find-parameter`
>   Returns the parameter list of *group* (see Section 2.10 [Group Parameters], page 22). If given a second parameter, returns the value of that parameter for *group*.

`gnus-group-set-parameter`
>   Takes three parameters; *group*, *parameter* and *value*.

`gnus-narrow-to-body`
>   Narrows the current buffer to the body of the article.

`gnus-check-backend-function`
>   Takes two parameters, *function* and *group*. If the back end *group* comes from supports *function*, return non-`nil`.

>            ```
            (gnus-check-backend-function "request-scan" "nnml:misc")
            ⇒ t
            ```

`gnus-read-method`
>            Prompts the user for a select method.

## 11.8.2 Back End Interface

Gnus doesn't know anything about NNTP, spools, mail or virtual groups. It only knows how to talk to *virtual servers*. A virtual server is a *back end* and some *back end variables*. As examples of the first, we have **nntp**, **nnspool** and **nnmbox**. As examples of the latter we have **nntp-port-number** and **nnmbox-directory**.

When Gnus asks for information from a back end—say **nntp**—on something, it will normally include a virtual server name in the function parameters. (If not, the back end should use the "current" virtual server.) For instance, **nntp-request-list** takes a virtual server as its only (optional) parameter. If this virtual server hasn't been opened, the function should fail.

Note that a virtual server name has no relation to some physical server name. Take this example:
            ```

```
(nntp "odd-one"
      (nntp-address "ifi.uio.no")
      (nntp-port-number 4324))
```

Here the virtual server name is 'odd-one' while the name of the physical server is 'ifi.uio.no'.

The back ends should be able to switch between several virtual servers. The standard back ends implement this by keeping an alist of virtual server environments that they pull down/push up when needed.

There are two groups of interface functions: *required functions*, which must be present, and *optional functions*, which Gnus will always check for presence before attempting to call 'em.

All these functions are expected to return data in the buffer **nntp-server-buffer** (' ***nntpd***'), which is somewhat unfortunately named, but we'll have to live with it. When I talk about *resulting data*, I always refer to the data in that buffer. When I talk about *return value*, I talk about the function value returned by the function call. Functions that fail should return **nil** as the return value.

Some back ends could be said to be *server-forming* back ends, and some might be said not to be. The latter are back ends that generally only operate on one group at a time, and have no concept of "server"; they have a group, and they deliver info on that group and nothing more.

Gnus identifies each message by way of group name and article number. A few remarks about these article numbers might be useful. First of all, the numbers are positive integers. Secondly, it is normally not possible for later articles to "re-use" older article numbers without confusing Gnus. That is, if a group has ever contained a message numbered 42, then no other message may get that number, or Gnus will get mightily confused.[1] Third, article numbers must be assigned in order of arrival in the group; this is not necessarily the same as the date of the message.

The previous paragraph already mentions all the "hard" restrictions that article numbers must fulfill. But it seems that it might be useful to assign *consecutive* article numbers, for Gnus gets quite confused if there are holes in the article numbering sequence. However, due to the "no-reuse" restriction, holes cannot be avoided altogether. It's also useful for the article numbers to start at 1 to avoid running out of numbers as long as possible.

Note that by convention, back ends are named **nnsomething**, but Gnus also comes with some **nnotbackends**, such as **nnheader.el**, **nnmail.el** and **nnoo.el**.

In the examples and definitions I will refer to the imaginary back end **nnchoke**.

11.8.2.1 Required Back End Functions

(nnchoke-retrieve-headers ARTICLES &optional GROUP SERVER FETCH-OLD)
> *articles* is either a range of article numbers or a list of **Message-IDs**. Current back ends do not fully support either—only sequences (lists) of article numbers, and most back ends do not support retrieval of **Message-IDs**. But they should try for both.

---

[1] See the function **nnchoke-request-update-info**, Section 11.8.2.2 [Optional Back End Functions], page 342.

The result data should either be HEADs or NOV lines, and the result value should either be `headers` or `nov` to reflect this. This might later be expanded to `various`, which will be a mixture of HEADs and NOV lines, but this is currently not supported by Gnus.

If *fetch-old* is non-`nil` it says to try fetching "extra headers", in some meaning of the word. This is generally done by fetching (at most) *fetch-old* extra headers less than the smallest article number in `articles`, and filling the gaps as well. The presence of this parameter can be ignored if the back end finds it cumbersome to follow the request. If this is non-`nil` and not a number, do maximum fetches.

Here's an example HEAD:

```
221 1056 Article retrieved.
Path: ifi.uio.no!sturles
From: sturles@ifi.uio.no (Sturle Sunde)
Newsgroups: ifi.discussion
Subject: Re: Something very droll
Date: 27 Oct 1994 14:02:57 +0100
Organization: Dept. of Informatics, University of Oslo, Norway
Lines: 26
Message-ID: <38o8e1$a0o@holmenkollen.ifi.uio.no>
References: <38jdmq$4qu@visbur.ifi.uio.no>
NNTP-Posting-Host: holmenkollen.ifi.uio.no
.
```

So a `headers` return value would imply that there's a number of these in the data buffer.

Here's a BNF definition of such a buffer:

```
headers        = *head
head           = error / valid-head
error-message  = [ "4" / "5" ] 2number " " <error message> eol
valid-head     = valid-message *header "." eol
valid-message  = "221 " <number> " Article retrieved." eol
header         = <text> eol
```

(The version of BNF used here is the one used in RFC822.)

If the return value is `nov`, the data buffer should contain *network overview database* lines. These are basically fields separated by tabs.

```
nov-buffer = *nov-line
nov-line   = field 7*8[ <TAB> field ] eol
field      = <text except TAB>
```

For a closer look at what should be in those fields, see Section 11.8.4 [Headers], page 350.

`(nnchoke-open-server SERVER &optional DEFINITIONS)`

server is here the virtual server name. *definitions* is a list of (`VARIABLE VALUE`) pairs that define this virtual server.

If the server can't be opened, no error should be signaled. The back end may then choose to refuse further attempts at connecting to this server. In fact, it should do so.

If the server is opened already, this function should return a non-`nil` value. There should be no data returned.

`(nnchoke-close-server &optional SERVER)`

Close connection to *server* and free all resources connected to it. Return `nil` if the server couldn't be closed for some reason.

There should be no data returned.

`(nnchoke-request-close)`

Close connection to all servers and free all resources that the back end have reserved. All buffers that have been created by that back end should be killed. (Not the `nntp-server-buffer`, though.) This function is generally only called when Gnus is shutting down.

There should be no data returned.

`(nnchoke-server-opened &optional SERVER)`

If *server* is the current virtual server, and the connection to the physical server is alive, then this function should return a non-`nil` value. This function should under no circumstances attempt to reconnect to a server we have lost connection to.

There should be no data returned.

`(nnchoke-status-message &optional SERVER)`

This function should return the last error message from *server*.

There should be no data returned.

`(nnchoke-request-article ARTICLE &optional GROUP SERVER TO-BUFFER)`

The result data from this function should be the article specified by *article*. This might either be a `Message-ID` or a number. It is optional whether to implement retrieval by `Message-ID`, but it would be nice if that were possible.

If *to-buffer* is non-`nil`, the result data should be returned in this buffer instead of the normal data buffer. This is to make it possible to avoid copying large amounts of data from one buffer to another, while Gnus mainly requests articles to be inserted directly into its article buffer.

If it is at all possible, this function should return a cons cell where the `car` is the group name the article was fetched from, and the `cdr` is the article number. This will enable Gnus to find out what the real group and article numbers are when fetching articles by `Message-ID`. If this isn't possible, `t` should be returned on successful article retrieval.

`(nnchoke-request-group GROUP &optional SERVER FAST INFO)`

Get data on *group*. This function also has the side effect of making *group* the current group.

If *fast*, don't bother to return useful data, just make *group* the current group.

If *info*, it allows the backend to update the group info structure.

Here's an example of some result data and a definition of the same:

```
          211 56 1000 1059 ifi.discussion
```

The first number is the status, which should be 211. Next is the total number of articles in the group, the lowest article number, the highest article number, and finally the group name. Note that the total number of articles may be less than one might think while just considering the highest and lowest article numbers, but some articles may have been canceled. Gnus just discards the total-number, so whether one should take the bother to generate it properly (if that is a problem) is left as an exercise to the reader. If the group contains no articles, the lowest article number should be reported as 1 and the highest as 0.

```
group-status = [ error / info ] eol
error        = [ "4" / "5" ] 2<number> " " <Error message>
info         = "211 " 3* [ <number> " " ] <string>
```

(nnchoke-close-group GROUP &optional SERVER)
:   Close *group* and free any resources connected to it. This will be a no-op on most back ends.

    There should be no data returned.

(nnchoke-request-list &optional SERVER)
:   Return a list of all groups available on *server*. And that means *all*.

    Here's an example from a server that only carries two groups:

```
ifi.test 0000002200 0000002000 y
ifi.discussion 3324 3300 n
```

On each line we have a group name, then the highest article number in that group, the lowest article number, and finally a flag. If the group contains no articles, the lowest article number should be reported as 1 and the highest as 0.

```
active-file = *active-line
active-line = name " " <number> " " <number> ' " flags eol
name        = <string>
flags       = "n" / "y" / "m" / "x" / "j" / "=" name
```

The flag says whether the group is read-only ('n'), is moderated ('m'), is dead ('x'), is aliased to some other group ('=other-group') or none of the above ('y').

(nnchoke-request-post &optional SERVER)
:   This function should post the current buffer. It might return whether the posting was successful or not, but that's not required. If, for instance, the posting is done asynchronously, it has generally not been completed by the time this function concludes. In that case, this function should set up some kind of sentinel to beep the user loud and clear if the posting could not be completed.

    There should be no result data from this function.

11.8.2.2 Optional Back End Functions

(nnchoke-retrieve-groups GROUPS &optional SERVER)

> *groups* is a list of groups, and this function should request data on all those groups. How it does it is of no concern to Gnus, but it should attempt to do this in a speedy fashion.
>
> The return value of this function can be either `active` or `group`, which says what the format of the result data is. The former is in the same format as the data from `nnchoke-request-list`, while the latter is a buffer full of lines in the same format as `nnchoke-request-group` gives.
>
> group-buffer = *active-line / *group-status

(nnchoke-request-update-info GROUP INFO &optional SERVER)

> A Gnus group info (see Section 11.8.6 [Group Info], page 352) is handed to the back end for alterations. This comes in handy if the back end really carries all the information (as is the case with virtual and imap groups). This function should destructively alter the info to suit its needs, and should return a non-nil value (exceptionally, `nntp-request-update-info` always returns `nil` not to waste the network resources).
>
> There should be no result data from this function.

(nnchoke-request-type GROUP &optional ARTICLE)

> When the user issues commands for "sending news" (`F` in the summary buffer, for instance), Gnus has to know whether the article the user is following up on is news or mail. This function should return `news` if *article* in *group* is news, `mail` if it is mail and `unknown` if the type can't be decided. (The *article* parameter is necessary in `nnvirtual` groups which might very well combine mail groups and news groups.) Both *group* and *article* may be `nil`.
>
> There should be no result data from this function.

(nnchoke-request-set-mark GROUP ACTION &optional SERVER)

> Set/remove/add marks on articles. Normally Gnus handles the article marks (such as read, ticked, expired etc.) internally, and store them in `~/.newsrc.eld`. Some back ends (such as IMAP) however carry all information about the articles on the server, so Gnus need to propagate the mark information to the server.
>
> *action* is a list of mark setting requests, having this format:
>
> (RANGE ACTION MARK)
>
> *range* is a range of articles you wish to update marks on. *action* is `add` or `del`, used to add marks or remove marks (preserving all marks not mentioned). *mark* is a list of marks; where each mark is a symbol. Currently used marks are `read`, `tick`, `reply`, `expire`, `killed`, `dormant`, `save`, `download`, `unsend`, and `forward`, but your back end should, if possible, not limit itself to these.
>
> Given contradictory actions, the last action in the list should be the effective one. That is, if your action contains a request to add the `tick` mark on article 1 and, later in the list, a request to remove the mark on the same article, the mark should in fact be removed.
>
> An example action list:

```
(((5 12 30) 'del '(tick))
 ((10 . 90) 'add '(read expire))
 ((92 94) 'del '(read)))
```

The function should return a range of articles it wasn't able to set the mark on (currently not used for anything).

There should be no result data from this function.

(nnchoke-request-update-mark GROUP ARTICLE MARK)

If the user tries to set a mark that the back end doesn't like, this function may change the mark. Gnus will use whatever this function returns as the mark for *article* instead of the original *mark*. If the back end doesn't care, it must return the original *mark*, and not **nil** or any other type of garbage.

The only use for this I can see is what **nnvirtual** does with it—if a component group is auto-expirable, marking an article as read in the virtual group should result in the article being marked as expirable.

There should be no result data from this function.

(nnchoke-request-scan &optional GROUP SERVER)

This function may be called at any time (by Gnus or anything else) to request that the back end check for incoming articles, in one way or another. A mail back end will typically read the spool file or query the POP server when this function is invoked. The *group* doesn't have to be heeded—if the back end decides that it is too much work just scanning for a single group, it may do a total scan of all groups. It would be nice, however, to keep things local if that's practical.

There should be no result data from this function.

(nnchoke-request-group-description GROUP &optional SERVER)

The result data from this function should be a description of *group*.

```
description-line = name <TAB> description eol
name             = <string>
description      = <text>
```

(nnchoke-request-list-newsgroups &optional SERVER)

The result data from this function should be the description of all groups available on the server.

```
description-buffer = *description-line
```

(nnchoke-request-newgroups DATE &optional SERVER)

The result data from this function should be all groups that were created after 'date', which is in normal human-readable date format (i.e., the date format used in mail and news headers, and returned by the function **message-make-date** by default). The data should be in the active buffer format.

It is okay for this function to return "too many" groups; some back ends might find it cheaper to return the full list of groups, rather than just the new groups. But don't do this for back ends with many groups. Normally, if the user creates the groups herself, there won't be too many groups, so **nnml** and the like are probably safe. But for back ends like **nntp**, where the groups have been created by the server, it is quite likely that there can be many groups.

`(nnchoke-request-create-group GROUP &optional SERVER)`

> This function should create an empty group with name *group*.
>
> There should be no return data.

`(nnchoke-request-expire-articles ARTICLES &optional GROUP SERVER FORCE)`

> This function should run the expiry process on all articles in the *articles* range (which is currently a simple list of article numbers.) It is left up to the back end to decide how old articles should be before they are removed by this function. If *force* is non-`nil`, all *articles* should be deleted, no matter how new they are.
>
> This function should return a list of articles that it did not/was not able to delete.
>
> There should be no result data returned.

`(nnchoke-request-move-article ARTICLE GROUP SERVER ACCEPT-FORM &optional LAST)`

> This function should move *article* (which is a number) from *group* by calling *accept-form*.
>
> This function should ready the article in question for moving by removing any header lines it has added to the article, and generally should "tidy up" the article. Then it should `eval` *accept-form* in the buffer where the "tidy" article is. This will do the actual copying. If this `eval` returns a non-`nil` value, the article should be removed.
>
> If *last* is `nil`, that means that there is a high likelihood that there will be more requests issued shortly, so that allows some optimizations.
>
> The function should return a cons where the `car` is the group name and the `cdr` is the article number that the article was entered as.
>
> There should be no data returned.

`(nnchoke-request-accept-article GROUP &optional SERVER LAST)`

> This function takes the current buffer and inserts it into *group*. If *last* in `nil`, that means that there will be more calls to this function in short order.
>
> The function should return a cons where the `car` is the group name and the `cdr` is the article number that the article was entered as.
>
> The group should exist before the back end is asked to accept the article for that group.
>
> There should be no data returned.

`(nnchoke-request-replace-article ARTICLE GROUP BUFFER)`

> This function should remove *article* (which is a number) from *group* and insert *buffer* there instead.
>
> There should be no data returned.

`(nnchoke-request-delete-group GROUP FORCE &optional SERVER)`

> This function should delete *group*. If *force*, it should really delete all the articles in the group, and then delete the group itself. (If there is such a thing as "the group itself".)
>
> There should be no data returned.

```
(nnchoke-request-rename-group GROUP NEW-NAME &optional SERVER)
```
This function should rename *group* into *new-name*. All articles in *group* should move to *new-name*.

There should be no data returned.

11.8.2.3 Error Messaging

The back ends should use the function **nnheader-report** to report error conditions—they should not raise errors when they aren't able to perform a request. The first argument to this function is the back end symbol, and the rest are interpreted as arguments to **format** if there are multiple of them, or just a string if there is one of them. This function must always returns **nil**.

```
(nnheader-report 'nnchoke "You did something totally bogus")
```

```
(nnheader-report 'nnchoke "Could not request group %s" group)
```

Gnus, in turn, will call **nnheader-get-report** when it gets a **nil** back from a server, and this function returns the most recently reported message for the back end in question. This function takes one argument—the server symbol.

Internally, these functions access *back-end*-status-string, so the **nnchoke** back end will have its error message stored in **nnchoke-status-string**.

11.8.2.4 Writing New Back Ends

Many back ends are quite similar. **nnml** is just like **nnspool**, but it allows you to edit the articles on the server. **nnmh** is just like **nnml**, but it doesn't use an active file, and it doesn't maintain overview databases. **nndir** is just like **nnml**, but it has no concept of "groups", and it doesn't allow editing articles.

It would make sense if it were possible to "inherit" functions from back ends when writing new back ends. And, indeed, you can do that if you want to. (You don't have to if you don't want to, of course.)

All the back ends declare their public variables and functions by using a package called **nnoo**.

To inherit functions from other back ends (and allow other back ends to inherit functions from the current back end), you should use the following macros:

nnoo-declare

> This macro declares the first parameter to be a child of the subsequent parameters. For instance:
>
> ```
> (nnoo-declare nndir
>   nnml nnmh)
> ```
>
> **nndir** has declared here that it intends to inherit functions from both **nnml** and **nnmh**.

defvoo   This macro is equivalent to **defvar**, but registers the variable as a public server variable. Most state-oriented variables should be declared with **defvoo** instead of **defvar**.

In addition to the normal `defvar` parameters, it takes a list of variables in the parent back ends to map the variable to when executing a function in those back ends.

```
(defvoo nndir-directory nil
  "Where nndir will look for groups."
  nnml-current-directory nnmh-current-directory)
```

This means that `nnml-current-directory` will be set to `nndir-directory` when an `nnml` function is called on behalf of `nndir`. (The same with `nnmh`.)

`nnoo-define-basics`

This macro defines some common functions that almost all back ends should have.

```
(nnoo-define-basics nndir)
```

`deffoo`   This macro is just like `defun` and takes the same parameters. In addition to doing the normal `defun` things, it registers the function as being public so that other back ends can inherit it.

`nnoo-map-functions`

This macro allows mapping of functions from the current back end to functions from the parent back ends.

```
(nnoo-map-functions nndir
  (nnml-retrieve-headers 0 nndir-current-group 0 0)
  (nnmh-request-article 0 nndir-current-group 0 0))
```

This means that when `nndir-retrieve-headers` is called, the first, third, and fourth parameters will be passed on to `nnml-retrieve-headers`, while the second parameter is set to the value of `nndir-current-group`.

`nnoo-import`

This macro allows importing functions from back ends. It should be the last thing in the source file, since it will only define functions that haven't already been defined.

```
(nnoo-import nndir
  (nnmh
   nnmh-request-list
   nnmh-request-newgroups)
  (nnml))
```

This means that calls to `nndir-request-list` should just be passed on to `nnmh-request-list`, while all public functions from `nnml` that haven't been defined in `nndir` yet should be defined now.

Below is a slightly shortened version of the `nndir` back end.

```
;;; nndir.el — single directory newsgroup access for Gnus
;; Copyright (C) 1995,1996 Free Software Foundation, Inc.


;;; Code:

(require 'nnheader)
```

```
(require 'nnmh)
(require 'nnml)
(require 'nnoo)
(eval-when-compile (require 'cl))

(nnoo-declare nndir
  nnml nnmh)

(defvoo nndir-directory nil
  "Where nndir will look for groups."
  nnml-current-directory nnmh-current-directory)

(defvoo nndir-nov-is-evil nil
  "*Non-nil means that nndir will never retrieve NOV headers."
  nnml-nov-is-evil)

(defvoo nndir-current-group ""
  nil
  nnml-current-group nnmh-current-group)
(defvoo nndir-top-directory nil nil nnml-directory nnmh-directory)
(defvoo nndir-get-new-mail nil nil nnml-get-new-mail nnmh-get-new-mail)

(defvoo nndir-status-string "" nil nnmh-status-string)
(defconst nndir-version "nndir 1.0")

;;; Interface functions.

(nnoo-define-basics nndir)

(deffoo nndir-open-server (server &optional defs)
  (setq nndir-directory
        (or (cadr (assq 'nndir-directory defs))
            server))
  (unless (assq 'nndir-directory defs)
    (push `(nndir-directory ,server) defs))
  (push `(nndir-current-group
          ,(file-name-nondirectory
            (directory-file-name nndir-directory)))
        defs)
  (push `(nndir-top-directory
          ,(file-name-directory (directory-file-name nndir-directory)))
        defs)
  (nnoo-change-server 'nndir server defs))

(nnoo-map-functions nndir
  (nnml-retrieve-headers 0 nndir-current-group 0 0)
  (nnmh-request-article 0 nndir-current-group 0 0)
```

```
      (nnmh-request-group nndir-current-group 0 0)
      (nnmh-close-group nndir-current-group 0))

   (nnoo-import nndir
     (nnmh
      nnmh-status-message
      nnmh-request-list
      nnmh-request-newgroups))

   (provide 'nndir)
```

11.8.2.5 Hooking New Back Ends Into Gnus

Having Gnus start using your new back end is rather easy—you just declare it with the **gnus-declare-backend** functions. This will enter the back end into the **gnus-valid-select-methods** variable.

gnus-declare-backend takes two parameters—the back end name and an arbitrary number of *abilities*.

Here's an example:

```
   (gnus-declare-backend "nnchoke" 'mail 'respool 'address)
```

The above line would then go in the **nnchoke.el** file.

The abilities can be:

mail   This is a mailish back end—followups should (probably) go via mail.

post   This is a newsish back end—followups should (probably) go via news.

post-mail
                This back end supports both mail and news.

none   This is neither a post nor mail back end—it's something completely different.

respool   It supports respooling—or rather, it is able to modify its source articles and
                groups.

address   The name of the server should be in the virtual server name. This is true for
                almost all back ends.

prompt-address
                The user should be prompted for an address when doing commands like *B* in the
                group buffer. This is true for back ends like **nntp**, but not **nnmbox**, for instance.

11.8.2.6 Mail-like Back Ends

One of the things that separate the mail back ends from the rest of the back ends is the heavy dependence by most of the mail back ends on common functions in **nnmail.el**. For instance, here's the definition of **nnml-request-scan**:

```
   (deffoo nnml-request-scan (&optional group server)
     (setq nnml-article-file-alist nil)
     (nnmail-get-new-mail 'nnml 'nnml-save-nov nnml-directory group))
```

It simply calls `nnmail-get-new-mail` with a few parameters, and `nnmail` takes care of all the moving and splitting of the mail.

This function takes four parameters.

method   This should be a symbol to designate which back end is responsible for the call.

exit-function
            This function should be called after the splitting has been performed.

temp-directory
            Where the temporary files should be stored.

group   This optional argument should be a group name if the splitting is to be performed for one group only.

`nnmail-get-new-mail` will call *back-end*-`save-mail` to save each article. *back-end*-`active-number` will be called to find the article number assigned to this article.

The function also uses the following variables: *back-end*-`get-new-mail` (to see whether to get new mail for this back end); and *back-end*-`group-alist` and *back-end*-`active-file` to generate the new active file. *back-end*-`group-alist` should be a group-active alist, like this:

```
(("a-group" (1 . 10))
 ("some-group" (34 . 39)))
```

11.8.3 Score File Syntax

Score files are meant to be easily parsable, but yet extremely malleable. It was decided that something that had the same read syntax as an Emacs Lisp list would fit that spec.

Here's a typical score file:

```
(("summary"
  ("Windows 95" -10000 nil s)
  ("Gnus"))
 ("from"
  ("Lars" -1000))
 (mark -100))
```

BNF definition of a score file:

```
score-file    = "" / "(" *element ")"
element       = rule / atom
rule          = string-rule / number-rule / date-rule
string-rule   = "(" quote string-header quote space *string-match ")"
number-rule   = "(" quote number-header quote space *number-match ")"
date-rule     = "(" quote date-header quote space *date-match ")"
quote         = <ascii 34>
string-header = "subject" / "from" / "references" / "message-id" /
                "xref" / "body" / "head" / "all" / "followup"
number-header = "lines" / "chars"
date-header   = "date"
string-match  = "(" quote <string> quote [ "" / [ space score [ "" /
                space date [ "" / [ space string-match-t ] ] ] ] ] ")"
```

```
score               = "nil" / <integer>
date                = "nil" / <natural number>
string-match-t      = "nil" / "s" / "substring" / "S" / "Substring" /
                      "r" / "regex" / "R" / "Regex" /
                      "e" / "exact" / "E" / "Exact" /
                      "f" / "fuzzy" / "F" / "Fuzzy"
number-match        = "(" <integer> [ "" / [ space score [ "" /
                      space date [ "" / [ space number-match-t ] ] ] ] ] ")"
number-match-t      = "nil" / "=" / "<" / ">" / ">=" / "<="
date-match          = "(" quote <string> quote [ "" / [ space score [ "" /
                      space date [ "" / [ space date-match-t ] ] ] ] ] ")"
date-match-t        = "nil" / "at" / "before" / "after"
atom                = "(" [ required-atom / optional-atom ] ")"
required-atom       = mark / expunge / mark-and-expunge / files /
                      exclude-files / read-only / touched
optional-atom       = adapt / local / eval
mark                = "mark" space nil-or-number
nil-or-number       = "nil" / <integer>
expunge             = "expunge" space nil-or-number
mark-and-expunge    = "mark-and-expunge" space nil-or-number
files               = "files" *[ space <string> ]
exclude-files       = "exclude-files" *[ space <string> ]
read-only           = "read-only" [ space "nil" / space "t" ]
adapt               = "adapt" [ space "ignore" / space "t" / space adapt-rule ]
adapt-rule          = "(" *[ <string> *[ "(" <string> <integer> ")" ] ")"
local               = "local" *[ space "(" <string> space <form> ")" ]
eval                = "eval" space <form>
space               = *[ " " / <TAB> / <NEWLINE> ]
```

Any unrecognized elements in a score file should be ignored, but not discarded.

As you can see, white space is needed, but the type and amount of white space is irrelevant. This means that formatting of the score file is left up to the programmer—if it's simpler to just spew it all out on one looong line, then that's ok.

The meaning of the various atoms are explained elsewhere in this manual (see Section 7.4 [Score File Format], page 219).

11.8.4 Headers

Internally Gnus uses a format for storing article headers that corresponds to the NOV format in a mysterious fashion. One could almost suspect that the author looked at the NOV specification and just shamelessly *stole* the entire thing, and one would be right.

Header is a severely overloaded term. "Header" is used in RFC 1036 to talk about lines in the head of an article (e.g., From). It is used by many people as a synonym for "head"— "the header and the body". (That should be avoided, in my opinion.) And Gnus uses a format internally that it calls "header", which is what I'm talking about here. This is a 9-element vector, basically, with each header (ouch) having one slot.

These slots are, in order: `number`, `subject`, `from`, `date`, `id`, `references`, `chars`, `lines`, `xref`, and `extra`. There are macros for accessing and setting these slots—they all have predictable names beginning with `mail-header-` and `mail-header-set-`, respectively.

All these slots contain strings, except the `extra` slot, which contains an alist of header/value pairs (see Section 3.1.2 [To From Newsgroups], page 47).

11.8.5 Ranges

GNUS introduced a concept that I found so useful that I've started using it a lot and have elaborated on it greatly.

The question is simple: If you have a large amount of objects that are identified by numbers (say, articles, to take a *wild* example) that you want to qualify as being "included", a normal sequence isn't very useful. (A 200,000 length sequence is a bit long-winded.)

The solution is as simple as the question: You just collapse the sequence.

```
(1 2 3 4 5 6 10 11 12)
```

is transformed into

```
((1 . 6) (10 . 12))
```

To avoid having those nasty '(13 . 13)' elements to denote a lonesome object, a '13' is a valid element:

```
((1 . 6) 7 (10 . 12))
```

This means that comparing two ranges to find out whether they are equal is slightly tricky:

```
((1 . 5) 7 8 (10 . 12))
```

and

```
((1 . 5) (7 . 8) (10 . 12))
```

are equal. In fact, any non-descending list is a range:

```
(1 2 3 4 5)
```

is a perfectly valid range, although a pretty long-winded one. This is also valid:

```
(1 . 5)
```

and is equal to the previous range.

Here's a BNF definition of ranges. Of course, one must remember the semantic requirement that the numbers are non-descending. (Any number of repetition of the same number is allowed, but apt to disappear in range handling.)

```
range            = simple-range / normal-range
simple-range     = "(" number " . " number ")"
normal-range     = "(" start-contents ")"
contents         = "" / simple-range *[ " " contents ] /
                   number *[ " " contents ]
```

Gnus currently uses ranges to keep track of read articles and article marks. I plan on implementing a number of range operators in C if The Powers That Be are willing to let me. (I haven't asked yet, because I need to do some more thinking on what operators I need to make life totally range-based without ever having to convert back to normal sequences.)

11.8.6 Group Info

Gnus stores all permanent info on groups in a *group info* list. This list is from three to six elements (or more) long and exhaustively describes the group.

Here are two example group infos; one is a very simple group while the second is a more complex one:

```
("no.group" 5 ((1 . 54324)))

("nnml:my.mail" 3 ((1 . 5) 9 (20 . 55))
                  ((tick (15 . 19)) (replied 3 6 (19 . 3)))
                  (nnml "")
                  ((auto-expire . t) (to-address . "ding@gnus.org")))
```

The first element is the *group name*—as Gnus knows the group, anyway. The second element is the *subscription level*, which normally is a small integer. (It can also be the *rank*, which is a cons cell where the `car` is the level and the `cdr` is the score.) The third element is a list of ranges of read articles. The fourth element is a list of lists of article marks of various kinds. The fifth element is the select method (or virtual server, if you like). The sixth element is a list of *group parameters*, which is what this section is about.

Any of the last three elements may be missing if they are not required. In fact, the vast majority of groups will normally only have the first three elements, which saves quite a lot of cons cells.

Here's a BNF definition of the group info format:

```
info          = "(" group space ralevel space read
                [ "" / [ space marks-list [ "" / [ space method [ "" /
                space parameters ] ] ] ] ] ")"
group         = quote <string> quote
ralevel       = rank / level
level         = <integer in the range of 1 to inf>
rank          = "(" level "." score ")"
score         = <integer in the range of 1 to inf>
read          = range
marks-lists   = nil / "(" *marks ")"
marks         = "(" <string> range ")"
method        = "(" <string> *elisp-forms ")"
parameters    = "(" *elisp-forms ")"
```

Actually that 'marks' rule is a fib. A 'marks' is a '<string>' consed on to a 'range', but that's a bitch to say in pseudo-BNF.

If you have a Gnus info and want to access the elements, Gnus offers a series of macros for getting/setting these elements.

`gnus-info-group`
`gnus-info-set-group`
        Get/set the group name.

`gnus-info-rank`
`gnus-info-set-rank`
        Get/set the group rank (see Section 2.7 [Group Score], page 19).

```
gnus-info-level
gnus-info-set-level
          Get/set the group level.
```

```
gnus-info-score
gnus-info-set-score
          Get/set the group score (see Section 2.7 [Group Score], page 19).
```

```
gnus-info-read
gnus-info-set-read
          Get/set the ranges of read articles.
```

```
gnus-info-marks
gnus-info-set-marks
          Get/set the lists of ranges of marked articles.
```

```
gnus-info-method
gnus-info-set-method
          Get/set the group select method.
```

```
gnus-info-params
gnus-info-set-params
          Get/set the group parameters.
```

All the getter functions take one parameter—the info list. The setter functions take two parameters—the info list and the new value.

The last three elements in the group info aren't mandatory, so it may be necessary to extend the group info before setting the element. If this is necessary, you can just pass on a non-**nil** third parameter to the three final setter functions to have this happen automatically.

11.8.7 Extended Interactive

Gnus extends the standard Emacs **interactive** specification slightly to allow easy use of the symbolic prefix (see Section 9.3 [Symbolic Prefixes], page 250). Here's an example of how this is used:

```
(defun gnus-summary-increase-score (&optional score symp)
  (interactive (gnus-interactive "P\ny"))
  ...
  )
```

The best thing to do would have been to implement **gnus-interactive** as a macro which would have returned an **interactive** form, but this isn't possible since Emacs checks whether a function is interactive or not by simply doing an **assq** on the lambda form. So, instead we have **gnus-interactive** function that takes a string and returns values that are usable to **interactive**.

This function accepts (almost) all normal **interactive** specs, but adds a few more.

'y'   The current symbolic prefix—the **gnus-current-prefix-symbol** variable.

'Y'   A list of the current symbolic prefixes—the **gnus-current-prefix-symbol** variable.

'`A`'	The current article number—the `gnus-summary-article-number` function.
'`H`'	The current article header—the `gnus-summary-article-header` function.
'`g`'	The current group name—the `gnus-group-group-name` function.

11.8.8 Emacs/XEmacs Code

While Gnus runs under Emacs, XEmacs and Mule, I decided that one of the platforms must be the primary one. I chose Emacs. Not because I don't like XEmacs or Mule, but because it comes first alphabetically.

This means that Gnus will byte-compile under Emacs with nary a warning, while XEmacs will pump out gigabytes of warnings while byte-compiling. As I use byte-compilation warnings to help me root out trivial errors in Gnus, that's very useful.

I've also consistently used Emacs function interfaces, but have used Gnusey aliases for the functions. To take an example: Emacs defines a `run-at-time` function while XEmacs defines a `start-itimer` function. I then define a function called `gnus-run-at-time` that takes the same parameters as the Emacs `run-at-time`. When running Gnus under Emacs, the former function is just an alias for the latter. However, when running under XEmacs, the former is an alias for the following function:

```
(defun gnus-xmas-run-at-time (time repeat function &rest args)
  (start-itimer
    "gnus-run-at-time"
    `(lambda ()
       (,function ,@args))
    time repeat))
```

This sort of thing has been done for bunches of functions. Gnus does not redefine any native Emacs functions while running under XEmacs—it does this `defalias` thing with Gnus equivalents instead. Cleaner all over.

In the cases where the XEmacs function interface was obviously cleaner, I used it instead. For example `gnus-region-active-p` is an alias for `region-active-p` in XEmacs, whereas in Emacs it is a function.

Of course, I could have chosen XEmacs as my native platform and done mapping functions the other way around. But I didn't. The performance hit these indirections impose on Gnus under XEmacs should be slight.

11.8.9 Various File Formats

11.8.9.1 Active File Format

The active file lists all groups available on the server in question. It also lists the highest and lowest current article numbers in each group.

Here's an excerpt from a typical active file:

```
soc.motss 296030 293865 y
alt.binaries.pictures.fractals 3922 3913 n
comp.sources.unix 1605 1593 m
comp.binaries.ibm.pc 5097 5089 y
no.general 1000 900 y
```

Here's a pseudo-BNF definition of this file:

```
active       = *group-line
group-line   = group spc high-number spc low-number spc flag <NEWLINE>
group        = <non-white-space string>
spc          = " "
high-number  = <non-negative integer>
low-number   = <positive integer>
flag         = "y" / "n" / "m" / "j" / "x" / "=" group
```

For a full description of this file, see the manual pages for 'innd', in particular 'active(5)'.

11.8.9.2 Newsgroups File Format

The newsgroups file lists groups along with their descriptions. Not all groups on the server have to be listed, and not all groups in the file have to exist on the server. The file is meant purely as information to the user.

The format is quite simple; a group name, a tab, and the description. Here's the definition:

```
newsgroups   = *line
line         = group tab description <NEWLINE>
group        = <non-white-space string>
tab          = <TAB>
description  = <string>
```

11.9 Emacs for Heathens

Believe it or not, but some people who use Gnus haven't really used Emacs much before they embarked on their journey on the Gnus Love Boat. If you are one of those unfortunates whom "*C-M-a*", "kill the region", and "set **gnus-flargblossen** to an alist where the key is a regexp that is used for matching on the group name" are magical phrases with little or no meaning, then this appendix is for you. If you are already familiar with Emacs, just ignore this and go fondle your cat instead.

11.9.1 Keystrokes

- Q: What is an experienced Emacs user?
- A: A person who wishes that the terminal had pedals.

Yes, when you use Emacs, you are apt to use the control key, the shift key and the meta key a lot. This is very annoying to some people (notably **vile** users), and the rest of us just love the hell out of it. Just give up and submit. Emacs really does stand for "Escape-Meta-Alt-Control-Shift", and not "Editing Macros", as you may have heard from other disreputable sources (like the Emacs author).

The shift keys are normally located near your pinky fingers, and are normally used to get capital letters and stuff. You probably use it all the time. The control key is normally marked "CTRL" or something like that. The meta key is, funnily enough, never marked as such on any keyboard. The one I'm currently at has a key that's marked "Alt", which is the meta key on this keyboard. It's usually located somewhere to the left hand side of the keyboard, usually on the bottom row.

Now, us Emacs people don't say "press the meta-control-m key", because that's just too inconvenient. We say "press the *C-M-m* key". *M-* is the prefix that means "meta" and "*C-*" is the prefix that means "control". So "press *C-k*" means "press down the control key, and hold it down while you press *k*". "Press *C-M-k*" means "press down and hold down the meta key and the control key and then press *k*". Simple, ay?

This is somewhat complicated by the fact that not all keyboards have a meta key. In that case you can use the "escape" key. Then *M-k* means "press escape, release escape, press *k*". That's much more work than if you have a meta key, so if that's the case, I respectfully suggest you get a real keyboard with a meta key. You can't live without it.

11.9.2 Emacs Lisp

Emacs is the King of Editors because it's really a Lisp interpreter. Each and every key you tap runs some Emacs Lisp code snippet, and since Emacs Lisp is an interpreted language, that means that you can configure any key to run any arbitrary code. You just, like, do it.

Gnus is written in Emacs Lisp, and is run as a bunch of interpreted functions. (These are byte-compiled for speed, but it's still interpreted.) If you decide that you don't like the way Gnus does certain things, it's trivial to have it do something a different way. (Well, at least if you know how to write Lisp code.) However, that's beyond the scope of this manual, so we are simply going to talk about some common constructs that you normally use in your ˜/.gnus.el file to customize Gnus. (You can also use the ˜/.emacs file, but in order to set things of Gnus up, it is much better to use the ˜/.gnus.el file, See Section 1.6 [Startup Files], page 7.)

If you want to set the variable **gnus-florgbnize** to four (4), you write the following:

```
(setq gnus-florgbnize 4)
```

This function (really "special form") `setq` is the one that can set a variable to some value. This is really all you need to know. Now you can go and fill your `~/.gnus.el` file with lots of these to change how Gnus works.

If you have put that thing in your `~/.gnus.el` file, it will be read and `evaled` (which is Lisp-ese for "run") the next time you start Gnus. If you want to change the variable right away, simply say *C-x C-e* after the closing parenthesis. That will `eval` the previous "form", which is a simple `setq` statement here.

Go ahead—just try it, if you're located at your Emacs. After you *C-x C-e*, you will see '4' appear in the echo area, which is the return value of the form you `evaled`.

Some pitfalls:

If the manual says "set **gnus-read-active-file** to **some**", that means:

```
(setq gnus-read-active-file 'some)
```

On the other hand, if the manual says "set **gnus-nntp-server-file** to '/etc/nntpserver'", that means:

```
(setq gnus-nntp-server-file "/etc/nntpserver")
```

So be careful not to mix up strings (the latter) with symbols (the former). The manual is unambiguous, but it can be confusing.

11.10 Frequently Asked Questions

Abstract

This is the new Gnus Frequently Asked Questions list.

Please submit features and suggestions to the ding list.

11.10.1 Changes

- 2008-06-15: Adjust for message-fill-column. Add x-face-file. Clarify difference between ding and gnu.emacs.gnus. Remove reference to discontinued service.
- 2006-04-15: Added tip on how to delete sent buffer on exit.

11.10.2 Introduction

This is the Gnus Frequently Asked Questions list.

Gnus is a Usenet Newsreader and Electronic Mail User Agent implemented as a part of Emacs. It's been around in some form for almost a decade now, and has been distributed as a standard part of Emacs for much of that time. Gnus 5 is the latest (and greatest) incarnation. The original version was called GNUS, and was written by Masanobu UMEDA. When autumn crept up in '94, Lars Magne Ingebrigtsen grew bored and decided to rewrite Gnus.

Its biggest strength is the fact that it is extremely customizable. It is somewhat intimidating at first glance, but most of the complexity can be ignored until you're ready to take advantage of it. If you receive a reasonable volume of e-mail (you're on various mailing lists), or you would like to read high-volume mailing lists but cannot keep up with them, or read high volume newsgroups or are just bored, then Gnus is what you want.

This FAQ was maintained by Justin Sheehy until March 2002. He would like to thank Steve Baur and Per Abrahamsen for doing a wonderful job with this FAQ before him. We would like to do the same: thanks, Justin!

This version is much nicer than the unofficial hypertext versions that are archived at Utrecht, Oxford, Smart Pages, Ohio State, and other FAQ archives. See the resources question below if you want information on obtaining it in another format.

The information contained here was compiled with the assistance of the Gnus development mailing list, and any errors or misprints are the Gnus team's fault, sorry.

11.10.3 Installation FAQ

Question 1.1

What is the latest version of Gnus?

Answer

Jingle please: Gnus 5.10 is released, get it while it's hot! As well as the step in version number is rather small, Gnus 5.10 has tons of new features which you shouldn't miss. The current release (5.13) should be at least as stable as the latest release of the 5.8 series.

Question 1.2

What's new in 5.10?

Answer

First of all, you should have a look into the file GNUS-NEWS in the toplevel directory of the Gnus tarball, there the most important changes are listed. Here's a short list of the changes I find especially important/interesting:

- Major rewrite of the Gnus agent, Gnus agent is now active by default.
- Many new article washing functions for dealing with ugly formatted articles.
- Anti Spam features.
- Message-utils now included in Gnus.
- New format specifiers for summary lines, e.g., %B for a complex trn-style thread tree.

Question 1.3

Where and how to get Gnus?

Answer

Gnus is released independent from releases of Emacs and XEmacs. Therefore, the version bundled with Emacs or the version in XEmacs's package system might not be up to date (e.g., Gnus 5.9 bundled with Emacs 21 is outdated). You can get the latest released version of Gnus from `http://www.gnus.org/dist/gnus.tar.gz` or via anonymous FTP from `ftp://ftp.gnus.org/pub/gnus/gnus.tar.gz`.

Question 1.4

What to do with the tarball now?

Answer

Untar it via '`tar xvzf gnus.tar.gz`' and do the common '`./configure; make; make install`' circle. (under MS-Windows either get the Cygwin environment from `http://www.cygwin.com` which allows you to do what's described above or unpack the tarball with some packer (e.g., Winace from `http://www.winace.com`) and use the batch-file make.bat included in the tarball to install Gnus.) If you don't want to (or aren't allowed to) install Gnus system-wide, you can install it in your home directory and add the following lines to your ~/.xemacs/init.el or ~/.emacs:

```
(add-to-list 'load-path "/path/to/gnus/lisp")
(if (featurep 'xemacs)
    (add-to-list 'Info-directory-list "/path/to/gnus/texi/")
  (add-to-list 'Info-default-directory-list "/path/to/gnus/texi/"))
```

Make sure that you don't have any Gnus related stuff before this line, on MS Windows use something like "C:/path/to/lisp" (yes, "/").

Question 1.5

I sometimes read references to No Gnus and Oort Gnus, what are those?

Answer

Oort Gnus was the name of the development version of Gnus, which became Gnus 5.10 in autumn 2003. No Gnus is the name of the current development version which will once become Gnus 5.12 or Gnus 6. (If you're wondering why not 5.11, the odd version numbers are normally used for the Gnus versions bundled with Emacs)

Question 1.6

Which version of Emacs do I need?

Answer

Gnus 5.13 requires an Emacs version that is greater than or equal to Emacs 23.1 or XEmacs 21.1, although there are some features that only work on Emacs 24.

Question 1.7

How do I run Gnus on both Emacs and XEmacs?

Answer

You can't use the same copy of Gnus in both as the Lisp files are byte-compiled to a format which is different depending on which Emacs did the compilation. Get one copy of Gnus for Emacs and one for XEmacs.

11.10.4 Startup / Group buffer

Question 2.1

Every time I start Gnus I get a message "Gnus auto-save file exists. Do you want to read it?", what does this mean and how to prevent it?

Answer

This message means that the last time you used Gnus, it wasn't properly exited and therefore couldn't write its information to disk (e.g., which messages you read), you are now asked if you want to restore that information from the auto-save file.

   To prevent this message make sure you exit Gnus via 'q' in group buffer instead of just killing Emacs.

Question 2.2

Gnus doesn't remember which groups I'm subscribed to, what's this?

Answer

You get the message described in the q/a pair above while starting Gnus, right? It's another symptom for the same problem, so read the answer above.

Question 2.3

How to change the format of the lines in Group buffer?

Answer

You've got to tweak the value of the variable gnus-group-line-format. See the manual node "Group Line Specification" for information on how to do this. An example for this (guess from whose .gnus :-)):

```
(setq gnus-group-line-format "%P%M%S[%5t]%5y : %(%g%)\n")
```

Question 2.4

My group buffer becomes a bit crowded, is there a way to sort my groups into categories so I can easier browse through them?

Answer

Gnus offers the topic mode, it allows you to sort your groups in, well, topics, e.g., all groups dealing with Linux under the topic linux, all dealing with music under the topic music and all dealing with scottish music under the topic scottish which is a subtopic of music.

To enter topic mode, just hit t while in Group buffer. Now you can use 'T n' to create a topic at point and 'T m' to move a group to a specific topic. For more commands see the manual or the menu. You might want to include the %P specifier at the beginning of your gnus-group-line-format variable to have the groups nicely indented.

Question 2.5

How to manually sort the groups in Group buffer? How to sort the groups in a topic?

Answer

Move point over the group you want to move and hit 'C-k', now move point to the place where you want the group to be and hit 'C-y'.

11.10.5 Getting Messages

Question 3.1

I just installed Gnus, started it via 'M-x gnus' but it only says "nntp (news) open error", what to do?

Answer

You've got to tell Gnus where to fetch the news from. Read the documentation for information on how to do this. As a first start, put those lines in ~/.gnus.el:

```
(setq gnus-select-method '(nntp "news.yourprovider.net"))
(setq user-mail-address "you@yourprovider.net")
(setq user-full-name "Your Name")
```

Question 3.2

I'm working under Windows and have no idea what ~/.gnus.el means.

Answer

The ~/ means the home directory where Gnus and Emacs look for the configuration files. However, you don't really need to know what this means, it suffices that Emacs knows what it means :-) You can type 'C-x C-f ~/.gnus.el RET ' (yes, with the forward slash, even on Windows), and Emacs will open the right file for you. (It will most likely be new, and thus empty.) However, I'd discourage you from doing so, since the directory Emacs chooses will most certainly not be what you want, so let's do it the correct way. The first thing you've got to do is to create a suitable directory (no blanks in directory name please), e.g., c:\myhome. Then you must set the environment variable HOME to this directory. To do this under Windows 9x or Me include the line

```
SET HOME=C:\myhome
```

in your autoexec.bat and reboot. Under NT, 2000 and XP, hit Winkey+Pause/Break to enter system options (if it doesn't work, go to Control Panel -> System -> Advanced). There you'll find the possibility to set environment variables. Create a new one with name HOME and value C:\myhome. Rebooting is not necessary.

Now to create `~/.gnus.el`, say 'C-x C-f ~/.gnus.el RET C-x C-s'. in Emacs.

Question 3.3

My news server requires authentication, how to store user name and password on disk?

Answer

Create a file `~/.authinfo` which includes for each server a line like this

```
machine news.yourprovider.net login YourUserName password YourPassword
```

. Make sure that the file isn't readable to others if you work on a OS which is capable of doing so. (Under Unix say

```
chmod 600 ~/.authinfo
```

in a shell.)

Question 3.4

Gnus seems to start up OK, but I can't find out how to subscribe to a group.

Answer

If you know the name of the group say 'U name.of.group RET' in group buffer (use the tab-completion Luke). Otherwise hit ^ in group buffer, this brings you to the server buffer. Now place point (the cursor) over the server which carries the group you want, hit 'RET', move point to the group you want to subscribe to and say 'u' to subscribe to it.

Question 3.5

Gnus doesn't show all groups / Gnus says I'm not allowed to post on this server as well as I am, what's that?

Answer

Some providers allow restricted anonymous access and full access only after authorization. To make Gnus send authinfo to those servers append

```
force yes
```

to the line for those servers in `~/.authinfo`.

Question 3.6

I want Gnus to fetch news from several servers, is this possible?

Answer

Of course. You can specify more sources for articles in the variable gnus-secondary-select-methods. Add something like this in ~/.gnus.el:

```
(add-to-list 'gnus-secondary-select-methods
             '(nntp "news.yourSecondProvider.net"))
(add-to-list 'gnus-secondary-select-methods
             '(nntp "news.yourThirdProvider.net"))
```

Question 3.7

And how about local spool files?

Answer

No problem, this is just one more select method called nnspool, so you want this:

```
(add-to-list 'gnus-secondary-select-methods '(nnspool ""))
```

Or this if you don't want an NNTP Server as primary news source:

```
(setq gnus-select-method '(nnspool ""))
```

Gnus will look for the spool file in /usr/spool/news, if you want something different, change the line above to something like this:

```
(add-to-list 'gnus-secondary-select-methods
             '(nnspool ""
                        (nnspool-directory "/usr/local/myspooldir")))
```

This sets the spool directory for this server only. You might have to specify more stuff like the program used to post articles, see the Gnus manual on how to do this.

Question 3.8

OK, reading news works now, but I want to be able to read my mail with Gnus, too. How to do it?

Answer

That's a bit harder since there are many possible sources for mail, many possible ways for storing mail and many different ways for sending mail. The most common cases are these: 1: You want to read your mail from a pop3 server and send them directly to a SMTP Server 2: Some program like fetchmail retrieves your mail and stores it on disk from where Gnus shall read it. Outgoing mail is sent by Sendmail, Postfix or some other MTA. Sometimes, you even need a combination of the above cases.

However, the first thing to do is to tell Gnus in which way it should store the mail, in Gnus terminology which back end to use. Gnus supports many different back ends, the most commonly used one is nnml. It stores every mail in one file and is therefore quite fast. However you might prefer a one file per group approach if your file system has problems with many small files, the nnfolder back end is then probably the choice for you. To use nnml add the following to ~/.gnus.el:

```
(add-to-list 'gnus-secondary-select-methods '(nnml ""))
```

As you might have guessed, if you want nnfolder, it's

```
(add-to-list 'gnus-secondary-select-methods '(nnfolder ""))
```

Now we need to tell Gnus, where to get its mail from. If it's a POP3 server, then you need something like this:

```
(eval-after-load "mail-source"
  '(add-to-list 'mail-sources '(pop :server "pop.YourProvider.net"
                                    :user "yourUserName"
                                    :password "yourPassword")))
```

Make sure ~/.gnus.el isn't readable to others if you store your password there. If you want to read your mail from a traditional spool file on your local machine, it's

```
(eval-after-load "mail-source"
  '(add-to-list 'mail-sources '(file :path "/path/to/spool/file"))
```

If it's a Maildir, with one file per message as used by postfix, Qmail and (optionally) fetchmail it's

```
(eval-after-load "mail-source"
  '(add-to-list 'mail-sources '(maildir :path "/path/to/Maildir/"
                                        :subdirs ("cur" "new"))))
```

And finally if you want to read your mail from several files in one directory, for example because procmail already split your mail, it's

```
(eval-after-load "mail-source"
  '(add-to-list 'mail-sources
                '(directory :path "/path/to/procmail-dir/"
                            :suffix ".prcml")))
```

Where :suffix ".prcml" tells Gnus only to use files with the suffix .prcml.

OK, now you only need to tell Gnus how to send mail. If you want to send mail via sendmail (or whichever MTA is playing the role of sendmail on your system), you don't need to do anything. However, if you want to send your mail to an SMTP Server you need the following in your ~/.gnus.el

```
(setq send-mail-function 'smtpmail-send-it)
(setq message-send-mail-function 'smtpmail-send-it)
(setq smtpmail-default-smtp-server "smtp.yourProvider.net")
```

Question 3.9

And what about IMAP?

Answer

There are two ways of using IMAP with Gnus. The first one is to use IMAP like POP3, that means Gnus fetches the mail from the IMAP server and stores it on disk. If you want to do this (you don't really want to do this) add the following to ~/.gnus.el

```
(add-to-list 'mail-sources '(imap :server "mail.mycorp.com"
                                  :user "username"
                                  :pass "password"
                                  :stream network
                                  :authentication login
```

```
                              :mailbox "INBOX"
                              :fetchflag "\\Seen"))
```

You might have to tweak the values for stream and/or authentication, see the Gnus manual node "Mail Source Specifiers" for possible values.

If you want to use IMAP the way it's intended, you've got to follow a different approach. You've got to add the nnimap back end to your select method and give the information about the server there.

```
(add-to-list 'gnus-secondary-select-methods
             '(nnimap "Give the baby a name"
                      (nnimap-address "imap.yourProvider.net")
                      (nnimap-port 143)
                      (nnimap-list-pattern "archive.*")))
```

Again, you might have to specify how to authenticate to the server if Gnus can't guess the correct way, see the Manual Node "IMAP" for detailed information.

Question 3.10

At the office we use one of those MS Exchange servers, can I use Gnus to read my mail from it?

Answer

Offer your administrator a pair of new running shoes for activating IMAP on the server and follow the instructions above.

Question 3.11

Can I tell Gnus not to delete the mails on the server it retrieves via POP3?

Answer

Yes, if the POP3 server supports the UIDL control (maybe almost servers do it nowadays). To do that, add a `:leave VALUE` pair to each POP3 mail source. See see Section 6.4.4.1 [Mail Source Specifiers], page 154 for VALUE.

11.10.6 Reading messages

Question 4.1

When I enter a group, all read messages are gone. How to view them again?

Answer

If you enter the group by saying 'RET' in group buffer with point over the group, only unread and ticked messages are loaded. Say 'C-u RET' instead to load all available messages. If you want only the 300 newest say 'C-u 300 RET'

Loading only unread messages can be annoying if you have threaded view enabled, say

```
(setq gnus-fetch-old-headers 'some)
```

in `~/.gnus.el` to load enough old articles to prevent teared threads, replace 'some with `t` to load all articles (Warning: Both settings enlarge the amount of data which is fetched when you enter a group and slow down the process of entering a group).

If you already use Gnus 5.10, you can say '/o N' In summary buffer to load the last N messages, this feature is not available in 5.8.8

If you don't want all old messages, but the parent of the message you're just reading, you can say '^', if you want to retrieve the whole thread the message you're just reading belongs to, 'A T' is your friend.

Question 4.2

How to tell Gnus to show an important message every time I enter a group, even when it's read?

Answer

You can tick important messages. To do this hit 'u' while point is in summary buffer over the message. When you want to remove the mark, hit either 'd' (this deletes the tick mark and set's unread mark) or 'M c' (which deletes all marks for the message).

Question 4.3

How to view the headers of a message?

Answer

Say 't' to show all headers, one more 't' hides them again.

Question 4.4

How to view the raw unformatted message?

Answer

Say 'C-u g' to show the raw message 'g' returns to normal view.

Question 4.5

How can I change the headers Gnus displays by default at the top of the article buffer?

Answer

The variable gnus-visible-headers controls which headers are shown, its value is a regular expression, header lines which match it are shown. So if you want author, subject, date, and if the header exists, Followup-To and MUA / NUA say this in ~/.gnus.el:

```
(setq gnus-visible-headers
      '("^From" "^Subject" "^Date" "^Newsgroups" "^Followup-To"
        "^User-Agent" "^X-Newsreader" "^X-Mailer"))
```

Question 4.6

I'd like Gnus NOT to render HTML-mails but show me the text part if it's available. How to do it?

Answer

Say

```
(eval-after-load "mm-decode"
 '(progn
     (add-to-list 'mm-discouraged-alternatives "text/htnl")
     (add-to-list 'mm-discouraged-alternatives "text/richtext")))
```

in ~/.gnus.el. If you don't want HTML rendered, even if there's no text alternative add

```
(setq mm-automatic-display (remove "text/html" mm-automatic-display))
```

too.

Question 4.7

Can I use some other browser than w3m to render my HTML-mails?

Answer

Only if you use Gnus 5.10 or younger. In this case you've got the choice between shr, w3m, links, lynx and html2text, which one is used can be specified in the variable mm-text-html-renderer, so if you want links to render your mail say

```
(setq mm-text-html-renderer 'links)
```

Question 4.8

Is there anything I can do to make poorly formatted mails more readable?

Answer

Gnus offers you several functions to "wash" incoming mail, you can find them if you browse through the menu, item Article->Washing. The most interesting ones are probably "Wrap long lines" ('W w'), "Decode ROT13" ('W r') and "Outlook Deuglify" which repairs the dumb quoting used by many users of Microsoft products ('W Y f' gives you full deuglify. See 'W Y C-h' or have a look at the menus for other deuglifications). Outlook deuglify is only available since Gnus 5.10.

Question 4.9

Is there a way to automatically ignore posts by specific authors or with specific words in the subject? And can I highlight more interesting ones in some way?

Answer

You want Scoring. Scoring means, that you define rules which assign each message an integer value. Depending on the value the message is highlighted in summary buffer (if it's high, say +2000) or automatically marked read (if the value is low, say -800) or some other action happens.

There are basically three ways of setting up rules which assign the scoring-value to messages. The first and easiest way is to set up rules based on the article you are just reading. Say you're reading a message by a guy who always writes nonsense and you want to ignore his messages in the future. Hit 'L', to set up a rule which lowers the score. Now Gnus asks you which the criteria for lowering the Score shall be. Hit '?' twice to see all possibilities, we want 'a' which means the author (the from header). Now Gnus wants to know which kind of matching we want. Hit either 'e' for an exact match or 's' for substring-match and delete afterwards everything but the name to score down all authors with the given name no matter which email address is used. Now you need to tell Gnus when to apply the rule and how long it should last, hit 'p' to apply the rule now and let it last forever. If you want to raise the score instead of lowering it say 'I' instead of 'L'.

You can also set up rules by hand. To do this say 'V f' in summary buffer. Then you are asked for the name of the score file, it's name.of.group.SCORE for rules valid in only one group or all.Score for rules valid in all groups. See the Gnus manual for the exact syntax, basically it's one big list whose elements are lists again. the first element of those lists is the header to score on, then one more list with what to match, which score to assign, when to expire the rule and how to do the matching. If you find me very interesting, you could add the following to your all.Score:

```
(("references" ("hschmi22.userfqdn.rz-online.de" 500 nil s))
 ("message-id" ("hschmi22.userfqdn.rz-online.de" 999 nil s)))
```

This would add 999 to the score of messages written by me and 500 to the score of messages which are a (possibly indirect) answer to a message written by me. Of course nobody with a sane mind would do this :-)

The third alternative is adaptive scoring. This means Gnus watches you and tries to find out what you find interesting and what annoying and sets up rules which reflect this. Adaptive scoring can be a huge help when reading high traffic groups. If you want to activate adaptive scoring say

```
(setq gnus-use-adaptive-scoring t)
```

in ~/.gnus.el.

Question 4.10

How can I disable threading in some (e.g., mail-) groups, or set other variables specific for some groups?

Answer

While in group buffer move point over the group and hit 'G c', this opens a buffer where you can set options for the group. At the bottom of the buffer you'll find an item that allows you to set variables locally for the group. To disable threading enter gnus-show-threads as name of variable and **nil** as value. Hit button done at the top of the buffer when you're ready.

Question 4.11

Can I highlight messages written by me and follow-ups to those?

Answer

Stop those "Can I ..." questions, the answer is always yes in Gnus Country :-). It's a three step process: First we make faces (specifications of how summary-line shall look like) for those postings, then we'll give them some special score and finally we'll tell Gnus to use the new faces.

Question 4.12

The number of total messages in a group which Gnus displays in group buffer is by far to high, especially in mail groups. Is this a bug?

Answer

No, that's a matter of design of Gnus, fixing this would mean reimplementation of major parts of Gnus' back ends. Gnus thinks "highest-article-number − lowest-article-number = total-number-of-articles". This works OK for Usenet groups, but if you delete and move many messages in mail groups, this fails. To cure the symptom, enter the group via 'C-u RET' (this makes Gnus get all messages), then hit 'M P b' to mark all messages and then say 'B m name.of.group' to move all messages to the group they have been in before, they get new message numbers in this process and the count is right again (until you delete and move your mail to other groups again).

Question 4.13

I don't like the layout of summary and article buffer, how to change it? Perhaps even a three pane display?

Answer

You can control the windows configuration by calling the function gnus-add-configuration. The syntax is a bit complicated but explained very well in the manual node "Window Layout". Some popular examples:

Instead 25% summary 75% article buffer 35% summary and 65% article (the 1.0 for article means "take the remaining space"):

```
(gnus-add-configuration
 '(article (vertical 1.0 (summary .35 point) (article 1.0))))
```

A three pane layout, Group buffer on the left, summary buffer top-right, article buffer bottom-right:

```
(gnus-add-configuration
 '(article
   (horizontal 1.0
               (vertical 25
                         (group 1.0))
               (vertical 1.0
                         (summary 0.25 point)
                         (article 1.0)))))
(gnus-add-configuration
 '(summary
   (horizontal 1.0
               (vertical 25
                         (group 1.0))
               (vertical 1.0
                         (summary 1.0 point)))))
```

Question 4.14

I don't like the way the Summary buffer looks, how to tweak it?

Answer

You've got to play around with the variable gnus-summary-line-format. Its value is a string of symbols which stand for things like author, date, subject etc. A list of the available specifiers can be found in the manual node "Summary Buffer Lines" and the often forgotten node "Formatting Variables" and its sub-nodes. There you'll find useful things like positioning the cursor and tabulators which allow you a summary in table form, but sadly hard tabulators are broken in 5.8.8.

Since 5.10, Gnus offers you some very nice new specifiers, e.g., %B which draws a thread-tree and %&user-date which gives you a date where the details are dependent of the articles age. Here's an example which uses both:

```
(setq gnus-summary-line-format ":%U%R %B %s %-60=|%4L |%-20,20f
|%&user-date; \n")
```

resulting in:

```
:O      Re: [Richard Stallman] rfc2047.el          |  13 |Lars Magne
:O      Re: Revival of the ding-patches list       |  13 |Lars Magne
:R  >   Re: Find correct list of articles for a gro|  25 |Lars Magne
:O  \-> ...                                         |  21 |Kai Grossjohann
:R  >   Re: Cry for help: deuglify.el - moving stuf|  28 |Lars Magne
:O  \-> ...                                         | 115 |Raymond Scholz
:O    \-> ...                                       |  19 |Lars Magne
:O      Slow mailing list                           |  13 |Lars Magne
:O      Re: '@' mark not documented                 |  13 |Lars Magne
:R  >   Re: Gnus still doesn't count messages prope|  23 |Lars Magne
:O  \-> ...                                         |  18 |Kai Grossjohann
:O      \-> ...                                     |  13 |Lars Magne
```

Question 4.15

How to split incoming mails in several groups?

Answer

Gnus offers two possibilities for splitting mail, the easy nnmail-split-methods and the more powerful Fancy Mail Splitting. I'll only talk about the first one, refer to the manual, node "Fancy Mail Splitting" for the latter.

The value of nnmail-split-methods is a list, each element is a list which stands for a splitting rule. Each rule has the form "group where matching articles should go to", "regular expression which has to be matched", the first rule which matches wins. The last rule must always be a general rule (regular expression .*) which denotes where articles should go which don't match any other rule. If the folder doesn't exist yet, it will be created as soon as an article lands there. By default the mail will be send to all groups whose rules match. If you don't want that (you probably don't want), say

```
(setq nnmail-crosspost nil)
```

in ~/.gnus.el.

An example might be better than thousand words, so here's my nnmail-split-methods. Note that I send duplicates in a special group and that the default group is spam, since I filter all mails out which are from some list I'm subscribed to or which are addressed directly to me before. Those rules kill about 80% of the Spam which reaches me (Email addresses are changed to prevent spammers from using them):

```
(setq nnmail-split-methods
  '(("duplicates" "^Gnus-Warning:.*duplicate")
    ("XEmacs-NT" "^\\(To:\\|CC:\\).*localpart@xemacs.invalid.*")
    ("Gnus-Tut" "^\\(To:\\|CC:\\).*localpart@socha.invalid.*")
    ("tcsh" "^\\(To:\\|CC:\\).*localpart@mx.gw.invalid.*")
    ("BAfH" "^\\(To:\\|CC:\\).*localpart@.*uni-muenchen.invalid.*")
    ("Hamster-src" "^\\(CC:\\|To:\\).*hamster-sourcen@yahoogroups.
\\(de\\|com\\).*")
    ("Tagesschau" "^From: tagesschau <localpart@www.tagesschau.invalid>$")
    ("Replies" "^\\(CC:\\|To:\\).*localpart@Frank-Schmitt.invalid.*")
    ("EK" "^From:.*\\(localpart@privateprovider.invalid\\|
localpart@workplace.invalid\\).*")
    ("Spam" "^Content-Type:.*\\(ks_c_5601-1987\\|EUC-KR\\|big5\\|
iso-2022-jp\\).*")
    ("Spam" "^Subject:.*\\(This really work\\|XINGA\\|ADV:\\|XXX\\
|adult\\|sex\\).*")
    ("Spam" "^Subject:.*\\(\=\?ks_c_5601-1987\?\\|\=\?euc-kr\?\\|
\=\?big5\?\\).*")
    ("Spam" "^X-Mailer:\\(.*BulkMailer.*\\|.*MIME::Lite.*\\|\\)")
    ("Spam" "^X-Mailer:\\(.*CyberCreek Avalanche\\|.*http\:\/\/
GetResponse\.com\\)")
    ("Spam" "^From:.*\\(verizon\.net\\|prontomail\.com\\|money\\|
ConsumerDirect\\).*")
    ("Spam" "^Delivered-To: GMX delivery to spamtrap@gmx.invalid$")
    ("Spam" "^Received: from link2buy.com")
    ("Spam" "^CC: .*azzrael@t-online.invalid")
    ("Spam" "^X-Mailer-Version: 1.50 BETA")
    ("Uni" "^\\(CC:\\|To:\\).*localpart@uni-koblenz.invalid.*")
    ("Inbox" "^\\(CC:\\|To:\\).*\\(my\ name\\|address@one.invalid
\\|address@two.invalid\\)")
    ("Spam" "")))
```

Question 4.16

How can I ensure more contrast when viewing HTML mail?

Answer

Gnus' built-in simple HTML renderer (you use it if the value of mm-text-html-renderer is shr) uses the colors which are declared in the HTML mail. However, it adjusts them in order to prevent situations like dark gray text on black background. In case the results still have a too low contrast for you, increase the values of the variables `shr-color-visible-distance-min` and `shr-color-visible-luminance-min`.

11.10.7 Composing messages

Question 5.1

What are the basic commands I need to know for sending mail and postings?

Answer

To start composing a new mail hit 'm' either in Group or Summary buffer, for a posting, it's either 'a' in Group buffer and filling the Newsgroups header manually or 'a' in the Summary buffer of the group where the posting shall be send to. Replying by mail is 'r' if you don't want to cite the author, or import the cited text manually and 'R' to cite the text of the original message. For a follow up to a newsgroup, it's 'f' and 'F' (analogously to 'r' and 'R').

Enter new headers above the line saying "–text follows this line–", enter the text below the line. When ready hit 'C-c C-c', to send the message, if you want to finish it later hit 'C-c C-d' to save it in the drafts group, where you can start editing it again by saying 'D e'.

Question 5.2

How to enable automatic word-wrap when composing messages?

Answer

Starting from No Gnus, automatic word-wrap is already enabled by default, see the variable message-fill-column.

For other versions of Gnus, say

```
(unless (boundp 'message-fill-column)
  (add-hook 'message-mode-hook
            (lambda ()
              (setq fill-column 72)
              (turn-on-auto-fill))))
```

in `~/.gnus.el`.

You can reformat a paragraph by hitting 'M-q' (as usual).

Question 5.3

How to set stuff like From, Organization, Reply-To, signature...?

Answer

There are other ways, but you should use posting styles for this. (See below why). This example should make the syntax clear:

```
(setq gnus-posting-styles
  '((".*"
      (name "Frank Schmitt")
      (address "me@there.invalid")
```

```
(organization "Hamme net, kren mer och nimmi")
(signature-file "~/.signature")
("X-SampleHeader" "foobar")
(eval (setq some-variable "Foo bar")))))
```

The ".*" means that this settings are the default ones (see below), valid values for the first element of the following lists are signature, signature-file, organization, address, name or body. The attribute name can also be a string. In that case, this will be used as a header name, and the value will be inserted in the headers of the article; if the value is nil, the header name will be removed. You can also say (eval (foo bar)), then the function foo will be evaluated with argument bar and the result will be thrown away.

Question 5.4

Can I set things like From, Signature etc group based on the group I post too?

Answer

That's the strength of posting styles. Before, we used ".*" to set the default for all groups. You can use a regexp like "^gmane" and the following settings are only applied to postings you send to the gmane hierarchy, use ".*binaries" instead and they will be applied to postings send to groups containing the string binaries in their name etc.

You can instead of specifying a regexp specify a function which is evaluated, only if it returns true, the corresponding settings take effect. Two interesting candidates for this are message-news-p which returns t if the current Group is a newsgroup and the corresponding message-mail-p.

Note that all forms that match are applied, that means in the example below, when I post to gmane.mail.spam.spamassassin.general, the settings under ".*" are applied and the settings under message-news-p and those under "^gmane" and those under "^gmane\\.mail\\.spam\\.spamassassin\\.general$". Because of this put general settings at the top and specific ones at the bottom.

```
(setq gnus-posting-styles
      '((".*" ;;default
         (name "Frank Schmitt")
         (organization "Hamme net, kren mer och nimmi")
         (signature-file "~/.signature"))
        ((message-news-p) ;;Usenet news?
         (address "mySpamTrap@Frank-Schmitt.invalid")
         (reply-to "hereRealRepliesOnlyPlease@Frank-Schmitt.invalid"))
        ((message-mail-p) ;;mail?
         (address "usedForMails@Frank-Schmitt.invalid"))
        ("^gmane" ;;this is mail, too in fact
         (address "usedForMails@Frank-Schmitt.invalid")
         (reply-to nil))
        ("^gmane\\.mail\\.spam\\.spamassassin\\.general$"
         (eval (set (make-local-variable 'message-sendmail-envelope-from)
                    "Azzrael@rz-online.de")))))
```

Question 5.5

Is there a spell-checker? Perhaps even on-the-fly spell-checking?

Answer

You can use ispell.el to spell-check stuff in Emacs. So the first thing to do is to make sure that you've got either ispell or aspell installed and in your Path. Then you need ispell.el and for on-the-fly spell-checking flyspell.el. Ispell.el is shipped with Emacs and available through the XEmacs package system, flyspell.el is shipped with Emacs and part of XEmacs text-modes package which is available through the package system, so there should be no need to install them manually.

Ispell.el assumes you use ispell, if you choose aspell say

```
(setq ispell-program-name "aspell")
```

in your Emacs configuration file.

If you want your outgoing messages to be spell-checked, say

```
(add-hook 'message-send-hook 'ispell-message)
```

In your ~/.gnus.el, if you prefer on-the-fly spell-checking say

```
(add-hook 'message-mode-hook (lambda () (flyspell-mode 1)))
```

Question 5.6

Can I set the dictionary based on the group I'm posting to?

Answer

Yes, say something like

```
(add-hook 'gnus-select-group-hook
          (lambda ()
            (cond
             ((string-match
               "^de\\." (gnus-group-real-name gnus-newsgroup-name))
              (ispell-change-dictionary "deutsch8"))
             (t
              (ispell-change-dictionary "english")))))
```

in ~/.gnus.el. Change "^de\\." and "deutsch8" to something that suits your needs.

Question 5.7

Is there some kind of address-book, so I needn't remember all those email addresses?

Answer

There's an very basic solution for this, mail aliases. You can store your mail addresses in a ~/.mailrc file using a simple alias syntax:

```
alias al        "Al <al@english-heritage.invalid>"
```

Then typing your alias (followed by a space or punctuation character) on a To: or Cc: line in the message buffer will cause Gnus to insert the full address for you. See the node "Mail Aliases" in Message (not Gnus) manual for details.

However, what you really want is the Insidious Big Brother Database bbdb. Get it through the XEmacs package system or from bbdb's homepage. Now place the following in `~/.gnus.el`, to activate bbdb for Gnus:

```
(require 'bbdb)
(bbdb-initialize 'gnus 'message)
```

Now you probably want some general bbdb configuration, place them in ~/.emacs:

```
(require 'bbdb)
;;If you don't live in Northern America, you should disable the
;;syntax check for telephone numbers by saying
(setq bbdb-north-american-phone-numbers-p nil)
;;Tell bbdb about your email address:
(setq bbdb-user-mail-names
      (regexp-opt '("Your.Email@here.invalid"
                    "Your.other@mail.there.invalid")))
;;cycling while completing email addresses
(setq bbdb-complete-name-allow-cycling t)
;;No popup-buffers
(setq bbdb-use-pop-up nil)
```

Now you should be ready to go. Say 'M-x bbdb RET RET' to open a bbdb buffer showing all entries. Say 'c' to create a new entry, 'b' to search your BBDB and 'C-o' to add a new field to an entry. If you want to add a sender to the BBDB you can also just hit ':' on the posting in the summary buffer and you are done. When you now compose a new mail, hit 'TAB' to cycle through know recipients.

Question 5.8

Sometimes I see little images at the top of article buffer. What's that and how can I send one with my postings, too?

Answer

Those images are called X-Faces. They are 48*48 pixel b/w pictures, encoded in a header line. If you want to include one in your posts, you've got to convert some image to a X-Face. So fire up some image manipulation program (say Gimp), open the image you want to include, cut out the relevant part, reduce color depth to 1 bit, resize to 48*48 and save as bitmap. Now you should get the compface package from this site. and create the actual X-face by saying

```
cat file.xbm | xbm2ikon | compface > file.face
cat file.face | sed 's/\\/\\\\/g;s/\"/\\\"/g;' > file.face.quoted
```

If you can't use compface, there's an online X-face converter at http://www.dairiki.org/xface/. If you use MS Windows, you could also use the WinFace program, which used to be available from 'http://www.xs4all.nl/~walterln/winface/'. Now you only have to tell Gnus to include the X-face in your postings by saying

```
(setq message-default-headers
      (with-temp-buffer
        (insert "X-Face: ")
```

```
(insert-file-contents "~/.xface")
(buffer-string)))
```

in `~/.gnus.el`. If you use Gnus 5.10, you can simply add an entry

```
(x-face-file "~/.xface")
```

to gnus-posting-styles.

Question 5.9

Sometimes I accidentally hit r instead of f in newsgroups. Can Gnus warn me, when I'm replying by mail in newsgroups?

Answer

Put this in `~/.gnus.el`:

```
(setq gnus-confirm-mail-reply-to-news t)
```

if you already use Gnus 5.10, if you still use 5.8.8 or 5.9 try this instead:

```
(eval-after-load "gnus-msg"
  '(unless (boundp 'gnus-confirm-mail-reply-to-news)
     (defadvice gnus-summary-reply (around reply-in-news activate)
       "Request confirmation when replying to news."
       (interactive)
       (when (or (not (gnus-news-group-p gnus-newsgroup-name))
                 (y-or-n-p "Really reply by mail to article author? "))
         ad-do-it))))
```

Question 5.10

How to tell Gnus not to generate a sender header?

Answer

Since 5.10 Gnus doesn't generate a sender header by default. For older Gnus' try this in `~/.gnus.el`:

```
(eval-after-load "message"
        '(add-to-list 'message-syntax-checks '(sender . disabled)))
```

Question 5.11

I want Gnus to locally store copies of my send mail and news, how to do it?

Answer

You must set the variable gnus-message-archive-group to do this. You can set it to a string giving the name of the group where the copies shall go or like in the example below use a function which is evaluated and which returns the group to use.

```
(setq gnus-message-archive-group
        '((if (message-news-p)
              "nnml:Send-News"
            "nnml:Send-Mail")))
```

Question 5.12

I want Gnus to kill the buffer after successful sending instead of keeping it alive as "Sent mail to...", how to do it?

Answer

Add this to your ~/.gnus:

```
(setq message-kill-buffer-on-exit t)
```

Question 5.13

People tell me my Message-IDs are not correct, why aren't they and how to fix it?

Answer

The message-ID is an unique identifier for messages you send. To make it unique, Gnus need to know which machine name to put after the "@". If the name of the machine where Gnus is running isn't suitable (it probably isn't at most private machines) you can tell Gnus what to use by saying:

```
(setq message-user-fqdn "yourmachine.yourdomain.tld")
```

in ~/.gnus.el. If you use Gnus 5.9 or earlier, you can use this instead (works for newer versions as well):

```
(eval-after-load "message"
  '(let ((fqdn "yourmachine.yourdomain.tld"));; <-- Edit this!
     (if (boundp 'message-user-fqdn)
         (setq message-user-fqdn fqdn)
       (gnus-message 1 "Redefining `message-make-fqdn'.")
       (defun message-make-fqdn ()
         "Return user's fully qualified domain name."
         fqdn))))
```

If you have no idea what to insert for "yourmachine.yourdomain.tld", you've got several choices. You can either ask your provider if he allows you to use something like yourUser-Name.userfqdn.provider.net, or you can use somethingUnique.yourdomain.tld if you own the domain yourdomain.tld, or you can register at a service which gives private users a FQDN for free.

Finally you can tell Gnus not to generate a Message-ID for News at all (and letting the server do the job) by saying

```
(setq message-required-news-headers
  (remove' Message-ID message-required-news-headers))
```

you can also tell Gnus not to generate Message-IDs for mail by saying

```
(setq message-required-mail-headers
  (remove' Message-ID message-required-mail-headers))
```

, however some mail servers don't generate proper Message-IDs, too, so test if your Mail Server behaves correctly by sending yourself a Mail and looking at the Message-ID.

11.10.8 Old messages

Question 6.1

How to import my old mail into Gnus?

Answer

The easiest way is to tell your old mail program to export the messages in mbox format. Most Unix mailers are able to do this, if you come from the MS Windows world, you may find tools at http://mbx2mbox.sourceforge.net/.

Now you've got to import this mbox file into Gnus. To do this, create a nndoc group based on the mbox file by saying 'G f /path/file.mbox RET' in Group buffer. You now have read-only access to your mail. If you want to import the messages to your normal Gnus mail groups hierarchy, enter the nndoc group you've just created by saying 'C-u RET' (thus making sure all messages are retrieved), mark all messages by saying 'M P b' and either copy them to the desired group by saying 'B c name.of.group RET' or send them through nnmail-split-methods (respool them) by saying 'B r'.

Question 6.2

How to archive interesting messages?

Answer

If you stumble across an interesting message, say in gnu.emacs.gnus and want to archive it there are several solutions. The first and easiest is to save it to a file by saying 'O f'. However, wouldn't it be much more convenient to have more direct access to the archived message from Gnus? If you say yes, put this snippet by Frank Haun <pille3003@fhaun.de> in ~/.gnus.el:

```
(defun my-archive-article (&optional n)
  "Copies one or more article(s) to a corresponding 'nnml:' group, e.g.,
'gnus.ding' goes to 'nnml:1.gnus.ding'. And 'nnml:List-gnus.ding' goes
to 'nnml:1.List-gnus-ding'.

Use process marks or mark a region in the summary buffer to archive
more then one article."
  (interactive "P")
  (let ((archive-name
         (format
          "nnml:1.%s"
          (if (featurep 'xemacs)
              (replace-in-string gnus-newsgroup-name "^.*:" "")
            (replace-regexp-in-string "^.*:" "" gnus-newsgroup-name)))))
    (gnus-summary-copy-article n archive-name)))
```

You can now say 'M-x my-archive-article' in summary buffer to archive the article under the cursor in a nnml group. (Change nnml to your preferred back end)

Of course you can also make sure the cache is enabled by saying

```
(setq gnus-use-cache t)
```

then you only have to set either the tick or the dormant mark for articles you want to keep, setting the read mark will remove them from cache.

Question 6.3

How to search for a specific message?

Answer

There are several ways for this, too. For a posting from a Usenet group the easiest solution is probably to ask groups.google.com, if you found the posting there, tell Google to display the raw message, look for the message-id, and say 'M-^ the@message.id RET' in a summary buffer. Since Gnus 5.10 there's also a Gnus interface for groups.google.com which you can call with 'G W') in group buffer.

Another idea which works for both mail and news groups is to enter the group where the message you are searching is and use the standard Emacs search 'C-s', it's smart enough to look at articles in collapsed threads, too. If you want to search bodies, too try 'M-s' instead. Further on there are the gnus-summary-limit-to-foo functions, which can help you, too.

Of course you can also use grep to search through your local mail, but this is both slow for big archives and inconvenient since you are not displaying the found mail in Gnus. Here nnir comes into action. Nnir is a front end to search engines like swish-e or swish++ and others. You index your mail with one of those search engines and with the help of nnir you can search through the indexed mail and generate a temporary group with all messages which met your search criteria. If this sounds cool to you, get nnir.el from `ftp://ftp.is.informatik.uni-duisburg.de/pub/src/emacs/`. Instructions on how to use it are at the top of the file.

Question 6.4

How to get rid of old unwanted mail?

Answer

You can of course just mark the mail you don't need anymore by saying '#' with point over the mail and then say 'B DEL' to get rid of them forever. You could also instead of actually deleting them, send them to a junk-group by saying 'B m nnml:trash-bin' which you clear from time to time, but both are not the intended way in Gnus.

In Gnus, we let mail expire like news expires on a news server. That means you tell Gnus the message is expirable (you tell Gnus "I don't need this mail anymore") by saying 'E' with point over the mail in summary buffer. Now when you leave the group, Gnus looks at all messages which you marked as expirable before and if they are old enough (default is older than a week) they are deleted.

Question 6.5

I want that all read messages are expired (at least in some groups). How to do it?

Answer

If you want all read messages to be expired (e.g., in mailing lists where there's an online archive), you've got two choices: auto-expire and total-expire. Auto-expire means, that every article which has no marks set and is selected for reading is marked as expirable, Gnus hits 'E' for you every time you read a message. Total-expire follows a slightly different approach, here all article where the read mark is set are expirable.

To activate auto-expire, include auto-expire in the Group parameters for the group. (Hit 'G c' in summary buffer with point over the group to change group parameters). For total-expire add total-expire to the group-parameters.

Which method you choose is merely a matter of taste: Auto-expire is faster, but it doesn't play together with Adaptive Scoring, so if you want to use this feature, you should use total-expire.

If you want a message to be excluded from expiration in a group where total or auto expire is active, set either tick (hit 'u') or dormant mark (hit 'u'), when you use auto-expire, you can also set the read mark (hit 'd').

Question 6.6

I don't want expiration to delete my mails but to move them to another group.

Answer

Say something like this in ~/.gnus.el:

```
(setq nnmail-expiry-target "nnml:expired")
```

(If you want to change the value of nnmail-expiry-target on a per group basis see the question "How can I disable threading in some (e.g., mail-) groups, or set other variables specific for some groups?")

11.10.9 Gnus in a dial-up environment

Question 7.1

I don't have a permanent connection to the net, how can I minimize the time I've got to be connected?

Answer

You've got basically two options: Either you use the Gnus Agent (see below) for this, or you can install programs which fetch your news and mail to your local disk and Gnus reads the stuff from your local machine.

If you want to follow the second approach, you need a program which fetches news and offers them to Gnus, a program which does the same for mail and a program which receives the mail you write from Gnus and sends them when you're online.

Let's talk about Unix systems first: For the news part, the easiest solution is a small nntp server like Leafnode or sn, of course you can also install a full featured news server like inn. Then you want to fetch your Mail, popular choices are fetchmail and getmail. You should tell those to write the mail to your disk and Gnus to read it from there. Last but not least the mail sending part: This can be done with every MTA like sendmail, postfix, exim or qmail.

On windows boxes I'd vote for Hamster, it's a small freeware, open-source program which fetches your mail and news from remote servers and offers them to Gnus (or any other mail and/or news reader) via nntp respectively POP3 or IMAP. It also includes a smtp server for receiving mails from Gnus.

Question 7.2

So what was this thing about the Agent?

Answer

The Gnus agent is part of Gnus, it allows you to fetch mail and news and store them on disk for reading them later when you're offline. It kind of mimics offline newsreaders like Forte Agent. If you want to use the Agent place the following in `~/.gnus.el` if you are still using 5.8.8 or 5.9 (it's the default since 5.10):

```
(setq gnus-agent t)
```

Now you've got to select the servers whose groups can be stored locally. To do this, open the server buffer (that is press '^' while in the group buffer). Now select a server by moving point to the line naming that server. Finally, agentize the server by typing 'J a'. If you make a mistake, or change your mind, you can undo this action by typing 'J r'. When you're done, type 'q' to return to the group buffer. Now the next time you enter a group on a agentized server, the headers will be stored on disk and read from there the next time you enter the group.

Question 7.3

I want to store article bodies on disk, too. How to do it?

Answer

You can tell the agent to automatically fetch the bodies of articles which fulfill certain predicates, this is done in a special buffer which can be reached by saying 'J c' in group buffer. Please refer to the documentation for information which predicates are possible and how exactly to do it.

Further on you can tell the agent manually which articles to store on disk. There are two ways to do this: Number one: In the summary buffer, process mark a set of articles that shall be stored in the agent by saying '#' with point over the article and then type 'J s'. The other possibility is to set, again in the summary buffer, downloadable (%) marks for the articles you want by typing '@' with point over the article and then typing 'J u'. What's the difference? Well, process marks are erased as soon as you exit the summary buffer while downloadable marks are permanent. You can actually set downloadable marks in several groups then use fetch session ('J s' in the GROUP buffer) to fetch all of those articles. The only downside is that fetch session also fetches all of the headers for every selected group on an agentized server. Depending on the volume of headers, the initial fetch session could take hours.

Question 7.4

How to tell Gnus not to try to send mails / postings while I'm offline?

Answer

All you've got to do is to tell Gnus when you are online (plugged) and when you are offline (unplugged), the rest works automatically. You can toggle plugged/unplugged state by saying 'J j' in group buffer. To start Gnus unplugged say 'M-x gnus-unplugged' instead of 'M-x gnus'. Note that for this to work, the agent must be active.

11.10.10 Getting help

Question 8.1

How to find information and help inside Emacs?

Answer

The first stop should be the Gnus manual (Say 'C-h i d m Gnus RET' to start the Gnus manual, then walk through the menus or do a full-text search with 's'). Then there are the general Emacs help commands starting with C-h, type 'C-h ? ?' to get a list of all available help commands and their meaning. Finally 'M-x apropos-command' lets you search through all available functions and 'M-x apropos' searches the bound variables.

Question 8.2

I can't find anything in the Gnus manual about X (e.g., attachments, PGP, MIME...), is it not documented?

Answer

There's not only the Gnus manual but also the manuals for message, emacs-mime, sieve, EasyPG Assistant, and pgg. Those packages are distributed with Gnus and used by Gnus but aren't really part of core Gnus, so they are documented in different info files, you should have a look in those manuals, too.

Question 8.3

Which websites should I know?

Answer

The most important one is the official Gnus website.

Tell me about other sites which are interesting.

Question 8.4

Which mailing lists and newsgroups are there?

Answer

There's the newsgroup gnu.emacs.gnus (also available as gmane.emacs.gnus.user) which deals with general Gnus questions. If you have questions about development versions of Gnus, you should better ask on the ding mailing list, see below.

If you want to stay in the big8, news.software.readers is also read by some Gnus users (but chances for qualified help are much better in the above groups). If you speak German, there's de.comm.software.gnus.

The ding mailing list (ding@gnus.org) deals with development of Gnus. You can read the ding list via NNTP, too under the name gmane.emacs.gnus.general from news.gmane.org.

Question 8.5

Where to report bugs?

Answer

Say 'M-x gnus-bug', this will start a message to the gnus bug mailing list including information about your environment which make it easier to help you.

Question 8.6

I need real-time help, where to find it?

Answer

Point your IRC client to irc.freenode.net, channel #gnus.

11.10.11 Tuning Gnus

Question 9.1

Starting Gnus is really slow, how to speed it up?

Answer

The reason for this could be the way Gnus reads its active file, see the node "The Active File" in the Gnus manual for things you might try to speed the process up. An other idea would be to byte compile your ~/.gnus.el (say 'M-x byte-compile-file RET ~/.gnus.el RET' to do it). Finally, if you have require statements in your .gnus, you could replace them with eval-after-load, which loads the stuff not at startup time, but when it's needed. Say you've got this in your ~/.gnus.el:

```
(require 'message)
(add-to-list 'message-syntax-checks '(sender . disabled))
```

then as soon as you start Gnus, message.el is loaded. If you replace it with

```
(eval-after-load "message"
        '(add-to-list 'message-syntax-checks '(sender . disabled)))
```

it's loaded when it's needed.

Question 9.2

How to speed up the process of entering a group?

Answer

A speed killer is setting the variable gnus-fetch-old-headers to anything different from **nil**, so don't do this if speed is an issue. To speed up building of summary say

```
(gnus-compile)
```

at the bottom of your ~/.gnus.el, this will make gnus byte-compile things like gnus-summary-line-format. then you could increase the value of gc-cons-threshold by saying something like

```
(setq gc-cons-threshold 3500000)
```

in ~/.emacs. If you don't care about width of CJK characters or use Gnus 5.10 or younger together with a recent GNU Emacs, you should say

```
(setq gnus-use-correct-string-widths nil)
```

in ~/.gnus.el (thanks to Jesper harder for the last two suggestions). Finally if you are still using 5.8.8 or 5.9 and experience speed problems with summary buffer generation, you definitely should update to 5.10 since there quite some work on improving it has been done.

Question 9.3

Sending mail becomes slower and slower, what's up?

Answer

The reason could be that you told Gnus to archive the messages you wrote by setting gnus-message-archive-group. Try to use a nnml group instead of an archive group, this should bring you back to normal speed.

11.10.12 Glossary

~/.gnus.el   When the term ~/.gnus.el is used it just means your Gnus configuration file. You might as well call it ~/.gnus or specify another name.

Back End   In Gnus terminology a back end is a virtual server, a layer between core Gnus and the real NNTP-, POP3-, IMAP- or whatever-server which offers Gnus a standardized interface to functions like "get message", "get Headers" etc.

Emacs   When the term Emacs is used in this FAQ, it means either GNU Emacs or XEmacs.

Message   In this FAQ message means a either a mail or a posting to a Usenet Newsgroup or to some other fancy back end, no matter of which kind it is.

MUA   MUA is an acronym for Mail User Agent, it's the program you use to read and write e-mails.

NUA   NUA is an acronym for News User Agent, it's the program you use to read and write Usenet news.

12 GNU Free Documentation License

Version 1.3, 3 November 2008

Copyright © 2000, 2001, 2002, 2007, 2008 Free Software Foundation, Inc.
http://fsf.org/

Everyone is permitted to copy and distribute verbatim copies
of this license document, but changing it is not allowed.

0. PREAMBLE

The purpose of this License is to make a manual, textbook, or other functional and
useful document *free* in the sense of freedom: to assure everyone the effective freedom
to copy and redistribute it, with or without modifying it, either commercially or noncommercially. Secondarily, this License preserves for the author and publisher a way
to get credit for their work, while not being considered responsible for modifications
made by others.

This License is a kind of "copyleft", which means that derivative works of the document
must themselves be free in the same sense. It complements the GNU General Public
License, which is a copyleft license designed for free software.

We have designed this License in order to use it for manuals for free software, because
free software needs free documentation: a free program should come with manuals
providing the same freedoms that the software does. But this License is not limited to
software manuals; it can be used for any textual work, regardless of subject matter or
whether it is published as a printed book. We recommend this License principally for
works whose purpose is instruction or reference.

1. APPLICABILITY AND DEFINITIONS

This License applies to any manual or other work, in any medium, that contains a
notice placed by the copyright holder saying it can be distributed under the terms
of this License. Such a notice grants a world-wide, royalty-free license, unlimited in
duration, to use that work under the conditions stated herein. The "Document",
below, refers to any such manual or work. Any member of the public is a licensee, and
is addressed as "you". You accept the license if you copy, modify or distribute the work
in a way requiring permission under copyright law.

A "Modified Version" of the Document means any work containing the Document or
a portion of it, either copied verbatim, or with modifications and/or translated into
another language.

A "Secondary Section" is a named appendix or a front-matter section of the Document
that deals exclusively with the relationship of the publishers or authors of the Document
to the Document's overall subject (or to related matters) and contains nothing that
could fall directly within that overall subject. (Thus, if the Document is in part a
textbook of mathematics, a Secondary Section may not explain any mathematics.) The
relationship could be a matter of historical connection with the subject or with related
matters, or of legal, commercial, philosophical, ethical or political position regarding
them.

The "Invariant Sections" are certain Secondary Sections whose titles are designated, as
being those of Invariant Sections, in the notice that says that the Document is released

under this License. If a section does not fit the above definition of Secondary then it is not allowed to be designated as Invariant. The Document may contain zero Invariant Sections. If the Document does not identify any Invariant Sections then there are none.

The "Cover Texts" are certain short passages of text that are listed, as Front-Cover Texts or Back-Cover Texts, in the notice that says that the Document is released under this License. A Front-Cover Text may be at most 5 words, and a Back-Cover Text may be at most 25 words.

A "Transparent" copy of the Document means a machine-readable copy, represented in a format whose specification is available to the general public, that is suitable for revising the document straightforwardly with generic text editors or (for images composed of pixels) generic paint programs or (for drawings) some widely available drawing editor, and that is suitable for input to text formatters or for automatic translation to a variety of formats suitable for input to text formatters. A copy made in an otherwise Transparent file format whose markup, or absence of markup, has been arranged to thwart or discourage subsequent modification by readers is not Transparent. An image format is not Transparent if used for any substantial amount of text. A copy that is not "Transparent" is called "Opaque".

Examples of suitable formats for Transparent copies include plain ASCII without markup, Texinfo input format, LaTeX input format, SGML or XML using a publicly available DTD, and standard-conforming simple HTML, PostScript or PDF designed for human modification. Examples of transparent image formats include PNG, XCF and JPG. Opaque formats include proprietary formats that can be read and edited only by proprietary word processors, SGML or XML for which the DTD and/or processing tools are not generally available, and the machine-generated HTML, PostScript or PDF produced by some word processors for output purposes only.

The "Title Page" means, for a printed book, the title page itself, plus such following pages as are needed to hold, legibly, the material this License requires to appear in the title page. For works in formats which do not have any title page as such, "Title Page" means the text near the most prominent appearance of the work's title, preceding the beginning of the body of the text.

The "publisher" means any person or entity that distributes copies of the Document to the public.

A section "Entitled XYZ" means a named subunit of the Document whose title either is precisely XYZ or contains XYZ in parentheses following text that translates XYZ in another language. (Here XYZ stands for a specific section name mentioned below, such as "Acknowledgements", "Dedications", "Endorsements", or "History".) To "Preserve the Title" of such a section when you modify the Document means that it remains a section "Entitled XYZ" according to this definition.

The Document may include Warranty Disclaimers next to the notice which states that this License applies to the Document. These Warranty Disclaimers are considered to be included by reference in this License, but only as regards disclaiming warranties: any other implication that these Warranty Disclaimers may have is void and has no effect on the meaning of this License.

2. VERBATIM COPYING

You may copy and distribute the Document in any medium, either commercially or noncommercially, provided that this License, the copyright notices, and the license notice saying this License applies to the Document are reproduced in all copies, and that you add no other conditions whatsoever to those of this License. You may not use technical measures to obstruct or control the reading or further copying of the copies you make or distribute. However, you may accept compensation in exchange for copies. If you distribute a large enough number of copies you must also follow the conditions in section 3.

You may also lend copies, under the same conditions stated above, and you may publicly display copies.

3. COPYING IN QUANTITY

If you publish printed copies (or copies in media that commonly have printed covers) of the Document, numbering more than 100, and the Document's license notice requires Cover Texts, you must enclose the copies in covers that carry, clearly and legibly, all these Cover Texts: Front-Cover Texts on the front cover, and Back-Cover Texts on the back cover. Both covers must also clearly and legibly identify you as the publisher of these copies. The front cover must present the full title with all words of the title equally prominent and visible. You may add other material on the covers in addition. Copying with changes limited to the covers, as long as they preserve the title of the Document and satisfy these conditions, can be treated as verbatim copying in other respects.

If the required texts for either cover are too voluminous to fit legibly, you should put the first ones listed (as many as fit reasonably) on the actual cover, and continue the rest onto adjacent pages.

If you publish or distribute Opaque copies of the Document numbering more than 100, you must either include a machine-readable Transparent copy along with each Opaque copy, or state in or with each Opaque copy a computer-network location from which the general network-using public has access to download using public-standard network protocols a complete Transparent copy of the Document, free of added material. If you use the latter option, you must take reasonably prudent steps, when you begin distribution of Opaque copies in quantity, to ensure that this Transparent copy will remain thus accessible at the stated location until at least one year after the last time you distribute an Opaque copy (directly or through your agents or retailers) of that edition to the public.

It is requested, but not required, that you contact the authors of the Document well before redistributing any large number of copies, to give them a chance to provide you with an updated version of the Document.

4. MODIFICATIONS

You may copy and distribute a Modified Version of the Document under the conditions of sections 2 and 3 above, provided that you release the Modified Version under precisely this License, with the Modified Version filling the role of the Document, thus licensing distribution and modification of the Modified Version to whoever possesses a copy of it. In addition, you must do these things in the Modified Version:

A. Use in the Title Page (and on the covers, if any) a title distinct from that of the Document, and from those of previous versions (which should, if there were any, be listed in the History section of the Document). You may use the same title as a previous version if the original publisher of that version gives permission.

B. List on the Title Page, as authors, one or more persons or entities responsible for authorship of the modifications in the Modified Version, together with at least five of the principal authors of the Document (all of its principal authors, if it has fewer than five), unless they release you from this requirement.

C. State on the Title page the name of the publisher of the Modified Version, as the publisher.

D. Preserve all the copyright notices of the Document.

E. Add an appropriate copyright notice for your modifications adjacent to the other copyright notices.

F. Include, immediately after the copyright notices, a license notice giving the public permission to use the Modified Version under the terms of this License, in the form shown in the Addendum below.

G. Preserve in that license notice the full lists of Invariant Sections and required Cover Texts given in the Document's license notice.

H. Include an unaltered copy of this License.

I. Preserve the section Entitled "History", Preserve its Title, and add to it an item stating at least the title, year, new authors, and publisher of the Modified Version as given on the Title Page. If there is no section Entitled "History" in the Document, create one stating the title, year, authors, and publisher of the Document as given on its Title Page, then add an item describing the Modified Version as stated in the previous sentence.

J. Preserve the network location, if any, given in the Document for public access to a Transparent copy of the Document, and likewise the network locations given in the Document for previous versions it was based on. These may be placed in the "History" section. You may omit a network location for a work that was published at least four years before the Document itself, or if the original publisher of the version it refers to gives permission.

K. For any section Entitled "Acknowledgements" or "Dedications", Preserve the Title of the section, and preserve in the section all the substance and tone of each of the contributor acknowledgements and/or dedications given therein.

L. Preserve all the Invariant Sections of the Document, unaltered in their text and in their titles. Section numbers or the equivalent are not considered part of the section titles.

M. Delete any section Entitled "Endorsements". Such a section may not be included in the Modified Version.

N. Do not retitle any existing section to be Entitled "Endorsements" or to conflict in title with any Invariant Section.

O. Preserve any Warranty Disclaimers.

If the Modified Version includes new front-matter sections or appendices that qualify as Secondary Sections and contain no material copied from the Document, you may at your option designate some or all of these sections as invariant. To do this, add their titles to the list of Invariant Sections in the Modified Version's license notice. These titles must be distinct from any other section titles.

You may add a section Entitled "Endorsements", provided it contains nothing but endorsements of your Modified Version by various parties—for example, statements of peer review or that the text has been approved by an organization as the authoritative definition of a standard.

You may add a passage of up to five words as a Front-Cover Text, and a passage of up to 25 words as a Back-Cover Text, to the end of the list of Cover Texts in the Modified Version. Only one passage of Front-Cover Text and one of Back-Cover Text may be added by (or through arrangements made by) any one entity. If the Document already includes a cover text for the same cover, previously added by you or by arrangement made by the same entity you are acting on behalf of, you may not add another; but you may replace the old one, on explicit permission from the previous publisher that added the old one.

The author(s) and publisher(s) of the Document do not by this License give permission to use their names for publicity for or to assert or imply endorsement of any Modified Version.

5. COMBINING DOCUMENTS

You may combine the Document with other documents released under this License, under the terms defined in section 4 above for modified versions, provided that you include in the combination all of the Invariant Sections of all of the original documents, unmodified, and list them all as Invariant Sections of your combined work in its license notice, and that you preserve all their Warranty Disclaimers.

The combined work need only contain one copy of this License, and multiple identical Invariant Sections may be replaced with a single copy. If there are multiple Invariant Sections with the same name but different contents, make the title of each such section unique by adding at the end of it, in parentheses, the name of the original author or publisher of that section if known, or else a unique number. Make the same adjustment to the section titles in the list of Invariant Sections in the license notice of the combined work.

In the combination, you must combine any sections Entitled "History" in the various original documents, forming one section Entitled "History"; likewise combine any sections Entitled "Acknowledgements", and any sections Entitled "Dedications". You must delete all sections Entitled "Endorsements."

6. COLLECTIONS OF DOCUMENTS

You may make a collection consisting of the Document and other documents released under this License, and replace the individual copies of this License in the various documents with a single copy that is included in the collection, provided that you follow the rules of this License for verbatim copying of each of the documents in all other respects.

You may extract a single document from such a collection, and distribute it individually under this License, provided you insert a copy of this License into the extracted document, and follow this License in all other respects regarding verbatim copying of that document.

7. AGGREGATION WITH INDEPENDENT WORKS

A compilation of the Document or its derivatives with other separate and independent documents or works, in or on a volume of a storage or distribution medium, is called an "aggregate" if the copyright resulting from the compilation is not used to limit the legal rights of the compilation's users beyond what the individual works permit. When the Document is included in an aggregate, this License does not apply to the other works in the aggregate which are not themselves derivative works of the Document.

If the Cover Text requirement of section 3 is applicable to these copies of the Document, then if the Document is less than one half of the entire aggregate, the Document's Cover Texts may be placed on covers that bracket the Document within the aggregate, or the electronic equivalent of covers if the Document is in electronic form. Otherwise they must appear on printed covers that bracket the whole aggregate.

8. TRANSLATION

Translation is considered a kind of modification, so you may distribute translations of the Document under the terms of section 4. Replacing Invariant Sections with translations requires special permission from their copyright holders, but you may include translations of some or all Invariant Sections in addition to the original versions of these Invariant Sections. You may include a translation of this License, and all the license notices in the Document, and any Warranty Disclaimers, provided that you also include the original English version of this License and the original versions of those notices and disclaimers. In case of a disagreement between the translation and the original version of this License or a notice or disclaimer, the original version will prevail.

If a section in the Document is Entitled "Acknowledgements", "Dedications", or "History", the requirement (section 4) to Preserve its Title (section 1) will typically require changing the actual title.

9. TERMINATION

You may not copy, modify, sublicense, or distribute the Document except as expressly provided under this License. Any attempt otherwise to copy, modify, sublicense, or distribute it is void, and will automatically terminate your rights under this License.

However, if you cease all violation of this License, then your license from a particular copyright holder is reinstated (a) provisionally, unless and until the copyright holder explicitly and finally terminates your license, and (b) permanently, if the copyright holder fails to notify you of the violation by some reasonable means prior to 60 days after the cessation.

Moreover, your license from a particular copyright holder is reinstated permanently if the copyright holder notifies you of the violation by some reasonable means, this is the first time you have received notice of violation of this License (for any work) from that copyright holder, and you cure the violation prior to 30 days after your receipt of the notice.

Termination of your rights under this section does not terminate the licenses of parties who have received copies or rights from you under this License. If your rights have been terminated and not permanently reinstated, receipt of a copy of some or all of the same material does not give you any rights to use it.

10. FUTURE REVISIONS OF THIS LICENSE

The Free Software Foundation may publish new, revised versions of the GNU Free Documentation License from time to time. Such new versions will be similar in spirit to the present version, but may differ in detail to address new problems or concerns. See `http://www.gnu.org/copyleft/`.

Each version of the License is given a distinguishing version number. If the Document specifies that a particular numbered version of this License "or any later version" applies to it, you have the option of following the terms and conditions either of that specified version or of any later version that has been published (not as a draft) by the Free Software Foundation. If the Document does not specify a version number of this License, you may choose any version ever published (not as a draft) by the Free Software Foundation. If the Document specifies that a proxy can decide which future versions of this License can be used, that proxy's public statement of acceptance of a version permanently authorizes you to choose that version for the Document.

11. RELICENSING

"Massive Multiauthor Collaboration Site" (or "MMC Site") means any World Wide Web server that publishes copyrightable works and also provides prominent facilities for anybody to edit those works. A public wiki that anybody can edit is an example of such a server. A "Massive Multiauthor Collaboration" (or "MMC") contained in the site means any set of copyrightable works thus published on the MMC site.

"CC-BY-SA" means the Creative Commons Attribution-Share Alike 3.0 license published by Creative Commons Corporation, a not-for-profit corporation with a principal place of business in San Francisco, California, as well as future copyleft versions of that license published by that same organization.

"Incorporate" means to publish or republish a Document, in whole or in part, as part of another Document.

An MMC is "eligible for relicensing" if it is licensed under this License, and if all works that were first published under this License somewhere other than this MMC, and subsequently incorporated in whole or in part into the MMC, (1) had no cover texts or invariant sections, and (2) were thus incorporated prior to November 1, 2008.

The operator of an MMC Site may republish an MMC contained in the site under CC-BY-SA on the same site at any time before August 1, 2009, provided the MMC is eligible for relicensing.

ADDENDUM: How to use this License for your documents

To use this License in a document you have written, include a copy of the License in the document and put the following copyright and license notices just after the title page:

```
Copyright (C)  year  your name.
Permission is granted to copy, distribute and/or modify this document
under the terms of the GNU Free Documentation License, Version 1.3
or any later version published by the Free Software Foundation;
with no Invariant Sections, no Front-Cover Texts, and no Back-Cover
Texts.  A copy of the license is included in the section entitled ''GNU
Free Documentation License''.
```

If you have Invariant Sections, Front-Cover Texts and Back-Cover Texts, replace the "with...Texts." line with this:

```
with the Invariant Sections being list their titles, with
the Front-Cover Texts being list, and with the Back-Cover Texts
being list.
```

If you have Invariant Sections without Cover Texts, or some other combination of the three, merge those two alternatives to suit the situation.

If your document contains nontrivial examples of program code, we recommend releasing these examples in parallel under your choice of free software license, such as the GNU General Public License, to permit their use in free software.

13 Index

N

14 Key Index

I

J

K

L

M

U

T

V

www.ingramcontent.com/pod-product-compliance
Lightning Source LLC
LaVergne TN
LVHW060120070326
832902LV00019B/3043